INTERNATIONAL FINANCIAL
AND MANAGERIAL
ACCOUNTING

INTERNATIONAL
FINANCIAL
AND MANAGERIAL
ACCOUNTING

Ahmed Riahi-Belkaoui

QUORUM BOOKS
Westport, Connecticut • London

Library of Congress Cataloging-in-Publication Data

Riahi-Belkaoui, Ahmed, 1943–
    International financial and managerial accounting / Ahmed Riahi-Belkaoui.
      p. cm.
    Includes bibliographical references and index.
    ISBN 1-56720-416-3 (alk. paper)
    1. International business enterprises—Finance. 2. Accounting. 3. Managerial
accounting. I. Title.
    HF5686.I56R528   2002
    658.15'99—dc21   2001041799

British Library Cataloguing in Publication Data is available.

Library of Congress Catalog Card Number: 2001041799
ISBN: 1-56720-416-3

First published in 2002

Quorum Books, 88 Post Road West, Westport, CT 06881
An imprint of Greenwood Publishing Group, Inc.
www.quorumbooks.com

Printed in the United States of America

∞™

The paper used in this book complies with the
Permanent Paper Standard issued by the National
Information Standards Organization (Z39.48–1984).

10 9 8 7 6 5 4 3 2 1

Copyright Acknowledgments

The author and publisher gratefully acknowledge permission for use of the following material:

Exhibits from Baber et al., "Profit-Volume Exchange Rate Analysis for Planning International Operations," *Journal of International Financial Management Accounting* 7 (1996), pp. 95–96.

Exhibits from Kirsch, Robert J., and Wayne Johnson, "The Impact of Fluctuating Exchange Rates on Budgeting and Performance Evaluation of Foreign Subsidiaries," *IJOA* 26, no. 3 (1991), 154–155, 164, 169–172.

To Dimitra

Contents

Exhibits

Preface

Multinational as well as domestic firms need to be aware of the linkages, ram-
ifications, conditions, and demands of the global economy. One way of fulfilling
this requirement is to produce accounting information that reflects this international reality. International accounting is aimed at the production of this new
type of information for both external reporting, to "international users," and
internal reporting, to managers operating in different nations and/or cultures.

This book covers the international accounting issues that are crucial to the
efficient running of multinational firms. The content of each chapter covers the
issues by providing practical solutions and exposing the readers to the literature
coverage of the subject. The organization of the material is intended to stress,
not only the descriptive, but also the normative, solutions to international accounting problems, thus giving to international accounting the status of a legitimate multidisciplinary line of inquiry.

Chapter 1, "International Accounting: The Rise of a Paradigm" examines the
environmental factors in the global economies as they affect the definition, dimensions, and conduct of international accounting.

Chapter 2, "International Taxation and Value-Added Taxation," deals with
the international issues of taxation philosophies, types of taxes, systems of tax
administration, tax treaties, tax havens, U.S. international taxation, and value
added taxation.

Chapter 3, "Exchange Rate Risk Management and Economic Exposure," examines the issues surrounding the determination and estimation of exchange
rates and the management of economic exposure.

Chapter 4, "Transaction Exposure for Multinational Operations," elaborates on the techniques used in international arbitrage and the management of transaction exposure.

Chapter 5, "Organizational and Performance Evaluation of Multinational Operations," examines the issues facing multinational firms when deciding on a choice of organizational structure and evaluating decisional performance.

Chapter 6, "Analyzing Foreign Financial Statements and Disclosure Innovativeness," examines the use and misuse of accounting information for analyzing financial statements, as well as the innovative information that can be found in the financial statements of multinational firms.

Chapter 7, "Capital Budgeting for Multinational Firms and Political Risk" examines the specific issues of capital budgeting techniques by multinational corporations in analyzing the financial benefits and costs of a potential investment. It also examines the problems associated with the management of political risks that can be faced when investing internationally.

Chapter 8, "Accounting for Foreign Currency Transactions, Translation, Derivative Instruments, and Hedging Activities," examines the accounting treatments associated with foreign currency translation, foreign currency transactions and future contracts.

Chapter 9, "Pricing Strategies and Transfer Pricing for Multinational Firms," examines the accounting and tax issues involved in the determination of transfer prices by multinational firms.

Chapter 10, "Accounting for Inflation Internationally," examines the various asset valuation and income determination models available for dealing with inflation internationally.

International Financial and Managerial Accounting should be of interest to financial and management accountants in multinational firms, as well as undergraduate and graduate students in international accounting classes. Many people helped in the development of this book. I received considerable assistance from students at the University of Illinois at Chicago, especially Shahrzad Ghatan, Ewa Tomaszewska, and Vivian Au. I also thank Eric Valentine, Lori Ewen, and the entire production team at Greenwood Publishing Group for their continuous and intelligent support.

1

International Accounting:
The Rise of a Paradigm

INTRODUCTION

Since early history, accounting has been a vehicle for the facilitation of international business. From the Italian city-states of the fourteenth and fifteenth centuries, which attempted to expand international business, and the eighteenth- and nineteenth-century colonization efforts of the European countries, to the increasing world trade of the twentieth century, accounting has been transmitted from one country to another, in the process generating specific national accounting systems that have exhibited both similarities and differences. This international tradition led gradually to the growth of international accounting as an important subdiscipline of the field and practice of accounting. The realities of modern business have made it a necessity for international accounting to develop as a full-fledged area of practice and inquiry. The conditions for this growth of international accounting as well as the resulting dimensions are explained in this chapter.

ENVIRONMENTAL FACTORS

Global Economy

The global economy is best characterized by a new economic and corporate world, in which national boundaries are losing their importance. Emerging characteristics of this global economy include the following:

1. Partnerships are forming between firms of different nationalities, which are willing to forget their rivalries in order to share in the profit opportunities of a

world market, to share the material and labor costs and risks associated with the development of products, to reduce the impact of fluctuating currencies around the world, and to avoid protectionism and government-imposed obstacles such as tariffs, import limits, and regulations. The most noticeable global strategy emanating from these partnerships is the desire to be present in three major markets—Japan, the United States, and Europe. This strategy is labeled "triad power," and it involves allocating manufacturing, marketing, financing, and administrative operations among the three markets.[1]

2. Progress is taking place toward international integration in the form of a global capital market. The obstacles to the global capital market remain the persistent existence of different rules concerning the regulation of stocks, voting rights, corporate control, antitrust policies, and accounting policies, to name only a few. As more harmonization takes place among nations, the globalization of stocks and commodities will flourish. One evidence of increased globalization relates to the increasing number of stock markets: by 1992, there were almost two per time zone. The three most important markets, forming what is known as the "golden triangle," are the New York Stock Exchange (NYSE), the London Stock Exchange (LSE), and the Tokyo Stock Exchange (TSE). These markets open at different times, allowing the great trading houses—Merrill Lynch and Solomon Brothers in the United States; Nomura Securities International, Inc., in Japan; and Barclay's Bank, PLC, in the United Kingdom—to trade stocks, bonds, and currencies around the clock and around the world.

3. The rise of the global economy is also evident in the increase in commodity trades and, especially, the creation of big trading blocs. The world seems to be edging toward the following trading blocs:

a. In North America, a trading bloc was created by the signing of the North American Free Trade Agreement, in 1992, by the United States, Canada, and Mexico.

b. In Central and South America, trading blocs have been created by the Andean Pact, signed in 1991 by Colombia, Ecuador, Bolivia, Peru, and Venezuela, and the Mercosur Pact, signed in 1991 by Argentina, Brazil, Paraguay, and Uruguay.

c. In Europe, blocs were created by the establishment of the European Community (EC) in 1957 and the European Free Trade Association (EFTA), set up in 1960 by Liechtenstein, Switzerland, Sweden, Finland, Norway, Iceland, and Austria.

d. In Southeast Asia, a bloc was created by the Association of Southeast Asian Nations Free Trade Area, which was signed in 1992 by Thailand, Indonesia, Malaysia, the Philippines, Singapore, and Brunei. Vietnam and Laos have also expressed interest in joining the pact.

e. In Africa, a bloc was created by the Maghreb countries, an agreement having been signed by Morocco, Algeria, Tunisia, Mauritania, and Libya.

The North American Free Trade Agreement, between the United States, Mexico, and Canada, was announced in August 1992, thereby creating the world's largest trading bloc. The benefits to the U.S. public are best stated as follows:

"Consumers: In all three nations, consumers should come out ahead, as tariffs, which raise prices, are lowered and eliminated. Consumers also should find greater choices of goods and services.

Business: Businesses should profit by gaining access to bigger markets and the ability to integrate operations throughout the continent. Some also would benefit by shifting production to low-cost Mexico.

Labor: The outlook is mixed for American workers. While as many as 500,000 low-skilled jobs could be transferred to Mexico to save costs, other companies could hire as many U.S. workers to produce products for a modernized Mexico."[2]

The agreement is intended to liberalize trade and investment throughout North America.

These regional trade agreements are the subject of an intense debate. Some subscribe to the idea that these arrangements may lead to an undermining of global free-trade negotiations under the General Agreement on Tariffs and Trade, the 103-nation pact that has set the world's free-trade rules since 1947, and an increase in protectionism, as countries use regional agreements to steer business toward their allies instead of buying from whatever country produces most cheaply. Some, however, feel that regional free-trade deals are better than no free trade at all in forcing some countries to open their markets to foreign products.

4. The key words arising from this new economic order are *competitiveness* and *survival*. A new paradigm maintains that competitiveness itself motivates the success of nations. Such is the thesis of Porter, who maintains that the ability of a nation to upgrade its existing advantages to the next level of technology and productivity is the key to international success.[3] Four factors, called the "diamond" of national competitive advantages, are presented as the key to the success of nations:

a. factor conditions (a nation's ability to turn factor endowment into a specialized advantage)

b. demand conditions (the existence of demanding, sophisticated customers)

c. related and supporting industries that provide supplies clusters to firms

d. company, strategy, structure, and rivalry (conditions governing how firms in a nation are created and nurtured during times of intense competition)

Porter's single, home-based diamond is relevant for larger triad economies like the United States and Japan. For other countries, the model needs to incorporate the effects of multinational activities. A much more relevant concept may prevail in small open economies, named the "double diamond." Basically, a nation's competitiveness depends partly on the domestic diamond and partly on the "international" diamond relevant to its firms. Exhibit 1.1 shows the home-based single diamond and Exhibit 1.2 shows the double diamond. In Exhibit 1.2, the large diamond $(F_g T_g D_g S_g)$ represents a global diamond and the small one

Exhibit 1.1
The Home-Based Single Diamond

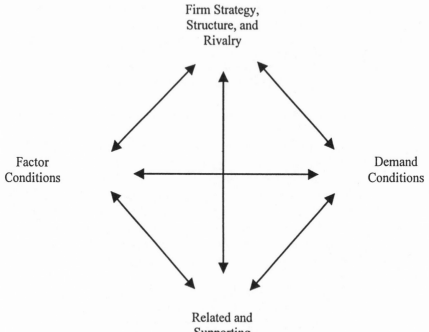

Firm Strategy,
Structure, and
Rivalry

Factor
Conditions

Demand
Conditions

Related and
Supporting
Industries

$(F_dT_dD_dS_d)$, a domestic diamond. Although the size of the global diamond is fixed for a given period, the size of the domestic diamond varies according to the country's size and competitiveness.[4]

The differences in competitiveness internationally may also be attributed to the differences in corporate ownership and corporate objectives in various parts of the world. In the United States, for example, transient owners such as institutional investors, pension funds, mutual funds, and money managers focus on short-term objectives rather than long-term growth.

It also appears that the American system of capital allocation relies heavily on external capital provided by transient owners, comprised of institutional investors, pension funds, mutual funds, and other money managers, who are mainly interested in short-term gains. These owners/agents are very motivated by the market performance of their stocks, at the expense of direct interest in the company, its goals, or its level of international competitiveness. As a result, American managers place their major focus on earning high returns on investments and maximizing current stock prices.

Exhibit 1.2
The New Double Diamond

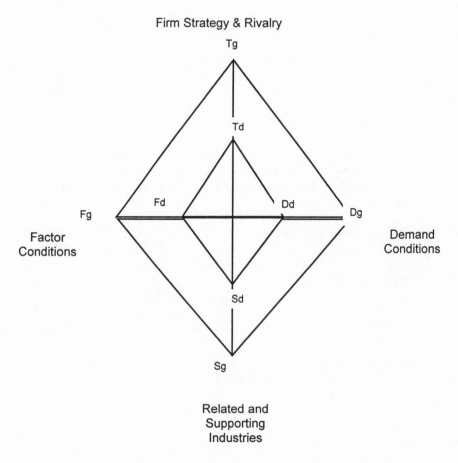

Firm Strategy & Rivalry

Factor
Conditions

Demand
Conditions

Related and
Supporting
Industries

The external and internal capital location systems are different in Japan and Germany, where the dominant owners not agents but rather principals, who seek long-term growth and have a special relationship with the firm. This special relationship translates into access to inside information and greater influence on managerial behavior.

5. International rules are being written to regulate and tame the global economy. They include:

a. The creation of the World Trade Organization to regulate foreign trade.

b. The writing of rules governing investment around the world by multinational corporations, to be known as the Multinational Agreement on Investment.

c. The writing of accounting standards for firms that want to register their stock on global stock markets.

d. The issuance by the Bank for International Settlements, which coordinates the world's central banks, of a new "core principle," guiding, but not binding on, bank examiners in all countries.

e. The increased settlements of global business disputes, not in the courts, but in private tribunals run by arbitrators chosen by the litigants and dominated by American lawyers. The Big Three of international arbitration centers are the International Chamber of Commerce in Paris, the London Court of International Arbitration, and the American Arbitration Association in New York.

What is still lacking is a kind of global Internal Revenue Service to curb tax evasion and the establishment of global labor and environmental standards.

6. The faces of capitalism are changing. One may distinguish four types of capitalism, as follows:[5]

1. *Consumer capitalism*, as practiced in the United States, Britain, Canada, Australia; characterized by greater laissez-faire, open borders, small government, and profit mentality, potentially leading to problems of income inequality, low saving rates, and weak central governments.

2. *Producer capitalism*, as practiced in Germany, France, Japan, and Mexico; characterized by a focus on production, employment, and statist policies, potentially leading to such problems as the fraying of the social safety net, the slowing of innovation, and consumer dissatisfaction.

3. *Family capitalism*, as practiced in Taiwan, Malaysia, Thailand, and Indonesia; created by the Chinese diaspora, as characterized by extended clans dominating business, and by capital flows, potentially leading to social resentment from other, non-Chinese ethnics.

4. *Frontier capitalism*, as practiced by China and Russia; characterized by government's support of for-profit business activities and by the sprouting of an entrepreneurial class, potentially leading to a rise in criminal activity. In fact, there are three stages to frontier capitalism, as follows:

   a. Stage One: Statist economies collapse or fade away. Black marketeers profit enormously, with some becoming gangsters, and government corruption spreads.

   b. Stage Two: Small-scale entrepreneurs, often financed by family loans, flourish. Rule of law remains weak, but businesspeople start evolving their own rules of commerce.

   c. Stage Three: Economic growth is brisk, but hard to measure. Financial markets begin to evolve, tapping savings and attracting foreign institutional investors, and a clearer legal code appears.[6]

Capitalism itself may be facing a crisis, as illustrated by the following theses:

A. One thesis is that the capitalist system will not cope with twenty-first-century pressures. Lester C. Thurow's evaluation of capitalism's current dilemma arises from both punctuated equilibrium and plate tectonics.[7] Punctuated equilibrium refers to the occasional suddenness of biological evolution and here is used to mean that winners can sometimes quickly become losers. Plate tectonics refers to the invisible slow movements of the continental plates floating on the earth's core and here is used to mean that the causes of events may be difficult to determine and long-lasting. Five economic events are presented, each of which produces changes that threaten capitalism:

1. the collapse of communism, creating a vast supply of cheap and educated labor
2. the primacy of technology, creating a knowledge-based economy
3. the demographic issue of an aging population in the rich North facing a tide of immigration from the poor South
4. the growth of the global economy and the consequent decline in wages
5. the disappearance of a single globally dominant power

B. Another thesis is that nations go through periods of rise and decline, providing a case for successive primacies. Kindleberger advances this thesis in two books: *Manias, Panics, and Crashes: A History of Financial Crises*[8] and *World Economic Primacy: 1500–1900*.[9] The thesis is very much in line with that of a Spanish professor of juriprudence who asserted in 1799 that all nations of the world, following the steps of nature, have been weak in their infancy, ignorant in their puberty, warlike in their youth, philosophic in their manhoods, legists in their old age, and superstitious and tyrannical in their decrepitude. It is also much in line with the "law of interrupted progress," which holds that any country pioneering a new, more developed phase of civilization reaches a threshold or barrier beyond which it is extremely difficult to proceed, with the result that the next step forward in the progress of humankind has to be made in another part of the world. Examples of nations following the cycle of eventual declines include: (a) the Italian city-states of Venice, Florence, Genoa, and Milan; (b) Portugal and Spain, following their wealth in the fifteenth and sixteenth centuries; and (c) France, Britain, Germany, the United States, and Japan's recent history of economic wealth turning into rigidity and resistance to change. Kindleberger cites the decline of the team player, the polarization of races and classes, and the shattering of American confidence following the Vietnam War as the reason why the United States seems to be going in the direction of sclerosis and decline.

C. Another thesis argues for the rise of big emerging markets. The United States used to worry about economic competition from abroad by focusing on advanced industrialized democracies like Japan and Germany. Today, however, a new era for the world economy dictates otherwise. The big emergent market hypothesis is also called the "big ten hypothesis," as advanced by Jeffrey E. Garten,[10] and stipulates that the main agents of change are a group of ten countries that are important enough to affect the entire world economy. These countries are Argentina, Brazil, China, India, Indonesia, Mexico, Poland, South Africa, South Korea, and Turkey. They are potentially wealthy enough to play a major role in the entire world economy, providing producers everywhere with huge new markets and opportunities for profit and job creation. They are in agreement with the United States in the adoption of free-market practices while in disagreement with the United States in the role of governmental policies in influencing trade and investment flows, the rights of workers and consumers, and environmental policies. Do these ten countries provide a threat to the dominance of the United States or do they need American technology, American capital, and an American market that represents fully 25 percent of the world economy? This hypothesis will need verification in the years to come.

D. Another debate goes on about the U.S. model thesis versus the clash of cultures thesis. According to the U.S. model thesis, as advocated by Francis Fukuyama, this is the "end of history," as marked by the universal triumph of American-style liberal democracy as the final form of government. The end result is not very reassuring. As stated by Fukuyama:

The end of history will be a very sad time. The struggle for recognition, the willingness to risk one's life for a purely abstract goal, the worldwide ideological struggle that called forth daring, courage, imagination, and idealism, will be replaced by economic calculation, the endless solving of technical problems, environmental concerns, and the satisfaction of sophisticated consumer demands. In the post-historical period there will be neither art nor philosophy, just the perpetual caretaking of the museum of human history. I can feel in myself, and see in others around me, a powerful nostalgia for the time when history existed. Such nostalgia, in fact, will continue to fuel competition and conflict even in the post-historical world for some time to come. Even though I recognize its inevitability, I have the most ambivalent feelings for the civilization that has been created in Europe since 1945, with its North Atlantic and Asian offshoots. Perhaps this very prospect of centuries of boredom at the end of history will serve to get history started once again.[11]

The second thesis argues that the course of events did not work according to the "end of history" scenario. According to the clash of culture hypothesis, as enunciated by Samuel P. Huntington,[12] the two blocs created by the Cold War split into "civilizations," based on common cultures and heritage, that are more likely to fight each other than to form a single world based on one culture. The eight civilizations are:

a. the Western one, led by the United States and Western Europe;

b. the Sinic, led by China;

c. the Hindi, led by India;

d. the Islamic, with no real leader;

e. Japan, a self-contained civilization;

f. the Orthodox, led by Russia; and

g. the African and Latin American civilizations, with no clear leaders.

Basically, in economics and politics there are no universal values.

7. With the increased level of business activities conducted by multinational firms, the international business literature raises the empirical question of whether multinationality does, in fact, add to the shared values commonly used to link multinationality to investment value, namely: the internalization theory, the imperfect capital markets theory, and the managerial objectives theory.

The internalization theory maintains that foreign direct investment will cause the increase of the market value of a firm relative to its accounting value only if the firm can internalize markets for certain of its intangibles. Examples of these firm-specific intangible assets include production skills, managerial skills, patents, market abilities, and consumer goodwill. These information-based, proprietary intangible assets cannot be copied or exchanged at arm's length; they can only be transferred to subsidiaries, thereby internalizing the markets for such assets. As a result, the market value of a multinational firm that possesses these intangibles and engages in foreign direct investment will be directly proportional to the firm's degree of multinationality.

The imperfect capital markets theory suggests that investors, who are restrained by institutional constraints on international capital flows and the information asymmetries that exist in global capital markets, invest in multinational firms to gain from the international diversification opportunities provided by these multinational firms. This direct valuation of multinational firms by investors as a means of diversifying their portfolios internationally is assumed to enhance the share price of multinational firms, independent of the information-based, proprietary intangible assets that they possess.

The managerial objectives theory rests on the assumption of differing motives between management and shareholders. The complexity of the multinational firm and the resulting difficulty for shareholders to monitor management's decisions allow management to act in its own self-interest. Management may favor international diversification because it reduces firm-specific risk, a situation that may reduce the market value of multinational firms.

8. The United States will be less secure by 2025, as concluded by a 1999 Pentagon-funded panel of experts. The main finding is the United States will have limited ability to impose its will and will be increasingly vulnerable to growing range of threats against American forces and citizens overseas as well as at home. While global economic growth will continue, serious and unexpected economic downturns, major disparities in wealth, volatile capital flows, increasing vulnerabilities in global electronic infrastructures, labor and social disruptions, and pressures for increased protectionism will also occur. Other findings include:

- An economically strong United States is likely to remain a primary political, military and cultural force through 2025. It will remain the principal military power.

- Much of the world will resent and oppose the United States, and reliable alliances will become more difficult to establish and sustain.

- World energy supplies will remain largely based on fossil fuels, and American dependence on foreign sources of energy will also grow over the next two decades.

- Weapons of mass destruction will proliferate, making the maintenance of a robust U.S. nuclear deterrent essential. Some important states will not be able to manage the challenges now emerging and could fragment or fail. New states, international protectorates, and zones of autonomy, as now seen in Kosovo, will increase, many of which will be born of violence.

- Weapons are likely to be put into space, which will become permanently manned.

- Pressures will increase substantially for the United States to reduce its military presence in Europe and Asia.

- New technologies will divide the world as well as draw it together, and an antitechnology backlash is possible.

- All national borders will be porous; some will bend and some will break. Traditional bonds between states and their citizens, including in the United States, can no longer be taken for granted.[13]

9. Trade is regulated by the World Trade Organization (WTO), a 135-nation group that sets the rules for international commerce. It is both traffic cop and top court of the global economy.[14] Its 36,000 pages of regulations reach into far-flung crannies of human existence. The main purpose remains free trade, with the resulting abolition of tariffs enabling consumers to profit globally from lower prices. It is, however, the arena for a world full of conflicts, where different players negotiate over a variety of issues. They include:[15]

a. Conflicts between Europe and Japan versus the United States and the emerging countries: the issue is that European and Japanese farmers are protected by government subsidies. The United States and the emerging economies want access to those markets. Europe and Japan maintain that the United States also aids its farmers, and they oppose America's genetically modified food.

b. Conflicts between the United States and the European Union versus the emerging countries: the issue is the low-cost labor from the emerging countries, which threatens jobs in the United States and Europe. Naturally, the emerging countries do not want outside interference in their labor markets.

c. Conflicts between the United States and the European Union (EU) versus the emerging countries: the issue is that the United States and the EU want to enforce environmental pacts—such as treaties restricting endangered species trade. The emerging countries oppose "enviro" (environmental) restrictions.

d. Conflicts between the United States versus everyone else: the issue is that the United States wants to slash barriers to several key industries, including health care, banking, education, insurance, and e-commerce (electronic commerce).

e. Conflicts between the United States versus Japan and the emerging countries: the issue is that the U.S. laws block countries from "dumping" subsidized products—such as steel, semiconductors, and textiles—on the American market. The emerging countries maintain that the laws are protectionist and the United States should import more.

The Role of the Multinational Corporation

Mueller gives the following accurate characterization of the multinational corporations: "The international corporation is emerging. This is a corporation which is internationally owned and controlled. It is not a domestic corporation with some foreign business. It is a business organization with a truly international organization for all its business functions, including management, production, marketing and finance."[16] The international firm is generally a domestic firm that expanded from the development of a strong product for domestic sales to a complex firm with a multinational management organization and a multinational ownership of equity securities. It can take one of two forms:

1. a world corporation format, which includes the merger of domestic and foreign operations for the functions of research and development, manufacturing, marketing and finance
2. an international division format, in which all foreign operations are separated from their domestic counterparts in an international division

The eclectic paradigm of international production by multinational firms argues that the initial act of foreign production by firms and the growth of such production depend crucially on the configuration of three elements: firm-specific (or ownership-specific) advantages, county-specific (locational) advantages, and internalization advantages.[17]

The ownership advantages include both proprietary know-how (unique assets) and transactional advantages that outweigh the costs of servicing an unfamiliar or distant environment. Basically, the firm has unique ownership advantages that its competitors lack.

The locational advantages include the benefits associated with locating certain activities in particular countries. When it is in the best interest of the multinational firm to locate its activities outside the home country, the firm uses its locational advantages to respond to a kind of spatial market failure, basically internalizing exogenous spatial imperfections.

The internalization advantages refer to the relative benefits associated with serving foreign markets. With internalization advantages present, it is to the advantage of the multinational firm to transfer its ownership advantages abroad rather than sell them. The perceived great costs of transactional failure lead the firm to transfer its advantages across national borders rather operate through contractual agreements with foreign firms. In a sense, the multinational firm "internalizes" the market for its use.

The multinational corporation (MNC) is best viewed as a collection of valuable options. Various benefits can be achieved through the MNC:

1. Significant arbitrage benefits can be obtained through:

   a. exploitation of financing bargains;

   b. reduction of taxes on financial flows;

   c. mitigation or shifting of risks to agents with a comparative advantage in bearing them;

   d. diversification of cash flows received through foreign operations;

   e. exploitation of various institutional perfections;

   f. capturing and appropriation of information.

2. Foreign operating options allow additional benefits through:

   a. location options, which are associated with location alternatives that enhance profits;

   b. timing options, which are connected with the exploitation of transient costs and exchange rate disparities;

   c. technology options, linking international cost disparities and flexible technologies for the exploitation of the short-term price changes; and

   d. staging options, which are associated with establishing a discernible presence in foreign markets.[18]

3. Other benefits include capital availability and a desirable cost of capital for a considerable range of the MNC's capital budget.[19]

The multinational corporation's objective is to maximize shareholder wealth, subject to environmental, regulatory, and ethical constraints. The objective may be difficult to achieve in cases where managers decide to maximize their own utility functions. This is the *agency problem*, in which the goals of the shareholders conflict with those of the managers. The problem may be more frequent in the case of multinational corporations, where managers of different subsidiaries are more inclined to maximize the value of their respective subsidiaries. The multinational corporation calls for specific performance evaluation and control techniques to alleviate the potential agency problems that arise from the divergent interests of subsidiaries and the multinational corporation. It also calls for specific accounting standards to deal with the unique pressures of accountability from domestic and foreign interest groups. Accordingly, Gray Shaw, and McSweeney argued that there is a case for applying standards to multinational corporations as follows:

The present lack of consistency in MNC accountability and the proliferation of national standards may lead to the conclusion that worldwide harmonization of MNC reporting— disclosure and measurement—is needed. Equally, there may be a major priority for international [domestic] enterprises with no foreign operations, because the needs of the international investment community, the main agency involved and relatively expert, could be met to a large extent by accounting policy disclosures. It is only when international companies become units of a supernatural economic ability, the MNC, that arguments of consistency and comparability in the interests of international constituencies of users become persuasive.[20]

Foreign Direct Investment

Foreign direct investment involves the transfer of capital, managerial, and technical assets of a firm from one country (the home country) to another (the host country) by or within the same firm. Firms engage in foreign direct investment and expand their markets by producing and selling abroad. Some of the reasons include the following:

- to reduce transportation costs
- because of a lack of domestic policy
- to achieve economies of scale in small-scale process technology
- to avoid trade or customer-imposed restrictions
- to follow customers and competitors
- to benefit from a different cost structure
- to achieve some vertical integration
- to rationalize production by taking advantage of varying costs of labor, capital, and raw materials
- to have access to production factors
- to take advantage of government investment incentives
- because of political motives
- to use a monopoly advantage over similar companies in the foreign countries
- to have better profitability and stable sales and earnings.[21,22]

Various models and theories can be used to explain foreign direct investment (FDI). They include international trade theory, location theory, investment theory, the theory of the firm, and industrial organization theory.

a. The international trade theory relies either on a comparative cost view or a product life cycle view.
b. The location theory relies on transportation costs.
c. The investment theory relies on either an imperfect capital markets view or a portfolio of foreign direct investments view.
d. A theory of the firm relies on a microeconomic perspective, including an "internalization" dimension.
e. The industrial organization theory relies on market imperfections that create oligopolies and the exploitation of company-specific advantages.

The International Monetary System

The international monetary system (IMS) constitutes the structure within which exchange rates are determined, international trade and capital flows are accumulated, and balance-of-payments adjustments are made. To better appreciate the exchange rate problem and how it affects international accounting practices, a good grasp of the IMS is essential.

The United Nations Monetary and Financial Conference, held in Bretton Woods, New Hampshire in 1944 with the objective of developing an IMS, created both the International Monetary Fund (IMF), and the International Bank for Reconstruction and Development, which is known as the World Bank. The IMF's objectives, as set by its charter, are:

"1. To promote international monetary cooperation . . . through consultation and collaboration.

2. To facilitate the expansion and balanced growth of international trade.

3. To promote exchange stability . . . and to avoid competitive exchange depreciation.

4. To assist in the establishment of a multilateral system of payments . . . and in the elimination of foreign exchange restrictions.

5. To give confidence to members by making the Fund's resources available to them . . . thus providing them with opportunity to correct [temporary] maladjustments in their balances of payments."

Soon, the fixed exchange rate system or par value based on gold and the U.S. dollar proved inadequate and needed improvement. This was accomplished by two actions:

1. Swap agreements, whereby instant reserves were created by a swap of credit lines between central banks, were facilitated.

2. A more lasting solution to the need for growth in world monetary reserves was provided by the creation of a new unit of reserve called the Special Drawing Right (SDR). This system allowed countries to borrow or withdraw SDRs from the IMF to buy other countries' currencies.

However, crisis in the IMS, caused by an overvalued dollar and growing U.S. balance-of-trade deficits, led, in December 1971, to the convening of another conference, which resulted in the Smithsonian Agreement and the devaluation of the U.S. dollar. A further devaluation of the dollar in 1973 showed the limits of the fixed rate system. From these crises there emerged the following exchange rate systems:

1. a fixed rate system, in which the value of the currency is "pegged" (fixed) to another currency or allowed to fluctuate only within very narrow boundaries;

2. a freely floating exchange rate system, in which the value of the currency is determined by market forces and not through intervention by government;

3. a managed-float exchange rate system, in which the value of the currency is allowed to fluctuate and governments intervene to ensure the value does not move too much in a given direction (also known as a "managed float" or "dirty float");

4. a pegged exchange rate system, used by members of the European Community to peg the value of their currencies to a basket of currencies expressed in European Currency Units (ECUs), and to limit fluctuations within established limits. (The system is also known as the "snake.") The 1991 Maastricht Agreement between the members of the European Community was to create, by 1999, a European Central Bank and a single currency (or national currencies "irrevocably" fixed with one another), with the provision that the central bank will conduct a single monetary policy.

However, beginning in January 1999 the Euro currency was introduced with the three-year goal of completely replacing the German marks, French franc, Italian lira, and Spanish pesata. The European Monetary Union (EMU) thus became the world's second largest economy, consisting of 288 million people and a gross domestic product of nearly 20% of the global's total. Among the repercussions are the following:

- "Business and individual consumers will find it much easier to buy and sell products and services across European borders. Intra-European trade and commercial competition will soar, companies will be forced to shape up, and a wave of megamergers will create powerful pan-European companies."

- "A Europewide capital market will emerge for the first time, offering enormous cross-border opportunities for borrowing and investing. Meanwhile, EMU will act as a catalyst for more flexible labor markets and for more harmonized European policies for everything from taxes to banking regulation."

- "The European Central Bank—which, by law, will be highly independent—will follow in the conservative footsteps of Germany's Bundesbank and create conditions for low inflation and healthier economic growth throughout the region."

- "The euro will become a powerful rival to the dollar for central banks' reserves and trade financing. Russia and all of Eastern Europe will be drawn into the new euro zone, bringing them under Western Europe's political sway. The European Union will gain substantial clout in the Group of Seven, the International Monetary Fund, and the World Trade Organization."[23]

The World Bank is an international, profit-oriented bank whose objective is to make loans to countries for economic development projects and to secure funds through the sale of bonds and other debt instruments to private investors and governments. Other such institutions include, to name only a few:

1. the International Financial Corporation (IFC), which is devoted to the promotion of private enterprise within countries

2. the International Development Association (IDA), which is devoted to the promotion of economic development for very needy nations

3. the Bank of International Settlements, "a central bank's central bank" devoted to facilitating international transactions among countries

4. regional development agencies, which are devoted to regional economic development, such as

   a. the Inter-American Development Bank

   b. the Asian Development Bank

   c. the African Development Fund

   d. the European Bank for Reconstruction and Development

THE NEED FOR INTERNATIONAL ACCOUNTING

These four new environmental factors—the global economy, the international monetary system, the multinational corporation, and foreign direct investment—have created an environment in which business transactions, and their conduct, measurement and disclosure take on new and distinctive forms that call for a specific accounting subdiscipline. That accounting subdiscipline is international accounting. The definition of international accounting, like the field itself, is subject to constant changes in order to adapt to different contexts, requirements, and expectations. One useful definition distinguished three approaches: a universal system, a comparative system, and accounting for subsidiaries.

The concept of universal or world accounting is by far the largest in scope. It directs international accounting to the formulation and study of a universally accepted set of accounting principles. It aims for a complete standardization of accounting principles internationally. The definition used by Weirich, Avery, and Anderson is as follows:

World Accounting. In the framework of this concept, international accounting is considered to be a universal system that could be adopted in all countries. A world-wide set of generally accepted accounting principles (GAAP), such as the set maintained in the United States, would be established. Practices and principles would be developed which were applicable to all countries. This concept would be the ultimate goal of an international accounting system.[24]

While very commendable, this goal is unlikely to be achieved in the near future and may be characterized as highly idealistic by some and even utopian by others. As will be seen in the rest of this book, pessimistic attitudes are a reflection of the many obstacles to a complete standardization of accounting principles. Chapter 2 examines in detail some of the factors determining accounting differences internationally.

The concept of comparative or international accounting directs international accounting to a study and understanding of national differences in accounting. It involves "(a) an awareness of the international diversity in corporate accounting and reporting practices, (b) understanding of the accounting principles and practices of individual countries, and (c) ability to assess the impact of diverse accounting practices on financial reporting."[25] There is a general consensus in accounting literature that the term "international accounting" refers to comparative accounting principles. The definition of Weirich, Avery, and Anderson is:

International Accounting. A second major concept of the term international accounting involves a descriptive and informative approach. Under this concept, international accounting includes all varieties of principles, methods and standards of accounting of all countries. This concept includes a set of generally accepted accounting principles established for each country, thereby requiring the accountant to be multiple principle conscious when studying international accounting. . . . No universal or perfect set of principles would be expected to be established. A collection of all principles, methods and standards of all countries would be considered as the international accounting system. These variations result because of differing geographic, social, economic, political and legal influences.[26]

The concept of parent–foreign subsidiary accounting, or accounting for foreign subsidiaries, is by far the oldest and narrowest in scope. It reduces international accounting to the process of consolidating the accounts of the parent company and its subsidiaries and translating foreign currency into local currency. The definition of Weirich, Avery, and Anderson is as follows:

Accounting for Foreign Subsidiaries. The third major concept that may be applied to "international accounting" refers to the accounting practices of a parent company and a foreign subsidiary. A reference to a particular country or domicile is needed under the concept for effective internal financial reporting. The accountant is concerned mainly with the translation and adjustment of the subsidiary's financial statement. Different accounting problems arise and different accounting principles are to be followed depending upon which country is used as a reference for translating and adjusting purposes.[27]

DIMENSIONS OF INTERNATIONAL ACCOUNTING

Areas of International Accounting

International accounting takes in all the technical accounting problems in financial, managerial, tax, and auditing areas that have a bearing on the conduct, measurement, and disclosure of foreign operations. There are issues relevant to international business that create special accounting problems and specific solutions that differ from the solutions adopted in a domestic context. They are generally perceived to be the general domain of international accounting. A good list of these issues is as follows:

A. Private sector accounting

   1. Comparative analysis

      a. National accounting, reporting, and auditing practice (principles, procedures, standards and disclosure)

      b. National accounting theory (including historical dimensions)

   2. Policy at the international level (standardization)

   3. Accounting for multinational operations

      a. Financial accounting (translation, consolidation, segmental, inflation accounting, disclosure, auditing)

      b. Managerial accounting (risk and exposure measurements, foreign investment analysis, information systems, transfer pricing, control and performance evaluation, operational, auditing, behavioral dimensions)

   4. Taxation (of international operations in different countries)

B. Public sector accounting

   1. Comparative analysis of national systems Gross National Product (GNP), measurement, balance of payments, balance of trade, employment statistics, and so on)

   2. Accounting for governmental agencies and public not-for-profit organizations (overlaps with the realm of private sector accounting because certain industries are nationalized in some countries.[28]

International Annual Reports

The rise of the global economy, the multinational corporation, the integration of capital markets, and the increased cosmopolitanism of investors suggest that there is a new type of information seeker—the international information seeker. This person's interests go beyond conventional information to include concerns about political risks, foreign exchange effects, and international performance, to name only a few. To meet the needs of these new, international information seekers, the annual reports of multinational companies have become more internationally oriented, including, in various cases, the translation of annual reports in one or more languages, the separate disclosure of the extent of international involvement, employee reporting, value-added reporting, social responsibility reporting, and other specific innovations. To meet the requirements of a multiple audience of interests from different countries, three identifiable approaches have been advocated:[29]

1. Primary and secondary financial statements: to meet the financial need of audiences of interest in more than one country, multiple sets of statements are prepared. Essentially, the secondary financial statements are prepared to meet the information need of audiences of interest in other countries. Secondary financial statements have one or more of the following characteristics:

- The reporting standards of a foreign country are followed.
- The statements are translated into a language that is not the language of the company's country of domicile.

• The auditor's report is expressed in a form not commonly used in the company's country of domicile."[30]

2. Single-domicile reporting: the argument of this school is that financial statements can reflect only one point of view, that of the company's country of domicile. Mueller gives the following explanation:

The notion of a single domicile for financial statements means that each set of financial statements necessarily has a nationality, reflects style and customs at a particular viewpoint or characteristic. Financial statements are anchored in a single set of underlying account data prepared within a framework of quite specific accounting standards, methods and procedures. Restatement of financial statements to a different set of accounting principles produces different relationships between individual account balances and financial ratios. The meaning and implications of these new relationships may convey an entirely different financial substance to statement readers in other countries.[31]

3. International reporting standards: this school of thought argues that internationally accepted accounting standards should be adopted by all countries in the preparation of their financial statements. It implies a complete international standardization of accounting standards. It is a worthwhile project that has been started and has generated much enthusiasm and participation.

Increase in Foreign Stock Listings

As firms enter foreign markets for either the purchasing or selling of products or services and for obtaining capital in these markets, they may find it advantageous to list their stock on a foreign stock exchange. Various benefits and costs are associated with listing on a foreign stock exchange. The benefits include:[32]

1. financial benefits associated with a reduced cost of capital, given that, in addition, some foreign capital markets offer lower transaction costs, narrower quotation spreads, and greater market stability than is the case domestically, and other financial benefits, including the facilitation of foreign acquisitions, mergers, stock swaps, and tender offers made possible by the supplies of shares that meet local regulatory requirements.
2. marketing and public relations benefits with a better name recognition in the foreign country.
3. political benefits, by complying with local ownership requirements
4. employee relations benefits, by aligning foreign employee and shareholder incentives and enabling foreign employees to trade shares acquired from employee stock ownership plans on a local exchange.

The costs of foreign listing are generated by the costs of increased accounting and disclosure requirements. They include the following:

1. adjustments of accounting procedures to meet local requirements
2. adjustments of auditing procedures to meet local requirements
3. changes in the frequency of reporting
4. costs resulting from more extensive foreign financial disclosures than are required for domestic competitors
5. monetary expense, time, and administrative effort in initial registration
6. recurring costs of compliance
7. possible foreign regulation in response to simultaneous offerings at home and abroad
8 foreign regulatory agency's jurisdiction over worldwide business practices[33]

Given that the benefits outweigh the costs, a pressure exists for the regulatory agencies in each country to protect investors with comprehensive disclosure requirements and yet attract foreign investment by increasing the competitiveness of their local stock exchanges through less costly disclosure requirements. The trade-off is difficult to achieve, but feasible. Examples include the U.S. Securities and Exchange Commission (SEC) adoption of the Integrated Disclosure System (IDS) in 1982, which includes the use of the foreign registrant's domestic GAAP in preparing financial statements, segment reporting timeliness of the financial statements incorporated in the prospectus, and disclosure of top management's compensation.[34]

Another example is the April 1990 SEC adoption of Rule 144A, which provides a safe harbor exemption from the registration requirements of the 1933 Securities Act for the resale of restricted securities to "qualified institutional buyers."[35] It allows traders to resell private-placement securities without registration or any waiting period. A Japanese example includes the December 1983 amendment to the Enforcement Order of the Securities and Exchange Law and the Ministerial Ordinance on the Audit Certificate of Financial Statements to eliminate the dual audit requirements for foreign companies listed on the Tokyo Stock Exchange.

The SEC requirements are, nonetheless, very demanding for non-U.S. firms. The registration statements for non-U.S. issuers making a distribution in the U.S. markets are Form F-1, used for the initial public offering; Forms F-2 and F-3, for issuers who had previously registered securities under the Securities Act or the Securities Exchange Act; Form F-4, for business combinations; and Form F-6, for the registration of American Depository shares evidenced by American depository receipts (ADR). The disclosure requirements set forth in Regulations S-K and S-X apply also to non-U.S. issuers. Basically, foreign issuers may elect to file the registration and reporting forms used by domestic issuers, as outlined in Exhibit 1.3. Alternately, they can also elect to file forms that are considered less stringent, such as Forms 20-F (similar to 10K) and 6-K (similar to 8-K). Issuers of ADRs are exempt from 8-K requirements. When using Form 20-F, foreign issuers are required to indicate the reporting principles

Exhibit 1.3
Corporate Filings: Securities and Exchange Commission

10-K Annual Report

Contents   (partial listing):
            Business of Company
            Properties
            Legal Proceedings
            Management Discussion and Analysis
            Changes or Disagreements with Auditors
            Financial Statements and Footnotes
            Investee Financial Statements (where applicable)
            Parent Company Financial Statements (where applicable)
            Schedules:
            I. Condensed Financial Information
            II. Bad Debt and Other Valuation Accounts
            III. Real Estate and Accumulated Depreciation
            IV. Mortgage Loans on Real Estate
            V. Supplementary Information Concerning Property-Casualty Insurance Oper-
               ations

Due Date: 3 months following end of fiscal year.

10-Q Quarterly Report

Contents   Financial Statements
            Management Discussion and Analysis

Due Date: 45 days following end of fiscal quarter. Not required for fourth quarter of fiscal
year.

8-K Current Report

Contents   (used to report important events):
            Change in Control
            Acquisitions and Divestitures
            Bankruptcy
            Change in Auditors
            Resignation of Directors

Due Date: 15 days following event.

used and the material differences from U.S. GAAP and to reconcile reported
income and stockholders' equity to U.S. GAAP.

he SEC took a first step toward a multijurisdictional disclosure system
(MJDS) when, in 1991, it entered into an agreement with Canadian regulators
allowing large Canadian firms to issue certain classes of securities in the United

States using financial statements prepared according to Canadian GAAP (and vice-versa).

Accounting Standards for the Multinational Corporation

Multinational corporations (MNCs) are faced with a diversity of accounting standards with which they must comply. First, MNCs need to comply with the local standards of their country of origin, which will differ in some respect from the standards required in other countries. As a result, they need to be sensitive to the requirements of *comparative international accounting*. Second, MNCs need to comply with the international accounting standards set by the Intertional Accounting Standards Committee (IASC), the international standard setting body. As a result, they need to be sensitive to the requirements of *standardized international accounting*. Third, MNCs need to comply with the reporting and disclosure requirements of regional or world political institutions. As a result they need to be sensitive to the requirements of *politicized international accounting*. Fourth, MNCs need to comply with the accounting techniques that can facilitate the conduct of their operations and ensure their success. As a result, they need to be sensitive to *operational international accounting*.[36]

Questions that will immediately arise for users, multinationals, and these potential standards setters include the following: should there be specific standards for MNCs? What should be required, and who should set them?[37]

The first question—whether there should be specific standards for MNCs— is usually answered in the affirmative. There now exist identifiable international constituencies, which demand specific information from multinational corporations. In fact, the existence of an international investor group from different countries has created various unique reporting audiences of interest. The following reasons have been proposed for such uniqueness.

- People living and working in different cultures have different characteristics, attitudes, lifestyles, and general behavior patterns. These differences make for differing standards of comparison and may lead to different decision processes.
- Investment institutions differ from country to country, thus causing differing information wants and usages.
- Accounting principles, as financial statement users understand them, differ from country to country.[38]

The second question—that of what should be required by the standards—is more difficult to answer, given the lack of knowledge of the decision requirements of the user groups involved. Although a minimal list of items of disclosure may easily be determined, more cooperation from the accounting profession and a substantial research effort, as well as a political effort, will be needed to develop general accounting standards for the multinational corporations and to resolve various issues. Examples of these issues include:

- defining user information needs
- the role of general-purpose reports versus special-purpose reports
- segmental information, particularly on a geographic basis, or multianalysis by activity and by country
- transfer pricing and its impact
- employment conditions and prospects
- foreign currency transactions and the translation of foreign currency financial statements
- accounting for groups and the consolidation of financial statements
- accounting for inflation
- accounting for taxation[39]

Examples of managerial accounting issues include:

- foreign exchange risk management
- consolidation of enterprise accounts
- investment planning
- external financial sourcing
- international taxation
- transfer pricing
- performance evaluation
- information control system[40]

The third question—concerning who should set the standards—is the most difficult and sensitive of the three. One alternative is to let the multinational corporations set the standards, assuming an existing enlightened self-interest on the part of the management of multinational interest groups that establish claims to disclosure by the multinational corporation about its worldwide or local activities.

If the first alternative is rejected, there remain only two alternative agencies, the political and the professional. Although the professional route would be preferable, developments in international accounting seem to show that the political approach has merits. Consider the following:

Matters of accountancy appear to have become too important to be left to accountancy bodies. If the levels of accountability are to be defined at the national level in the first instance and ultimately some form of supernational harmonization is to be achieved, then it is difficult to see any alternative to political agencies. At this stage, it also seems likely that such agencies will concentrate on the philosophy of information disclosure—why information is needed and in what form it is required—leaving detailed aspects to be worked out in cooperation with the professional accountancy organization.[41]

The Internationalization of the Accounting Profession

One important result of the rise of international accounting is the internationalization of the accounting profession. This can be seen in the development of international and regional accounting bodies making their entrance in the standards-setting arena and in the growing network of international firm partnerships and liaisons. In effect, various organizations have, in recent years, made some efforts to harmonize their accounting standards.

These organizations include the Accounting International Study Group (AISG), the International Accounting Standards Committee, the European Community (EC), the United Nations, the International Federations of Accountants, and the Union of European Accountants.

The internationalization of the accounting profession can be seen in the growing network of international firm partnerships and liaisons. These international accounting firms have developed, for the most part, to meet the needs of affiliates or subsidiaries of multinational companies.[42] Marshall proposes the following reasons for this:[43]

- *Common bases of reporting*: The foreign subsidiary is concerned, not only with meeting the accounting requirements of the host nation, but also with showing the consistent application of principles required by the parent company. An international accounting firm has the capability to secure both objectives.

- *Common auditing standards*: Again, the parent company would prefer to have its own international operations examined by firms applying similar standards and methods of auditing and to be judged by professionals applying common criteria and demands for accuracy. An international accounting firm can satisfy these requirements.

- *Reliance on the work of other auditors*: Because of the future goal of achieving common standards of reporting and auditing, the auditors of parent companies have to be careful in their reliance on the work of a foreign auditor, especially when they have to assume responsibility for all subsidiary companies included in the consolidation, irrespective of whether they have examined the accounts themselves or have relied on the work of other auditors. To correct this problem, accounting firms may decide to go international through one of two options: "First, impose their own auditing standards on the foreign professionals by issuing very specific instructions and requirements, with annual or at least periodic checks to insure compliance; second, assign the audit work to a firm with established standards equal to their own (an associated firm or possibly an associated form of another international firm with an acknowledged reputation or capability)."[44]

- *International financing requirements*: International financial institutions lend funds, provided that borrowers' financial statements are audited by firms whose auditing and reporting standards and professional training and judgment are reliable. However, the international lenders prefer only international accounting firms because of their reputations, known standards of work, and previous experience with the requirements of international lenders.

These international firms have several problems, however. One serious problem is the result of nationalism and the call for local control of all foreign operations. Marshall, for instance, expressed concern for the situation in most Latin American countries:

The profession in most Latin American countries exhibits extremely strong nationalistic feelings and, except for specific arrangements made under a very few international treaties, non-nationals generally are refused international recognition of their qualifications as well as their right to practice. In particular, international firms based in English-speaking countries have been under severe attack in respect of their rights to practice and to assign and transfer non-national personnel to countries as the needs arise.[45]

A second problem of these new international firms is to maintain good standards of fieldwork and quality-control procedures through careful international coordination. A third problem arises from the need to find high-caliber local staff in each country. A more serious problem arises from the antagonistic attitudes of some of the governments of these developing countries toward enterprise accounting generally.

An additional problem faced by these firms, as well as by other service firms, involves national restrictions on gambling, insurance, construction, engineering, consulting, data processing, tourism, shipping, and other activities that are included under the common heading of "service." What may be needed is regulation to eliminate some of the barriers on service exports. In short, a General Agreement on Tariffs and Trade (GATT) for services is needed. In fact it was with $350 billion a year international trade in services in mind that the U.S. National Study on Trade Representative (Bill Brock at the time) drafted the U.S. National Study on Trade and Services. The study was submitted to the eighty-nine-nation Council of GATT to provide a point of discussion.[46] The problem of restrictions on service exports is deeply felt by American industry. A Price Waterhouse study, conducted among companies included in the *Fortune* services 500 directory, revealed the following findings:

1. Seventy-two percent believed that foreign countries are taking unfair advantage of the U.S. open services trade policies.

2. Eighty-two percent believed that the United States should not become more restrictive in its services trade policies.

3. Eighty-six percent believed that other countries would retaliate if the United States instituted new restrictions on services trade.

4. Sixty-eight percent believed that the use of trade as a foreign-policy mechanism (for example, Soviet pipeline sanctions and grain embargoes) was counterproductive.

5. Seventy-three percent believed that the needs and problems of service organizations trading abroad were not adequately recognized by the U.S. government.[47]

In spite of these problems, the international accounting firms have been attempting to make adaptive transfers of accounting technology. Needles emphasizes that adaptive transfers of accounting technology can only be successful when they take as their starting point the social and economic objectives of the transferee nation.[48] Needles argues that national goals of countries combine with the social, political, and economic environment and general resources and constraints to influence the economic plan with a strategy for the transfer of accounting technology as a specific subplan of the overall economic plan. As a result, international accounting firms should recognize the national economic goals of host countries in their adaptive transfer of accounting technology. An interesting assessment of the future role of international firms follows:

Even if nationalistic regulation prohibits partnership interests across national borders or otherwise limits the participation of foreigners in national practices, international firms will still be able to deliver high-quality, consistent services to clients worldwide. One indication is an emerging trend toward "federalism," whereby national firms may affiliate with each other and with international firms on the basis of mutual agreements to meet specified standards of auditing, reporting, professional education, independence and ethics. These organizations each establish a central office to provide administrative and technical services to firms in the group and to act as an overall coordinating body. The format provides national firms of all sizes with a vehicle that both satisfies the legal and professional requirements of the various countries in which they practice and allays fears of national firms concerning the possible domination of international practice by any other firm in the group.[49]

Accounting and Economic Development

Before approaching the issue of accounting and economic development, it is important to notice the grotesque gap between the developed and developing countries as global inequalities in income and living standards have reached gigantic proportions. In 1999 the richest countries, such as the United States, have 20 percent of the world's people but 80 percent of its income, 91 percent of its Internet users, 81 percent of its exports, and 74 percent of its telephone lines. The 20 percent living in the poorest countries such as Ethiopia have about 1 percent of each of these commodities. In 1999 the three richest officers of Microsoft—Bill Gates, Paul Allen, and Steve Ballmer—have more assets (nearly $140 billion) than the combined national product of the 43 least-developed countries and their 600 million people. Obviously, competitive markets may be the best guarantee of efficiency, but they do not necessarily guarantee equity. Markets are neither the first nor the last word in human development. As a result, the 1999 United Nations Development Program (UNDP) report called for a "global architecture" that would include:

- "A global central bank to act as a lender of last resort to strapped countries and to help regulate finance markets.
- A global investment trust to moderate flows of foreign capital in and out of Third World countries and to raise development funds by taxing global pollution or short-term investments.
- New rules for the World Trade Organization, including anti-monopoly powers to enable it to keep global corporations from dominating industries.
- New rules on global patents that would keep the patent system from blocking the access of Third World countries to development, knowledge or health care.
- New talks on a global investment treaty that, unlike talks that failed last year, would include developing countries and respect local laws.
- More flexible monetary rules that would enable developing countries to impose capital controls to protect their economies.
- A global code of conduct for multinational corporations, to encourage them to follow the kind of labor and environmental laws that exist in their home countries. The report praised voluntary code adopted in Asia by Disney World and Mattel, the toy company."

"The leading industrial nations already are considering new global rules on investment, banking and trade. The UNDP report, in effect, endorsed these efforts but urged that they be broadened to include the needs of poorer nations."[50]

Accounting has a dual function in the economic development process, with a role at both the micro level and the macro level. At the micro level, accounting helps corporations and micro-governmental units in measuring, reporting, and disclosing information about their financial position and performance. It also helps in collecting and transforming economic and social data and disseminating relevant data for decision making by the same micro units. At the macro level, accounting helps governments and nations in measuring, reporting, and disclosing national economic performance. It also helps in measuring social indicators to assess the adequacy of planning in all the national areas of concern to the country (i.e., education, health, etc.).

In short, the role of accounting in economic development goes beyond the mere measurement of economic activity at the micro and macro levels to acquire a socioeconomic dimension; more explicitly, accounting plays an important role in the full implementation of economic development planning by providing the relevant information for its execution. Enthoven suggests the following possible contributions of accounting to development planning.

1. definition, classification, and valuation of transactions and stocks for all social accounts, in particular the national income and input output accounts
2. assessment of, and changes in, the components of input output data capital coefficients and shadow prices, the latter being the equilibrium, or true, factors of production
3. a uniform and standardized system of industrial accounts to assist in obtaining more comparable data and coefficients for different countries

4. up-to-date cost-accounting procedures for cost-benefit calculations at various sector levels

5. assistance in estimating future financial results and determination of how these will affect investments and the planning pattern

6. assistance in devising economic policies, measures, and programs; this may include help in elaborating tax or incentive provisions and other administrative policies to stimulate industrial growth

7. control and audit of the plan and reporting of its results[51]

In fact, a review of the relevant international accounting literature suggests the following main roles of accounting with regard to economic development. First, the skills and techniques that make up accounting are essential to the development of commerce, industry, and public administration. Second, economic development rests on a successful industrialization effort and the efficient mobilization of capital. Accounting helps in evaluating the success of both endeavors. According to Seidler: "Enterprise accounting is a supplier of information, a device for increasing the efficiency of resource allocations and a mechanism for controlling productive operations. It seems logical that these skills, normally considered to be tools of private enterprise management, should be equally useful to the management of the development process."[52]

Third, by ensuring the production of reliable and timely information, accounting is essential to the efficient functioning of a capital market, which is necessary to channel funds for development and investment, in the collection of taxes, and for the efficient allocation of scarce resources. Fourth, accounting information is needed by developing nations' governments, capital markets, and business firms. Governments need such information for implementing public policy, controlling and regulating private enterprise, controlling economic cycles, analyzing expenditures for social overhead, measuring national income, constructing input-output and flow-of-funds systems, disseminating information, and finally, collecting income taxes. Fifth, accounting information is seen as being vital to the emergence of a domestic private capital market, external public sources of capital, and a capital market consisting of funds from international agencies. Sixth, accounting information is necessary to assist management in its custodial functions, operating decisions, control of subsidiaries and branches, personnel control, real income measurement, budgeting and forecasting, and special management problems. Seventh, economic development depends on an efficient use of a country's economic resources. It rests on development planning to guide the efficient use of these resources. Finally, to be successful, development planning should be supported by an adequate supply of information, which is one of the prerogatives of accounting. The last point is eloquently addressed by Mirghani:

Since development planning represents a system of decision making under conditions of great uncertainty, it should be supported by an information system capable of generating the types of information necessary for reducing the amount of uncertainty surrounding the economic choices that must be made. The development planning process can be linked to the resource allocation process in a micro-organization. The management of any organization would attempt to select the package of alternative uses that would yield maximum benefits in view of the constraints operating in that organization's specific environment. Such an exercise would not be fruitful without an information system that would enable management to make rational choices among alternative uses.[53]

CONCLUSIONS

This chapter has focused on the need for international accounting by highlighting the roles of the new environmental factors in international business. These factors include:

1. the emergence of the global economy

2. the role of the multinational corporation

3. the increase in foreign direct investment

4. the developments in the international monetary system

Six dimensions of international accounting were also examined, including:

1. listing of the areas of international accounting

2. the nature of international annual reports

3. the increase in foreign stock listings

4. accounting standards for the multinational corporation

5. the international role of the accounting profession

6. the role of accounting in economic development

NOTES

1. Kenishi, Ohmae, *Triad Power: The Coming Stage of Global Competition* (New York: The Free Press, 1985).

2. Gunset, George, "Trade Accord Productive for Midwest Farms," *The Chicago Tribune*, August 13, 1992, p. 1.

3. Porter, M., *The Competitive Advantage of Nations* (New York: Free Press, 1989), pp. 98–110.

4. Moon, H. C., A. M. Rugman, and A. Verbeke, "A Generalized Double Diamond Approach to the Global Competitiveness of Korea and Singapore," *International Business Review* 7 (1998), pp. 135–150.

5. Farrell, Christopher, "The Triple Revolution," *Business Week*, Special 1994 Bonus Issue, p. 19.

6. Pennan, K., P. Gallagher, and K. L. Miller, "Capitalism in Transition," *Business Week*, Special 1994 Bonus Issue, p. 28.

7. Thurow, Lester C., *The Future of Capitalism: How Today's Economic Forces Shape Tomorrow's World* (New York: William Morrow and Company, 1996).

8. Kindleberger, Charles P., *Manias, Panics, and Crashes: A History of Financial Crises* (New York: John Wiley, 1996).

9. Kindlerberger, Charles P., *World Economic Primacy: 1500–1900* (Oxford: Oxford University Press, 1996).

10. Garten, Jeffrey E., *The Big Ten* (New York: Basic Books, 1997).

11. Fukuyama, Francis, "The End of History?" *The National Interest*, Summer 1989, p. 18.

12. Huntington, Samuel P., "The Clash of Civilizations and the Remaking of the World Order," *Foreign Affairs* 5 (1994), pp. 13–24.

13. Giacomo, Carol, "U.S. Will Be Less Secure by 2025, Experts Say," *The Chicago Tribune*, September 16, 1999, p. 6.

14. Hornblower, Margot, "The Battle in Seattle," *Time Magazine*, November 29, 1999, pp. 40–41.

15. Ibid.

16. Mueller, Gerhard G., "Whys and Hows of International Accounting," *The Accounting Review* 40 (April 1965), p. 386.

17. Dunning, John H., "The Eclectic Paradigm of International Production: A Restatement and Some Possible Extensions," *Journal of International Business Studies* 19 (1988), pp. 1–31

18. Tsetsekos, George P. "Multinationality and Common Stock Offering Dilution," *Journal of International Financial Management and Accounting* (Spring 1991), p. 2.

19. Baldwin, C., "The Capital Factor: Competing for Capital in Global Environment," in M. Porter (ed.), *Competition in Global Industries* (Boston: Harvard Business School Press, 1986), pp. 184–223.

20. Gray, S. J., J. C, Shaw, and B., McSweeney, "Accounting Standards for Multinational Corporations," *Journal of International Business Studies* 15 (Spring–Summer 1981), p. 127.

21. Daniels, J. D., and L. H. Radebaugh, *International Business: Environments and Operations* (Reading, Mass: Addison Wesley, 1989).

22. Miller, J. C., and B. Eras, "The Effect of Multinational and Export Diversification on the Profit Stability of U.S. Corporations," *Southern Economic Journal* 3 (1980), pp. 78–79.

23. Garter, Jeffrey E. "The Euro Will Turn Europe Into a Superpower," *Business Week*, May 4, 1998, p. 30.

24. Weirich, Thomas R., Clarence G. Avery, and Henry R., Anderson, "International Accounting: Varying Definitions," *International Journal of Accounting, Education, and Research* 10 (Fall 1971), p. 9.

25. Qureshi, Manhood, "Pragmatic and Academic Bases of International Accounting," *Management International Review* 2 (1979), p. 62.

26. Weirich, Avery, and Anderson, "International Accounting."

27. Ibid.

28. Schoenfield, Hanns-Martin W. "International Accounting: Development, Issues and Future Directions," *Journal of International Business Studies* 16 (Fall 1981), pp. 83–84.

29. Mueller, Gerhard G., and Lauren M. Walker, "The Coming of Age of Transnational Financial Reporting," *The Journal of Accountancy* 90 (July 1976), pp. 15–30.

30. Accountants International Study Group, *International Financial Reporting* (London: Accountants International Study Group, 1975), para. 39.

31. Mueller, Gerhard G. "The International Significance of Financial Statements," *Illinois CPA* Spring 1965, pp. 1–10.

32. Biddle, Gary C., and Shahrokh M. Sandagaran, "Foreign Stock Listings: Benefits Costs and the Accounting Policy Dilemma," *Accounting Horizons*, September 1991, pp. 70–71

33. Ibid., p. 72

34. Securities and Exchange Commission, *SEC Docket* 24, no. 15 (March 16, 1982), pp. 1262–1345.

35. Securities Act of 1933, Release No. 6862.

36. The four terms in italics were introduced in F. D. S. Choi and G. G. Mueller, *International Accounting*, 2nd ed. (Englewood Cliffs, NJ: Prentice-Hall, 1992), p. 12.

37. Gray, Shaw, and McSweeney, "Accounting Standards for Multinational Corporations," p. 122.

38. Mueller, and Walker, "The Coming of Age of Transnational Reporting."

39. Ibid., pp. 128–129.

40. Choi, F. D. S., "Multinational Challenges for Managerial Accountants," *Journal of Contemporary Business* 11 (Autumn 1975), p. 10.

41. Gray, Shaw, and McSweeney, "Accounting Standards for Multinational Corporations," p. 130.

42. Bavishi, V. B., and H. E. Wyman, *Who Audits the World? Trends in Worldwide Auditing Professions* (Storrs, CT.: Center for Transnational Reporting, 1984).

43. Marshall, A. T., "Public Accounting and Multinationalism," *Chartered Accountant Magazine*, December 1974, pp. 11–32.

44. Ibid.

45. Ibid.

46. This study shows that, of the 20 million jobs created in the United States in the last decade, 90 percent were in services, chiefly information services with high technological requirements.

47. " 'Fair Trade' Supported in Export Services," *The Journal of Accountancy* (February 1984), p. 32.

48. Needles, Belverd E., Jr., "Implementing a Framework for the International Transfer of Accounting Technology," *International Journal of Accounting, Education and Research* (Fall 1976), pp. 45–62.

49. Kanga, William S., "International Accounting: The Challenge and the Changes," *Journal of Accountancy* (November 1980), p. 56.

50. Quoted in Longworth, R. C., "A 'Grotesque' Gap," *The Chicago Tribune*, July 12, 1999, p. 8.

51. Enthoven, Adolph J. H., *Accountancy and Economic Development Policy* (Amsterdam: North Holland Publishing, 1973), pp. 168–169.

52. Seidler, Lee J., *The Function of Accounting in Economic Development: Turkey as a Case Study* (New York: Praeger, 1967).

53. Mirghani. Mohamed A., "A Framework for Linkage between Microaccounting and Macroaccounting for Purposes of Development Planning in Developing Countries," *The International Journal of Accounting, Education and Research* 18 (Fall 1982), pp. 57–68.

SELECTED READINGS

Dunning, J. H. "Toward an Eclectic Theory of International Production: Some Empirical Tests." *Journal of International Business Studies* 11 (1980), pp. 9–31.

————. "The Eclectic Paradigm of International Production: A Restatement and Some Possible Extensions." *Journal of International Business Studies* 19 (1988), pp. 1–31.

Mishra, C. S., and D. H. Gobeli. "Management Incentives, Internalization and Market Valuation of Multinational Firms." *Journal of International Business Studies* 29, no. 3 (1998), pp. 583–598.

Qureshi, M. "Pragmatic and Academic Bases of International Accounting." *Management International Review* 2 (1979), pp. 61–68.

Riahi-Belkaoui, Ahmed. *Multinationality and Financial Performance.* Westport, CT: Greenwood Publishing, 1996.

————. *Performance Results of Multinationality* Westport, CT: Greenwood Publishing, 1999.

Weirich, T. R., C. G., Avery, and H. R. Andersen. "International Accounting: Varying Definitions." *The International Journal of Accounting, Education and Research* 7 (Fall 1971), pp. 79–87.

2
International Taxation and
Value-Added Taxation

INTRODUCTION

The job of tax preparation for a multinational corporation is inordinately complex and expensive. As an example, it was reported that the Citigroup's 1998 return exceeded 30,000 pages in length, including computations for more than 2,000 companies located in 50 states and 100 countries. More than 200 tax professionals, both in the United States and abroad, were involved.

The managers of multinational corporations face different tax systems in different countries, which requires adequate tax planning. These differences make international taxation a changing, complex, and challenging topic, creating in the process demanding and costly problems for the international executive. These problems stem from the fact that the international executive must be a combination of an administrator, tax attorney, tax accountant, computer expert, and human being and must work within a framework of a society that he or she had very little to do with creating. The complications and intricacies of the U.S. tax laws are monumental. In addition, the international executive is faced with sophisticated tax treaties superimposed over U.S. law, which frequently negate the clear implication of the latter. The pyramid of levels of tax law priorities is further compounded by the invariable differences in local tax laws, which continually exert their influence in eroding the "bottom line" of international business. The dilemma is further enlarged by the fact that international U.S. law and foreign tax law are in a continuous flux.[1]

All the dilemmas require from the international tax executive a good appreciation of the important issues characterizing international taxation. The taxation issues examined in this chapter include taxation philosophies, types of taxes, systems of tax administration, tax treaties, and tax havens.

PHILOSOPHIES OF TAXATION

Taxation of business varies from one country to another. Not only are tax rates different, but opinions differ as to definitions of taxable income and the types of taxes to be used. This situation is due mainly to international differences in taxation philosophies. These differences center on the worldwide versus territorial assertions of taxation. According to the territorial approach, each country has the right to tax income earned inside its borders. Countries adopting such a philosophy include Hong Kong, Panama, Switzerland, Argentina, Venezuela, and many Central American and Caribbean lands.

Accounting to the worldwide approach, each country can claim the right to tax income arising outside its border if that income is received by a corporation domiciled, incorporated, or with its center of control within the country. Needless to say, the worldwide approach leads to double taxation. Fortunately, most countries adhering to the worldwide approach grant some form of relief from double taxation by taxing foreign subsidiary earnings only when they are sent home to the parent company. This is known as the *deferral principle*. The only exceptions under U.S. law are "Subpart F" and "Foreign Personal Holding Company" income, which are taxed even when not repatriated.

Central to the idea of granting some form of relief from double taxation is the notion of tax neutrality. Tax neutrality is considered an appropriate goal in forming transnational tax policy. It means that tax aspects should have no effect on investment decisions. Different views of tax neutrality exist, and there is no agreement as to which is best. These views include capital-export neutrality, which is achieved when a firm pays the same total tax on foreign profits as on domestic profits; capital-import neutrality, which is achieved when all firms, domestic or foreign, operating in the same industry in a given country pay the same total corporate tax on earnings; and national neutrality, which assumes that the total country returns of capital are shared by that country's government in the form of taxes and that local investors remain the same whether the capital is located at home or abroad.

Other views of neutrality include domestic and foreign neutrality. Under domestic neutrality, the objective is to tax the foreign income and domestic income of U.S. taxpayers similarly. Under foreign neutrality, the objective is to tax the foreign operations of U.S. taxpayers no more than the host-country competitors are taxed. This is designed to challenge the viability of the competition.[2]

Besides these different views of neutrality, countries also differ in their attempts to achieve tax neutrality. In particular, they differ in their treatment of tax-deferral privilege, foreign tax credits, provisions in tax treaties, and the treatment of intracompany transactions.

KINDS OF TAXES

Multinational companies face a variety of taxes in addition to corporate income taxes. James and Nobes provided an exhaustive classification of the important taxes,[3] which are classified generally as either direct or indirect.

Direct taxes are directly linked to a tax base. They include specific (regressive) taxes, such as the poll tax; current taxes, such as the generally progressive income tax and the generally proportional corporation tax and capital gains tax; and capital taxes, such as the inheritance tax and the wealth tax. Indirect taxes include the ad valorem, multirate value-added tax and the ad valorem and specific excise duties. Some of the important taxes are examined next.

Corporate Income Taxes

Corporate income tax is by far the most widely used tax in the world.

Corporations are taxed a certain percentage of their taxable income. They may be taxed either at a flat rate or on a graduated scale. In some countries, the taxable income corresponds to a certain extent to the accounting income. The United States relies heavily on corporate income tax as a major source of government revenue.

The rates are high in some developing countries, which rely exclusively on corporate income taxes as a source of government revenues, and low in other developing countries, which are eager to attract direct investment, whether foreign or local.

Other Direct Taxes

Other direct taxes include the poll tax, the inheritance tax, the wealth tax, and the capital gains tax. The poll tax, sometimes referred to as the head tax, is a lump-sum tax levied on each person. It does not vary with the amount of income earned. It is generally a "community charge" on all individuals set by a local authority, without regard to the ability to pay. It is generally perceived to be unfair and difficult to implement. The inheritance tax is a tax on wealth following a person's death.

The wealth tax is a tax on an individual's wealth. It is motivated by considerations of equity and efficiency, with the argument that a person with more wealth has a greater taxable potential than an individual with less wealth. It may, however, discourage savings. It is used in Europe, the Indian subcontinent, and Central and South America. Wealth taxes are sometimes deductible against income taxes.

The capital gains tax is a tax on the gain due to an increase in the value of capital or assets, generally financial assets. It is motivated by considerations of equity and efficiency, and it is fair to the wage and salary earners, who are taxed on their earnings.

Indirect Taxes

Indirect taxes include such taxes as consumption taxes, value added taxes, excise duties, estate and gift taxes, employment taxes, and different kinds of user fees.

The value added tax is the most prevalent indirect tax used in the world. First introduced in France in the 1950s, the value added tax (VAT)—or *taxes sur la valeur ajouté (TVA)*—is also levied at each stage of the production process, but only on the value added at that specific stage. Each firm invoices the VAT separately and passes it on until it is eventually paid by the final consumer. VAT is in force throughout the European Community, but at different rates in different countries. Other countries using VAT include Austria, Norway, Sweden, Argentina, Brazil, Chile, and Mexico. The excise tax is a tax levied on goods produced for home consumption.

Other Taxes

Other taxes include border, net worth, and withholding taxes. Border taxes are the most prevalent form of international taxes. They are used mainly to make domestic goods more competitive with imports. In most developing countries, they provide a great proportion of government revenues.

Net worth taxes are assessed on the undistributed earnings of a firm, as a way of encouraging firms to source finances for investment projects externally.

Withholding or remittance taxes are assessed on dividends, interest, and royalties. They range from a high of 30 percent in Australia to a low of 10 percent in Korea. Nationally, these taxes can be modified by tax treaties between the countries concerned.

Not everyone argues against double taxation, as noted from the following comment:

This double taxation of distributed corporate earnings may seem inequitable, but the alternatives are not necessarily equitable either. If a dividend received were not taxable income to individual, it would mean that, in effect, all individuals would have had their dividends taxed at the same rate (at the corporate level), a condition that is a violation of the progressive income taxes principle. If corporations were not taxed at all, but dividends were taxable to individuals, tax could be deferred indefinitively if corporations simply distributed no dividends.[4]

TAX SYSTEMS

In addition to differences in the types of taxes and taxation philosophies, countries differ in terms of systems of tax administration. There are basically three international systems of tax administration for corporate taxes: the classical, or separate, system; the partial integration system; and the fully integrated, assimilated system.

The Classical, or Separate, Corporate Tax System

The system used in the United States makes no distinction between the taxation of retained earnings and that of distributed earnings. Basically it taxes the income of corporations and the dividends paid to the shareholders separately. Needless to say, this leads to the so-called "economic double taxation" of dividends, given that they are taxed both by the corporation tax (income tax) and then by the personal income tax. There are two main circumstances of classical systems, which have been expressed as follows:

First, this double taxation is said to be inequitable when compared to the treatment of distributable income of unincorporated businesses. Income of such businesses, whether physically distributed or not, bears no corporation tax but bears current income tax in the hands of the owners of the business. . . .

The second case against economic double taxation is that it introduces a bias against the distribution of dividends. Since both total income and then distributed income are fully taxed, the larger the distribution, the larger is the total tax borne by a company and its shareholder.[5]

The Partial Integration System

This system consists of two possible subsystems: the split-rate system and the imputation, or tax credit, system. Under the split-rate system, retained profits are taxed at a higher rate than distributed profits. Countries using this method include Germany, Japan, and Norway. Under the imputation, or tax credit, system, the retained and distributed profits are taxed at the same rate but the shareholders receive a credit for the amount of tax paid or deemed to have been paid by the corporation. Countries using the imputation system include Italy, France, and the United Kingdom. A comparison of the classical and imputation systems is shown in Exhibit 2.1. The example is based on the British system from 1979 to 1983, with a corporation tax of 52 percent and a tax credit of $3/7$ of the dividend given to the shareholders. Notice that in the imputation system, the tax liability is computed on the cash dividend, which is "grossed up" with the tax credit. The total tax paid by the shareholder is 10,000 (8,000 + 1,200 + 800) under the classical system and 11,200 (10,400 + 800) under the imputation system. The imputation system recovers the double taxation. In 1994–1995, the British tax credit was 20/80 with a corporation tax of 33 percent, meaning that only 50.766 percent of the corporation tax paid by the companies is imputed to shareholders. In the United Kingdom, an advance corporation tax (ACT) equal to the size of the tax credits is added to the distribution. Basically, when distributing a dividend, a British corporation, remits

Exhibit 2.1
Classical and Imputation Systems

			Classical	Imputation
Company:				
Assumed Income			20,000	20,000
Corporation Tax			8,000	(52%) 10,400
Distributable Income			12,000	9,600
Assumed Distribution			4,000	
Less Income Tax Deducted at Source	(30%)	1,200		
	Net	2,800		2,800
Retained Income			8,000	6,800
Shareholders:				
Dividend Received			2,800	2,800
Income Tax Deducted at Source			1,200	0
Tax Credit Received (3/7)			0	1,200
Gross Dividend			4,000	Grossed-Up Dividend 4,000
Income Tax liability (50%)			2,000	2,000
Less Tax Already Deducted			1,200	0
Less Tax Credit			0	1,200
Tax Due			800	800
Total Tax (8,000+1,200+800)			10,000	11,200

a portion of it (20/80) to the British tax authorities as an advance corporation tax. It is then claimed as a credit by the shareholder against the tax liability on the distributed dividend. For example, the British shareholder receiving a dividend of £80 with an ACT of £20 reports a total dividend of £100 with a tax credit of £25 against the individual income tax liability on that £100. What results is a partial integration of the corporate and shareholder income source in the United Kingdom.[6]

The previous British-based example covers partial imputation versus the classical system. Imputation can also exist in the form of full imputation. To illustrate the differences between the classical, partial imputation, and full imputation systems, consider an example involving Germany, which has adopted a full imputation system; the United Kingdom, which has adopted a partial imputation system; and the United States, which relies on the classical system. The following information is provided:

1. Before-tax income $= m = 100$
2. Corporate tax rate (CTR):
   a. for Germany $= .30$
   b. for United Kingdom $= .33$

   c. for United States = .34
3. Person tax rate (PTR) = .40
4. Imputation rate (IR):
   a. for Germany = .30
   b. for United Kingdom = .20
   c. for United States = 0

The dividends received are equal to m $(1 - CTR)$. Under the classical system the total after tax dividends received are equal to m $(1 - CTR)$ $(1 - PTR)$. The gross up dividend is m $(1 - CTR)/(1 - IR)$. Because CTR = IR for full imputation, the grossed-up dividend is equal to the pretax income. The gross liability of the shareholders is (PTR) m $(1 - CTR)/(1 - IR)$. The net liability of the shareholder is (PTR $- IR$) m $(1 - CTR) / (1 - IR)$. As a result, the net dividend received after corporate and personal taxes is m $(1 - CTR) -$ (PTR $- IR$) m $(1 - CTR) / (1 - IR)$, or m $([1 - CTR] / [1 - IR]) (1 - PTR)$. Given that with full imputation, CTR = IR, the net dividends received are m $(1 - PTR)$, meaning that they are only taxed at the shareholder's personal marginal tax rates. The results for our simple example are shown in Exhibit 2.2.

The Fully Integrated, or Assimilated, System

Under such a system, no double taxation, with or without credit, is accepted. Proposals for fully integrated systems have been made in Canada, the United States, and Germany. Only Greece does not levy corporate tax on distributed profits. In the United States, an allowance of a given amount of investment income received is exempted for personal income tax. Sweden and Iceland rely on a "primary dividend" system, which permits firms to deduct a certain percentage of dividends in the computation of taxable incomes.

There is obviously a need in the United States for an integration of personal and corporate taxes and an elimination of the double tax on dividends. Two proposals were made in 1992 for a combination of the corporate and individual tax system: one by the Treasury[7] and one by the American Institute of Certified Public Accountants.[8] The Treasury study identified three major economic distortions caused by the classical two-tier tax system that integration would eliminate. They are (a) tax advantages to noncorporate forms of business, (b) a tax basis in favor of corporate debt financing, and (c) tax incentives for retaining, rather than distributing, corporate earnings.[9] The AICPA study added two more reasons: (a) coordination of the U.S. tax system with foreign tax system and (b) ease of administration.[10] Before integration is adopted, however, four questions need to be considered:

1. Should shareholders benefit from tax preferences allowed to corporations?
2. Should capital gain taxes be modified as part of integration?

Exhibit 2.2

Comparison of Partial Imputation, Full Imputation, and Classical Tax Systems

	Full Imputation: Germany	Partial Imputation: United Kingdom	Classical: United States
Corporate Level			
Pre-Tax Income	1000	1000	1000
Corporate Tax	(300)	330	340
Dividend	700	670	660
Individual Level			
Dividend	700	670	660
Individual Tax			
Gross-up Dividend	1000	837.50	----
Personal Tax	(400)	(335)	(264)
Imputation Credit	300	167.50	0
Net Individual Tax	100	167.50	(264)
Net Dividend	600	502.50	396

3. Should foreign investors reap the benefits of U.S. integration?

4. Should tax-exempt investors reap the benefits of integration?[11]

Four methods were identified in the Treasury study, namely, (a) a comprehensive business income tax (CBIT), (b) a dividend exclusion method, (c) a shareholder allocation method, and (d) an imputation credit method. Three methods were identified by the AICPA study, namely: (a) the flow-through, or partnership, method, (b) the dividend deduction method, and (c) the shareholder credit method. In a summary definition of one of the methods falling under the dividend exclusion, the shareholders are allowed an exclusion for dividend received. More precisely, the exclusion would be allowed only for dividends paid from income on which corporate taxes previously had been paid. The corporation would be required to maintain an excludable distributions account (EDA) and report to shareholders the amount of the available exclusion. The concept of accumulated earnings and profits, which currently measure the amount of corporate earnings available for dividend treatment, would be divided into two accounts. If an EDA approach were adopted, the corporation would record the equivalent amount of after-tax income based on the actual amount of taxes. The balance remaining in accumulated E & P would represent untaxed profits, to be treated as dividends but not excluded when paid to shareholders.[12]

TAX TREATIES

To create a favorable climate for foreign trade and foreign investment and to avoid or relieve the double taxation of profits, countries sign bilateral or multilateral agreements known as tax treaties. These treaties basically define the way in which joint income should be allocated between national taxing jurisdictions and are intended, in particular, to limit taxation by the source country.

The most important provision of these treaties focuses on the term *permanent establishment*. In the various U.S. treaties, the permanent establishment may take the form of an office or a fixed place of business, or it may be a resident agent of the taxpayer with authority to enter into contractual relationships or who fills orders from a stock of goods located in the foreign country. Besides these two principles, the treaty generally enumerates the types of activities that do and do not constitute a permanent establishment. In addition to the concept of permanent establishment, most treaties have provisions limiting the amount of withholding tax on various items, such as interest, dividends, and royalties.

Types of Treaties

Basically, three types of treaties have emerged. First, in 1977 the United States published a model income tax treaty to be used as a basis for its future treaty negotiations. This treaty includes articles on the general scope, the taxes covered, the residence, the permanent establishment, the income from real property (immovable property), business profits, shipping and air transport, associated enterprises, dividends, interest, royalties, gains, independent personal services, dependent personal services, limitations on benefits, artists and athletes, pensions, annuities, alimony and child support, government service, students and trainees, other income, capital relief from double taxation, nondiscrimination, mutual-agreement procedures, exchange of information and administrative assistance, diplomatic agents and consular officers, entry into force, and termination.

Second, in 1963 the Organization for Economic Cooperation and Development (OECD) proposed a model treaty for the elimination of double taxation. The OECD treaty has, in fact, greatly influenced the U.S. model. Detailed differences between the two focus on either the permanent establishment article or the dividend withholding article. Whereas the Treasury model requires twenty-four months before a building site is considered a permanent establishment, the OECD model requires only twelve months. Similarly, whereas the Treasury model requires only 10 percent of the voting stock to qualify for the 5 percent limitation on withholding, the OECD model requires 25 percent of the capital. Other significant differences between the two models include differences in personal scope, taxes covered, interest, investments in holding companies, and relief from double taxation.

Third, the United Nations has also proposed a draft model for a double taxation convention between developed and developing countries. When it comes to developing countries, "tax sparing" and "investment credit" are the major inducements or concessions sought, in order to provide some form of tax reduction or "tax holiday" to attract foreign investment.

Unfortunately, the U.S. Senate refuses to recognize tax-sparing provisions. U.S. arguments used against tax sparing include:

1. Tax sparing is inequitable, in that those investing capital in the United States must pay a full tax, whereas those investing in a "tax-sparing" country are taxed by neither the foreign government nor the United States on the income spared.

2. Tax sparing is "capricious," in that the benefit depends on the nominal rate of tax in the less-developed country. A country that does not have a tax holiday may need the foreign investment more than another that has one.

3. Tax sparing encourages the repatriation of earnings. If a tax incentive such as a tax holiday without tax sparing is used by the foreign country in which a subsidiary is operating, a U.S. tax will be payable upon remitting the earnings to the U.S. parent. A sparing provision removes this restraint on the remittance of earnings.

4. Tax sparing encourages less-developed countries to compete against each other in offering tax incentives. This is undesirable, as it lessens the revenue.[13]

Another complete view on tax sparing is as follows:

The United States' resistance to tax sparing has been based on a number of considerations. First, tax sparing rewards investment abroad at the expense of investment in the United States. There is also concern that developing countries should not be encouraged to provide tax holidays because the loss of revenues may not be worth the additional investment attached thereby. Moreover, the practice of offering tax holidays leads poor countries to compete with one another to give up badly needed revenues. In response to these latter concerns, leaders of such countries are likely to note that they have not asked [the] United States' leaders to determine their economic and fiscal policies; and the leaders of developing countries are not necessarily enthusiastic about helping to address the deficit in the United States Treasury.[14]

Unlike tax sparing, investment credit provisions were found acceptable by the U.S. Senate as a form of making inducements to developing countries. These provisions allow a certain percentage of a qualified investment to be used as a credit against U.S. taxes. Needless to say, more work needs to be done to find formulas that are acceptable to both developing and developed countries. The OECD model is now the norm rather than the exception. In 1976 and 1981, the U.S. Treasury issued model income tax treaties conforming, to a great extent, to the provisions of the OECD model. However, when it comes to the developing countries, some, like China, prefer to follow the UN model. It has become difficult for the United States to conclude tax treaties with developing countries because it has not been prepared to grant major incentives such as tax-sparing credits. Of the forty-two income tax treaties signed by the United States and in effect in 1992, only about one-quarter were with developing countries.

Elements generally found in these treaties include (1) a definition of the affected taxpayers and determination of the fiscal domicile (i.e., corporate residency) on the basis of criteria including state of incorporation, domicile, residency, and place of management; (2) the taxes included in the treaty; (3) a nondiscrimination clause that guarantees that the taxes levied on foreign corporations are no heavier than those levied on local corporations; (4) a clause that preserves the availability to the foreign taxpayers of exclusions, credits, and deductions that otherwise might be limited by the tax treaty; and (5) a saving clause that allows a country the right to tax its own citizens and residents as if the treaty had not come into effect.

Treaty Shopping

One noticeable difference between the U.S. and the OECD tax treaty models is that the United States has included some form of Article 16 in all its treaties. Article 16 has always required that a corporation have some degree of local ownership if it is to enjoy treaty benefits. In fact, Article 16 of the latest version of the model treaty provides generally that corporations resident in a treaty country do not get its treaty benefits unless (1) at least 75% of its shares are owned directly or indirectly by individuals resident in that country or in the United States and (2) the corporation's income is not used substantially, whether directly or indirectly, to meet liabilities to residents of a country other than the United States or the treaty partner. The idea behind Article 16 is to discourage what is known as treaty shopping, which is, basically, the use of a tax treaty by the resident of a third country in his or her tax planning. This is accomplished by forming a corporation in a country that is party to a beneficial treaty. The U.S. Treasury view is that tax treaties are intended to protect tax revenues and not to benefit residents of third countries. In general, the Treasury gives the following reasons why Article 16 is needed:

- Treaty shopping causes a loss of revenue and encourages tax avoidance.
- Treaty shopping grants residents of nontreaty companies treaty benefits, and these countries then see little need to grant U.S. residents concession via a tax treaty with the United States.
- U.S. internal law is violated by treaty shopping: for example, interest withholding is eliminated unlawfully when treaties are invoked by third-country residents.[15]

To prevent treaty shopping, U.S. treaties generally include an article that limits the benefits of the treaty to residents of the two contracting countries. In addition, the U.S. Internal Revenue Service (IRS) disallows treaty benefits obtained through the use of intermediary entries by involving the judicial doctrine of substance over form.[16]

TAX HAVENS

A tax haven can be defined as "a place where foreigners may receive income or own assets without paying higher rates of taxes upon them." In fact, tax havens can be classified in various categories:

1. traditional tax havens with virtually no taxes at all, such as the Bahamas, Bermuda, and the Cayman Islands

2. tax havens that impose a relatively low rate, such as the British Virgin Islands and Jersey

3. tax havens that tax income from domestic sources but exempt all income from foreign sources, such as Hong Kong, Liberia, and Panama

4. tax havens that allow special privileges, such as Brazil, Luxembourg, and the Netherlands[17]

A tax haven is used by setting up a subsidiary in the tax haven country and channeling income to it, thereby shifting income form high-tax to tax-haven places. "For example, a British manufacturer could sell directly to a dealer in Germany and concentrate the profit in Britain, or it could sell the goods to a tax haven subsidiary at cost and then sell the goods to the German dealer, thus concentrating the profits in the tax haven corporation."[18]

Most non-U.S. multinational corporations have subsidiaries that act as tax havens for corporate funds awaiting a decision on reinvestment or repatriation, but the U.S. Revenue Act of 1962 made it difficult for U.S. multinational corporations to use tax havens. The popularity of tax havens decreased in the United States when the Revenue Act of 1962 added Subpart F in order to tax concurrently the sham transactions of a controlled foreign corporation (CFC). However, despite increased U.S. crackdowns, the use of Caribbean tax havens has continued to increase. It is reasonable to assume that a great deal of activity designed to violate the tax and other laws of the United States still takes place in the Caribbean Basin havens. Estimates of revenue lost cannot be calculated with any accuracy, because of difficulties in obtaining data. The gravity of the situation can be expressed as follows:

As of 1988, 833 of the largest 7,500 CFC's had Subpart F income. Almost 50% of these CFC's with Subpart F income were based in tax havens; for example, Switzerland (with an effective tax rate of 9%) was the home of 96 of these CFC's. Five countries (Bermuda, Netherlands Antilles, Netherlands, Panama, and Switzerland) accounted for 81% of the $7 billion of 1988 tax haven Subpart F income.[19]

Tax havens depend on inconsistencies in U.S. tax laws and, therefore, can be wiped out overnight. For example, because U.S. companies can raise capital from overseas more cheaply if they have a Netherlands Antilles address, about 2,500 of them set up "subsidiaries" there. Though rarely little more than a mailbox, these subsidiaries have issued $40 billion of corporate bonds to over-seas investors. European corporations with U.S. tax exposure also have found that the Antilles financing units can save them money. U.S. corporations have set up units on the islands because bonds issued from those units are tax free to overseas investors. That makes the bonds a cheaper source of capital than U.S.-issued bonds, which are not tax-free. Not only do U.S. companies benefit through their access to cheaper capital—in addition, the parent corporations can credit any tax to the Antilles against the IRS bill. All these advantages of the Antilles can be wiped out, however, because a 1984 U.S. law permits U.S. companies as well as the government to directly offer tax-free bonds to overseas investors. This will eliminate the need to circumvent the IRS by issuing bonds through the Netherlands Antilles. The law serves as an incentive for foreign investors and has eliminated the 30 percent withholding taxes that foreigners had been paying on interest from American securities. In addition, to attract individual foreigners to invest in treasury bonds without having to supply their names and addresses when investing, the Treasury Department announced in August 1984 that it would issue a new type of security available only to for-eigners and that overseas buyers of the new bonds would not have to disclose their names to the U.S. authorities. Needless to say, this provides another way for some American investors to dodge taxes, by buying the new bond from a foreign dealer.

Another persistent problem is the failure of foreign firms operating in the United States to pay their fair share of taxes. A report issued by the Internal Revenue Service, on April 9, 1992, expressed suspicion that hundreds of foreign businesses were underpaying corporate tax, to an estimated overall extent of $30 billion a year. The study followed a 1990 House Ways and Means Committee investigation into thirty-six foreign companies in the United States that found that more than half of these firms paid little or no federal income tax over the course of a decade, despite selling $35 billion worth of goods to Americans annually. This led the IRS in 1991 to examine the returns of more than 1,300 foreign-owned corporations, representing some 3 percent of the 45,000 firms doing business in the United States.

Most Caribbean islands offer an array of attractive inducements to companies and investors, including low or nonexistent taxes, secretive banking arrange-ments, and less rigorous regulation for both companies and their securities. With relocation to a tax haven as an objective, in 1999 Fruit of the Loom completed a reorganization and became a subsidiary of Fruit of the Loom, Ltd., a Caymen islands holding company. In fact more than 59,000 companies are registered in the Caymans, including 600 banks and trust companies. The British Virgin Is-lands has a population of only about 19,000, but more than 300,000 companies are registered there. They do not have to hold annual meetings, and they do not have to reveal financial information.[20]

To conclude and give an idea of the importance of tax havens, it is generally estimated that one-third of the world's wealth flows through tax havens. The

Organization of Economic Cooperation and Development estimated in 1999 that the tax havens account for 15 percent of the direct investment made today by U.S. companies and individuals. One may also argue that the Caymans and other tax havens simply represent an opportunity to practice pure capitalism, with few or no taxes and little regulation. Witness the following comments about the Caymans, made in 1999: "Home to 59,000 companies, 600 of the world's top banks, 9,900 mutual funds, at least another 16,000 closed funds, thousands of insurance companies and the latest financial schemes dreamed up by lawyers and savvy investors, the Caymans are the world's fifth-largest financial center."[21] This is a country of roughly 39,500 people occupying 260 square miles. In addition, although the world's prosperity depends on a fluid and unfettered financial system, the lack of control has created a shadow economy of money-laundering, serving customers from cocaine cartels to tax-dodging companies and leading the IRS to claim in 1989 that the tax cheats skim as much as $50 billion a year from legitimate cash-generating businesses, to be laundered to avoid detection. Various laundering schemes are used. My favorite one concerns a banker in Willemstad, Netherlands Antilles, and an American visitor who is expecting a six-figure cash windfall that he wants to bring "quietly" into the United States. After the banker is assured that the money is not "tainted," the banker states that he can set up a so-called "Dutch sandwich."

The Paris bank would set up a corporation for the customer in Rotterdam, where he would deposit his cash in the bank's local branch. The American would control the newly created Dutch corporation through an Antilles trust company, but his identity as the owner would be protected by the island group's impenetrable secrecy laws. The Caribbean branch would then "lend" the American his own money held in Rotterdam. If the American were questioned . . . he could point to his loan from a respected international bank.[22]

U.S. TAXATION OF FOREIGN INCOME

U.S. taxation of foreign income is mitigated by the need to avoid double taxation and to ensure at the same time adequate levying of taxes on foreign income. This section provides procedures for the computation of the foreign tax credit as well as an explanation of the crucial issues affecting the U.S. taxation of foreign income.

Foreign Tax Credit

The foreign tax credit (FTC) provisions were enacted by the U.S. Congress to provide relief from double taxation. The provisions include both a direct and an indirect credit. Basically, the direct and indirect credits are available for the taxes either paid directly by a U.S. individual or corporation to a foreign government or deemed to have been paid to it.

The direct foreign tax credit (Section 901 of the U.S. Internal Revenue Code) includes income tax paid on foreign branch earnings; any taxes withheld at the source, such as dividends, interest, and royalties remitted to a U.S. investor; and other forms of passive income.

The indirect foreign tax credit or the deemed paid credit (Section 902 of the U.S. Internal Revenue Code) is recognized when dividends are received or deemed to have been received from foreign corporations. The reported dividends on a U.S. tax return would be grossed up to include the deemed tax paid plus any applicable foreign withholding taxes. The allowable foreign indirect tax credit (deemed paid credit) is computed as follows:

$$\frac{\text{Dividend (including withholding taxes)}}{\text{Earnings Net of Foreign Income Tax}} \times \text{Creditable Foreign Tax}$$

The operation of the individual credit may be illustrated by the following examples.

In example 1, assume that company XYZ owns 50 percent of foreign subsidiary FS, which earns $200,000 in the foreign country, where it pays 30 percent income taxes and a total dividend of $140,000. Therefore, XYZ receives $70,000 in dividends from FS. The following steps can be used:

Step 1: The foreign tax credit or amount deemed paid:

$$\frac{\$70,000}{\$140,000} \times (\$200,000 \times 30\%)$$
$$= \frac{\$70,000}{\$140,000} \times 60,000 = \$30,000$$

Step 2: Gross-up of dividend:

$$\$70,000 + \$30,000 = \$100,000$$

Step 3: The U.S. tax on the grossed-up amount:

$$\$100,000 \times 34\% = \$34,000$$

Step 4: The net tax to be paid:

$$\$34,000 - \$30,000 = \$4,000$$

In example 2, assume the following data for FS:

Income	$200,000
Local tax (30%)	60,000
Earnings after tax	140,000

Dividend   40,000

Withholding on dividend (10%)   4,000

Let us also assume that XYZ owns 50 percent of FS and receives $18,000, which amounts to dividends of $20,000 less withholding taxes of $2,000. The tax interaction for XYZ is illustrated as follows:

$$\text{XYZ tax deemed paid} = \frac{\$20,000}{\$140,000} \times \$60,000 = \$8,571$$

XYZ grossed-up income =	$28,571
U.S. tax at 34%	9,714
Direct credit	$ 2,000
Indirect credit	8,571
Total credit	10,571
Excess foreign tax credit	856

The third example shown in Exhibit 2.3 is also used to evaluate the impact of both credits. Withholding taxes on dividend payments is assumed to be 20 percent in country Y; income tax rates in countries X and Y are assumed to be 40 percent. The branch earnings are "grossed up," meaning that they are included in U.S. income before deducting foreign taxes. The allowable foreign indirect tax credit for the subsidiary in country Y is $40, resulting in an excess foreign tax credit of $18 to be used to offset U.S. taxes or other foreign earnings.

The United States, however, generally limits the amount of foreign tax creditable in any one year. Japan also uses a worldwide limitation, whereas Germany, Denmark, and Canada employ a country-by-country limitation. The U.S. foreign tax limitation is determined as follows:

Overall Limitation = U.S. Tax on Worldwide Income before FTC
$$\times \frac{\text{Foreign-Source Taxable Income}}{\text{Worldwide Taxable Income}}$$

The foreign-source income includes only income that is deemed to be repatriated in a particular tax year, which comes from the source as dividend income and passive income (subpart F1). The worldwide income is the sum of foreign and domestic source income. Assume that the XYZ company's total world income is $10 million, its U.S. tax liability is $4 million, and the foreign-source income is $5 million. The overall limitation may be computed as follows:

Exhibit 2.3
U.S. Taxation of Foreign-Source Income

	Branch in country X	Subsidiary in country Y
Segment (branch or subsidiary)		
Before-tax earnings	$200	$200
Foreign income taxes (40%)	80	80
After-tax earnings	120	120
Dividends paid	0	60
Foreign withholding taxes (20%)	0	12
Foreign credible taxes		
Direct credit	(80)	(12)
Deemed paid (60/120 × 80)	---	(40)
Total Creditable taxes	(80)	(52)
Included in U.S. income		
Income	200	60
Plus foreign deemed paid taxes (i.e. grossed up)	---	40
Taxable income	200	100
U.S. taxes at 34%	68	34
Less foreign tax credit	(80)	(52)
U.S. tax payable	($12)	($18)

$$\text{Overall limitation} = \frac{\$5,000,000}{\$10,000,000} \times \$4,000,000 = \$2,000,000$$

Thus, if the foreign tax paid were $3 million, only $2 million would be allowed as a tax credit; the excess $1 million can be carried back two years and forward five years, as long as the foreign tax credit remains within limitations in the recomputed carryover years.

However, the limitations create excess credits. One way of eliminating the excess credits is to rely on a cross-crediting strategy. The strategy consists of blending low-tax and high-tax foreign-source income within a simple limitation. The result is that the excess limitation on the low-tax income will cover the excess credits on the high-tax income. To prevent cross-crediting between lightly taxed passive foreign investment income and more heavily taxed active foreign business profits, separate income limitations were enacted by the IRS. The formula for the separate income limitation is as follows:

$$\text{Pro-credit U.S. tax} \times \frac{\text{Separate category foreign-source taxable income}}{\text{Worldwide taxable income}}$$

The separate limitation can be used for each of the following categories of income:

1. passive income (e.g., investment-type income)
2. financial service income
3. high withholding tax interest (interest subject to withholding tax equal to or greater than 5 percent
4. shipping income
5. dividends from controlled foreign corporations (10 to 50 percent U.S.-owned foreign corporations)
6. dividends from domestic international sales corporations (DISCs)
7. foreign trade income from a foreign sales corporation (FSC)
8. distribution from an FSC
9. general limitation income, a residual category for income not assigned to one of the other income categories

For example, let us assume the case of the XYZ company, which has $24 million in U.S. taxable income, $16 million in foreign-source general limitation taxable income on which $6 million in foreign taxes were paid, and $4 million in foreign-source passive taxable income on which $.8 million in foreign taxes were paid. The U.S. tax rate is assumed to be 35 percent.

A. Under a single overall limitation, all of the XYZ company's foreign taxes are creditable as follows:
   1. Creditable foreign taxes ($6 million + $800,000) = $6.8 million
   2. Foreign tax credit limitation
      a. Total taxable income ($24 million + $16 million + $4 million) = $44 million
      b. Precredit U.S. tax ($44 million × 35%) = $15.4 million
      c. Foreign-source taxable income: ($16 million + $4 million) = $20 million
      d. Overall limitation $15.4 million × ($20 million / $44 million) = $6.99 million
   3. Foreign tax credit = $6.8 million

B. Under the separate income limitation, the XYZ company's foreign taxes are creditable as follows:

1. Total taxable income = $44 million

2. Precredit U.S. tax ($44 million × 35%) = $15.4 million

3. Foreign tax credit on general limitation income

   a. Foreign-source general limitation income = $16 million

   b. Foreign taxes = $6 million

   c. Limitation ($15.4 million × ([$16 million / $44 million])

   d. Allowable credit = $5.59 million

4. Foreign tax credit on passive income

   a. Foreign-source passive income = $4 million

   b. Foreign taxes = $.8 million

   c. Limitation ($15.4 million × ([$4 million / $44 million]) = $1.4 million

   d. Allowable credit = $.8 million

5. Total allowable credit = $6.39 million

C. The difference in the total allowable credit between the single overall limitation and the separate income limitation is $.41 million ($6.80 million−$6.39 million).

It is appropriate to add that to apply the separate category of income limitations, the foreign income taxes must be allocated among the nine income categories using the following formula:

Foreign income taxes related to more than one income category

$$\times \frac{\text{Net income subject to the foreign tax}}{\text{Total net income subject to the foreign tax}}$$

In addition, a U.S. citizen can use foreign tax credits to offset not only his or her regular income tax but also the alternative minimum tax (AMT). AMT is applicable if the U.S. taxpayer's tentative minimum tax exceeds the regular tax for the year.

The United Kingdom also has an item-by-item FTC limitation. These basket limitations are motivated by the desire to prevent corporations from undermining the limitations. Witness the following example:

For example if a firm faced a severe FTC limitation, it would have incentives to "stuff" income-earning assets into subsidiaries located in tax-haven countries (where tax rates are very low). And to avoid the implicit taxes that often result from investing in active business in low-tax countries, there would be a particularly strong incentive to invest in passive assets, such as Eurobonds. This would reduce the average tax rate on foreign-source income and give rise to larger refunds of the foreign tax paid in high-tax countries.[23]

The foreign tax credit mechanisms do not eliminate double taxation in a variety of circumstances, examples of which include the following: Taxes other than those on income (for example, property taxes, value-added taxes, and excise taxes) are not eligible for the FTC, although they are deductible as business expenses for U.S. tax purposes. In addition, the income tax rate in some foreign countries exceeds that in the United States, and the FTC limitation may prove restrictive here, because the United States will not refund more in taxes than would have been paid if the income were earned in the United States. Finally, the foreign country may use different source of income rules (that is, whether income is deemed to be earned by the foreign corporation of the U.S. corporation), as well as different rules for income recognition and deduction (for example, depreciation rules) than in the United States.[24]

In the United States, an individual claiming a foreign tax credit must attach Form 1116, Foreign Tax Credit, to his or her tax return, whereas a corporation claiming the same credit must attach Form 1118, Foreign Tax Credit–Corporations.

Foreign Corporations Controlled by U.S. Firms

The deferral principle allows income from a foreign branch to be deferred from U.S. taxation until it is received as a dividend or liquidation distribution. This principle was questioned, however, and 1962 legislation attempted to distinguish between the "legitimate" deferral of U.S. taxation in foreign operations and deferral resulting from a manipulation of U.S. tax rules. The decision was to curtail deferral through the so-called Subpart F provisions for foreign operations. Basically, the decision calls for exclusion from the deferral principle of a certain class of income (Subpart F income) of a certain type of corporation (controlled foreign corporation, or CFC),

A CFC is a foreign corporation of which more than 50 percent of the total combined voting power of all classes of stock entitled to vote is owned, directly, indirectly, or constructively, by U.S. shareholders on any given day during the taxable year of such foreign corporations. For tax purposes, a U.S. shareholder is one owning 10 percent or more of the voting power. Subpart F income includes the following five components:

1. income from insurance of U.S. risks

2. foreign-base company income

3. certain international boycott-related income

4. illegal bribes and kickbacks

5. income from ostracized countries

Foreign-base company income includes the following five categories:

1. foreign personal holding company income
2. foreign-base company sales income
3. foreign-base company services income
4. foreign-base company shipping income
5. foreign-base company oil-related income

Foreign personal holding company income includes (a) rents, (b) royalties, (c) dividends, (d) interest, (e) gains from sale of securities, (f) foreign currency gains, (g) commodity transactions, and (h) sale of property producing passive or no income.

Unitary Taxation

Most businesses operate in a multivariate environment, which may lead them to face up to forty-seven different state tax provisions, even though most states "piggyback" onto the federal income tax base. Although each state has the right to tax a business incorporated in that state, for a state to be permitted to tax a business not incorporated in that state depends on the business having a sufficient nexus established with that state. A nexus is the degree of activity needed before a state can impose a tax or an entity's income. Unless a corporation has business activities in more than one state and has established sufficient means with these states, it must allocate and apportion its income among them. The difference between apportionment and allocation is that apportionment involves the division of income among states, whereas allocation is the direct assignment of an income to a state. Apportionment is generally based either on a three-factor formula that especially weights sales, property, and payroll or on a modified three-factor formula, in which the sales factor is assigned a double weight. To illustrate both formulas, we assume that the Alvertos Corporation has realized $1 million in taxable income from sales in states X and Y, which were established as the firm's nexus for income tax purposes. The following data on sales, payroll, and property are provided:

	State X	State Y	Total
Sales	$2,000,000	$2,000,000	$4,000,000
Property	5,000,000	0	5,000,000
Payroll	1,000,000	0	1,000,000

A. If state Y uses an equally weighted, three-factor formula, $166,600 of Alvertos Corporation's taxable income is apportioned to state Y, computed as follows:

Sales ($2,000,000 / $4,000,000)	50%
Property ($0 / $5,000,000)	-0-
Payroll ($0 ~ 1,000,000)	-0-
Sum of the three factors	50%
Average (divided by)	3
Apportionment factor for state Y	16.66%
Taxable income	$1,000,000
Income apportioned to state Y	$166,600

B. If state Y uses a double-weighted, sales factor–based, three-factor formula, $333,300 of Alvertos Corporation's taxable income is apportioned to state Y, computed as follows:

Sales ($2,000,000 / $4,000,000) × 2	100%
Property ($0 / $5,000,000)	-0-
Payroll ($0 / $1,000,000	-0-
Sum of the three factors	100%
Average (divided by)	3
Apportionment factor for state Y	33.33%
Income apportioned to state Y	$333,300

The principle used is the unitary theory, which justifies the apportionment and allocation. This principle views the business as a unitary business, an entity that cannot be segregated into independently operating divisions.

The serious problem with unitary taxation involves foreign multinational corporations. The question is whether an individual state should be allowed to impose income taxes on foreign-source income. Proponents of the unitary-tax method answer the question positively. What is the unitary tax and why has it stirred up so much controversy? The concept of unitary taxation is relatively simple: corporations are perceived as single, worldwide units and are taxed by a state based on the proportion of the total operation that is located within that state. A unitary formula, previously devised to measure the income of a functionally related enterprise that operated in several states, is used to compute the state corporate tax. Previously, state tax was calculated by taking state sales, payroll, and property and averaging them in relation to national figures for the same categories. Now, however, worldwide sales, payroll, and property are used. Basically, the state calculates the tax by multiplying the percentage of business a company does in that state by its worldwide income, which supposedly will give the state more revenues than when only national income was used. California has been using the unitary-tax method for the last forty-five years.

Needless to say, the unitary tax method is not popular with most multinational corporations, and various arguments are used by its critics. The first argument is that because the state unitary method has no provision for credits for foreign tax paid, the worldwide unitary method leads to international double taxation. A second argument is that because it is the federal government, and not the states, that conducts the nation's foreign relations, any state action that interferes with internal commerce threatens the federal uniformity ordained by the Founding Fathers.[25] A third argument is related to the legitimacy of a state levying taxes on business conducted in another country. What allows a state to consider any sale made outside its borders as a state sale, whether that sale is made in another state or another country? To be more critical, how can a state claim it has the right to tax profits that a Mexican company with a Californian subsidiary makes on a sale in Canada?

In a landmark decision, the Supreme Court affirmed the constitutionality of a state's authority to require worldwide combined reporting of U.S. parent firms with the income of its foreign subsidiaries.[26] To avoid an international crisis, however, most states using unitary taxation permit a multinational company to choose water's edge unitary reporting as an alternative to worldwide unitary reporting. This concept is explained as follows:

The water's edge provision permits a multinational corporation to elect to limit the reach of the state's taxing jurisdiction over out-of-state affiliates to activities occurring within the boundaries of the United States. The decision to make a water's edge election may have a substantial effect on the tax liability of a multinational corporation. For instance, a water's edge election usually cannot be revoked for a number of years without permission from the appropriate tax authority. Moreover, corporations making this election may be assessed an additional tax for the privilege of excluding out-of-state entities from the combined report.[27]

U.S. TAXATION ISSUES

Branch versus Subsidiary Status

An important decision when planning a foreign operation is the choice of the most advantageous form (branch or subsidiary) in which to operate. The tax implications of either option may weigh heavily on the final decision. If a branch is chosen to carry on foreign operations, the income earned abroad is simply subject to U.S. taxation, reduced by the foreign income tax paid or accrued under the foreign tax credit rules. If a subsidiary is chosen to carry on foreign operations, the foreign subsidiary's income is normally not subject to U.S. taxation until distributed as a dividend to the U.S. parent company, but is subject to foreign taxes in the country where its operations are located.

Advantages of operating as a foreign branch rather than a foreign subsidiary include the following:

1. Losses from foreign operations are immediately deductible against U.S. domestic income. This is especially important for start-up operations, which can reasonably be

expected to generate losses. Moreover, it is possible to incorporate the branch once operations turn profitable in order to shield future income from U.S. taxation. The cost, however, is that the firm must recapture, as income, previously deducted losses.

2. The U.S. tax law applies to the specific character of a variety of overseas activities. For example, the rules reserve favorable tax treatment to certain investment activities, such as natural resource mining (for example, immediate deduction of intangible drilling costs).

3. Income repatriated from a foreign branch is not considered to be a dividend. As a result, a branch avoids the withholding taxes on dividends that are often paid by a foreign subsidiary (often in addition to a tax levied on the earnings of the subsidiary).

4. Property can be transferred to a branch without fear of current taxation on appreciation. Some transfers of property to foreign subsidiaries, however, are taxable.[28]

Disadvantages of operating as a foreign branch include the following:

1. There is no deferral of U.S. tax on the earnings of the branch. In many cases, this is the most important consideration, especially when the host country's tax rate is below that of the United States. However, this factor became less important for U.S. multinationals following passage of the 1986 Tax Act.

2. Some countries may require the disclosure of data on worldwide operations to tax authorities. This may not only be administratively burdensome but may also require disclosing sensitive competitive information.[29]

Strategies for U.S. Multinationals

To deal with the complex international tax system, U.S. multinationals are adopting the following various tax strategies.[30]

Same Country Holding Company and Debt Push-Down

This technique for repatriating cash and reducing future taxes involves setting up a holding company in the same country as a high-tax operating subsidiary and funding that holding company to buy shares of the operating company from the U.S. parent, thus allowing for the direct repatriation of future earnings without payment of withholding taxes. The consolidation of the returns of the holding company and the operating company allow, not only the deduction of the new interest, but also the reduction of future foreign taxes. The U.S. law, through Section 304 of the International Revenue Code, considers this taxation as a dividend distribution rather than a sale because the ultimate ownership of the operating company has not changed. Foreign countries have generally levied on this as a sale by a foreign corporation, with no foreign tax on any capital gain.

Regional Holding Companies

This variation involves a regional or other multicountry holding company. Given that intercompany dividends between European Community (EC) countries are going to be tax free, a subsidiary in one country will borrow to buy shares of another subsidiary in another European country. Burge elaborated on the benefits of this technique as follows:

The use of regional holding companies within Europe has many benefits, especially if the funds from one country are needed for expansion in Europe. For this purpose, you need a holding company in a country that does not tax dividend income or capital gains and that has a low withholding rate on dividends back to the U.S. In the EC, both the Netherlands and Luxembourg (and, perhaps, even Belgium) would fit the bill.[31]

Finance Corporation

In view of the tax incentives given to finance companies in Belgium and Ireland, U.S. multinationals may establish finance companies in these countries to manage group cash and currency exposure and to channel funds within Europe without bringing them back to the parent company. Burge gives the following example:

For example, if you have excess cash in Germany, you may want to finance a subsidiary in exchange for preferred shares in the finance company. The German company reduces its cash, which may be particularly useful if it cannot pay dividends due to an insufficiency of earnings or reluctance to pay withholdings tax.[32]

Escaping Tax on Profits in the United States

The federal tax on profits from the sale of stock, land, or other assets—known as the capital gains tax—can be easily avoided by the richest U.S. taxpayers, thanks to a large arsenal of Wall Street techniques designed to delay or entirely avoid taxes on investment gains. These include:

- Owners of a private business can sell it to their employees without paying capital gains taxes as long as they put the proceeds in certain investments—which Wall Street is eager to provide.

- Real estate owners can swap properties without the capital gain taxes required when a sale is made, allowing them to diversify their holdings and raise cash for other purposes.

- Large shareholders can use any of several complex Wall Street strategies to raise cash and lock in their stock market profits without actually selling their shares, which would create a tax bill.[33]

The first technique consists of selling a company and paying no capital gains taxes as long as it is sold to an employee stock ownership plan (ESOP) and the proceeds are reinvested in corporate securities. The deal is possible with the Section 1042 tax break, which allows the owner of a private business to sell between 30 and 100 percent of it to an ESOP and pay no capital tax gains as long as the proceeds are reinvested in corporate securities during his or her lifetime. This is a great exit strategy for owners.

The second technique, which involves new and improved loopholes, calls for the arrangement of an umbrella partnership real estate investment trust (generally labeled a UPREIT). This system combines the tax break provided by Section 1031 of the tax code, which allows the swapping of one property for another similar one without the incurrence of a capital gain tax, with the loophole offered by Section 721, which allows partners to transfer property to their own partnership without the incurrence of a capital gains tax. Basically, a developer can swap a property of an umbrella partnership and allow a real estate investment trust that is a partner to sell shares to the public, raise cash, and use the money for operating or investment purposes.

The third technique allows shareholders to get rid of the risk without getting rid of their stocks. Basically, this was the advertisement used by Bankers Trust in *Barron's Magazine* in July 1994. It calls for the shareholders to surrender to Bankers Trust all the economic rewards and risks of stocks but to keep the titles. In return, Bankers Trust may offer to pay a return on an equal alternative investment, minus the bank's fee, and reimburse the shareholder for any decline in the stock's price over the term of the swap.

The fourth technique consists of "shorting against the tax." Basically, large shareholders are allowed to lock in the profit on their shares by simply borrowing an identical number of shares from a broker and selling them short. If the price goes down, a profit is realized, and the shareholder uses his or her own shares to replace the borrowed shares, without any taxes being paid. In addition, the shareholder may withdraw his or her short-term profits through an inexpensive loan from the banker.

A fifth technique involves the use of debt that is exchangeable in common stocks. Assume a company Y owns shares of a company X. A deal originated by Salomon Brothers consists of issuing a new form of exchangeable notes indirectly by shares of company X and then paying a substantial part of the note proceeds to company Y, allowing company Y to lock in its profit and use the cash as if it had sold the shares in company X, but without incurring the capital gains taxes. The transaction initiated by Salomon in June 1993 is called a debt exchangeable into common stock (DECS) note. (Similar products now offered by Merrill Lynch and Goldman, Sacks are called Strypes and AGES, respectively.) When the note matures, company Y can pay Salomon with either cash or the shares in company X. If the payment is in cash, no taxes are paid, as company Y accepts the ownership of shares in company X in addition to having had the privilege of using the cash raised if the note is free of capital gains taxes.

Exhibit 2.4
Computation of the Value-Added Tax for a Retailer

Profit and Loss Statement		VAT computed at 10%	
Sales	$10,000	+ $1,000	VAT debit on sales
Less Purchases	$5,000	- $500	VAT credit on purchases
Value Added	$5,000	$500	VAT net due
Less Labor and other costs	$2,000		
Profit before Tax	$3,000		

VALUE-ADDED TAXATION

Definition and Computation

The value-added tax (VAT) is basically a tax on the value added by a firm in the course of its operations. The value added can be defined by using either the subtractive method (the difference between the sales and purchases) or the additive method (the sum of the wages, rent, interest, and profits). Because of its practicality, the subtractive method is generally favored for the computation of VAT in European countries. The calculation of VAT is, as a result, a double process, involving a tax on a firm's sales and a credit received by the firm for the VAT paid on its purchases. Exhibits 2.4 and 2.5 show the computation for the retailer and wholesaler.

Exhibit 2.4 uses the subtractive method to compute the value added. In that case, the value added due ($500) is computed as the difference between the value added due on sales ($1,000) and the VAT credit on purchases ($500). Assume a simple tax rate; the VAT in this case could be directly obtained by taking 10 percent of the tax base of $5,000, resulting in a $500 VAT.

Exhibit 2.5 uses the subtractive method to compute the value added throughout the chain of production and distribution formed by the manufacturer, wholesaler, and retailer. The VAT due at each stage is: $1,000 for the manufacturer, $2,000 for the wholesaler, and $2,000 for the retailer.

VAT Collection Methods

There are two possible VAT collection methods: the cash-collection, or tax-credit, method and the invoice-collection, or additive, method. The cash-collection, or tax-credit, method recognizes VAT liability in sales and VAT credits on purchases at the time of cash payment. Under this method the VAT must be determined and shown separately on all merchandise invoices. One of

Exhibit 2.5
Computation of the Value-Added Tax for a Manufacturer, Wholesaler,
and Retailer

	Profit And Loss	VAT Computed at 10%		
		VAT Computation	Net VAT due at Each Stage	Cumulative VAT due to the Government
Manufacturer *Sales*	$10,000	$1,000		
Less Purchase	-0	0		
Value Added	$10,000	$1,000	$1,000	
Less Other Costs	5,000			
Profit	$5,000			$1,000
Wholesaler Sales	$30,000	$3,000		
Less Purchases	10,000	-1,000		
Value Added	20,000	$2,000	$2,000	$3,000
Less Other Costs	17,000			
Profit	3,000			
Retailer Sales	$50,000	$5,000		
Less Purchases	$30,000	$3,000		
Value Added	$20,000	$2,000	$2,000	
Less Other Costs	10,000	---		$5,000
Profit	10,000			
Price to *Consumer*	$50,000	$5,000		$55,000
Value Added	$50,000			

the method's advantages is that it is self-policing: a merchant (manufacturer, wholesaler, or retailer) collects the VAT on its sales, as with any other sales tax, and then pays the taxing authority that amount, minus any allowable offsets. (The allowable offsets are the VAT paid by the merchant on purchases.) Thus, the individual's net tax due is determined on the basis of, and traceable to, sales and purchase invoices. Any buyer of goods, therefore, has a direct interest in ensuring that the amount of VAT charged and reported by his or her supplier is correct, as that charge becomes his or her tax credit. This system relies less on voluntary compliance than does an income tax system.[34]

The invoice-collection, or additive, method recognizes VAT liability on sales and VAT credits on purchases at the time of invoicing. It is similar to the Michigan business tax (the only American VAT), where the same result is achieved by having taxpayers add up the individual components of their value added: compensation paid, depreciation, depletion, and other capital cost recovery allowances; taxable income (other than dividends received); interest, rent, and royalties paid in excess of interest; and rent and royalties received. They then deduct purchases of investment goods.

Type of VAT: Consumption, Income, and Gross Product

Because the purchases may include both purchases of goods and purchases of capital assets, the alternative methods of treating purchases of capital assets generate three possible types of VAT—namely, consumption VAT, income VAT, and gross product VAT.

With consumption VAT, the VAT credit or purchases include both purchases of goods and capital assets. This is labeled a consumption-type VAT because its economic base is total private consumption. Under income-type VAT, the VAT credit on purchases includes both the purchases of goods and the amortization value of the capital assets for the year. It is labeled an income-type VAT because its economic base is net national income.

Under gross product VAT, the VAT credit on purchases includes only the purchases of goods and does not include any credit for capital assets, in total or in part. It is called the gross product type because the economic base is the gross national product, which is equivalent to consumption plus investment. Exhibits 2.6 and 2.7 illustrate the computation of VAT for the three types: consumption, income, and gross national product.

Other Characteristics of VAT

The examples used up to now have assumed that a single rate of VAT is used and no adjustments are made. In fact, however, most existing VAT systems include at least one of the following adjustments:

1. multiple rates applicable to different categories of goods
2. specific exemptions from VAT, to include, for example:
   a. exemption of a separated product
   b. exemption of products for political or social reasons
   c. exemption given to certain retailers
   d. exclusion of some of the stages in the production and distribution process[35]
3. a reduced taxable base

Exhibit 2.6
Alternative Methods of Value-Added Tax Computation for 10 Percent VAT Rate

Method	Firm A	Firm B	Firm C	Firm D
1. Subtraction Method				
Net Sales	$300	$500	$700	
Less:				
Purchases	-0-	300	500	
Capital Acq'n	100	50	-0-	
Net VAT base	$200	$150	$200	$700
VAT at 10%	$20	$15	$20	$70
2. Addition Method				
Payments to Productive Factors: Payroll/Int.				
Rent	$200	$100	$100	
Profit	100	100	100	
Total Payments	$300	$200	$200	
Less:				
Change in Inv.	-0-	-0-	-0-	
Cap. Acquisition	100	50	-0-	
Net VAT at Base	$200	$150	$200	$700
VAT at 10%	$20	$15	$20	$70
3. Invoice Method				
Invoiced VAT	$30	$50	$70	
Less:				
Invoiced VAT on Purchase	$10	$35	$20	$70
Net VAT due	$20	$15	$20	$70

With regard to exemptions, we may include items of consumption that are intrinsically difficult to tax under VAT or any other consumption tax, such as domestic services and expenditures abroad by Americans. The most important services that are difficult to tax under VAT are the services of financial inter-

Exhibit 2.7
Value-Added Transactions and Alternative Tax Bases

Facts:	Firm A	Firm B	Firm C	Firm D
Sales	$300	$500	$700	
Input Purchases	-0-	300	500	
Value Added	$300	$200	$200	
Labor/rent/interest	200	100	100	
Profit	$100	$100	$100	
Capital acq. (5-yr. Life)	$100	$50	-0-	
Fraction of Value Added	3/7	2/7	2/7	
Alternative VAT Bases				
1. Consumption type VAT				
Sales	$300	$500	$700	
Less:				
Purchases	-0-	300	500	
Capital acq'n	100	50	-0-	
Net VAT base	$200	$150	$200	$700
2. Income type VAT				
Sales	$300	$500	$700	
Less:				
Purchases	-0-	300	500	
Depreciation on cap acq.	20	10	-0-	
Net VAT base	$280	$190	$200	$700
3. Gross product type VAT				
Sales	$300	$500	$700	
Less:	-0-	300	500	
Purchases				
Net VAT base	$300	$200	$200	$700

mediaries, including insurance companies. The following quote illustrates the difficulty:

Banks, insurance companies, and other financial institutions are exempt from the Danish value-added tax simply, it is said, because of the difficulty of applying to them the concept of total sales and total purchases. Interest as such is of course not subject to the consumption-type of value-added tax; but "interest" as a payment for services rendered by a bank free of direct charge (e.g., free checkbook and checking services) is in principle taxable. Such a service would have to be given an imputed households, so that the tax levied on the service rendered to firms could be taken by those firms as a credit against the tax on their own sales. An approximate solution would be to tax the financial institution on its payroll, and divide this tax between the two groups of customers on some relevant basis, perhaps number of checks handled, but Denmark has been unwilling to attempt this or any other rough substitute. Meanwhile the exclusion of these financial institutions from the value-added tax system has caused some difficulty. The banks have set up a cooperative electronic data processing institute to perform services for the smaller banks, but these services are held taxable, and the small banks get no tax credit, being themselves exempt. The larger banks perform their own EDP [electronic data processing] services, and pay no tax on that value added.[36]

Some suggest a retail sales tax as an alternative to VAT. There are fundamental differences between VAT and the retail sales tax, although both are consumption taxes. While VAT is collected at every level of the business process, the retail sales tax is only levied at the point of final sale. There are also administrative and political differences underlying the comparison between the sales retail tax and VAT. First, VAT requires more paperwork than a national sales tax. Second, evasion is more difficult under VAT, given that it is limited to the level of production where it occurred whereas under a retail sales tax, the whole potential tax revenue is eliminated. Finally, most states in the United States have a sales tax and would not welcome the imposition of a VAT by the federal government.

SOME IDEAS FROM THE LEFT

The left wing, both in Europe and the United States, has always wanted to ensure that the current economic boom of globalization serves social ends rather than leading, as its critics maintain, to a growing inequality of wealth between nations and within nations, a reduction of health and social benefits, and greater job insecurity. It searches for a "third way" between socialism and American-style capitalism, accepting the basic structure of capitalism while working for a more democratic and egalitarian form. Some of the proposals made by the left include:

(1) The "Tobin tax," a proposed tax on foreign currency and international financial transactions. By most estimates, some $1.3 trillion changes hands each day in foreign currency transactions. The suggested Tobin tax would raise about

$250 billion a year—more than five times the current level of all international aid. In France, the ATTAC (the Association for the Taxation of Financial Transactions for the Aid of Citizens) is the main advocate of the Tobin tax.

(2) The stakeholder proposal made by Bruce Akerman[37] would give every eighteen-year-old person $80,000 to invest, a contemporary version of the nineteenth-century homesteading notion of awarding 40 acres and a mule. The end result would be to make everybody a potential capitalist.

(3) The end of work proposal made by Jeremy Rifkin[38] consists of a thirty-five-hour work week, which is now French law.

CONCLUSIONS

As this chapter has shown, international taxation involves a complex array of rules and conventions. To minimize and avoid unnecessary taxes, multinational corporations must try to achieve an orderly and systematic approach to tax planning. Some firms have adopted the following procedures:

1. explicitly stating the objectives of tax planning in international operations
2. assigning definite responsibilities, at both headquarters and the subsidiaries, for various aspects of the planning
3. acquiring a thorough knowledge of variables in international taxation, preferably in an information-gathering system designed to routinely generate the necessary information
4. determining what decisions and operating procedures are affected by tax considerations and how they are affected and ensuring the dissemination of this information to the decision makers
5. defining the procedures that will ensure the efficient interaction of the tax planners with the decision makers
6. evaluating the impact of the tax considerations on international operating and investment decisions and on operating procedures

Implementing elaborate tax-planning systems such as these may be the first step toward developing a comprehensive approach to international taxation.

NOTES

1. Kalish, Richard H. and J. P. Casey, "The Dilemma of the International Tax Executive," *Columbia Journal of World Business* 10 (Summer 1975), p. 67.

2. Scholes, M. S., and M. A. Wolfson, *Taxes and Business Strategy: A Planning Approach* (Englewood Cliffs, NJ: Prentice-Hall, 1992), p. 247.

3. James, Simon, and Christopher Nobes, *The Economics of Taxation*, 4th ed. (Englewood Cliffs, NJ: Prentice-Hall, 1992), p. 13.

4. Holt, P. E., and C. D. Hein, *International Accounting* (Houston, TX: Dame Publications, 1996), p. 152.

5. Nobes, C., and R. Parker, *Comparative International Accounting*, 4th ed. (Englewood Cliffs, NJ: Prentice-Hall, 1995), p. 472.

6. Freeman, H., and R. Griffiths, "Surplus ACT—A Solution in Flight," *Fiscal Studies*, November 1993, pp. 58–73.

7. United States Department of the Treasury (DOT), *Report of the Department of the Treasury of Integration of the Corporate and Shareholder Tax Systems Corporate Tax Systems* (Washington, DC: U.S. DOT, 1992).

8. American Institute of Certified Public Accountants (AICPA), *Statement of Tax Policy: Integration of the Corporate and Shareholder Tax Systems* (Washington, DC: AICPA, 1993).

9. Thomas, D. W., and K. F. Sellers, "Eliminate the Double Tax on Dividends," *Journal of Accountancy* (November 1994), pp. 86–90.

10. Ibid., pp. 86–87.

11. Ibid., p. 87.

12. Ibid., p. 88.

13. Kirby, V. N., and W. H. Pedricks, *The Study of Federal Tax Law*, 1983–1984 (Chicago, IL: Commerce Clearing House, 1983), p. 228.

14. Gustafson, C. H., and R. C. Pugh, *Taxation of International Transactions 1991–1993* (Chicago, IL: Commerce Clearing House, 1991), p. 486.

15. Nick Hammer, "Tax Treaty Developments," *Price Waterhouse International Tax Review*, January/February 1984, p. 7.

16. Neldman, R. E., and M. S. Schadewald, *A Practical Guide to U.S. Taxation of International Transactions* (Chicago, IL: Commerce Clearing House, 1996), p. 245.

17. Doucet, Jean, and Kenneth J. Good, "What Makes a Good Tax Haven?" *Banker*, May 1973, p. 493.

18. Gray, S. J., and L. H. Radebaugh, *International Accounting and Multinational Enterprises* (New York: John Wiley and Sons, 1997), p. 620.

19. Hoffman, W. H., W. A. Raabe, J. E. Smith, and D. M. Maloney, *West's Federal Taxation* (Minneapolis, MN: West Publishing, 1997), pp. 9–39.

20. "Paradise Lost," *Chicago Tribune*, April 9, 2000, Sect. 5.

21. Franklin, Stephen, "Tax Havens under Increasing ###," *Chicago Tribune*, April 9, 2000, Sect. 5.2.

22. Beaty, J., and R. Hornile, "A Torrent of Dirty Dollars," *Time*, December 18, 1985, p. 50.

23. Scholes, Myron S., and Mark A. Wolfson, *Taxes and Business Strategy: A Planning Approach* (Englewood Cliffs, NJ: Prentice-Hall, 1992), p. 286.

24. Ibid., p. 267.

25. This point was not, however, supported in court. In December 1983, the Supreme Court refused to consider an appeal by Shell Petroleum (supported by the ten member nations of the European Community) that California's unitary method violates the commercial treaty between the United States and the Netherlands.

26. *Container Corporation of America v. Franchise Tax Board*, 103 S. Ct. 2933 (1983).

27. Hoffman, Raabe, Smith, and Maloney, *West's Federal Taxation*, pp. 15–31.

28. Scholes and Wolfson, *Taxes and Business Strategy*, p. 249.

29. Ibid., p. 21.

30. Burge, Marianne, "Foreign Taxes: How You Can Pay Less," *Price Waterhouse Review* 1 (1992), pp. 15–23.

31. Ibid., p. 21.

32. Ibid., p. 22.

33. Hennigues, Diana B., and Floyd Norris, "Wealthy, Helped by Wall St., Find New Ways to Escape Tax on Profits," *New York Times*, December 1, 1996, p. 1.

34. Reckess, P. M., and Bates., H. L., "Ready for VAT?" *Financial Executive*, February 1980, p. 25.

35. Smith, Dan Throop, Weber, James B., and Cerf, Carol M., *What You Should Know about Value Added* (Homewood, IL: Dow Jones, 1977) p. 8.

36. Shoup, Carl S., "Experience with Value-Added Tax in Denmark and Prospects in Sweden," *Finanzarchiv*, March 1969, p. 25.

37. Akerman, Bruce, and Anne Alstote, *The Stakeholder Society* (New Haven, CT: Yale University Press, 2000).

38. Rifkin, Jeremy, *The Age of Access: The New Culture of Hypercapitalism, Where All Life Is a Paid-for-Experience* (New York Pitman Publishing Group, 2001).

SELECTED READINGS

Jacobs, Fred A., and Ernest R. Larkins. "Management Control for a Foreign Sales Corporation: Some Special Considerations." *Journal of Management Accounting Research* 5 (Fall 1992), pp. 99–115.

Larkins, Ernest R. "Alternative Tax Vehicles for Exportation (Part I)." *The Tax Adviser*, March 1991, pp. 183–190.

———. "Alternative Tax Vehicles for Exportation (Part II)." *The Tax Adviser*, April 1991, pp. 247–256.

Larkins, Ernest R., and Fred A. Jacobs. "Tax Incentives for Small Businesses with Export Potential: A Capital Budgeting Decision Analysis." *Accounting Horizons*, June 1996, pp. 32–50.

Moore, M. L., and R. L. Parish. "DISC, FSC, and Small FSCs Alternatives—Dealing with the Financial and Tax Considerations." *International Tax Journal* 10 (Spring 1986), pp. 181–199.

Neldman, Robert E., and Michael S. Schadewald. *A Practical Guide to U.S. Taxation of International Transactions*. Chicago, IL: Commerce Clearing House, 1996.

Norcross, K. J. "Interest Change DISCs and Small FSCs: A Comparison of the Tax Benefits." *Taxes—The Tax Magazine*, 5 (February 1985), pp. 134–139.

O'Keefe, W. Timothy. "Small Business Acceptance of Foreign Sales Corporation Incentives." *American Journal of Small Business* 7 (Summer 1986), pp. 43–51.

3
Exchange Rate
Risk Management and
Economic Exposure

INTRODUCTION

Firms engaged in international operations face various risks associated with the fluctuations of unstable exchange rates. To counteract the negative effect of these risks, these firms need to (1) have an appreciation of the economic equilibrium relationship affecting the behavior of exchange rates, (2) resort to various forms of exchange rate forecasting, and (3) deal with the risk exposures created by the exchange rate fluctuations. One risk exposure examined in this chapter is the economic exposure (or operating exposure). Transaction exposure will be examined in Chapter 4, and translation exposure will be examined in Chapter 8.

THE WORLD OF FOREIGN EXCHANGE MARKETS

Spot and Forward Exchange Rates

Countries have their own national currency. Foreign exchange refers to the national currency of another country. Each national currency has its own relative value or exchange rate. An exchange rate of a currency is initially determined as a function of its content or by the reserves of other currencies held in the central bank to support its international exchange ability. Foreign exchange markets are used in the determination of the values of foreign exchange and for the facilitation of its sales and purchases. These markets establish foreign exchange as a commodity whose value is subject to the laws of supply and demand. Basically, foreign exchange markets determine the rate at which one national currency is exchanged for another. The resulting exchange rates are the basis for the exchange prices used for international business transactions. Within these foreign exchange markets, a forward market is used to hedge against the exchange rate risks arising from holding open-ended account balances.

There are basically two types of foreign exchange rate: the spot rate and the forward rate. The spot rate is the rate quoted for currency transactions to be delivered within two days and is determined by trade flows, inflation, seasonal demand for the currency, and arbitrage. The forward rate is the rate quoted for forward exchange contracts. These are contracts, between a foreign exchange trader and a customer or between two foreign traders, which specify the delivery of a certain sum in foreign currency at a future date and at a given rate. Various reasons motivate the use of forward contracts, including to hedge a transaction, to speculate on currency movements, to hedge a net investment in a foreign entity, and to hedge a foreign currency commitment.

The designated rate in the forward contracts is the forward rate. The forward rate may be equal to, or different from, the spot rate at the time when the contract is made. The difference between the two rates is known as the "spread."

The Foreign Exchange Market in the United States

A distinction should be made between internal and external credit markets. Internal credit markets are markets for deposits by local residents, which are governed by rules and institutional conventions of the local country. External credit markets trade interest rate contracts that are denominated in a single currency but traded outside the borders of that country issuing the currency. Hence, Eurodollars are dollar-denominated deposits held in a country other than the United States. The transfers between international banks are accomplished through a network of telephone lines leased by the Society of Worldwide Interbank Financial Telecommunications (SWIFT). Efficiencies of the foreign exchange markets include:

1. allocational efficiency, referring to how the market channels capital toward its most productive uses
2. operational efficiency, referring to how large an influence transaction costs and other market functions have in the operations of the market
3. information efficiency, referring to whether prices reflect "true" value[1]

It is interesting to note the absence of government interference in the Eurocurrency transactions in the external market. In particular, it has:

• no reserve requirements
• no interest rate regulations or caps
• no withholding taxes
• no deposit insurance requirements

- no regulations influencing credit allocation decisions
- less stringent disclosure requirements[2]

The foreign exchange market in the United States includes both a spot market, for the intermediate exchange of one currency for another, and a forward foreign exchange, where currencies are sold for a future exchange at a fixed price. Forward contracts are similar to future contracts, except that future contracts have fixed sizes and preestablished maturity dates. Future contracts are three-, six-, or twelve-month contracts maturing on the third Wednesday of January, March, April, June, July, September, October, and December.

Foreign exchange dealings involve the following actions and stages:

1. an entity that desires to buy a given currency on either the spot or forward market
2. a local bank that offers the entity (a client) the foreign exchange service (major banks develop trading (or dealing) desks for spot and forward foreign exchange transactions.)
3. the local bank entering the interbank market, which consists of several major banks specializing in foreign exchange and forming an association of commercial banks in foreign exchange dealings, called the Clearing House Interbank Payment System (CHIPS), or entering the brokers' market, which consists of several foreign exchange brokers seeking to match buyers and sellers of foreign currencies.

Exchange rates are quoted either in Europe, on the "continental basis," as units of foreign currency per dollar, or in the United States, on the "American basis," as units of dollars per unit of foreign exchange. Therefore, in a deutsch mark–dollar trade, DM1.8225/$ is stated on the continental basis, whereas $0.5487/DM is stated on the American basis.

A quotation of a home currency price of one unit of foreign currency is a "direct quote." Quotation of the foreign currency price of one unit of home currency price of one unit of home currency is an "indirect quote." Therefore:

- DM1.8225/$ is a direct quote in Europe and an indirect quote in the United States.
- $0.5487/DM is a direct quote in the United States and an indirect quote in Europe.

As another example:

- S ($/£) = 1.5683, or $1.5683/£, is a direct quote in the United States and an indirect quote in Europe.
- S (£/$) = .6376, or £ .6376/$, is a direct quote in Europe and an indirect quote in the United States.

Note that the American and European term quotes are reciprocals of one another. That is:

$$S(£/\$) = \frac{1}{S(\$/£)}$$

$$0.6376 = \frac{1}{1.5683}$$

The forward premium or discount is now computed as follows.
With indirect quotes:

$$\text{Forward premium or discount} = \frac{Spot - Forward}{Forward} \times \frac{12}{n} \times 100$$

With direct quotes:

$$\text{Forward premium or discount} = \frac{Forward - Spot}{Spot} \times \frac{12}{n} \times 100$$

The forward premiums and discounts have different implications depending on whether they are expressed as direct or indirect quotes.

1. If they are experienced as direct quotes, the following applies:

   a. A currency in the denominator of a foreign exchange quote is trading at a forward premium if the nominal value of that currency in the forward market is higher than in the spot market.

   b. A currency in the denominator of a foreign exchange quote is trading at a forward discount if the nominal value of that currency in the forward market is lower than in the spot market.

2. If experienced as indirect quotes, the following applies:

   a. A currency in the numerator of a foreign exchange quote is trading at a forward premium if the nominal value of that currency in the forward market is lower than in the spot market.

   b. A currency in the numerator of a foreign exchange quote is trading at a forward discount if the nominal value of that currency in the forward market is higher than in the spot market.

As an example, assume that the ninety-day Japanese yen forward rate is .008304 and the spot rate for the Japanese yen is .008193. In this case, the ninety-day forward premium or discount for the Japanese yen versus the U.S. dollar is

$$f_{90, \text{ ¥ or \$}} = \frac{0.008304 - 0.008193}{0.008193} \times \frac{360}{90} = 0.0542$$

This means that the ninety-day forward premium is .0542, or 5.42 percent. More precisely, the Japanese yen is trading at a 5.42 percent premium versus the U.S. dollar for delivery in ninety days.

An outright quotation means that the full price is stated. A three-month forward rate quotation of SF 2.2818/$ is an outright quote. Those who deal with foreign exchange on a daily basis, as in the case of bankers, express foreign exchange rates in terms of "points," also referred to as the "swap rate." A point is equal to the difference between the spot rate and the forward rate, expressed to the number of decimal points traditional for trading between two countries. For example, the spot rate may be SF 2.1823 and the one-year, thirty-day forward may be expressed as +35. This means that the forward rate is 35 points above the spot rate.

An interbank exchange rate quotation is made as a two-digit number/lid with the receding numbers assumed. For example, a British quote of 40/70 means that an actual price of:

- £1.79640 is bid to buy one U.S. dollar
- £1.79670 is asked when selling one U.S. dollar.

The bid/ask spread is equal to:

$$\frac{\text{Ask rate} - \text{Bid rate}}{\text{Ask rate}} = \frac{1.7967 - 1.7964}{1.7967} = 0.000167$$

Because about 50 percent of all spot and forward transactions occur through London banks, the London Interbank Bid Rate (LIBD) and the London Interbank Offer Rate (LIBOR) are the most frequently quoted rates. They are quoted for all major countries. Remember that, in order to be competitive, the interbank Eurocurrency market pays more interest in deposits and accepts less interest on loans than the domestic market. Therefore, the LIBOR is inferior to the domestic lending rate and the LIBD is higher than the domestic rate.

A bank buys foreign currency while simultaneously selling another currency. It has a long position in a given currency when it has purchased it in the spot or forward market. It is in a short position after it has sold that currency. A summary of transactions gives it its net position in each currency and at each forward rate.

DETERMINATION OF THE EXCHANGE RATE

Reliance on Fundamental Economic Relationships

Exchange rates fluctuate. A decline in their value is called a depreciation. An increase in their value is called an appreciation. A percentage change in the spot rate (e_f) at this specific point is computed as:

$$e_f = \frac{S_t - S_{t-1}}{S_t}$$

where

S_t = spot rate at time t

S_{t-1} = spot rate at time $t - 1$

The strength or weakness of a given currency is also generally measured by analysis with an index, where several currencies are consolidated into a single composite. Each currency in the index is designated a weight, which is determined by its relative importance in international trade and/or finance. Examples of such indices are the International Monetary Fund (IMF) index and the Federal Reserve Board (FRB) exchange rate index.

The equilibrium exchange rate is determined by the intersection of the demand and supply functions of a given currency. Because of the lack of information on both the demand and supply curves for each exchange market participant and the failure of anticipating government constraints in the exchange market, fundamental economic relationships that underlie exchange rate determination are used instead. They are examined next.

Purchasing Power Parity

The purchasing power parity (PPP) theory maintains that the percentage change in the value of a currency (rate of change in the spot exchange rate) is equal to the difference between the inflation rates in both countries. The formula is as follows:

$$e_f = \frac{(1 + I_h)}{(1 + I_f)} - 1$$

where

e_f = percentage change in the value of the foreign currency

I_f = inflation rate in the foreign country

I_h = inflation rate in the home country

The formula shows that:

• If $I_h > I_f$, e_f is positive and the foreign currency will appreciate.
• If $I_h < I_f$, e_f is negative and the foreign currency will depreciate.

For example, if the home currency experiences a 6 percent inflation rate while the foreign currency experiences a 4 percent inflation rate, the percentage change in the value of the foreign currency is:

$$e_f = \frac{1 + 0.06}{1 + 0.04} - 1 = 0.0192 \text{ or } 1.92\%$$

In other words, the foreign currency will appreciate by 1.92 percent as a result of the higher inflation rate in the home country.

The formula can be used to forecast the new value of the spot exchange rate of a given currency as function of the initial spot rate (S_t) and the inflation differential. In other words:

$$S_{t+1} = S_t \frac{(1 + I_h)}{(1 + I_f)}$$

or, as an approximate version:

$$S_{t+1} = S_t \left[1 + \left(I_h - I_f \right) \right]$$

For example, if the equilibrium value of the French franc is U.S. $.27 and the U.S. experiences a 7 percent inflation rate, then, according to the PPP theory, the spot rate of the franc will change as follows:

$$S_{t+1} = \$.27 \left[1 + \left(0.02 - 0.07 \right) \right]$$
$$= \$0.2565$$

Note that a less precise formula for the PPP theory is:

$$e_f = I_h - I_f$$

Two reasons why the PPP theory may not work all times are the influence of other factors in addition to the inflation differentials and the case in which there are no substitute goods at home.

When PPP holds and the differential inflation rates between countries are offset by the same differential in exchange rates, the competitive export positions of both countries are not affected by the exchange rate changes. In case of deviation from the PPP, changes in nominal rates lead to changes in real exchange rates and in the international competitive positions of the countries involved. If PPP does not hold, then the real exchange rate, R, can be defined as follows:

$$R = \frac{1 + I_h}{(1 + e_j)(1 + I_j)}$$

For example, if the annual inflation rate is 5.0 percent in the United States and 3.5 percent in the United Kingdom and the dollar depreciates by 5.5 percent against the pound, then the real exchange rate is:

$$R = (1.05) / (1.055)(1.035) = 0.96$$

Basically, the dollar depreciates by more than is dictated by PPP, resulting in a strengthening of U.S. industries. The possible relationships can be summarized as follows:

$R = 1$: competitiveness of the domestic country is unchanged

$R < 1$: competitiveness of the domestic country improves

$R > 1$: competitiveness of the domestic country worsens

International Fisher Effect (IFE)

The International Fisher Effect (IFE), also called Fisher Open, holds that the rate of change in the spot exchange rate is a function of interest rate differentials. The formula is as follows:

$$e_f = \frac{(1 + i_h)}{(1 + i_f)} - 1$$

where

e_f = percentage change in the value of the foreign currency

i_h = domestic interest rate

i_f = foreign interest rate

The formula shows that:

- If $i_h > i_f$, e_f is positive and the foreign currency will appreciate.
- If $i_h < i_f$, e_f is negative and the foreign currency will depreciate.

For example, if the domestic interest rate is 10 percent and the foreign interest rate is 13 percent, the percentage change in the value of the foreign currency is:

$$e_f = \frac{(1 + .10)}{(1 + .13)} - 1 = -0.026 \text{ or } -2.6\%$$

note that a less precise formula of IFE is:

$$e_f = i_h - i_f$$

The Fisher Effect

The Fisher Effect holds that the nominal interest rate in a country is equal to the interest rate plus the expected rate of inflation. For two countries, it would imply the following relationships:

$$\text{Home interest rate } i_h = R_h + I_h \tag{1}$$

$$\text{Foreign interest rate } i_f = R_f + I_f \tag{2}$$

Subtracting equation (1) from equation (2) gives:

$$i_h - i_f = (R_h - R_f) + (I_h - I_f)$$

Given that investors can buy interest-bearing securities in many different countries, the real rates of return should tend toward equalities between any two countries. The Fisher Effect holds, then, that the nominal interest rates will vary by the difference in the expected rates of inflation between two countries. Therefore, the following equality holds:

$$i_h - i_f = I_h - I_f$$

For example, if nominal interest rates in Italy and the United States on one-year maturities were respectively, 16 and 10 percent, this would be consistent with the differences in inflation rates of, 11 percent in Italy and 17 percent in the United States.

Interest Rate Parity (IRP)

The theory of interest rate parity holds that the difference in nominal interest rates should be equal, but opposite in sign, to the forward exchange rate premium. Basically:

$$\text{Forward Premium or Discount} = \frac{F_t - S_t}{S_t} = i_h - i_f$$

where

F_t = forward exchange rate
S_t = spot rate

i_h = nominal interest rate in the home country

i_t = nominal interest rate in the foreign country

A more precise formula is:

$$\text{Forward Premium or Discount} = \frac{F_t - S_t}{S_t} = \frac{(1 + i_h)}{(1 + i_f)} - 1$$

For example, assume that the nominal interest rate in the foreign country is 12 percent and the same rate in the home country is 8 percent. According to the IRP theory, the forward rate premium of the foreign country with respect to the U.S. dollar (assumed to be the home country) should be:

$$\text{Forward Premium} = \frac{(1 + 0.08)}{(1 + 0.12)} - 1 = -0.035 \text{ or } -3.5\% \text{ (not analyzed)}$$

The foreign currency is exhibiting a forward discount of 3.5 percent, which means that U.S. investors expect 3.5 percent less when selling the foreign currency forward six months from now than the spot rate they pay now. If the foreign currency's spot rate is $.20, a forward discount of 3.5 percent means that the six months forward rate is

$$\begin{aligned} F &= S\,(1 + \text{Discount}) \\ &= \$.20\,(1 - 0.035) \\ &= \$0.193 \end{aligned}$$

Basically, the discount offsets the interest rate advantage of the foreign currency. Note that when the International Fisher Effect is combined with IRP, that is;

$$\frac{F_t - S_t}{S_t} = i_h - i_f$$

we obtain

$$\frac{F_t - S_t}{S_t} = \frac{S_{t+n} - S_t}{S_t}$$

This is referred to as forward parity. Forward parity holds that any forward premium or discount is equal to the expected change in the exchange rate. Assuming that investors are risk neutral, forward parity will hold as long as the foreign exchange market is informally efficient.[3]

The Forward Rate as an Unbiased Predictor of the Future Spot Rate

Assuming an efficient foreign exchange market, it may be asserted that the forward rate acts as an unbiased predictor of the future spot rate. In other words, a 6 percent one-year forward premium on the French franc will appreciate by 6 percent during the next year.

Combined Economic Equilibrium Relationships

Assuming that there are no government foreign exchange controls or transaction costs, the five equilibrium relationships can be portrayed as in Exhibit 3.1. Various factors, including uncertainty, pure speculation, and a country's balance of payments, to name only a few, can affect these relationships and the foreign exchange rate, calling for the need for models for forecasting exchange rates.

EXCHANGE RATE FORECASTING

Forecasting exchange rates is essential to the conduct of various managerial functions, including (1) hedging decisions, (2) short-term financing, (3) short-term investment decisions, (4) long-term financing, and (5) earnings assesments. Exchange rate forecasting methods include technical methods, fundamental methods, and market-based methods.

1. Technical methods rely on the historical exchange rate to predict future rates. The methods rely on the use of a past-time series of observations on the exchange rate to determine whether some nonrandom behavior can be detected by the use of a time-series model such as spector analysis or the Box Jenkins model. The use of these models can sometimes allow speculations in the foreign exchange market to generate some spectacular profits. Do they work all the time? The answer is probably no.

2. Fundamental methods rely on hypothesized relationships between exchange rates and various economic variables. The general approach consists in regressing the exchange rate against economic variables that are assumed to have an impact on the exchange rate. The regression equation can be defined as:

$$ER_t = A_0 + A_1X_1 + A_2X_2 \ldots + A_nX_n$$

where

ER_t = exchange rate at time t

$X_1 \ldots X_n$ = economic variables

Exhibit 3.1
Combined Economic Equilibrium Relationships

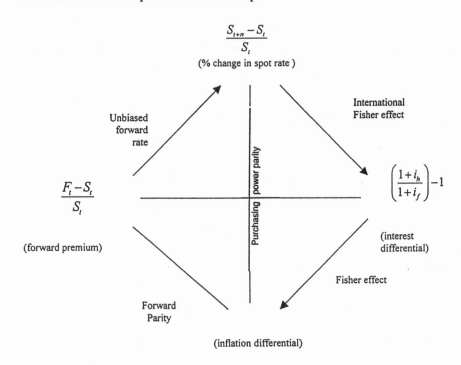

Examples of economic variables considered in the literature include (a) interest rate differentials, (b) relative inflation rates, (c) balance-of-payments flow, (d) reserve asset positions and (e) a measure of the statement of foreign exchange market participation as reflected in their portfolio asset compositions.

Eun and Reswick formulated a monetary approach in the following empirical form.[4]

$$s = \alpha + \beta_1 (m - m^*) + \beta_2 (v - v^*) + \beta_3 (y^* - y) + u$$

where

s = natural logarithm of the spot exchange rate

$m - m^*$ = natural logarithm of domestic/foreign money supply

$v - v^*$ = natural logarithm of domestic/foreign velocity of money

$y^* - y$ = natural logarithm of foreign/domestic output

u = random error term, with a mean of zero

$\alpha s, \beta s$ = model parameters

To generate forecasts using the fundamental approach, the following three steps are suggested:

Step 1: Estimation of the structural model to determine the numerical values for the parameters such as αs and βs.

Step 2: Estimation of future values of the independent variables such as $(m - m^*)$, $(v - v^*)$, and $(y^* - y)$.

Step 3: Substituting the estimated values of the independent variables into the estimated structural model to generate the exchange rate forecasts.[5]

The empirical evidence is not favorable to the monetary approach; in fact, it shows that the fundamental models developed based on the monetary approach did worse than the random walk model even if realized (true) values were used for the independent variables.

Four limitations of fundamental forecasting are worth mentioning. They are:

"• Uncertain timing of impact,
• Forecasts needed for factors with instantaneous impact,
• Omissions of other relevant factors from model,
• Change in sensitivity of currency movements to each factor over time."[6]

3. Market-based methods rely on market indicators to forecast either the spot rate or the forward rate. For example, based on the theory that the forward rate is an unbiased predictor of the spot rate, a market-based method will rely on a regression between the spot and forward rate, as follows:

$$S_t = A_0 + A_1 F_{t-1} + M_t$$

where

S_t = Spot rate at time t

F_{t-1} = Forward rate at time $t - 1$

M_t = Error term

A_0 = Intercept

A_1 = Regression coefficient

Three results are possible:

1. The results show that $A_o = 0$ and $A_1 = 1$; in this case, the forward rate is unbiased.
2. The results show that $A_o = 0$ and $A_1 < 1$; in this case, the forward rate systematically underestimates the spot rate.
3. The results show that $A_o = 0$ and $A_1 > 1$; in this case, the forward rate systematically overestimates the spot rate.

If the underestimation is expected to persist in the future, it can be used for the spot rate.

4. The accuracy of the exchange rate forecast can be evaluated by the absolute forecast error as a percentage of the realized value, computed as follows:

Absolute forecast value (as a percentage of realized value)
$$= \frac{\text{Forecast value} - \text{Realized value}}{\text{Realized value}}$$

For example, suppose you are hired to assess a multinational firm's ability to forecast the values of the yen and British pound. Information on four periods' point forecasts for the two currencies follows:

Period	Yen forecast	Actual yen value	Pound forecast	Actual pound value
1	$0.0042	$0.0043	$1.48	$1.52
2	0.0052	0.0051	1.47	1.50
3	0.0059	0.0053	1.43	1.48
4	0.0043	0.0042	1.52	1.49

The absolute forecast error as a percentage of the realized value follows:

Period	Yen Forecast	Pound forecast
1	0.023255	0.026315
2	0.019607	0.02
3	0.018867	0.033783
4	0.023809	0.044025
Mean	0.021385	0.031031

Given that the mean absolute forecast error of the yen is lower than that of the pound, the yen was forecasted with greater accuracy.

TYPES OF FOREIGN EXCHANGE EXPOSURE

Foreign exchange risk results from the change in foreign exchange rates and the effect that this has on the profitability, financial position, and transactions of a firm. As such, there are three types of foreign exchange exposure: translation, transaction, and economic.

- *Transaction exposure* arises whenever a firm has a receivable, a payable, a revenue or expense, or a forward contract that is denominated in other than its functional currency, which is usually the local currency or the currency in which the firm does most of its business. If a U.S. firm has a payable in the French franc, for example, and the French franc depreciates relative to the dollar, the number of dollars needed for payment by the U.S. firm decreases, resulting in an exchange gain. If, instead, the French franc appreciates relative to the dollar, the number of dollars needed for payment by the U.S. firm increases, resulting in an exchange loss. The transaction exposure is present whenever a cash flow in a specific transaction is affected by the changes in the foreign exchange rate.

- Translation exposure, which is also called "accounting exposure," results from the necessity of periodically consolidating or aggregating parent companies' and subsidiaries' financial statements. To do so, subsidiaries' financial statements have to be translated into their parent companies' currency before being consolidated with the parent companies' financial statements. Translation exposure results from the possibility that a change in exchange rates will create an exchange rate used for the translation of individual items in the balance sheet and income statement. The items to be translated at the historical exchange rate are unexposed, whereas the items to be translated at the current exchange rate are considered exposed and their translation results in translation losses or gains. These losses and gains do not involve any cash flows but rather result from the desire to value earnings in a single *numeraire* (reference currency).

- Economic exposure, also called "operating exposure" or "residual foreign exchange exposure," results from the possibility that a firm's economic value will change as a result of a change in the future operating cash flows following an unexpected change in the foreign exchange rate. The economic exposure results from the impact of a currency change on the cost of a firm's inputs and the price and volume of its output, which will affect its competitive strength.

The classification of foreign exchange exposure into economic, transaction, and translation exposure rests on the selection of foreign exchange risk as a discriminatory factor. Other discriminatory factors result in other classifications of foreign risk. The classification may be done in terms of:

1. before- or after-tax exposure, when tax is the discriminating factor

2. currency or country exposure and subsidiary or corporate exposure, when organizational structure is the discriminating factor

3. pro forma or actual exposure, when planning is used as the discriminating factor

4. long-, medium-, or short-term exposure, when the time frame is used as the discriminating factor

5. diversifiable or undiversifiable exposure, when diversifiability is used as the discriminating factor

6. actual or contingent exposure, when contingency is used as the discriminating factor

7. on-balance-sheet or off-balance-sheet exposure, when relation to the balance sheet is used as the discriminating factor

These classifications are not mutually exclusive.

ECONOMIC EXPOSURE

Nature of Economic Exposure

Economic exposure results from the impact of unexpected changes in exchange rates as a firm incorporates the expected changes in its investment, production, financing, and pricing decisions. Only the unexpected changes are assumed to cause the market value of a firm to change, as the expected changes are assumed, under an efficient market hypothesis, to be impounded in the market value.

Economic exposure may be separated into two components: a competitive effect and a conversion effect. As stated by Eugene Flood, Jr., and Donald Lessard:

The competitive effect is the sensitivity of the local currency cash flows to changes in exchange rate, which is shown to depend on the competitive structure of the markets in which the firm sells its products and the sources of its inputs. The conversion effect is purely the one-for-one mapping of the resulting local currency cash flows into dollars. White dollar cash flows are, by definition, not subject to the conversion effect, they may be subject to a competitive effect.[7]

Although the economic exposure affects mainly firms involved in international business, it has an effect on domestic firms as well. A domestic producer that sells only domestically, for example, may be affected by a change in the foreign exchange rate if a foreign competitor's price decreases as a result of a depreciation in the exchange of the foreign currency and the customer abandons the local company to benefit from the lower prices of the foreign producer.

The economic exposure can also be indirect. Consider, for example, the case of a U.S. importer of a good with payments denominated in U.S. dollars. If the foreign currency depreciates, the U.S. importer does not face direct economic exposure. It is possible, however, for the foreign exporter to decide to charge a higher price in order to offset the devaluation in the foreign currency. In that case, the U.S. importer will face an indirect economic exposure.

Impact of Economic Exposure

The impact of economic exposure depends on whether impact costs and output prices are determined locally and globally, as follows:

1. If the operating expenses and the revenues are defined locally, then, given the segmentation of local markets from global markets, the impact of economic exposure will be minimal.
2. If the operating expenses are determined globally while the revenues are determined locally, importers will have a *negative* exposure to foreign currency values.
3. If the operating expenses are determined locally while the revenues are determined globally, exporters will have a *positive* exposure to foreign currency values.
4. If the operating expenses and the revenues are determined globally, the multinational firm can have either a *positive* or *negative* exposure to foreign currency values, depending on the particular products and markets in which it competes.[8]

The effects of operating exposure are shown in Exhibit 3.2. In fact, the following generalizations may be made:

- A real appreciation of the foreign currency helps exporters and hurts importers.
- A real depreciation of the foreign currency helps importers and hurts exporters.
- A real appreciation of the local currency helps importers and hurts exporters.
- A real depreciation of the local currency helps exporters and hurts importers.

The impact of economic exposure varies, depending on the types of activities of a particular multinational corporation. Examples of the contingent impact of economic exposure include the following:

1. An increasingly strong U.S. dollar vis-à-vis other foreign currencies can result in a reduction of market share for U.S. exports as well as for local sales of foreign subsidiaries of U.S. multinationals. A foreign subsidiary's competitive position in the local markets can be such that increasing prices to offset an exchange rate depreciation can result in a loss of sales.
2. Credit policies can be such that the larger the credit term that is granted, the greater is the risk for economic loss resulting from exchange depreciation. The more the exchange risk can be passed to, or shared with, a customer, the less economic risk will be absorbed by the corporation.
3. The more the corporation can pass on to the customer increasing costs due to inflation and foreign exchange, the less the economic risk will be, and the reverse also holds true.

Exhibit 3.2
Economic Exposure

A. The Economic Exposure of U.S. Companies

	Base case	Per unit revenue or cost in dollars at $.0120/¥				
	In Dollars	At $.010/¥	Local	Importer	Exporter	Global
Revenue	$ 2,000	¥ 200,000	$ 2,000	$ 2,000	$ 2,400	$ 2,400
Cost	$ 1,600	¥ 160,000	$ 1,600	$ 1,920	$1,600	$ 1,920
Profit	$ 400	¥ 40,000	$ 400	$ 80	800	480
Percentage Change			0%	-80%	100%	20%

B. The Economic Exposure of Japanese Companies

	Base case	Per unit revenue or cost in dollars at $.0120/¥				
	In Dollars	At $.010/¥	Local	Importer	Exporter	Global
Revenue	¥ 200,000	$ 2,000	¥ 200,000	$ 2,000	¥166,666	¥166,666
Cost	¥ 160,000	$ 1,600	¥ 160,000	$ 1,920	¥160,000	¥133,333
Profit	¥ 40,000	$ 400	¥ 40,000	$ 80	¥ 6666	¥ 33,333
Percentage Change			0%	66%	-83%	-16%

4. The lower the level of working capital, the lower the level of economic risk will be, and the reverse also holds true.

5. The more contractual prices can be adjusted for inflation and foreign exchange, the less economic risk there will be.

6. The more local earnings are repatriated through dividend payments, the less economic risk there will be.

7. The more volatile the foreign exchange and capital markets are, the more uncertain the cost of financing will be, as measured by the sum of interest expense and debt-related transaction-translation gain or loss.[9]

Various factors affect the impact of economic exposure on an MNC. First, the impact of economic exposure depends on whether the foreign exchange rate has depreciated or appreciated. In the case of a local currency appreciation, for example, the local cash inflow is diminished by:

1. a decrease in local sales as foreign substitutes become cheaper
2. a decrease in foreign exports denominated in the local currency as a result of the increase in the price of its products in foreign countries
3. a decrease in its foreign exports denominated in foreign currency as the value of its exports converted in local currency declines
4. a decrease in any interest or dividends from foreign investments, due to their reduced value when converted into the local currency

Similarly, in the case of a local currency appreciation, its local cash outflows will be decreased by:

1. a decrease in the valve of the important supplies denominated in foreign currency
2. a decrease in any interest or dividends to pay foreign investors due to the reduced value of these payments when converted into the local currency

In the case of a local currency depreciation, the opposite may happen, with an increase in overall cash outflows and inflows.

Second, the impact of the economic exposure on a firm's expected cash flows depends on the time horizon used to determine the firm-level impact: short-run, medium-run equilibrium case, medium-run disequilibrium case, and the long run.[10]

1. In the short run, little can be done about the change in the exchange rates, resulting in a difference between realized cash flows and budgeted cash flows.
2. In the medium run, as expressed in two- to five-year budgets and assuming an equilibrium condition among foreign exchange rates, national inflation rates, and national interest rates, the firm is in a position to adjust prices and costs to maintain the expected cash flows, with the result of a minimum to zero economic exposure.
3. In the medium run and the disequilibrium case, the firm is unable to adjust its prices and costs, resulting in a difference between the expected and realized cash flows.
4. In the long run, all firms are subject to economic exposure if the foreign exchange markets are not continually in equilibrium.[11]

Measuring Economic Exposure

The measurement of economic exposure can be accomplished by one of three methods: (1) applying economic exposure formulas, (2) using regression analysis models, or (3) assessing the income statement sensitivity to potential exchange rate changes. One formula for the computation of economic exposure is based on the difference between the firm's net present values before and after the predicted change in the exchange rate. For example, the economic exposure in dollars to a firm operating in a foreign country with a fluctuating foreign currency (FC) is:

$$\text{Economic Exposure} = \sum \frac{\text{Original FC Cash Flow} \times ER_t}{(1 + r)^n}$$
$$- \sum \frac{\text{Adjusted FC Cash Flows} \times ER_{ai}}{(1 + r)^n}$$

where

ER_i = series of exchange rates expected before the change in the value of the exchange rate

ER_{ai} = series of exchange rates expected before the change in the value of the exchange rate

The adjusted FC cash flows are those cash flows that do not adjust proportionally to the change in the exchange rate. In other words, a 100 percent adjustment in cash flow results in zero economic exposure. There is, however, a small exchange loss even when there is a 100 percent adjustment in the cash flows. Assume, for example, that the cash flow foreign subsidiary for one year is FC 100 = $100.00. Two possible situations are examined next.

1. If the devaluation of the FC is 10 percent and the percentage adjustment in cash in cash flow is 100 percent, the economic exposure is zero. However, the change in FC cash flow may be 10 percent, with a new exchange rate of 90 percent, a new FC cash flow of FC 110 (FC 100 × 1.10), and a new dollar cash flow of $99 (FC 110 × 0.90). Therefore the exchange loss is $1.00 (original $100.00 − new dollar cash flow of $99.00).

2. If the devaluation of the FC remains 10 percent and the percentage adjustment is reduced to 60 percent, the economic exposure is 40 percent (100 percent − 60 percent). The change in FC cash flow is 6 percent (60 percent of 10 percent); the new exchange rate is 90 percent (10 percent of FC 100), resulting in a new FC cash flow 106.00 (FC 100 × 1.06) and a new dollar cash flow of $95.40 (FC 106 × 0.90). Therefore, the exchange loss is equal to $4.60 ($100.00 − $95.40). Using this analysis, R. M. Rodriguez and E. E. Carter proposed the following formula for economic exposure:[12]

FC economic exposure = ([Original FC cash flow] [1 − percentage adjustment in cash flows] + [expected change in FC cash flows])(expected percentage change in exchange rate)

In other words, the economic exposure resulting from a devaluation of 10 percent and an adjustment of cash flow of 60 percent is equal to:

$$
\begin{aligned}
\text{Economic exposure} &= (100\ [1 - 60\%] + 6\%)\ 10\% \\
&= (40 \times 10\%) + (6\% \times 10\%) \\
&= 4 + 0.60 \\
&= \$4.60
\end{aligned}
$$

The \$4.60 loss is due to a 10 percent loss in the economic exposure of FC 40 plus the 10 percent loss in the increased cash flow of FC 6. Similarly, the economic exposure resulting from a devaluation of 10 percent and a percentage adjustment of 100 percent is equal to:

$$
\begin{aligned}
\text{Economic exposure} &= (100\ [1 - 100\%] + 10)\ 10\% \\
&= 0 + 1 \\
&= \$1
\end{aligned}
$$

The \$1 loss is due to a 10 percent loss on the economic exposure of FC 0 plus the 10 percent on the increase cash flow of FC 10.11.

Applying Regression Analysis Models

Regression analysis models can be also used to measure economic exposure. A first model involves the regression of the historical percentage changes in inflation-adjusted cash flows, measured in the firm's home currency against an index reflecting the percentage change in either the exchange rate of one currency or a composite of currencies, in which the weight assigned to each currency amounts to the proportion of total foreign cash flows denominated in that currency. The model can be expressed in two ways:

$$
CCFP_t = A_0 + A_1 ERC_t + M_t
$$

where

$CCFP_t$ = percentage change in inflation-adjusted cash flows at time t

ERC_t = percentage change in the exchange rate of one currency at time t

A_0 = intercept

A_1 = regression coefficient = economic exposure coefficient

or

$$
CCFP_t = A_0 + A_1 IERC_t + M_t
$$

where

$IERC_t$ = index of percentage change in several currencies

If the impact of currency changes is lagged, the equation becomes:

$$CCFP_t = A_0 + A_1 IERC_t + A_2 IERC_{t+1} + M_t$$

An improvement on this first model to have a better sense of the sensibility of a firm's operating cash flows to currency risks is to unbundle the revenues and costs and examine the sensitivity of each to changes in the foreign exchange rates, as follows:

$$PCR_t = A_0 + A_1 ERC_t + M_t$$
$$PCC_t = A_0' + A_1' ERC_t + M_t$$

where

PCR_t = percentage change in revenues at time t

PCC_t = percentage change in costs at time t

A second model invoices the regression of the percentage change in stock prices as a proxy for a firm's value against both the percentage change in the market index of stocks and the percentage change in the value of a currency or an index of currencies. It may be expressed as:

$$PCS_t = A_0 + A_1 PCIS_t + A_2 PCVC_t + M_t$$

where

PCS_t = percentage change in the stock price of a company

$PCIS_t$ = percentage change in the market index of stocks

$PCVC_t$ = percentage change in the value of a currency or a composite of currencies

A_1 = systematic risk coefficient

A_2 = economic exposure coefficient

This model can also be lagged, as follows:

$$PCS_t = A_0 + A_1 PCIS_t + A_2 PCVC_t + A_3 PCVC_{t-1} + A_4 PCVC_{t-2} + M_t$$

An example of the second model is provided in article by Jonion.[13] In this model, the estimates of the exposure coefficient can be obtained from the following time-series regression:

$$R_{it} = \beta_{0i} + \beta_{2i} R_{st} + \beta_{3i} R_{mt} + \varepsilon_{it}, t = 1, \dots, T$$

where

R_{it} = rate of return on the *ith* company's common stock

R_{st} = rate of change via the trade-weighted exchange rate, measured as the dollar price of the foreign currency and derived from the weights in the Multinational Exchange Rate Model (MERM), computed by the International Monetary Fund

R_{mt} = rate of return in the CRSP value-weighted market index.

β_{2i} = economic exposure

β_{3i} = systematic risk

Another example of the second model is provided in an article by Bartov and Bodnar.[14] Their model is written as follows:

$$ASP_{i,t} = a_0 + \sum_{j=0}^{n} c_j VCUR_{i,t-j} + \varepsilon_{i,t}$$

where

$ASP_{i,t}$ = the abnormal stock performance for security i in period t (in percentage form)

$VCUR_{i,t-j}$ = the percentage change in a trade-weighted U.S. dollar exchange rate index for the period t to j

a_0, c_j = parameters to be estimated

$\varepsilon_{i,t}$ = error term for firm i in period t

Abnormal stock performance of firm i over a measurement period T is defined as follows:

$$ASP_{i,T} = \left(\prod_{k=t1}^{t2} (1 + AR_{i,k}) \right) - 1 \left([t_1, \ldots, t_2] \in T \right)$$

where

$AR_{i,t}$ = abnormal return for security i, from day $t-1$ to day t (in percentage form)

The daily abnormal returns ($AR_{i,t}$) are computed using the market model:

$$AR_{i,t} = r_{i,t} - a_i - b_i r_{m,t}$$

where

$r_{i,t}$ = the realized return for security i from day $t-1$ to day t

$r_{m,t}$ = the realized equally weighted market return, from day $t-1$ to day t

Exhibit 3.3
Budgeted Income Statement: The Tomaszewska Company

	French Business	Tunisian Business
Sales	FF 250	TD 50
Cost of goods sold	-50	-20
Gross profit	FF 200	TD 30
-Operating expenses	-50	-10
Earnings before	FF 200	TD 20
interest & taxes	-60	-5
- Interest expenses		
Earnings before taxes	FF 140	TD 15

Note: Millions, in French Francs (FF) and Tunisian Dinars (TD)

a_i, b_i = ordinary least squares (OLS) estimates of the intercept coefficient and the market beta for security i

Another method of measuring economic exposure consists of predicting the impact of the changes in exchange rates on each of the income statement items. This method requires:

1. the use of the budgeted income statement—for example, that of the Tomaszewska Company, a French-based company with a Tunisian subsidiary, as shown in Exhibit 3.3

2. making different estimates on the potential changes in the exchange rate, with the assumption that the expected exchange values of the Tunisian dinar are, respectively, FF 0.90 and FF 0.80

3. assuming that the sales in local currency will increase, following an increase in the value of the foreign currency

The assumptions in this example are as follows:

Expected exchange rate	Expected French sales
FF 0.90	300
FF 0.80	200

The impact of the potential changes of the exchange rate in the earnings of the Tomaszewska Company is shown in Exhibit 3.4. The example shows that a stronger Tunisian dinar affects the financial performance of the Tomaszewska Company positively. The analysis described for the Tomaszewska Company can be extended to more than one year if a forecast of the income statement for more than a one-year period is available.

Exhibit 3.4
Impact of Expected Exchange Rate on Financial Performance of the Tomaszewska Company

	TD = FF0.90	TD = FF0.80
Sales		
(1) French	FF 300	FF 200
(2) Tunisian	TD 50 = FF 45	TD 50 = FF 40
(3) Total	FF 345	FF 240
Cost of goods sold		
(1) French	FF 50	FF 50
(2) Tunisian	TD 20 = FF 18	TD 20 = FF 16
(3) Total	FF 68	FF 66
Gross profit	FF 277	FF 174
Operating expenses		
(1) French	FF 50	FF 50
(2) Tunisian	TD 10 = FF 9	TD 10 = FF8
(3) Total	FF 59	FF 58
Earnings before interest & taxes	FF 218	FF 116
Interest		
(1) French	FF 60	FF 60
(2) Tunisian	TD 5 = FF 4.5	TD 5 = FF 4
(3) Total	FF 64.5	FF 64
Earnings before taxes	FF 153.5	FF 52

Managing Economic Exposure

Economic exposure is considerably more important to the multinational firm than translation or transaction exposure. It is more difficult to detect, given that it depends on the estimation procedures used to forecast cash flows. It does not result, however, from the idiosyncrasies of the accounting process, but rather from economic analysis and planning. As such, it requires from management an integrated planning process involving strategies in finance, marketing, production, and so forth. The planning has to start at the strategic rather than the management or operational levels, and it must be preventive rather than reactive. This might require the integration of operating and financial responsibilities from the policy-making level down to the implementation and performance evaluation levels.

Reacting to economic exposure requires strategic planning in the functional marketing, finance, and production. Marketing strategies may involve the careful planning of pricing, product promotion, and distribution strategies to be implemented in the event of exchange rate change. Production strategies may involve securing alternative sources and plants to be used for changes in production techniques and locations in the event of exchange rate changes. Similarly, financial strategies may involve securing alternative lines of credit in various countries to be used in the event of exchange rate changes. In short, the management of economic exposure rests on the firm's proper and timely diversification of its operations and financing base.

By diversifying its operations intentionally, a firm will be in a position to detect disequilibrium when it occurs and to react to worldwide competitive changes by altering its production, sourcing, and sales policies. A purely domestic firm, on the other hand, is not in a position to detect disequilibrium in a timely fashion or to manage the economic exposure it suffers from international competitors from countries with undervalued currencies.

By diversifying its financing sources, a firm can take advantage of unexpected interest differentials resulting from temporary deviations from the International Fisher Effect and can reduce default risk by matching the mix of currencies it borrows to the mix of currencies to be realized through its operations.

Eun and Reswick selected the following firm strategies for managing operating exposure:[15]

1. selecting low-cost production sites, whereby (a) the firm establishes and maintains production facilities in various countries and (b) it may shift production to deal with the effect of exchange rate changes

2. using a flexible sourcing policy, whereby the firm may elect to source from locations where input costs are low

3. diversification of the market for the firm's products by diversifying the export market

4. increasing investment in research and development (R&D) and product differentiation

5. using financial hedging to stabilize the firm's cash flow

USE OF PROFIT-VOLUME–EXCHANGE RATE ANALYSIS

Conventional profit-volume analysis relies on the variable/fixed cost classification, with volume as the key variable. Assuming that x is the volume in physical units, P is the unit selling price, V is the unit variable cost, and F is the total fixed cost, the breakeven profit, Π_x, is computed as follows:

$$\Pi_x = Px - Vx - F$$

If we set the contribution margin percent as $M = P - V$, then:

$$\Pi_x = Mx - F$$

Setting $\Pi_x = 0$, the breakeven x^0 is obtained as follows:

$$x^0 = F/M$$

Baker and colleagues propose a profit-exchange rate analysis that relies on a global cost/local cost classification with the exchange rate as the key variable.[16] The variables denominated in the global currency include P, the unit price; V, the global variable cost; and F, the global fixed costs. The variables denominated in the local currency include v, the local variable costs, and f, the local fixed cost. Given an exchange rate, r, expressed as the local-to-global currency units (the indirect quote), the profit, Π_r, which is a function of the exchange rate, is:

$$\Pi_r = Pr - Vr - v \text{ (assuming all costs are variable)}$$

The firm breaks even when the exchange rate, r^0, is:

$$r^0 = v / (P - V) = v / M$$

Baker and colleagues also developed a profit-volume-exchange rate analysis that holds on both the variable/fixed and the global/local classifications.[17] In such a case, the profit, Π_{rx}, which is a function of both exchange rate and volume, is stated in the local currency unit as:

$$\Pi_{rx} = Mrx - vx - Fr - f$$

Four new variables may be now introduced:

1. $x = x - F / M$ is "excess volume."
2. $r = r - v / M$ is "excess exchange rate."
3. $K = Fv / M + f$ is a "contribution margin requirement."
4. $s = rx$ is "rate volume."

Using these new variables, Π_{rx} may be restated as:[18]

$$\Pi_{rx} = Mrx - K$$

At breakeven, when $\Pi_{rx} = 0$, we obtain the following breakeven results:

$$s^0 = (rx)^o = K / M$$
$$x^0 = (K / M) / r$$
$$r^o = (K / M) / x$$
$$x^0 = (K / M) / (r - v / M) + F / M$$
$$r^o = (K / M) / (x - F / M) + v / M$$

The last two expressions are the most important, as they give the breakeven volume, x^0, and the breakeven exchange rate, r^o. The two variables can be depicted graphically as the volume and exchange rate combinations that achieve the breakeven profit. For example, consider the following example:

$P = \$500$

$V = \$300$

$F = \$5000$

$v = ¥20,000$

$f = ¥200,000$

The breakeven volume x^0, for a given exchange rate, as well as the breakeven exchange rate, r^o, for a given volume of x are depicted in Exhibit 3.5. The combination of volume and exchange rate to achieve a breakeven profit is depicted graphically in Exhibit 3.6.

CONCLUSIONS

This chapter has examined (1) the fundamentals of a world of foreign exchange, (2) the economic equilibrium models underlying the determination of exchange rates, (3) the forecasting of exchange rates, and (4) the measurement of economic exposure.

Economic exposure results from the floating of currencies and the resulting economic instability. In fact, when currencies float, some economies may sink. This is due to the prevailing orthodoxy in monetary policy, which advocates floating exchange rules. There is, however, a movement toward the view that smaller countries should replace the central bank with a currency board. The new system would allow a country to issue currency but would require by law

Exhibit 3.5
Breakeven Volume as a Function of Exchange Rate

Exchange Rate r (¥/$)	"Excess" Rate r: r = r -v/M(100¥/$)	"Excess" Volume x: x = 3500 (¥/$)/r units	Breakeven Volume $x^0 = x + F/M$ (=25) units
100	0	∞	∞
110	10	350	375
120	20	175	200
130	30	117	142
140	40	88	113
150	50	70	95
160	60	58	83
170	70	50	75
180	80	44	69
190	90	39	64
200	100	35	60

Note: M is the global contribution margin, global price less global variable cost, per unit (in $); F is total global fixed cost (in $); v is local variable cost per unit (in ¥); x is volume of production and sales in units; r is exchange rate (¥/$); x is "excess" volume over and above the volume needed to break even in a simple, volume-based breakeven analysis; and r is "excess" exchange rate over and above the exchange rate needed to break even in a simple rate-based breakeven analysis.

Source: Baber, William, Yuji, Ijirii, and Sok-Hyon Kang, "Profit-Volume-Exchange Rate Analysis for Planning International Operations," *Journal of International Management and Accounting* (Summer 1996), p. 95. Reprinted with permission.

that the central bank exchange the currency at a present rate for dollars or another strong foreign currency. Countries such as Hong Kong, Argentina, El Salvador, and Bulgaria have opted for currency boards. What may finally happen is a division of the world into two or three currency zones, ruled by currencies like the dollar, the Euro, the yen, or the yuan. It implies that many countries will have to sacrifice sovereignty over areas of monetary management, which may be hard to achieve. The new system would be better than the present system

Exhibit 3.6
Rate-Volume Trade-off at Breakeven (Rate − 100) × (Volume − 25) = 3,500

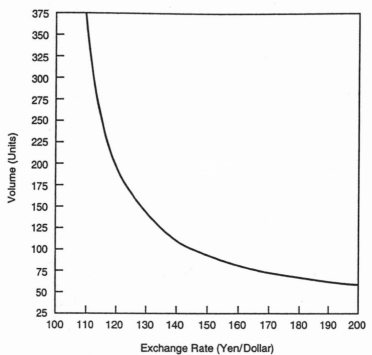

Source: Baber, William, Yuji Ijiri, and Sok-Hyon Kang, "Profit-Volume-Exchange Rate Analysis
for Planning International Operations," *Journal of International Financial Management and
Accounting* (Summer 1996), p. 96. Reprinted with permission.

of up to 175 small currencies, of which few are trustworthy. For investors, it
will eliminate the risks of devaluation and the need for expensive hedging strategies.

NOTES

1. Butler, Kirt C., *Multinational Finance* (Cincinatti, Ohio: South-Western College
Publishing, 1997), pp. 59–60.

2. Ibid., p. 62.

3. Eun, Cheol S., and Bruce G. Reswick, *International Financial Management* (Boston: Irwin-McGraw Hill, 2000), p. 125.

4. Ibid., p. 117.

5. Meese, Richard, and Kenneth Rogoff, "Empirical Exchange Rate Models of the
Seventies: Do They Fit Out of Sample?" *Journal of International Economics* 14 (1983),
pp. 3–24.

6. Madura, Jeff, *International Financial Management* (St. Paul, MN: West Publishing Company, 1995), p. 243.

7. Flood, Eugene, Jr., and Donald R. Lessard, "On the Measurement of Operating Exposure to Exchange Rates, A Conceptual Approach," *Financial Management*, Spring 1986, p. 76.

8. Butler, *Multinational Finance*, p. 612.

9. Srinivasuku, S. L., "Classifying Foreign Exchange Exposure," *Financial Executive*, February 1983, p. 38.

10. Stonehill, Arthur, I. Rawn, and N. Dullum, "Management of Foreign Exchange Exposure," in Goran Bergedahl, (ed.), *International Financial Management* (Stockholm: Norstadt, 1982), pp. 128–148.

11. Eiteman, D. D., and A. I. Stonehill, *Multinational Business Finance* (Reading, MA: Addison-Wesley, 1989), pp. 174–175.

12. Rodriguez, R. M., and E. E. Carter, *International Financial Management* (Englewood Cliffs, NJ: Prentice-Hall, 1984), p. 310.

13. Jonion, Philippe, "The Exchange-Rate Exposure of U.S. Multinationals," *Journal of Business* 63 (1990), p. 356.

14. Bartov, Eli, and Gordon M. Bodnar, "Firm Valuation, Earnings Expectations, and the Exchange-Rate Exposure Effect," *Journal of Finance* 15 (December 1994), pp. 1762–1763.

15. Eun and Reswick, *International Financial Management*, p. 304.

16. Baker, W. R., Yugi Ihiri, and Sok-Hyon Kang, "Profit-Volume-Exchange Rate Analysis for Planning International Operations," *Journal of International Financial Management and Accounting* 7 (1996), pp. 85–101.

17. Ibid.

18. $\Pi_{rx} = Mrx - vx - Fr - f$

This equation can be restated by adding and subtracting Fv/M and regrouping terms, verifying that:

$$M(r - v / M)(x - F / M) = Mrx - vx - Fr + Fv / M, \text{ namely:}$$
$$\Pi_{rx} = Mrx - vx - Fr - f = Mrx - vx - Fr + Fv/M - Fv/M - f$$
$$= M (r - v / M) (x - F / M) - (Fv / M + f)$$
$$= Mrx - K$$

SELECTED READINGS

Abuaf, Niso. "The Nature and Management of Foreign Exchange Risk." *Midland Corporate Finance Journal* 11 (Fall 1986), pp. 30–44.

Adler, Michael, and Bernard Dumas. "The Exposure of Long-Term Foreign Currency Bonds." *Journal of Financial Quantitative Analysis* 21 (November 1980), pp. 973–994.

———. "Exposure to Currency Risk: Definition and Measurement." *Financial Management* 15 (Spring 1984), pp. 41–50.

Baker, W. R., Yugi, Ijiri, and Sok-Hyong Kang. "Profit-Volume-Exchange Rate Analysis for Planning International Operations." *Journal of International Financial Management and Accounting* 7 (1996), pp. 85–101.

Bar:ov, Eli, and Gordon M. Bodnar, "Firm Valuation, Earnings Expectations, and the Exchange-Rate Exposure Effect." *Journal of Finance* (December 1994), pp. 175X–85.

Eiteman, D. D., and A. I., Stonehill. *Multinational Business Finance* (Reading, MA: Addison-Wesley, 1989).

Flood, Eugene, Jr., and Donald R., Lessard. "On the Measurement of Operating Exposure to Exchange Rates: A Conceptual Approach." *Financial Management*, Spring 1986, pp. 25–36.

George, Abraham. "Cash Flow versus Accounting Exposures to Currency Risk." *California Management Review*, Summer 1978, pp. 50–45.

Giddy, Ian H., "Exchange Risk: Whose View?" *Financial Management*, Summer 1977, pp. 23–33.

Heckman, Christine R. "Don't Blame Currency Values for Strategic Errors." *Midland Corporate Finance Journal* (September–October 1983), pp. 59–65.

Jacque, L. L. "Management of Foreign Exchange Risk." *Journal of International Business Studies* (Spring–Summer 1981), pp. 81–101.

Jonion, Philippe. "The Exchange-Rate Exposure of U.S. Multinationals." *Journal of Business* 63 (1990), pp. 331–345.

Kwok, Chuch C. Y. "Hedging Foreign Exchange Exposure: Independent vs. Integrative Approaches." *Journal of International Business Studies* (Summer 1987), pp. 33–52.

Lessard, Donald R., and S. B. Lightstone. "Volatile Exchange Rates Can Put Operations at Risk." *Harvard Business Review* (July–August 1986), pp. 107–114.

Madura, Jeff. *International Financial Management* (St Paul, MN: West Publishing, 1992).

APPENDIX 3.1: MAJOR MARKET INDEXES (WEDNESDAY, NOVEMBER 29, 2000)

North America

Symbol	Name	Last	Change	%	Date/Time
.IRV	13 Week Treasury Bill Index	60.40	⇓ -0.60	-0.98	Nov 29 13:33
.FVX	5 Year Treasury Note Index	54.87	⇓ -0.80	-1.44	Nov 29 13:34
.TNX	10 Year Treasury Note Index	55.47	⇓ -0.42	-0.75	Nov 29 13:34
.TYX	30 Year Treasury Note Index	56.70	⇓ -0.02	-0.04	Nov 29 13:34
.XOI	AMEX Oil and Gas Index	513.89	⇓ -17.77	-3.34	Nov 29 13:35
.XAX	AMEX Composite	860.68	⇓ -13.00	-1.49	Nov 29 13:34
.INX2	CBOE Internet	247.48	⇓ -4.12	-1.64	Nov 29 13:34
.TXX	CBOE Technology	743.75	⇓ -23.09	-3.01	Nov 29 13:34
.DJI	Dow Jones Industrial Average	10564.65	⇑ 57.07	0.54	Nov 29 13:34
.DJT	Dow Jones Transportation	2798.10	⇑ 1.69	0.06	Nov 29 13:34
.DJU	Dow Jones Utilities	392.70	⇓ -2.50	-0.63	Nov 29 13:34
.XAU	Gold and Silver Index	46.19	⇓ -0.90	-1.91	Nov 29 13:34
.GTC	Goldman Sachs Tech Index Composite	318.12	⇓ -10.30	-3.14	Nov 29 13:34
.IIX	Inter@ctive Week Internet Index	317.79	⇓ -10.30	-3.14	Nov 29 13:34
.XMI	Major Markets Index	1044.24	⇑ 3.37	0.32	Nov 29 13:35
.VIX	Market Volatility Index	30.74	⇑ 0.35	1.15	Nov 29 13:34
.MID	Mid Cap Index	485.37	⇓ -6.69	-1.36	Nov 29 13:34
.MSH	Morgan Stanley High Tech 35	718.45	⇓ -24.42	-3.29	Nov 29 13:35
.NDX	Nasdaq 100 Index	2668.25	⇓ -118.28	-4.24	Nov 22 17:15

.IXBK	Nasdaq Banking	1745.09	⇑ 33.04	1.93	Nov 29 13:34
.IXB	Nasdaq Combined Biotech	1100.70	⇓ -0.37	-0.03	Nov 29 13:33
.IXIC	Nasdaq Composite	2662.99	⇓ -71.99	-2.63	Nov 29 13:34
.IXK	Nasdaq Computer	1522.42	⇓ -55.79	-3.54	Nov 29 13:35
.IXIS	Nasdaq Insurance	1952.42	⇑ 26.30	1.37	Nov 29 13:35
.IXI	Nasdaq/NMS Industrial Index	600.45	⇓ -9.75	-1.60	Nov 29 13:34
.NYA	NYSE Composite	634.92	⇑ 0.59	0.09	Nov 29 13:34
.NFA	NYSE Financial Index	591.05	⇑ 8.66	1.49	Nov 29 13:34
.PSE	Pacific Stock Exch High Tech Index	832.16	⇓ -16.89	-1.99	Nov 29 13:34
.SOXX	Philadelphia Semiconductor Index	561.79	⇓ -15.33	-2.66	Nov 29 13:34
.RUT	Russell 2000	453.68	⇓ -5.34	-1.16	Nov 29 13:35
.OEX	S&P 100	707.80	⇓ -0.67	-0.09	Nov 29 13:34
.SPX	S&P 500	1333.01	⇓ -3.08	-0.23	Nov 29 13:34
.SML	S&P 600 Small Cap	200.11	⇓ -1.81	-0.90	Nov 29 13:34
.STI.N	Short Term Trading Index	1.06	⇓ -0.04	-3.37	Nov 29 13:34
.TSE35	Toronto	542.71	⇓ -7.67	-1.39	Nov 29 13:34
.WSX	Wilshire Small Cap Index	727.66	⇓ -11.73	-1.59	Nov 29 13:33

South America

Symbol	Name	Last	Change	%	Date/Time
.MERV	Argentina Merval Index	411.05	⇑ 4.56	1.12	Nov 29 13:33
.MXX	Bolsa	5919.13	⇓ -15.80	-0.27	Nov 29 13:35
.BVSP	Brazil Index	N/A	N/A	N/A	N/A
.IGPA	Chile Index	4855.24	⇓ -3.22	-0.07	Nov 29 13:34

Europe

Symbol	Name	Last	Change	%	Date/Time
.FCHI	CAC 40	6060.65	⇓ -8.57	-0.14	Nov 29 11:54
.GDAX	DAX	N/A	N/A	N/A	N/A
.FTSE	FT-100	6164.90	⇓ -84.90	-1.36	Nov 29 11:37
.CIFR	France-CI	1946.94	⇓ -1.79	-0.09	Nov 29 12:48
.HEX	Helsinki HEX General 50	13468.44	⇑ 13.36	0.10	Nov 29 11:00
.SMSI	Madrid SE Index	908.29	⇑ 9.33	1.04	Nov 29 11:39
.NTOT	Oslo SE Total	1402.68	⇓ -7.39	-0.52	Nov 29 10:00
.SSMI	Swiss	N/A	N/A	N/A	N/A

Asia Pacific Rim

Symbol	Name	Last	Change	%	Date/Time
.SSEB	China Shanghai B	74.09	⇓ -1.01	-1.35	Nov 29 02:00
.SSEC	China Shanghai Composite Index	2067.49	⇓ -11.90	-0.57	Nov 29 02:00
.HSLR	Hang Seng L R I Index	14115.64	⇓ -53.42	-0.38	Nov 29 10:30
.HIS	Hang Seng	14169.06	⇓ -397.16	-2.73	Nov 29 03:00
.KLSE	Malaysian Index	732.25	⇓ -6.17	-0.84	Nov 29 04:02
.N225	Nikkei 225	14507.64	⇓ -151.23	-1.03	Nov 29 01:00
.SETI	Thailand Set Index	282.90	⇓ -0.77	-0.27	Nov 29 05:00

4
Transaction Exposure for Multinational Operations

INTRODUCTION

The foreign exchange market presents (1) cases where the quoted prices of currencies vary from what the market price should be, and (2) cases where the fluctuating exchange rates change the value of a firm's transactions. The first type of case creates opportunities for the use of international arbitrage to cause a realignment of the currencies. The second type of case creates a transaction exposure that needs to be corrected or reduced. Accordingly, this chapter elaborates on the various techniques used in international arbitrage and in the management of transaction exposure.

INTERNATIONAL ARBITRAGE

Arbitrage involves the simultaneous exchange and sale of a commodity or asset in parent markets in order to capitalize on a discrepancy in quoted prices. Three types of international arbitrage are examined next: (1) locational arbitrage, (2) triangular arbitrage, and (3) covered interest arbitrage.

Locational Arbitrage

Spatial or locational arbitrage can be used when the foreign exchange rate quotations differ among different locations. Exhibit 4.1 shows the bid/ask spread for German marks at two banks, A and B. Locational arbitrage is possible in this case to capitalize on the differential exchange rates between the two loca-

Exhibit 4.1
Currency Quotes for Locational Arbitrage: First Example

	Bank A	Bank B
Bid price of German marks	$.565	$.605
Ask price of German marks	$.585	$.795

tions. A firm could buy German marks at $.585 at Bank A and sell them at $.605 to Bank B, in one "round-trip" transaction. The news of the potential in locational arbitrage will lead to a high demand for marks at Bank A and a higher supply at Bank B, leading Bank A to raise its price and Bank B to lower its price. Exhibit 4.2 shows the bid/ask spread for German marks when it is no longer possible to profit from a locational arbitrage. Note that in comparing Exhibits 4.1 and 4.2, it appears that locational arbitrage is only possible when the bid price at one location is higher than the ask price in another location.

Triangular Arbitrage

The value of a currency X relative to another currency Y is as follows:

$$\text{Value of } X \text{ relative to } Y = \frac{X}{Y}$$

Similarly, the value of Y relative to X can be determined from the cross–exchange rate formula:

$$\text{Value of } Y \text{ relative to } X = \frac{Y}{X}$$

Triangular arbitrage involves one exchange rate traded at two different prices—a direct price and an indirect price. For example, consider three currencies—the dollar, the pound sterling, and the mark. No profit opportunities exist if

$$(\$/£) = (\$/DM)_t (DM/£)_t$$

where the left side is the direct price of sterling in terms of dollars and the right side is the indirect price. Triangular arbitrage is warranted if the difference between the direct and indirect prices is positive. By definition, triangular ar-

Exhibit 4.2
Currency Quotes for Locational Arbitrage: Second Example

	Bank A	Bank B
Bid price of German marks	$.565	$.604
Ask price of German marks	$.604	$.795

bitrage is the process of trading out of a first currency into a second currency and then trading that for a third currency, which is in turn traded for the first currency. It amounts to earning an arbitrage profit via trading from the second to the third currencies when the direct exchange between the two is not in alignment with the cross-exchange rate.

For example, assume the following quotes:

1 British pound = $2.20/£
1 French franc = $0.22/FF

The relative values of these currencies are:

Value of British pound relative to French franc = $2.20 / $0.22 = 10
Value of French franc relative to British pound = $0.22 / $2.20 = 0.1

Now, suppose that the bank's rate is 1 pound = 12 francs. In such a case, it is worthwhile to buy British pounds with U.S. dollars, convert the pounds to francs, and then sell the francs for U.S. dollars. A person holding $22,000 can do the following:

1. Buy £10,000 ($22,000 / $2.20 per pound).
2. Convert the £10,000 to francs, obtaining 120,000 francs (£10,000 × 12 francs per pound).
3. Sell the 120,000 francs at the rate of 1 franc = $0.22, to obtain $26,400 (120,000 × $0.22).

The triangular arbitrage results in a gain of $4,400 ($26,400 − $22,000). However, the profit opportunities will eventually disappear with a realignment of the three currency values to reflect the values obtained by the cross-exchange formula.

Here is a second example of triangular arbitrage. Assume the following information is given:

Dutch guilders per U.S. dollar: fl1.9055/$

Canadian dollars per US dollar: C$1,3050/$

Dutch guilders per Canadian dollar: fl1.5400/C$

The cross-rate between Dutch guilders and Canadian dollars is:

$$\text{Cross-rate} = \frac{\text{fl}1.9055}{\text{C\$}1.3050} = \text{fl}1.4601/\text{C\$}$$

The cross-rate is, therefore, different from the actual quotation of fl1.5400/C$. Thus, an opportunity for arbitrage arises. For example, an investor with fl500,000 will proceed as follows in the spot market:

1. Exchange the sum of fl500,000 into for U.S. $262,398.32 (fl500,000/fl1.9055)

2. Exchange the U.S. dollars for Canadian dollars and obtain C$342,429.8 U.S. $262,398.32 × 1.3050)

3. Exchange the Canadian dollars for Dutch guilders and obtain fl527,341.89 (C$342,429.8 × 1.5400). The arbitrage profit amounts to fl527,341.89 − fl500,000 = fl27,341.89.

For a third example of triangular arbitrage, assume that the cross-trader at Bank A observes the following:

1. Bank B is buying dollars at S(FF/$) = 6.4080, the same as Bank A's bid price.

2. Bank C is offering dollars at S($/£) = 1.5680, the same as Bank A.

3. Bank D had a current ask price between the franc and the pound at S(FF/£) = 10.0090

Using the cross-rate formula, the cross-trader concludes that the FF/£ bid price should be no lower than S(FF/£) = 1.5680 × 6.4080 = 10.047. Given that Bank D is offering to sell British pounds at 10.0090, a triangular arbitrage profit exists. Using a given sum of $5,000,000, the trader proceeds with the following Bank A arbitrage strategy:

1. Sell the U.S. dollars for French francs: $5,000,000 × 6.4080 = £3,201,118.99.

2. Sell French francs for British pounds: FF32,040,000 / 10.090 = £3, 201,118.99.

3. Sell British pounds for U.S. dollars £3,201,118.99 × 1.5680 = $5,019,354.58.

4. Realize an arbitrage profit of $5,019,354.58 − 5,000,000.00 = $19,354.58.

Covered Interest Arbitrage

Covered interest arbitrage can be used if the differential in interest rates between the two countries is not approximately reflected in the differences between the exchange rate of the two countries. It involves investing in the foreign country and at the same time covering against exchange risk. In what follows, let us examine two cases: case 1, where covered interest arbitrage is not possible, and case 2, where it is possible.

Case 1. Make the following assumptions about exchange rates and interest rates between the United States and France:

Spot exchange rate: FF6.4251/1$

Three-month forward rate: FF6.4878/$

Three-month U.S. interest rate: 12 percent per annum or 3 percent per quarter

Three-month French interest rate: 16 percent per annum or 4 percent per quarter

Transaction size: $1,000,000

An American multinational company may elect to invest $1,000,000 for three months, yielding $1,030,000. Alternately, it may elect to purchase FF6,425,100 at today's spot rate (FF6.4251) and invest it in a three-month French security that will yield FF6,682,104 in three months. The same amount could, at the same time, be sold forward at the forward exchange rate of FF6.48748, which would yield $1,030,000 in three months and thus eliminate the exchange risk. This situation is typical of an equilibrium caused by an interest rate parity.

Case 2. When the market is not in equilibrium, as described by interest rate priority, there is a potential for "riskless," or arbitrage, profits. The arbitrageurs will invest in the currency offering the highest return in a covered basis. This is called covered interest arbitrage (CIA). Assume, however, that the French interest rate has increased to 20 percent per annum, or 5 percent per quarter. In such a case a profit can be generated through a covered interest arbitrage as follows.

Today

1. Borrow $1,000,000 at 3 percent per quarter for three months.
2. Acquire FF6,425,100 at the spot market after exchanging the $1,000,000 ($1,000,000 × FF6.4251).
3. Invest the FF6,425,100 in France at 5 percent interest per quarter, which in three months will yield FF6,746,355 (FF6,425,100 × (1.05))
4. Assume the transaction costs to be $500.
5. Sell the FF6,746,355 forward three months at FF6.4878.

Three Months from Now

6. Receive FF6,746,355 from the French bank for the investment.
7. Complete the forward contract by delivering FF6,746,355 at FF6.48748 and receive $1,039,903.70 (FF6,746,355 / FF6.4878).
8. Deliver to the U.S. bank the amount of $1,030,000 for the three-month loan.

What results from the transaction is the following:

Return from forward contract	$1,039,903.70
Minus reimbursed loan	1,030,000.00
Minus transaction cost	500.00
Net yield before tax	$ 9,403.70

Let us examine another example of covered interest arbitrage as it affects the daily work of a Hong Kong arbitrageur. Suppose that he or she reads the following information in the "Morning Quotation Box."[11]

Eurodollar rate	= 10% per annum
Euroyen rate	= 6% per annum
Spot rate	= ¥145/$
Six-month forward rate	= ¥143/$

The artibrageur decides to do the following:

1. Borrow ¥145,000,000 from a Japanese bank and convert at the spot rate of Y145/$ to $1,000,000.
2. Invest the proceeds in a Eurodollar account for six months at 5 percent per six months.
3. Simultaneously sell the proceeds ($1,050,000) forward for yen at the six-month forward rate of ¥143/$, which will give gross yen revenues of ¥150,150,000.
4. Compute the cost of funds at the Euro-yen rate of 3 percent per six months, which amount to ¥149,350,000. The profit in the covered interest arbitrage amounts to ¥800,000 (¥150,150,000 − ¥149,350,000).

Now suppose that the arbitrageur faces the same situation in the afternoon, with the six-month forward rate declining to Y125/$. He or she now decides to do the following:

1. Borrow $1,000,000 from an American bank and convert the amount at the spot rate of ¥45/$, to ¥45,000,000.
2. Invest the proceeds, ¥145,000,000 in a Euro-yen account for six months at 3 percent per six months.

3. Simultaneously sell the proceeds (¥149,350,000) forward for U.S. dollars at the new 180 forward rate of ¥125/$, earning gross dollar revenues of $1,194,800.

4. Compute the cost of funds at the Eurodollar rate of 5 percent per six months, amounting to $1,050,000. The profit in the covered interest arbitrage amounts to: $1,194,800 − $1,050,000 = $144,800.

The covered interest arbitrage should continue until the interest rate parity is maintained again, given that the arbitrageurs can make risk-free profits by repeating the cycle as often as necessary.

NATURE OF TRANSACTION EXPOSURE

Transaction exposure arises whenever the future cash transactions of a firm are affected by potential exchange rate fluctuations. A firm faces a transaction exposure whenever it has a receivable, a payable, a revenue, an expense, or a forward contract denominated in other than the functional currency in which it does most of its business. In all these transactions, the firm faces a situation of uncertainty because it does not know the exact exchange rate at the time of the settlement of these transactions. Transactions that create the potential for a transaction exposure include:

1. the purchase or sale of goods, services, or assets to be settled in foreign currencies
2. the borrowing or lending of funds to be settled in foreign currencies
3. the buying of a forward exchange contract

Suppose that a U.S. firm sells equipment worth $20.0 million to a French firm for FF140 million, with payment to be made in francs six months after the date of sale. The current exchange rate is FF7/$. At the payment date, the exchange rate is EF8/$, and the French firm remits FF140 million as contracted. The U.S. firm finds itself experiencing a transaction loss because the FF received amounted to $17.5 million (FF140 million/FF8/$), $2.5 million less than the amount receivable of $20.0 million. The $2.5 million is a transaction loss arising from a transaction exposure. The U.S. firm could have avoided the loss by asking for a payment in U.S. dollars. In this way, the transaction exposure is not eliminated but rather is shifted to the French firm.

HEDGING TRANSACTION EXPOSURE

The question of whether hedging is desirable arises. Hedging relies on forward contracts, and if the forward rate underestimates or overestimates the future spot rate, hedging results in higher costs in some periods, and lower costs in others. If this underestimation or overestimation happens with equal frequency, hedging is not desirable. Hedging is desirable if the firm hedges future payables when it expects appreciation of the currency denominating the payables and hedges, future receivables when it expects depreciation of the currency denominating the receivables.

Assuming that the firm finds hedging to be desirable, it has to choose among the following hedging techniques:

1. forward contract hedge
2. money market hedge
3. currency option hedge

Forward Contract Hedge

Nature of the Financial Instrument. The forward contract is a legal contract between two parties to purchase and sell a specific quantity of foreign currency at a price specified now, with delivery and settlement at a specified future date. Contracts can be tailored by banks to the specific needs of clients. Currency futures are similar to forward contracts except that they are traded in face-to-face transactions on one of the trading floors at the International Monetary Market (IMM), by special brokers. The seven most widely traded currencies at the IMM are:

Australian dollar (100,000 units per contract)

British pound (62,500 units per contract)

Canadian dollar (100,000 units per contract)

French Franc (250,000 units per contract)

German mark (125,000 units per contact)

Japanese Yen (12,500,000 units per contact)

Swiss franc (125,000 units per contact)

The typical settlement dates are the third Wednesdays in March, June, September, and December. Specific differences between forward and futures contracts are shown in Exhibit 4.3. Margin requirements are required for these contracts to cover fluctuations in term values.

A forward contract hedge, or forward exchange market hedge, consists of arranging for delivery and payment, at or around the desired future date (i.e., at a "fixed" date, or during a "delivery-date option" period usually not exceeding thirty days), of an amount of foreign currency at a contractual forward rate. The contract enables the firm to avoid the uncertainty of the future spot rate by locking in the rate it will pay or receive at forward rate. The important point to remember is that the forward contract hedge involves a contract between a firm and a bank. A firm uses the forward contract to hedge either a payable or a receivable denominated in foreign currency, rather than hedging the transaction. Although most forward contracts are short term, multinationals are now relying

Exhibit 4.3
Comparison of the Forward and Futures Markets

	Forward	Futures
Size of the contract	Tailored to individual needs.	Standardized.
Delivery date	Tailored to individual needs.	Standardized.
Participants	Banks, brokers, and multinational companies.	Banks, brokers, and multinational companies.
	Public speculation not encouraged.	Qualified public speculation encouraged.
Security deposit	None as such, but compensating bank balances or lines of credit required.	Small security deposit required.
Clearing operation	Handling contingent on individual banks and brokers. No separate clearing-house function.	Handled by exchange clearing-house. Daily settlements to the market price
Marketplace	Over the telephone worldwide.	Central exchange floor with worldwide communications.
Regulation	Self-regulating	Commodity Futures Trading Commission; National Futures Association.
Liquidation	Most settled by actual delivery. Some by offset, at a cost.	Most by offset: very few by delivery.
Transaction costs	Set by "spread" between bank's buy and sell price.	Negotiated brokerage fees, quoted for entry and exit.

on long-term forward contracts with a maturity of up to ten years or more. In addition, given that several cash flows of the same currency are generally expected to arrive at different times during the financial year, the financial manager is advised to hedge these cash flows independently rather than include them under one integrative hedging plan. One can elect to buy (take a long position) or sell (take a short position) foreign exchange forward. The following two examples illustrate the decision to hedge either a payable or a receivable.

The Hedging of a Payable. To hedge a payable using a forward (futures) hedge, the firm should purchase a forward (currency futures) contract representing the currency and amount related to the payables. Assume that a U.S. firm buys an asset for £200,000, to be paid in thirty days. The thirty-day forward

Exhibit 4.4
Probabilistic Analysis of Hedging Payables

Potential Spot Rate	Prior Probability	Nominal cost of payables Without Hedging	Nominal Cost of Hedging	Real Cost of Hedging
$1.35	0.20	$270,000	$290,000	$20,000
$1.30	0.15	$260,000	$290,000	$30,000
$1.34	0.22	$268,000	$290,000	$22,000
$1.41	0.18	$282,000	$290,000	$8,000
$1.46	0.20	$292,000	$290,000	-$2,000
$1.47	0.05	$294,000	$290,000	-$4,000

Note: Expected value of RCHP = 0.20 ($20,000) + 0.15 ($30,000) + 0.22 ($22,000) + 0.18 ($8,000) + 0.20 (−$2,000) + 0.05 (−$4,000) = $4,000 + $4,500 + $4,840 + $1,440 − $400 − $200 = $14,180

rate at the time of the purchase is $1.45/£. The nominal cost of hedging is, therefore, $290,000 (200,000 × $1.45/£). If the spot rate at the time of payment is $1.30, the nominal cost of the payable without hedging is $260,000 (200,000 × $1.30). In other words, the real cost of hedging payable is:

$$RCHP = NCHP - NCPW$$

where

$RCHP$ = real cost of hedging payables
$NCHP$ = nominal cost of hedging payables
$NCPW$ = nominal cost of payables without hedging.

This analysis of the real cost of hedging payables can only take place after the fact and at the date of payment of the payable. The management of the multinational firm may, however, develop an a priori probability distribution of the future spot rate at the time of the purchase transaction. Such a probability distribution is shown in Exhibit 4.4. Notice here that the real cost of hedging the payable differs depending on the estimated future spot rate. Under these conditions of uncertainty and on the basis of the knowledge of the prior probability distribution of the future spot rate, the firm may compute the expected value of the real cost of hedging payables as follows:

$$\text{Expected value of } RCHP = \sum P_i \times RCHP_i$$

The expected value of the real cost of hedging of $14,180, coupled with the probabilistic information included in Exhibit 4.4, facilitate the decision of whether to hedge the payables. Exhibit 4.4 shows that there is a 25 percent chance that hedging will be more cost-effective than not hedging. The degree of risk aversion espoused by the management of the multinational firm will determine the final decision. For an extra cost, the firm may elect to acquire additional information, and update the a priori probability distribution to obtain an a posteriori probability through the use of Bayes' Theorem.

The Hedging of a Receivable. To hedge receivables using a forward (futures) hedge, the firm should sell a forward (currency futures) contract representing the currency and amount related to the receivables. In the case of a receivable, the formula for determination of the real cost of hedging receivables $(RCHR)$ is equal to:

$$RCHR = NRWH - NRHR$$

where

$NRWH$ = nominal revenues denominated in home currency received without hedging

$NRHR$ = nominal revenues denominated in home currency received with hedging

The procedure is the same as with hedging payables in that the firm may elect to determine an a priori probability distribution of $NRWH$ and compute an expected value of $RCHR$. It may also elect to use additional information to update the prior probability distribution to improve its decision of whether or not to hedge. It is important to realize in both the hedging of a payable and the hedging of a receivable that the transaction exposure arises at the first moment (t_1) or quote in foreign currency terms is made by the seller to the buyer. Suppose that:

1. Time t_2 is the moment when the buyer places a firm order with a seller at the price agreed on at time t_1.
2. Time t_3 is the moment when the seller ships product and bills the buyer.
3. Time t_2 is the moment when the buyer settles the account receivable with cash issuing the foreign currency terms agreed on at time t_1.

The total transaction exposure is made up of:

1. a quotation exposure arising between t_1 and t_2
2. a backlog exposure arising between t_2 and t_3 and
3. a billing exposure arising between t_3 and t_4.

Money Market Hedge

The money market hedge involves the use of surplus or borrowed money to hedge a receivable or payable and invest the proceeds of the transaction in a money market. Money market hedges on payables and receivables are illustrated next.

Money Market Hedge on Payables. Assume that the XYZ company, an American importer of machinery, has a payable of DM3,371,769.3 that comes to term in one year. The management of the firm decides to use its actual surplus of cash to buy a one-year German security earning 6 percent per year. The amount to be used for the German security amounts to

DM3,371,769.3 / (1 + 0.06%) = DM3,180,914.50

If the German spot rate at the time of the transaction is \$0.505/DM, the amount needed by the firm to buy the German security is equal to \$1,606,361,80 (DM3,180,914.50 × \$0.505/DM). What happened in this money market hedge is that the XYZ firm used \$1,606,361.80 of its surplus cash to invest in a DM3,180,914.50 German security that earns 6 percent per year and that, at the end of the year, will generate the DM3,371,769.3 needed to pay the payable.

The previous example assumes that the XYZ firm has surplus cash. If the firm does not have surplus cash, it will proceed by borrowing the amount needed through a loan and investing it in the German short-term security. Using the previous example, the XYZ firm needs to:

1. Borrow \$1,606,361.80 from a U.S. branch, assuming a 4 percent interest rate per year.
2. Convert the \$1,606,361.80 into DM3, 108,914.50.
3. Invest in a DM3,108,914.50 German security earning 6 percent per year, which will yield DM3,371,769.3 in a year.
4. Repay the \$1,606,361.80 loan and interest, which will amount to \$1,670,616.272 at the end of the year.

Basically, to hedge payables with a money market hedge, the firm should borrow local currency, convert it to currency-denominated payables, and invest these funds until they are needed to cover the payables.

Money Market Hedge on Receivables. Assume that the ABC Company, a German exporter of machinery, has a receivable of \$1,616,000 to be received in a month. A money market hedge on this receivable will include the following steps:

1. Borrow U.S. dollars. Assuming a U.S. interest rate of 0.7 percent per month, the German firm needs to borrow (\$1,616,000 / [1 + .007]) = \$1,604,766.60.

2. Convert the $1,604,766.6 borrowed to DM at a rate of DM1.98/$ and receive DM 3,177,437.868.

3. Invest the proceeds in a German security earning 0.8 percent per month, which, at the end of the month, will be worth DM3,202,857.371.

4. Use the receivables to pay the loan in a month.

What results from this transaction is that the payment of the receivable to the German firm at the end of the month will cover the loan, and the investment in the one-month German security will yield a final amount of DM 3,202,857.371.

Basically, to hedge receivables using a money market hedge, the firm should borrow the currency denominating the receivables, convert it to local currency, and invest it before paying off the loan with cash inflows from the receivables.

Currency Options Hedge

Nature of the Financial Instrument. Currency options are classified as calls or puts. A currency call option to be used for the hedging of a payable involves the right to buy a given currency at a given price (the price, or exercise price) within a given period of time. A currency put option, to be used for the hedging of a receivable, involves the right to sell a given currency at a given price within a given period of time. Currency options are available in Amsterdam, Montreal, Philadelphia, and Chicago. In Chicago, both the Chicago Mercantile Exchange and Chicago Board Options Exchange provide a market for currency options.

The premium of either a call option or a put option is affected by three main factors:

1. "Level of existing spot price relative to strike price. The higher the spot rate relative to the strike price, the higher will be the option price. This is due to the higher probability of buying the currency at a substantially lower rate than what you would sell it for. . . .

2. Length of time before the expiration date. It is generally expected that the spot rate has a greater chance of rising high above the strike price if it has a longer period of time to do so. . . .

3. Potential variability of currency. The greater the variability of the currency, the higher the probability is that the spot rate will be above the strike price."[1]

Currency options hedges or options market hedges may be preferable to futures forward hedges and money market hedges in the event that the latter fail due to appreciation of the payables currency or depreciation of the receivables currency over the hedged period. Both currency options hedges protect the firm from adverse exchange rate changes and create benefits to the firm in case of favorable exchange rate changes. Specific terminology about options follows:

1. The buyer of an option is referred to as the long and the seller as the writer, or the short.

2. Depending on their exercise characteristics, options are of two types: American and European. European options are exercised only at the maturity or expiration date of the option, whereas American options are exercised anytime during the contract.

The Philadelphia Stock Exchange (PHLX) trades options on foreign currency. Similarly, the Chicago Mercantile Exchange trades American options on the futures contracts it offers.

The basic pricing relationships for an American call or put option at a time t prior to expiration are:

$$C_a = Max\ (S_t - E,\ 0)$$

and

$$P_a = Max\ (E - S_t,\ 0)$$

where

C_a = the value of the American call at expiration

S_t = the equation date spot price

E = the exercise price per unit of foreign currency

P_a = the value of the American put at expiration

Basically, a call (put) option with $S_t > E(E > S_t)$ expires in-the-money and will be exercised. If $S_t = E$, the option expires at-the-money. If $S_t < E(E < S_t)$, the call (put) option expires out-of-the-money and will not be exercised.

As an example of the expiration value of an American call option, assume that a SF62,500 American call option has a premium of 30 cents per SF and an exercise price of 68 cents per SF. At the expiration date, the spot rate is \$0.71/ SF. As a result, the call option has the exercise value of 3 cents (71–68) per each of the SF62,500 of the contract, or \$1,800. In other words, the call owner can buy SF60,000, worth \$44,375 (=SF62,500 × \$0.71) in the spot market for \$42,500 (=SF62,500 × \$0.68). Therefore, the owner should exercise the option. The same call option from the buyer's and the seller's perspectives is graphed, respectively, in Exhibits 4.5 and 4.6.

As an example of the expiration value of an American put option, assume that a Euro-denominated, EUR62,500 American put option has a premium of 3 cents per EUR and an exercise price of \$105. At the expiration date, the spot rate is \$104.5 per EUR. As a result, the put option has an exercise value of .5 cents (105–104.5) per EUR for each of the EUR62,500 of the contract, or \$312.50. In other words, the put owner can sell EUR62,500, worth \$65,312.5

Exhibit 4.5
Graph of 105 September EUR Put Option: Buyer's Perspective

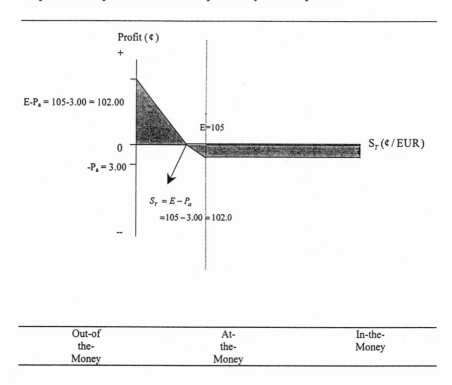

Out-of the- Money	At- the- Money	In-the- Money

(= EUR62,500 × 1.045) in the spot market, for $65,625 (EUR62,500 × 1.05). Therefore, the owner should exercise the option. The same put option from the buyer's and the seller's perspectives is graphed, respectively, in Exhibits 4.7 and 4.8.

Options Market Hedge for Payables. To hedge a payable using currency options, a firm must buy a currency call option that gives it the right to buy a specified amount of a particular currency at a specified price (the exercise price) within a given period. At the end of the period the firm may elect to exercise the option on the Philadelphia Stock Exchange or from a bank. Assume that the XYZ Company, an American importer of British machinery, has to pay £200,000 thirty days from now. Also assume that the firm faces two alternatives:

1. Buy a call option on the Philadelphia Stock Exchange for a strike price of $1.65, a premium cost of $0.035/pound, and a contract size of lb12,500.

2. Buy the call option in the over-the-counter (bank) market for a strike price of $1.65 and a premium of 2 percent when the spot rate is $1.67.

Exhibit 4.6
Graph of 105 September EUR Put Option: Writer's Perspective

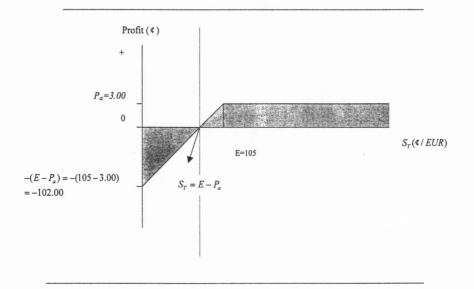

The cost of the first alternative is as follows:

Premium costs per option $(0.035 \times 12{,}500) = \$437.50$
Brokerage cost per option $= \$30.00$
Total cost per option $= \$467.50$
Options cost per pound $(\$467.50 / 12{,}500) = \$0.0374$
Number of options needed $(£200{,}000 / \text{lb}12{,}500) = 16$

The cost of the second alternative is as follows:

Size of the option $\times$ premium $\times$ spot rate $=$ cost of the option
£200,000 $\times$ 0.02 $\times$ 1.67 $=$ \$6,680

In this case, the XYZ firm would purchase the call option with the lower cost. Given that it is a three-month option, the premium cost of the option in three months, and assuming a cost of capital of 8 percent (2 percent per quarter), will be $\$6{,}680\ (1.2) = \$6{,}813.60$, or 0.034068 per pound ($\$6{,}813.60$).

The fate of the call option depends on the potential spot rate of the pound when the payables are due. Assume that there are three possible scenarios for the spot rate: $1.62, $1.66, and $1.68. The effects of each of the spot rates on the cost of XYZ payables differ depending on the potential spot rates:

Exhibit 4.7
Graph of 68 September SF Call Option: Buyer's Perspective

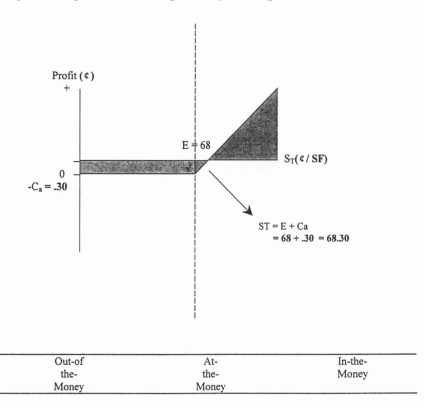

Out-of the- Money	At- the- Money	In-the- Money

1. Under the first scenario, the spot rate is $1.62, and XYZ would prefer to let the option expire and buy pounds in the spot market at $1.62. In such a case, the dollar amount paid by XYZ including the premium would be ($1.62 − 0.034068) × £200,000) = $330,813.60.
2. Under the second and third scenarios, the spot rate is either $1.66 or $1.68 and XYZ would prefer to exercise the option and purchase the pounds at $1.65. The dollar amount paid by XYZ including the premium would be ($1.65 + $0.034068) × £200,000) = $336,813.60 under both scenarios.

Basically, to hedge payables using a currency option hedge, the firm should purchase a currency call option representing the currency and the amount related to the payables.

Options Market Hedge for Receivables. To hedge a receivable using currency options, a firm must buy a currency put option that gives it the right to sell a specified amount of particular currency at a specified price (the exercise price) within a given period. At the end of the period, if the spot rate is higher

Exhibit 4.8
Graph of 68 September SF Call Option: Writer's Perspective

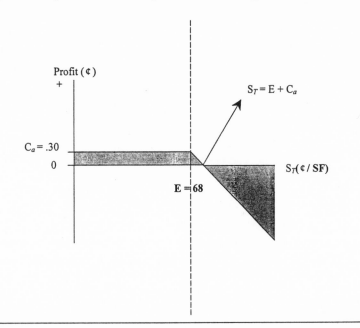

than the exercise price, the firm may elect to sell the currency at the spot rate and let the option expire. If the spot rate is lower than the exercise price, however, the firm will elect to exercise the option.

Assume that the ABC Company, an American exporter of machinery to the United Kingdom, has a receivable of £200,000 due in three months. To avert the risks of a depreciation of the pound against the dollar, the ABC Company decides to buy a put option that has an exercise price of $1.60 and a premium of $0.04 per unit.

Again, the fate of the put option depends on the potential spot rates at the time when the receivables are due. Assume that there are three possible scenarios for the spot rate: $1.58, $1.59, and $1.62. The effects of the spot rate on the cost of ABC's receivables differ depending on each of the scenarios:

1. Under the first scenario, the spot rate is $1.58 and the ABC Company prefers to exercise the option and sell the pounds at the exercise price of $1.60. In such a case, the dollar amount received from hedging the receivables after accounting for the premium paid is ($1.60 − $0.04) × 200,000 = $312,000.

2. Under the second scenario, the spot rate is $1.59 and the ABC Company prefers to exercise the option and sell the pounds at the exercise price of $1.60. In such a case, the dollar amount received from hedging the receivables after accounting for the premium price remains ($1.60 − $0.04) × 200,000 = $312,000.

3. Under the third scenario, the spot rate is $1.62 and the ABC Company prefers to let the option expire and sell the pounds at $1.62. In such a case the dollar amount received from hedging the receivables after accounting for the premium paid is ($1.62 − $0.04) × 200,000 = $316,000.

Basically, to hedge receivables using a currency option hedge, the firm should purchase a currency put option representing the currency and amount related to the receivables.

Currency Option Pricing Models. The exact European call and put pricing formulas are:[2]

$$C_e = S_f e^{-r_i T} N(d_1) - E e^{-r_{us} T} N(d_2)$$

and

$$P_e = E e^{-r_{us} T} N(-d_2) - S_f e^{-r_i T} N(-d_1)$$

where

$$d_1 = \frac{\ln(F / E) + .5\sigma^2 T}{\sigma / \sqrt{T}}$$

$d_2 = d_1 - \sigma \sqrt{T}$

S = the underlying spot exchange rate

$C (O)$ = the price of the currency call option

P = the price of the currency put option

E = the exercise price

r_{us} = the U.S. riskless rate of interest

r_i = the foreign riskless rate of interest

σ = the instantaneous standard deviation of the return on a holding of foreign currency

T = the time to option maturity, expressed as a fraction of a year

$N(\cdot)$ = the standard normal distribution function

As an example of using the European options pricing model, consider the following information for an SF call.[3]

1. The option has an exercise price of $67.

2. The option will expire 66 days from the quotation date, or $T = 66 / 365 = .1808$.

3. The September forward rate is F($/SF) = 0.6433.

4. The U.S. rate, r_{us}, is the annualized two-month Eurodollar bid rate of 5⅛ percent.

5. The estimated volatility is 10.8 percent.

Therefore, the values are:

$$d_1 = \frac{1n(64.33 \, / \, 67) + .5(.107)^2 \, (.1808)}{(.107)\sqrt{.1808}} - .8713$$

$$d_2 = -.8713 - (.107)\sqrt{.1808} = -.9168$$
$$N(-.8713) = .1918$$
$$N(-.9168) = .1796$$

and finally

$$C = (64.33[.19180 - 67].1796)e^{-(0.05125)(.1808)}$$
$$= (12.3385 - 12.0332)(.9908)$$
$$= .\ 30 \text{ cents per DM}$$

OPERATING STRATEGIES TO REDUCE TRANSACTION EXPOSURE

In certain cases, hedging may not completely eliminate the transaction exposure because the firm may not know the exact amount of revenues or expenditures arising from a transaction denominated in foreign currency. Various operating strategies may be used in such cases to reduce transaction exposure.

Leading and Lagging

To offset existing foreign exchange exposure, firms sometimes elect to use the operating strategy of leading and lagging. Leading and lagging consists of speeding up collections or lagging payments in payables denominated in a foreign currency. It is sometimes known as an "operating hedge." The basic idea is that when a firm expects a currency to appreciate, it speeds up payments of imports and debts and slows the collection of export receipts. When it expects a currency to depreciate, it reverses the tactic, slowing import payments and accelerating collections. Leading and lagging may be more feasible between affiliates, given the common set of goals for the consolidated group, and more adaptable to a firm operating on an integrated worldwide basis. Although possible with a 100 percent-owned affiliate, it may be unfair to minority stockholders in cases in which the affiliate is not wholly owned. It also may be unfair to 100 percent–owned profit centers when their performance evaluation is adjusted to take into account the sacrifices created by their acceptance of leading and lagging between affiliates. Leading and lagging is possible between independent firms if arrangements and adjustments are made in advance.

Although seemingly straightforward, the leading and lagging techniques for reducing transaction exposure end up shifting the burden to a single firm or affiliate in a particular country, which may explain the limits imposed by some governments on the allowed rate. *Netting* refers to the process of offsetting intragroup transactions (between parent and subsidiary or one subsidiary and another) to reduce transfer values and thus to only reflect and account for the net balance.[4]

Borrowing and Lending

Another way of minimizing translation and transaction exposure is to use foreign currency credits, such as foreign bank loans, overdrafts, and lines of credit, to finance repayables in foreign currencies. Yet another way is to borrow in a local currency in anticipation of a devaluation and to convert the proceeds into a strong currency. Finally, the firm may borrow in a local currency and use the proceeds to buy commodities from that country before their prices increase as a result of devaluation. This action is known as a *commodity hedge*.

Three obstacles may arise against the use of borrowing and lending. First, some countries limit the amount of local money that foreigners can borrow. Second, companies may hold too much foreign currency and end up scrambling to convert their local currency deposits and receivables into more usable bond currency—such as pounds, dollars, and marks—and then repatriating the cash to the United States. Third, some countries may become inclined to impose stricter controls on lending by their banks at home through their foreign subsidiaries.

Hedging against Fluctuating Interest Rates

In recent years, corporate treasurers have started to hedge against fluctuating interest rates much as were already doing against currency shifts. Although some still use regulated financial futures markets in Chicago and London, others off-market through the London banks. Off-market futures hedging is simpler and more flexible than futures hedging in the regulated markets. As an example, a corporate treasurer who must borrow $3 million three months from now to finance inventory buildup will want to lock in low current interest rates. To do so, he or she finds a bank willing to offer an acceptable rate. When the time comes to borrow, if interest rates have risen, the bank will pay the company any difference in the interest rates; if, on the other hand, interest rates have fallen, the company will pay the bank the difference. In the regulated financial futures market, the hedger pays a little every day, whereas off-market, payment is due only at the end of the transaction. Most banks participating in such a hedge feel that they are offering a simpler way to hedge than in the futures markets.

Gold Hedge

The shortage of foreign currencies in the developing countries means that overseas subsidiaries of multinational companies may end up loaded with weak currencies like Brazilian curzeiros and Mexican pesos. In 1982, for example, a growing number of U.S. multinational firms bought gold on the Brazilian market to protect their corporate assets against the country's runaway inflation. A loss of confidence in the dollar-pegged government bonds led to the move to gold. Gold, in fact, presents much less political risk and yields a better return than government-indexed bonds. Moreover, gold has a tax advantage over bonds because it can be carried as an unrealized gain until resale. The key to the gold hedge is the existence of a direct relationship, in the short run as well as in the long run, between the dollar price per unit of other major foreign currencies and the dollar price of gold, which suggests a certain degree of interchangeability of the two assets.[5]

An evaluation of the gold hedge was made as follows:

The adequacy of gold as a means of store value is limited during periods of high inflation rates since it does not pay interest or dividends. Its price fluctuations have been so great that it has either appreciated or depreciated more than the inflation rate. Despite its inability to serve as [an] inflation hedge, the store value function of gold had been of significant importance to investors worldwide. Its qualities as a hedge against monetary devaluations, political or economic uncertainty, and crises resulting from military confrontation, social upheaval, and terrorism have made it an insurance policy against disaster.[6]

Reinvoicing Centers

The reinvoicing center rests on the idea of creating a centralized unit that has all the transaction exposure of multinational firms. In a sense, the affiliates of such a firm are encouraged to trade among themselves and to be paid by the reinvoicing center in their own currency. The units that bought or sold are physically transferred from one affiliate to another, whereas the affiliate seller receives payment from the reinvoicing center in its own currency and the affiliate buyer pays the reinvoicing center in its own currency. What results is that both the affiliate buyer and the seller, whatever their countries, are allowed to deal in their own currency and thus to avoid all transaction exposure. The transaction exposure is centralized in the reinvoicing center and is calculated at cost, plus a commission for services to avoid the shifting of profits from operating affiliates.

The concept of a reinvoicing center is possible if the center acquires a nonresident status, as, generally, a finance subsidiary not doing business in a country is spared some taxes, such as interest withholding taxes and capital formation taxes, and is not perceived by local authorities as a taxpayer. The advantages of the reinvoicing center include the centralization of foreign exchange taxation exposure, and the ability of affiliates to operate successfully without worrying about transaction exposure.[7] Similarly, a firm with a portfolio of currency positions is better off hedging residual exposure. This "exposure netting" is better accomplished with a reinvoicing center.

Cross-Hedging

There are instances when the firm cannot hedge a position in a given currency X, since the known hedging techniques are not available. In that case, the firm may consider determining another currency Y that is highly correlated with currency X and then set up a forward contract on the currency Y. When the forward contract is due, the firm will convert the currency Y into currency X. Cross-hedging is, therefore, the use of a futures contract in a currency to reduce the risk position related to a cash position in another currency. This technique of cross-hedging will, of course, fail if the two currencies move in different directions against the dollar as a result of an unexpected event or phenomenon. When only two currencies are involved, the technique is referred to as a single cross-hedge. When more than two currencies are involved, the technique is referred to as a multiple cross-hedge. For example, to hedge a Tunisian dollar cash position, a firm may elect to use both a French franc and a U.S. dollar futures contract. An assessment of cross-hedging follows:

Cross-hedging is important because it greatly expands the opportunity set of hedging alternatives. There are only a limited number of currencies which are traded actively in futures markets or for which bank forward contracts are typically available. In general, currencies for which no organized futures or forward market exists are also currencies of countries with poorly developed capital markets. Consequently, alternative hedging techniques such as borrowing or lending in those currencies are also more limited. If effective cross-hedging strategies can be identified then the risk related to billing cash positions in those currencies can be reduced.[8]

Currency Diversification

Currency diversification is yet another technique that is used to reduce transaction exposure. When a dollar-denominated firm has receivables and payables from different countries that are denominated in one or two currencies, a sudden depreciation of these currencies against the dollar will adversely affect the inflows of cash and positively affect the outflows. The firm may elect to reduce the risk associated with exposure to currencies by diversifying the number of currencies in which payables and receivable are denominated. This strategy of currency diversification will reduce the impact of a sudden depreciation in any one of the currencies of the inflows. The diversification will work best as a strategy for reducing transaction exposure if the currencies that are chosen are not highly correlated.

Swaps

A firm may use swaps to reduce foreign exchange exposure. Swaps are a set of parallel transactions operating in opposite directions. In other words, a swap is an agreement between two entities to exchange one currency for another immediately and provides dates on which to give back the original amount swapped. Types of swaps include forward swaps, "back-to-back" or "parallel" loans, currency swaps, credit swaps, and interest swaps.

Swaps have evolved over the years because of (1) financial arbitrage, (2) tax regulatory arbitrage, (3) exposure management, and (4) competing markets. Swaps take place to benefit from the differentials in cost and tax regulations of their exposure interest rates, currency prices, or commodity prices and to enable market participants to fill gaps left by missing markets.

To get an idea of the size of the interest rate and currency swap markets, Exhibit 4.9 provides statistics on their size as measured by national principal, a reference amount of principal determining interest payments. The swap bank may act as either a broker or a dealer. As a broker, the swap bank facilitates the matching of counterparties, without itself assuming any risk, and receives a commission. As a dealer or market maker, the swap bank accepts the risk of the currency swap to either lay it off later or match it with a counterparty.

Back-to-back Loans A back-to-back or parallel loan is an agreement between firms to borrow each other's currency for a certain period at a given time in the future, without at any time going through the foreign exchange market. Like the parallel loan, the back-to-back loan involves two parties instead of four.

As an example of parallel loan, suppose that the four parties include a British parent and its Canadian subsidiary and a Canadian parent and its British subsidiary. The parallel loan involves the British company borrowing from a British lender and lending the amount to the British subsidiary of the Canadian parent while the Canadian parent borrows from a Canadian lender lends the amount to the Canadian subsidiary of the British parent. See Exhibit 4.10. The deal is good for both companies for at least two reasons:

1. The parent companies can borrow at a more attractive rate in their own countries than their subsidiaries in the foreign countries.
2. The companies are able to avoid any taxes associated with exchange controls and avoid violating any foreign exchange restrictions of either country.

As an example of a back-to-back loan, the British and the Canadian parent companies will lend directly to one another. See Exhibit 4.11 for the same

Exhibit 4.9
Size of Interest Rate and Currency Swap Markets: Total Notional Principal in Millions of U.S. Dollars

Year	Total New Business	Total Outstanding
A: Interest Rate Swaps		
1987	387,856	682,888
1988	568,113	1,010,203
1989	833,535	1,539,320
1990	1,229,241	2,311,544
1991	1,621,779	3,065,065
1992	2,822,635	3,850,800
1993	4,104,666	6,177,352
1994	6,240,890	8,815,561
1995	8,698,790	12,810,736
1996	13,678,173	19,170,909
1997	17,067,106	22,291,312
B: Currency Swaps		
1987	85,824	182,807
1988	122,661	316,821
1989	169,631	434,849
1990	212,763	577,535
1991	328,394	807,167
1992	301,858	860,387
1993	295,191	899,618
1994	379,303	914,885
1995	455,108	1,197,395
1996	759,051	1,559,636
1997	1,135,391	1,823,632

example as before, except that the British parent is borrowing at 11 percent and the Canadian parent at 12 percent. As Exhibit 4.11 shows, each firm will annually pay the other firm its annual debt service plus, at the maturity date of the debt, the principal sum.

Currency Swaps. A currency swap is similar to a back-to-back loan, except that it does not appear in any of the firm's balance sheets and does not involve any interest. Two firms agree to exchange a given amount of two countries' currencies for a specific period. Brokers in large banks act as middleman for matching firms' needs and creating currency swaps, for a fee. The accounting treatment of currency swaps in the United States is that of a foreign exchange transaction. The obligation to reverse the swap at some later date is treated as a forward exchange contract.

If both interest rates are fixed, the swap is known as a fixed currency swap.

Exhibit 4.10
Parallel Loan

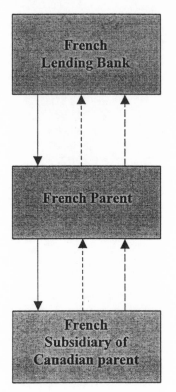

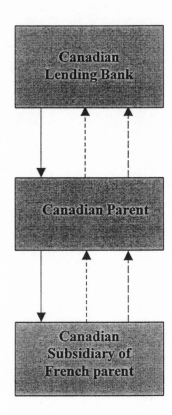

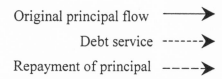

Original principal flow ⟶
Debt service ------➤
Repayment of principal ----➤

When one of the interest rates is fixed and the other is variable, the swap is known as either a simple interest swap or a currency coupon swap. Swaps can also be denominated in commodities, resulting in commodity swaps.

An example of a currency swap is portrayed in Exhibit 4.12. The assumption is that both the U.S. subsidiary of a French company and the French subsidiary of a U.S. company need an amount $X for financing projects. The U.S. parent borrows from a U.S. bank or capital market at 8 percent, while the French parent borrows the same amount from a French bank or capital market at 6 percent. Each remits the amount borrowed to a swap bank, which, in return, delivers the

Exhibit 4.11
Back-to-Back Loan

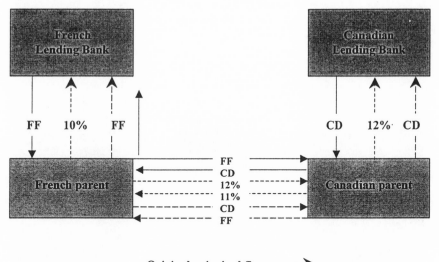

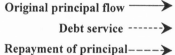

Original principal flow ⟶
Debt service ------▶
Repayment of principal----▶

French currency amount to the U.S. parent and the U.S. currency to the French parent.

The U.S. parent lends the French currency it received to the U.S. subsidiary of the French parent at 7.5 percent, the rate the U.S. parent would have been charged if it borrowed the amount in the French market or by issuing Euro-franc bonds. The French parent lends the dollar amount received to the French subsidiary of the U.S. parent at 8.5 percent, the rate the French parent would have been charged if it had borrowed the amount in the U.S. market. Annually, the debt service is channeled through the swap bank. At the debt realization date, the principal is again channeled through the swap bank, as indicated in Exhibit 4.12.

Credit Swaps. A credit swap involves the exchange of currency between a firm and a bank, to be reversed at a later date. For example, a French franc parent firm deposits a given amount in the Parisian subsidiary of a U.S. bank; in return, the U.S. bank in New York makes an equal loan to the French firm's affiliate in New York. At a later date, the transaction is reversed, with the affiliate in New York repaying the loan and the Parisian subsidiary of the U.S. bank returning the original French franc deposit. The French firm is allowed to

Exhibit 4.12
Currency Swap (U.S. Dollars for French Francs)

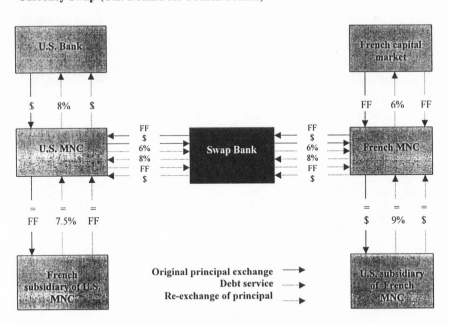

recover its deposit no matter what happened to the exchange rate, and the U.S. bank is allowed to receive an interest-free French franc deposit with the Parisian subsidiary.

Interest Rate Swaps. An interest rate swap is an agreement between two parties for an exchange of a given interest rate for another on the same agreed-upon currency amount. The exchange may be from a fixed to a floating rate, from a floating a fixed rate, or from one floating index to another. The party paying the variable rate is known as the floating rate payer. The floating rate payment is generally based on the London Interbank Offered Rate (LIBOR), the Treasury Bill rate, the commercial paper composite rate, or the J. J. Kenny rate. The interest swap takes place because of differential information and institutional restrictions across national boundaries. As stated by James Bicksler and Andrew Chen:

For example, in contrast to the U.S. corporate bond market, there is virtually no registration of disclosure requirement for issuing new corporate bonds in the Eurobond market. However, issuing a new bond issue in the Eurobond markets requires a large underwriting cost and a larger credit premium. Thus, it is generally more difficult for a relatively small and unknown bank or business firm to issue new bonds in the Eurobond markets. In the floating-rate markets, the U.S. short-term interest rates are usually lower than those in the European markets due, in part, to the presence of government insurance on deposits.[9]

As a first example, suppose that a given company XYZ has outstanding 100 million noncallable bonds, which carry a fixed rate of 14 percent and have six years to maturity. The company elects to enter into an interest rate swap with a bank, under which it agrees to pay the prime rate of 9.5 percent plus fifty basis points and to receive 13.0 percent from a fixed-rate payer. The company benefits from the swap since it obtains a net floating-rate cost of 11.0 percent and an economic gain of 3.0 percentage points in the cost of borrowed funds.

As a second example, assume that an AAA-rated firm is able to obtain fixed-rate financing at the lowest available market rate of 8 percent, whereas a BBB-rate firm would have to pay 12 percent for fixed-rate financing (assuming that it could obtain it at all). The AAA-rated firm has a "comparative credit advantage." However, the spread on the floating-rate financing available in the capital market is not nearly as wide. The AAA-rated firm can borrow at the prime rate, and the BBB-rated firm can borrow at the prime rate plus three percent. If firm A agrees to pay firm B prime plus 2.5 percent in exchange for firm B paying A an 11.0 percent fixed rate, both firms will lower their cost of borrowing. Firm A will pay 250 basis points (2.5 percent) over prime for the floating rate debt received from firm B but will receive 11.0 percent for the fixed rate debt it swapped to firm B. Because firm A's cost in the fixed rate financing was only 8.0 percent, it is receiving 300 basis points (3.0 percent) over its cost. The net gain from the swap for firm A is 50 basis points (0.5 percent), which is computed by deducting the 250 basis points it made by swapping the fixed-rate debt with firm B (11.0 percent–8.0 percent). Firm B will receive prime plus 2.5 percent for the floating-rate debt transferred to Firm A, for which it paid prime plus 3.0 percent, but will pay only 11.0 percent for the fixed-rate debt, which would normally have cost it 12.0 percent. The net savings to Firm B is also 50 basis points, or 0.5 percent.

As a third example, assume a company X has $300 million floating liability at prime plus 2 percent, and a company Y has $300 million of bonds outstanding at 14 percent. Also assume that the two firms agreed to swap their debt, with X agreeing to pay $2 million a year (14 percent × $300 million) and Y agreeing to pay X an amount equal to the prime plus 2 percent on $300 million. If the prime is equal to 12 percent, the swap yields identical receivables and payables for each firm. If the interest rate rises above 14 percent, company X has now a fixed interest rate of 14 percent while company Y has offsetting receivables and payables at 14 percent plus a net remaining payable at prime plus 2 percent.[10]

As a final example of a plain, variable-interest-rate swap, assume that Bank X is an AAA-rated international bank that needs an amount $X either at a fixed rate of 10 percent or at a floating rate equal to the LIBOR. Also note that company Y is a BBB-rated U.S. bank that needs the same amount $X, either at a fixed rate of 11.75 percent or at floating rate equal to the LIBOR plus .50 percent. A swap bank C is asked to arrange a fixed for floating-interest-rate swap that would benefit the three parties. A first step is to ensure that a qualified

Exhibit 4.13
Interest Swap: Fixed Rate for Floating Rate

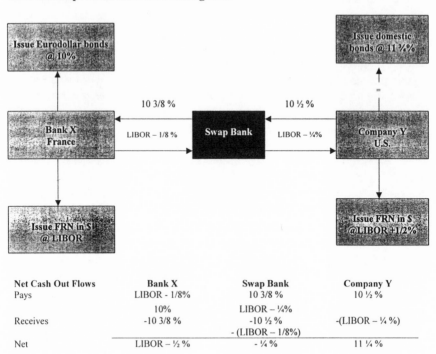

Net Cash Out Flows	Bank X	Swap Bank	Company Y
Pays	LIBOR - 1/8%	10 3/8 %	10 ½ %
	10%	LIBOR – ¼%	
Receives	-10 3/8 %	-10 ½ %	-(LIBOR – ¼ %)
		- (LIBOR – 1/8%)	
Net	LIBOR – ½ %	- ¼ %	11 ¼ %

spread differential (QSD) exists. A QSD is the difference between the default-risk premium differential in the fixed-rate debt and the default-risk premium differential on the floating-rate debt. In this case, it can be computed as follows:

	Company Y	*Bank X*	*Differential*
Floating-rate	LIBOR + .50%	LIBOR	.50%
Fixed-rate	11.75%	10.00%	1.75%
			QSD = 1.25%

Exhibit 4.13 shows one possible fixed for floating-interest-rate swap scenario, which is made possible by splitting the QSD in one way among the three parties so as to lower the all-in cost (interest expense, transaction costs, and service changes) for all the parties. As Exhibit 4.13 shows, the scenario entails the following:

1. Bank X issuing eurodollar bonds at 10 percent. In addition, it pays the swap bank LIBOR minus ⅛ percent and receives 10⅜ percent from the swap bank. The resulting all-in cost is LIBOR minus ½ percent. The result is a savings of ½ percent.

2. Company Y issues floating-rate notes at LIBOR plus ½ percent. It pays the swap bank 10 percent and receives from the swap bank LIBOR minus ¼ percent, with a resulting all-in cost of 11¼ percent. The result is a savings of ½ percent.

3. The swap bank pays 10⅜ to Bank X and LIBOR minus ¼ percent to company Y. It receives LIBOR minus ⅛ percent from Bank X and 10½ percent from Company Y. The result is an earnings of ¼ percent.

Basically, what is illustrated in Exhibit 4.13 is one allocation of the QSD of 1.25% between the three parties, with Bank X saving ½ percent, Company Y saving ½ percent, and the swap bank earning ¼ percent. Other allocations are obviously feasible as well.

Hedging and speculation with regard to interest-rate or currency-value fluctuations can be obtained by a swap. For example, if a given firm X believes interest rates will rise but firm Y believes they will fall, firm X will be willing to trade its variable-rate interest payments for firm Y's fixed-rate interest payments. Similarly, if firm X expects a significant devaluation of the dollar to occur, it will seek to swap dollar-based interest payments for interest payments based on what it considers to be a more stable currency. This rationale is explicated as follows:

At the inception of a swap agreement, the parties exchange promises that they perceive as equivalent in value. As interest rates change, however, the swap contract increases in value for one party and decreases in value for the other. A counterparty may attempt to capitalize on favorable interest rate shifts or to escape from an unfavorable swap arrangement by effectively terminating the agreement (by selling its position to another entity or agreeing with the other counterparty to cancel the agreement for a fee) or by entering into another swap, one that offsets the first agreement (engaging in a "reverse" swap or "unwinding" a swap).[11]

The swaps can be unmatched, which means that the company entering into the swap has no other asset or liability related to the swap transaction. The motivations are generally speculative. "The swap agreement may have been entered into for the speculative purpose or to hedge the enterprise's overall exposure to interest rate risk (so-called macro-hedging) or as a temporary position before establishing a matched, hedged or offsetting position."[12]

In an unmatched, or speculative, position, the interest-rate swap serves to create interest rate-risk and the user expects to gain from favorable changes in interest rates. In a matched, or linked, swap, the interest-rate swap is specifically linked to an asset or liability. Source swaps may be unmatched but are still considered to be hedged if the firm in some way reduces or eliminates the risk posed by the agreement. An example involves offsetting the interest-rate risk inherent in an unmatched swap position by purchasing or selling Treasury securities.[13] The swamp can be hedged if the firm takes any position that offsets the interest-rate risk in an unmatched swap.

Another swap, called the offsetting swap, occurs when an intermediary arranges two swap positions that counterbalance each other, thus maintaining a "matched book" of swaps and eliminating interest-rate risk. The intermediary retains the credit risk if either party should default.

Other types of swaps include the following:

- the commodity swap, which is similar to the basis swap except that one of the indexes is tied to a commodity (i.e., silver)
- the basis swap, whereby floating-rate debt is exchanged for floating-rate debt based on a different index (e.g., T-bill versus LIBOR)
- the circus swap, whereby fixed debt is swapped for floating-rate debt valued in a different currency (i.e., yen versus dollar)
- the reverse swap, whereby if interest rates change so that the company could profit or escape loss by terminating the swap, it can enter into another swap that reverses or "unwinds" the original swap
- the assets swap, which converts a fixed-rate asset into a floating-rate asset (or vice versa) by creating a synthetic floating rate through a swap
- the amortizing swap, whereby the principal decreases over the term of the swap
- the options or swaps or swaptions, which give the purchaser of the option the right (but not the obligation) to enter into an interest rate swap at predetermined rates
- forward swaps, which are swaps that become effective at some future time.

The advantage of interest-rate swaps include the following:

- Confidentiality: The swap is a "silent" form of financing.
- New funding source: Fixed-rate funding is obtained without resorting to the public or private capital markets.
- Flexibility: A swap contract can be sold or assigned to another party at any time.
- Reduction of interest-rate sensitivity: Corporations often arrange interest-rate swaps to match debt costs against projected revenues.
- Interest rate management: Interest-rate swaps allow a company to manage its interest rate exposure actively by switching from mixed-rate to floating-rate debt and back again, depending on its forecast of interest rates or hedging needs.
- "Cash out" convenience: Companies can use interest rate swaps to "cash out" of older, fixed-rate debt in cases where they have realized substantial gains due to a change in interest rates.[14]

Other advantages of interest swapping include the ability (1) to secure inexpensive, fixed-rate financing for firms with poor credit ratings, (2) to hedge against interest-rate exposure by converting floating-rate debt to fixed-rate debt without a renegotiation of the debt instrument, (3) to lock in a desired interest rate, and (4) to benefit from market imperfections and secure a low fixed or floating interest rate. Banks also take advantage of interest-rate swapping to close the maturity gaps between the assets and liabilities on their balance sheets, thus eliminating interest-rate exposure, and to manage basis risk by swapping floating-rate debt based on one index with floating-rate debt based on a more advantageous index.

There are, however, some risks in interest rate swaps, namely: (1) there is a credit risk if the counterparty required to make payments under the interest rate swap fails to do so, (2) there may be a market risk due to changing interest rates, and (3) there is a market liquidity risk because most interest-rate swaps are over-the-counter contracts and there is limited liquidity.

Yield Curve Notes

Yield curve notes can be very useful to a multinational firm for creating debt portfolios with a stable yield. The main characteristic of these notes is that their interest rate varies inversely with the level of some key interest rates, such as the LIBOR. For example, a yield curve note that pays 12 percent minus the LIBOR will have an interest rate of 2 percent if the LIBOR rises to 10 percent and an interest rate of 10 percent if the LIBOR falls to 2 percent. A firm facing a variable-rate portfolio that wishes to convert to a fixed-rate portfolio will use the yield curve note as follows.[15] Suppose the XYZ firm has $4 million in a Eurobond paying LIBOR. If the firm uses $2 million to buy a yield curve note paying 12 percent minus LIBOR, with the rest invested in LIBOR, the portfolio yield will be:

$$0.5(12 - \text{LIBOR}) + 0.5(\text{LIBOR}) = 6\% \text{ fixed}$$

Commodity Swaps

One innovative financial instrument is the commodity swap. It is a hedging contract between buyers and sellers, with a bank acting as a middleman, in which the price is locked over time and the contract is ultimately settled in cash. Assume that an oil producer X wants to lock in the price of oil at $20 a barrel and, in the process is willing to give up any profit if the price in the spot market climbs beyond $20. Also assume that an oil user Y is willing to lock in the purchasing price at $20 a barrel and in the process to give up any cost savings if the price in the spot market falls under $20. A bank may be interested in acting as a middleman between X and Y in exchange for the payment of fees from both parties. Basically, the bank sets up a contract between X and Y, whereby both agree to enter into a contract covering 20,000 barrels of oil for a locked-in price of $20. Two scenarios are possible:

1. If the price of oil increases to $25, for example, the contract is executed by X giving up $100,000 ($5 × 20,000) in profit to the bank to be used by Y. Basically, Y is

required to buy the oil at $25 but will receive compensation of $100,000 from the bank.

2. If the price of oil decreases to $17, for example, the contract is executed by X, who receives $40,000 ($2 × 20,000) from Y. Basically, Y buys the oil more cheaply but has to send the cost savings of $40,000 to X through the bank.

A good example of commodity swaps was provided by gold producers. In 1999, while gold prices continued to slide, Anglogold, the giant South African mining company posted respectable earnings by hedging, or agreeing ahead of time to sell production at set prices higher than the current ones. Jewelry makers and other gold consumers took the other side of these contracts to ensure a future flow of gold at reasonable prices—even if that meant passing up cheaper metal today in the spot market. In the first half of the year, forward contracts enabled Anglogold to sell its gold at $312 an ounce, 11 percent higher than average market prices.

Equity Swaps

Equity swaps, which are mostly used by multinational firms, involve exchanging long-term bonds that the multinational firm is holding for equity in the firm. They are generally used by developing countries that are eager to reduce their foreign debt. In 1988, for example, Chile used $4.6 billion in deals to reduce its foreign debt to $19.5 billion. In September 1988, the swap of debt for equity led to $20 million in investment by Citicorp, Scott Paper, and Royal Dutch/ Shell Group in a wood products company, an unfinished pulp mill, and a eucalyptus forest. The way in which an equity swap works is best illustrated by the situation in which Manufacturers Hanover Trust, which had loaned $2 billion to Brazil, decided to undertake an equity debt swap by exchanging some of the debt in shares in Companhia Suzano de Papel e Celulose, Brazilian a pulp and paper company. What took place includes the following steps:

1. Manufacturers Hanover Trust delivered $115 million in Brazilian government guaranteed bonds to Multuplic, a São Paulo broker.

2. A monthly debt auction at the Brazilian central banks led to the valuation of the debt at 86 cruzados on the dollar, netting $100 million worth of Brazilian cruzados for Manufacturers Hanover and a $150,000 commission for the broker.

3. Manufacturers Hanover Trust used the cruzados to buy 10 percent of the pulp and paper company.[16]

Another hypothetical debt-for-equity is illustrated in Exhibit 4.14. The exhibit indicates that the MNC has bought $200 million of Venezuelan debt from a creditor bank, at a discount of 30 percent, at $140 million. The MNC then

Exhibit 4.14
Debt-for-Equity Swap Illustration

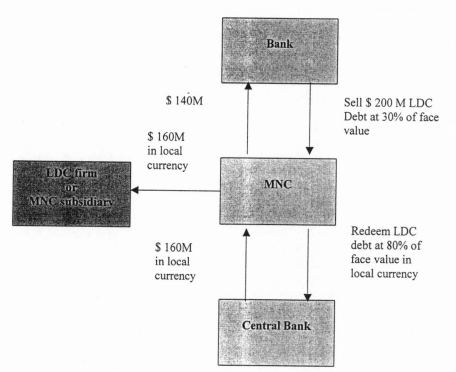

redeemed the debt at 80 percent of face value in local currency (for the equivalent of $160 million) from the Venezuelan central bank, to invest in its own Venezuelan subsidiary or in an equity position in another Venezuelan firm.

CONCLUSION

This chapter has dealt with international arbitrage and the problems of managing transaction exposure. The methods available for international arbitrage include locational arbitrage, triangular arbitrage, and covered interest arbitrage.

The methods available for managing transaction exposure are both imaginative and useful to the multinational firm. They include: (1) the forward contract hedge, (2) the money market hedge, (3) currency options, and (4) various operating procedures. The multinational firm must first conduct a cost-benefit analysis about the desirability of hedging and then conduct a second cost-benefit analysis to determine the best hedging techniques to be used for the particular situation and environment.

NOTES

1. Madura, Jeff, *International Financial Management* (St Paul, MN: West Publishing, 1992), pp. 130–131.

2. Riger, Nahum, and John Hull, "The Valuation of Currency Options," *Financial Management* 12 (1983), pp. 24–28; Garman, Mark, and Steven Kohlhagen, "Foreign Currency Option Values," *Journal of International Money and Finance* 2 (1983), pp. 231–238; Grabbe, J. Ozhin, "The Pricing of Call and Put Options on Foreign Exchange," *Journal of International Money and Finance* 2 (1983), pp. 239–254.

3. Eun, Cheol S., and Bruce G. Reswick, *International Financial Management* (Boston: Irwin McGraw-Hill, 2001), p. 227.

4. International Federation of Accountants, *Foreign Currency Exposure and Risk Management*, Study no. 2 (New York: International Federation of Accountants, 1986), p. 17.

5. Johnson, L. J., and C. H. Walther, "The Effectiveness of Forward and Gold Market Hedges Against Currency Risk," *Management International Review* 4 (1985), pp. 5–16.

6. Ibid., p. 6.

7. Eitman, D. K., and A. I. Stonehill, *Multinational Business Finance* (Reading, MA: Addison-Wesley, 1989), p. 205.

8. Eaker, Mark R., and Dwight M. Grant, "Cross-Hedging Foreign Currency Risk," *Journal of International Money and Finance* 6 (1987), p. 86.

9. Bicksler, James, and Andrew H. Chen, "An Economic Analysis of Interest Rate Swaps," *Journal of Finance* 16 (July 1986), p. 646.

10. Wilshon, Keith, and Lorin S. Chevalier, "Interest Rate Swaps—Your Rate or Mine?" *Journal of Accountancy* 13 (September 1985), p. 64.

11. Ibid., p. 65.

12. Ibid., p. 74.

13. Ibid.

14. Gambino, Anthony J., "Cash Management, Interest Rate Swaps, Risk Management Addressed by CPAs in Industry," *Journal of Accountancy* 13 (August 1985), pp. 66, 68.

15. Edmonds, John, and S. E. Moeller, "Interest Rate Swaps and Yield Curve Notes: Innovative Techniques in International Finance," *Issues in International Business*, Summer 1988, pp. 75–78.

16. Ryser, J., and E. Weiner, "How an Equity Swap Works," *Business Week*, October 3, 1988, p. 116.

SELECTED READINGS

Arak, Marcelle, Arturo Estrella, Laurie Goodman, and Andrew Silver. "Interest Rate Swaps: An Alternative Explanation." *Financial Management*, (Summer 1988), pp. 12–18.

Arnold, Tanya S. "How To Do Interest Rate Swaps." *Harvard Business Review* (September/October 1984), pp. 96–101.

Babbel, Dabid F. "Determining the Optimum Strategy for Hedging Currency Exposure." *Journal of International Business Studies* 5 (Spring/Summer 1983), pp. 133–139.

Batra, Raveendra, N., Shabtai Donnenfeld, and Josef Hadar. "Hedging Behavior by Multinational Firms." *Journal of International Business Studies* 4 (Winter 1982), pp. 59–70.

Bicksler, James, and Andrew H. Chen. "An Economic Analysis of Interest Rate Swaps." *Journal of Finance* 13 (July 1986), pp. 646–655.

Edmonds, John, and S. E. Moeller. "Interest Rate Swaps and Yield Curve Notes: Innovative Techniques in International Finance." *Issues in International Business*, 2 (Summer 1988).

Folks, William R., Jr. "Decision Analysis for Exchange Risk Management." *Financial Management*, Winter 1972, pp. 101–112.

Gambino, Anthony J. "Cash Management, Interest Rate Swaps, Risk Management Addressed by CPAs in Industry." *Journal of Accountancy* 10 (August 1985), pp. 66, 68.

International Federation of Accountants. *Foreign Currency Exchange and Risk Management.* Study no. 2. New York: International Federation of Accountants, 1986.

Jacque, Laurent L. "Management of Foreign Exchange Risk: A Review Article," *Journal of International Business Studies* 3 (Spring/Summer 1981), pp. 81–89.

Johnson, L. J., and C. H. Walther. "The Effectiveness of Forward and Gold Market Hedges against Currency Risk." *Management International Review* 1 (1985), pp. 5–16.

Kwok, Chuck C. Y. "Hedging Foreign Exchange Exposure: Independent vs. Integrative Approaches." *Journal of International Business Studies* 7 (Summer 1987), pp. 33–52.

Makin, John H. "The Portfolio Method of Managing Foreign Exchange Risk." *Euromoney*, August 1976, pp. 58–64.

———. "Portfolio Theory and the Problem of Foreign Exchange Risk." *Journal of Finance* 33 (May 1978), pp. 517–534.

Naidu, G. W., and Tai, Shim. "Effectiveness of Currency Futures Market in Hedging Foreign Exchange Risk." *Management International Review* 21, no. 4 (1981), pp. 5–16.

Park, Yoon S. "Currency Swaps as a Long-Term International Financing Technique." *Journal of International Business Studies* 6 (Winter 1984), pp. 47–54.

Ryser, J., and E. Weiner. "How an Equity Swap Works," *Business Week*, October 3, 1988, p. 116.

Sheperd, Sidney A. "Forwards, Futures, and Currency Options as Foreign Exchange Risk Protection." *Canadian Banker*, December 1983, pp. 22–25.

Smith, C. W., Jr., C. W. Smithson, and L. M. Wakeman. "The Evolving Market for Swaps." *Midland Corporate Finance Journal* 4 (Winter 1986), pp. 20–32.

Tumbull, S. M. "Swaps: A Zero Sum Game?" *Financial Management*, (Spring 1987), pp. 15–21.

Wheelright, Steven. "Applying Decision Theory to Improve Corporate Management of Currency-Exchange Risks." *California Management Review*, (Summer 1975), pp. 41–49.

Wilshon, Keith, and Lorin S. Chevalier. "Interest Rate Swaps—Your Rate or Mine?" *Journal of Accountancy* 10 (September 1985), pp. 63–84.

APPENDIX 4.1: REVIEW OF TECHNIQUES FOR HEDGING TRANSACTION EXPOSURE

Assume the Karabatsos Corporation expects to need 2,000,000 Norwegian krones (NOK) in one year. The following information is provided to facilitate the management of transaction exposure:

■ Spot rate of NOK as of today =$0.1419

■ One-year forward rate of NOK as of today =$0.1410.

■ Interest rates are as follows:

	US	Norway
Deposit Rate	8%	5%
Borrowing Rate	9%	6%

■ A call option on NOK that expires in one year has an exercise price of $0.1413 and a premium of $0.0003.

■ A put option on NOK that expires in one year has an exercise price of $0.1413 and a premium of $0.0003.

■ The Karabatsos Corporation forecasted the following future spot rates in a year:

$0.1411

$0.1412

$0.1415

Assume also that the Karabatsos Corporation expects to receive 2,000,000 Norwegian krones (NOK) in one year.

In both cases, assume that Karabatsos is considering (1) a forward hedge, (2) a money market hedge, (3) an option hedge, or (4) remaining unhedged.

The management of transaction exposure proceeds as follows:

1 In the case of management of transaction exposure arising from the 2,000,000 NOK

payables:

a. *Forward hedge*

Purchase 2,000,000 NOK one year forward: NOK 2,000,000 x $0.1410 = $282,000

b. *Money market hedge*

- Need to invest NOK (NOK 2,000,000/1.05) = NOK 1,904,761.9.

- Need to borrow $270,285.71 (NOK 1,904.761.9 x 0.1419) = $270,285.71.

- Will need $294,611.42 to repay the loan in one year ($270,285.71 x 1.09) = $294,611.42

c *Call option hedge* (exercise price =$0.1413; premium=$.0003)

Possible spot rate per unit	Option premium	Exercise option	Amount per unit (including the premium)	Total amount paid for 2,000,000 NOK
$0.1411	0.0003	No	$0.1414	$282,800
$0.1412	0.0003	No	$0.1415	$283,000
$0.1415	0.0003	Yes	$0.1416	$283,200

The optimal hedge is the forward hedge.

2 In the case of management of transaction exposure arising from the 2,000,000 NOK

receivables:

a. *Forward hedge*

Sell NOK 2,000,000 one year *forward:* NOK 2,000,000 x $0.1410 = $282,000.

b. *Money market hedge*

- Borrow NOK 1,886,792.4 (NOK 2,000,000/1.06 = NOK 1,886,792.4).

- Convert NOK 1,886,792.4 to $267,735.84 (at $0.1419).

- Invest the $267,735.84 at 8% to earn $289,154.7 by the end of the year.

c. *Put option hedge* (exercise price = $0.1413; premium = $.0003)

Possible spot rate per unit	Option premium	Exercise option	Amount per unit (after accounting for the premium)	Total amount received for 2,000,000 NOK
$0.1411	0.0003	Yes	0.1410	$282,000
$0.1412	0.0003	Yes	0.1410	$282,000
$0.1415	0.0003	No	0.1412	$282,400

The money market hedge is the optimal hedge.

5

Organizational and Performance Evaluation of Multinational Operations

INTRODUCTION

Multinational corporations strive to achieve superior economic performance and benefits from the economic opportunities present in the international environment. To benefit from these opportunities, these firms need to find the appropriate fit between their organizational structure and the environmental characteristics. At the same time they need to maintain adequate control over their multinational operations through the implementation of an appropriate control and performance evaluation system.

GENESIS OF THE MULTINATIONAL FIRM

Theories of Organizational Change and the Firm

Five theories of organizational change may be used to explain the genesis of the multidivisional form, namely, (1) strategy-structure, (2) transaction analysis, (3) population-ecology theory, (4) control theory based on power, and (5) organizational homogeneity theory.[1]

The first theory was enunciated in A. D. Chandler's seminal work, *Strategy and Structure*,[2] in which strategy is defined as "the determination of long-term goals and objectives of an enterprise, and the adoption of courses of action and the allocation of resources necessary for carrying out these goals."[3] These include either horizontal or vertical strategies or else diversification in related or unrelated markets. Chandler maintained that a horizontal strategy called for a unitary structure, characterized by manufacturing, sales and marketing, and fi-

nance departments, a vertical strategy called for a functional structure, characterized by departments organized along discrete task lines; and a diversification
strategy called for a multidivisional structure, in which a firm is organized into
product divisions and each division contains a unitary structure.

The second theory, transaction cost analysis, was enunciated by O. Williamson.[4] His work on understanding the economics of organization relied on three
related concepts: transaction costs, bounded rationality, and opportunism. Transaction cost is the cost of performing an economic exchange, bounded rationality
is a view that constrains individuals in their ability to process their knowledge,
and opportunism is a view that people, not only act out of self-interest, but also
act with guile. Given high transaction costs, bounded rationality, and opportunism in the market (referred to as the "market failures approach"), firms choose
to contract activities with the markets or build hierarchies to perform the same
task. Williamson concluded that firms may be inclined to choose the multidivisional form because the continuous expansion of the unitary or functional
structure creates "cumulative control loss" effects, which have "internal efficiency consequences."[5] As size increases, people reach their limits of control as
a result of bounded rationality and start resorting to opportunism, thereby threatening efficiency and profitability. The multidivisional form is one solution for
these problems.

The third theory, termed population-ecology, was enunciated by Hamman and
Freeman.[6] They elaborated on the link between organizational niche, age, inertia,
and the possibility of organizational change. As organizations age and reach
high levels of accountability and reliability of performance, they move to a state
of "structural inertia." Fligstein pointed out that if the population-ecology argument is used, one would expect that younger and smaller firms would be
more likely to adopt the multidivisional form than older and larger ones.[7]

The fourth theory, control based on power, was enunciated by several authors
and most recently by Jeffrey Pfeffer.[8] In the allocation of scarce resources in an
organization, no optimal mechanism exists. Power enters in all important organization decisions and must be based on some structural claim over resources.
When it comes to profit-oriented organizations, over time there has been a shift
of power from production to sales and marketing and to finance personnel.
Therefore, the multidivisional form will be favored by these new power holders,
(sales and marketing and finance personnel), as the multidivisional form allows
for growth through both product-related and product-unrelated strategies.

The fifth theory, organizational homogeneity, was enunciated by Paul Di-
Maggio and Walter Powell.[9] They argued that large organizations begin to re-
semble one another as a result of three kinds of environmental pressure: (1) the
cultural expectations of competitors, suppliers, and the state, (2) environmental
uncertainty, and (3) a particular worldview of appropriate behavior created by
the professionalization of managers. As a result of these three kinds of environmental pressure, large organizations start mimicking one another structurally by
adopting the multidivisional form (MDF). Fligstein noted:

The MDF spreads to various organizations as a response to other firms' behavior. The examples of successful firms such as Du Pont or General Motors provided the role models for other firms. The MDF has also become the accepted form for large firms. Business schools have taught the MDF as an important organizational tool, and managers have come to implement it.[10]

The M-Form Hypothesis

The multidivisional (M-Form) structure has evolved as a better solution to the problems of managing growth and diversity within a centralized (U-Form) structure. In a major historical study of American enterprise, Chandler noted that in the early 1920s, the M-form was adopted as a response to the increasingly complex administrative problems encountered within a U-form, as firm size and diversity increased.[11] Building on Chandler's analysis, Williamson suggested that because of two problems encountered by expanding multiproduct firms— cumulative control loss and the compounding of strategic and operating decision making—there is the risk of failure to achieve behavior to attain least-cost profit maximization.[12] He maintained that as size increases, people reach their limits of control as a result of bounded rationality and start resorting to opportunism, thereby threatening efficiency and profitability. The M-Form is presented as a unique structural framework that overcomes these difficulties and favors goal-oriented pursuits and least-cost behavior, as associated with the neoclassical profit-making hypothesis.

Building on Williamson, researchers investigated a hypothesis of links between the M-Form and better performance. Results to date have provided either a support of the proposition that the M-Form implementation improves performance, regardless of other contingencies, or mixed results. The studies did not differentiate between the firms on the basis of their diversification strategy. One exception by Hoskisson provided evidence in support of a contingency view of the relationship between improved performance and implementation of an M-Form structure.[13] The type of diversification strategy—vertical, related, or unrelated—is assumed to mediate the results. The impact of these strategies is examined next.

First, firms may opt for a strategy of vertical integration to increase the economies of scale and efficiency.[14] Each stage of the production process is organized as a separate division that must, however, buy or sell from other separate divisions of the firm. The need to coordinate these transfers requires the use of a system of transfer prices and, most often, top-level operational control. Top management of the firm maintains a hands-on approach. It requires that incentives be based on overall economic performance, rather than on objective financial performance criteria and implementation of an internal capital market.[15] Because the investment opportunities affect the whole corporation rather than one or some of the divisions, top management must formulate the investment opportunities.[16] In vertically integrated firms, the corporate strategic control as well as the operational controls keep a certain degree of centralization in the implementation of the M-Form structure.

Second, firms may also opt for an unrelated diversification. The implementation of the M-Form following a strategy of unrelated diversification requires both divisionalization—the creation of distinct divisions—and decentralization— the delegation of managerial and operating responsibility to the divisions. Because the divisions are operating in different business, top management may feel the need for an integrative effort. In such a case, it was found that too much integrative effort disturbs the divisional autonomy and accountability, resulting in poorer performance.[17] A successful performance is more likely if the M-Form enterprise is implemented following a strategy of unrelated diversification and managed as a holding company.[18]

Third, firms may opt for a related diversification. A strategy of related diversification is used by firms to increase economies of scope or the sharing of resources and capabilities among a related set of businesses.[19] As in vertically integrated firms, each division needs to coordinate its activities with the other related divisions through a system of transfer prices and information transfer. Similarly, the incentives need to be based on both objective and subjective criteria rather than only on objective financial performance criteria and the implementation of an internal capital market.[20, 21] Top management needs to centralize information flows and have a certain knowledge of the operating activities of the divisions to be able to formulate opportunities in each division that may have some benefits for the others. This activity can be handled at the corporate level or at the intermediate level of strategic business unit (SBU) structures to ensure the development of synergy among divisions. In firms pursuing a strategy of related diversification, the information flows need to be centralized to achieve the economies of scope in the implementation of the M-Form structure. The managers of the divisions find themselves pursuing two objectives: one of sharing information with top management for coordinating purposes and another of pursuing independent opportunities in the marketplace.

The central proposition of a study by Riahi-Belkaoui was that the implementation of a multidivisional structure leads to different productive efficiency in firms that employ the different strategic diversification approaches of unrelated diversification, vertical integration, and related diversification. The results of this study support the contingency view of the relationship between productive efficiency and the implementation of this M-Form.

The first result suggests that the implementation of M-Form controls tends to lead to a decrease in productive efficiency for vertically integrated firms. These results may be due to the different problems of coordinating the activities of interdependent divisions and the resort to heavy-handed control. The results parallel most of the earlier work supporting a decrease in rate of return for vertically integrated firms.

The second result suggests that the implementation of the M-Form controls tends to lead to an increase in productive efficiency for related-diversified firms.

The M-Form appears to be an efficient structure for related diversified firms. The synergistic economies of scope added to the M-Form controls created a good environment for productivity. Those results do not parallel earlier work supporting a decrease in rate of return for vertically integrated firms. One explanation may be related to the respective problems of measuring the accounting profit and the assets allocated to each division.

The third results suggests that, like related diversified firms, unrelated diversifiers demonstrated an increase in productivity, although it was not statistically significant. One explanation may be the difficulty in successfully exposing the unrelated acquisitions to the control and monitoring of an efficient internal capital market.

The fourth result showed that firms using related diversification strategies had a higher productive efficiency than unrelated or vertically integrated firms, following the implementation of the M-Form structure. The M-Form appears as a more efficient structure for related diversified firms than other diversification strategies for the improvement of productive efficiency.

ORGANIZATIONAL STRUCTURE AND INFORMATION PROCESSING

Organizational Structure of Multinational Firms

Various conventional structures have been proposed as adequate for multinational firms. They include the use of a separate international division, the use of a product division structure, the use of a geographical division structure, the use of a functional division structure, the matrix organization, and the use of a strategy matrix. Each of these types of structures will be discussed further, including the strategy and structure of multinational firms.

The Use of a Separate International Division. Multinational firms may rely on a separate division to handle all the international activities. This is ideal for those firms whose international activities and assets are still immaterial compared to the domestic activities.[22] This form of organizational structure is more prevalent in the United States than in Europe, as U.S. firms are generally more concerned about the impact of their domestic divisions.[23] The creation of a separate international division gives the offshoot equal footing and power with its domestic counterparts, although it may have to compete, and even depend on, the same domestic divisions for crucial responses in terms of personnel, technology, and other resources. With the creation of an international division, international expertise, data on foreign opportunities, as well as the freedom to make international decisions, are centralized in a semiautonomous unit. The major manufacturing and related functions remain in the hands of the domestic division to allow for more economies of scale. Coordination between the domestic and international divisions is necessary to avoid the conflict arising from the geographical orientation of the international division and the product or functional orientation of the domestic divisions.[24]

Product Division. Various multinational firms opt instead for a product-oriented organizational structure, with the product divisions operating in different countries and completely independent of one another. Basically, they select a global organizational structure that gives product divisions the international responsibility for production and marketing. Cost efficiency is assumed to be obtained by the centralization of production activities and the ability to react quickly to needed product-specific changes.[25] This type of structure is particularly useful in those cases in which the products are technologically sophisticated, custom designed, and in need of extensive capital investment. As Drake and Caudill explain: "The product groups of these companies often represent worldwide businesses which lend themselves to a limited number of product development and production facilities, worldwide marketing strategies, and (following from these conditions) centralized planning."[26]

Geographical (Area) Division. Various multinational firms with very large foreign operations that are not concentrated in a single country have opted for a geographical division structure. This global organizational structure gives complete manufacturing and marketing responsibilities to geographical or area divisions. Having narrow product lines geared to be used by specific foreign users is the main motivation behind the geographical divisional structure. Witness the following comments from a survey of multinational firms:

For geographic markets of significance and/or importance, at a great distance from the parent headquarters, special organizational and reporting arrangements typically have been established. These arrangements give recognition to unique marketing and business conditions, distinctive managerial styles, the intensity of local competition, and the problem of managing a local company from afar. Brazil, Japan, and (for European-based companies) the United States are three markets in which the need for such arrangements is particularly evident.[27]

Functional Division. Various multinational firms have opted for a functional division structure, with each functional division operating in different countries or geographic areas. They have opted for a global organization structure that gives international responsibilities to the various functional areas of production, marketing, finance, and personnel. Strategy emanates from the top, or strategic apex.[28] The consequence is a low participation of subunits in foreign subsidiaries in the strategic formulation process. As stated by Egelhoff:

The functional structure should be most suitable when the information required to formulate strategy already exists in the strategic apex of the parent and when strategy can be formulated more on a worldwide than a subsidiary-by-subsidiary basis (e.g., where a product tends to sell more in a uniform worldwide market than undifferentiated, local markets).[29]

Matrix Organization. Some multinational firms have opted for a matrix organization to allow all the major perspectives, groups, functions, or areas to be represented in a strategic as well as operational decision making. The matrix organization is basically an integration of the functional, geographical, and product structures, which in turn constitute different and multiple commands, which still have to report to the matrix structure manager. The manager serves as coordinator, facilitator of communications, and potential arbiter in case of conflicts. The matrix organization favors the creation of a global network organization whereby the various subsidiaries report, not only to headquarters, but to other subsidiaries. Numerous matrix patterns have been found used by multinational companies:

- The current matrix pattern in each company reflects present needs and particular circumstances.
- Each company's matrix pattern reflects the managerial style and culture of headquarters, as well as of its foreign-based management terms.
- The matrix pattern is influenced by the special emphasis given to large and particularly attractive geographic markets.
- The matrix is inherently unstable; it must shift continually in response to new business and new environmental and competitive conditions.[30]

Strategy Matrix. Some multinational companies have opted for the style of management known as the strategy matrix. This is a participatory planning and management system involving the integration of matrix management and strategic planning.[31] Matrix management involves team building and a multiple command system, whereas strategic planning involves the determination of corporate and business unit objectives, goals, and strategies in response to environmental scanning. Therefore, the strategy matrix as adopted by an MNC involves an extension of the scope of matrix management beyond short-term project management to long-term international strategic management, as well as the extension of strategic planning, not only within business units, but also across multiple business units.[32] The international strategy matrix is seen as inevitable to the running of multinational companies, even if the formal structure adopted is a divisional management structure. As Naylor states:

The international strategy matrix can accommodate the multidimensional nature of international management problems much more easily than traditional single dimensional hierarchical approaches can. Indeed, it can be argued that when companies attempt to force divisionalized management structures as their international business, success often comes only by virtue of the fact that informal teams and matrices emerge among the interdependent businesses and countries. Thus, whether or not senior management formally introduces the matrix into a multinational company, there remains the strong possibility that an informal matrix structure will eventually evolve as a natural response to the multinational interdependencies.[33]

The preceding discussion concerned various types of organizational structures. There is, however, no consensus about the best form for multinational corporations. What has been noted in practice are various experimentations in general and five basic patterns of organization in particular. The five basic patterns are:

1. Functionally organized—with foreign operations integrated into the functional units (Tata Chemicals Limited, India; Inocenti, Italy).

2. Functionally organized—with foreign operations assembled into one separate, overall international unit (AKU, Netherlands; Volkswagen, Germany).

3. Product organization—with foreign operations integrated into product divisions or groups (ICI, United Kingdom; Fiat, Italy).

4. Product organization—with foreign operations reporting directly to top management or assembled as a separate international unit (Ericsson Telephone, Sweden; Dunlop Rubber Co., United Kingdom).

5. Regional organization—with foreign and domestic operations grouped into components under regional heads (Singer, United States; Standard Oil Company, United States).[34]

What seems to be taking place is a search for the form of organizational structure that is most efficient for operating and financial control purposes. A rise of centralized and decentralized activities has appeared more recently as a way of meeting the different objectives of the various functions and goals of multinational companies. Centralization in production and logistics, for example, has become easier with the advent of international computer-linked communications systems. Similarly, centralized purchasing or "common sourcing" may make it easier to obtain purchaser quantity discounts, greater bargaining power for supplies, benefits from price differentials, and other economies of scale.[35] Naturally, the appropriate mix of centralized and decentralized activities differs from one multinational company to another because of differences in industries and environments. However, there seem to be common factors in the search for the correct mix:

1. The major decisions affecting the entire system, which previously may have been made locally, now tend to be made centrally, in a coordinated fashion. For example, foreign affiliates typically now have decreased discretion over the reinvestment of their earnings, as headquarters, which is aware of all competing alternatives, allocates resources in a balanced fashion for the global system.

2. Local managers retain considerable authority in largely local matters and in other matters where it is necessary to maintain flexibility and immediacy or response at the operating levels.

3. Financial control systems are changing from the emphasis on profits under the profit-center concept to control via budgets and budget variances; additionally, other evaluation techniques are increasingly used supplementally. These new control systems

are designed to permit control centrally, even though a great deal of authority is left at the local level.

4. New systems for centralized coordination and for cooperative management are emerging. That is, a bevy of new central coordination techniques, many requiring extensive interaction with cooperation from local managers, is emerging. For example, operations research techniques (particularly simulation and network analysis) are used for coordination; formal, frequent, and lengthy meetings of managers from around the world are reaching new heights of sophistication as a coordination technique; top-management policy guidelines have been refined for extensive use as a means to guide local managers in decision making in situations that are important for global coordination but too complex to permit promulgation of rigid decision rules; and behind each of these new developments, the accounting and management information system must be redesigned, altered, and expanded to accommodate information flows resulting from the use of the new techniques.[36]

Multinational firms are known to experiment with various organizational structures. Various organizational characteristics are believed to influence multinational structure.

1. After showing that diversity influenced organizational design,[37] Chandler hypothesized that foreign involvement is also an influencing variable.[38] Both variables were later found to be strong predictors of multinational structure.[39, 40]

2. Case studies of U.S. multinationals have shown that changes in organizational parameters such as size, diversity, foreign activity, and personnel deployment may lead to a change of structure.[41, 42]

3. Following the principle of isomorphism, multinational firms have been formed to change their structure to imitate a leader.[43]

4. In evaluating important fits between elements of strategy and type of organizational structure, Egelhoff formed the following elements of strategy to differentiate significantly between types of structure: (a) foreign product diversity, (b) product modification differences between subsidiaries, (c) product change, (d) size of foreign operations, (e) size of foreign manufacturing, (f) number of foreign subsidiaries, (g) extent of outside ownership in foreign subsidiaries, and (h) extent of foreign acquisitions.[44] The fits are summarized as follows:

Five fits are important for firms with worldwide functional divisional structures: a narrow and highly consistent worldwide product line, a limited number of foreign subsidiaries, a low level of outside ownership in foreign subsidiaries, a few foreign acquisitions. . . . The international division structure has a single dominant fit with the firm's international strategy. It is appropriate when foreign operations are relatively low . . . For companies with geographical region structures, the most important fits are a sufficiently large foreign operations and a high percentage of foreign manufacturing . . . Companies with worldwide product division structures also have large foreign operations and are distinguished from other structures by high level of product diversity and product change.[45]

5. Multinational firms are constantly evolving in their search for the best organizational design. Over time, specific trends emerge. Davis reported on the following trends:

a. Worldwide functional structures are showing definite instabilities.

b. Corporations organized by country are exploring how and where to place product management more adequately in their framework.

c. Firms with worldwide product groups require better coordination within countries and regions than their structures provide.

d. Corporate planning and development activities have led some companies to organize around markets rather than geography.

e. Some companies are experimenting with global matrix management and structure.

U.S. multinationals go through three phases as their foreign business becomes material: (a) a phase of "ignoring the system's potential," in which international financial management is left to a small staff that monitors quasi-independent affiliates, (b) a phase of "exploiting the system's potential," in which the international financial management is centralized in a more coherent and capable and experienced unit, and (c) a phase of "compromising with flexibility," in which the large central international unit is now delegating responsibility to foreign-based subsidiaries through detailed "rule books."[46]

Information Processing and the Multinational Firm

Information processing involves data collection, transforming data into information, and communication and storage of the information.[47] As defined by Egelhoff:

Information processing is largely represented in terms of the capacities of different kinds of organizational structures and processes to transfer information within an organization, to move it across the boundaries of an organization, and to access specific kinds of knowledge and decision making capabilities needed to transform data or information.[48]

Viewing organizations from an information-processing perspective highlights technologies and environments as major sources of uncertainties that lead to differences in organizations. Galbraith defined uncertainty from an information-processing perspective as the difference between the amount of information required to perform the task and the amount of information already processed by the organization.[49] The implication is that effective organizations will attempt to design their information-processing capabilities to fit the amount of uncertainty that they face. In the case of multinational firms, Egelhoff relied on two structural dimensions: one reflecting the purpose and perspective of information processing (whether strategic or tactical) and one reflecting the subject and content of information processing (whether it deals with product matters or company and country matters).[50]

These two structural dimensions of information processing are generated from types of information processing in the form of:

1. tactical information processing for company and country matters
2. strategic information processing for company and country matters
3. tactical information processing for product matters
4. strategic information processing for product matters

This set of information-processing dimensions works well to distinguish where in an organization different kinds of knowledge and different kinds of decision making capabilities lie. It helps to identify which carts of an organization need to be linked together in order to solve a given problem or address a specific decision-making situation. In other words, these dimensions are useful for measuring the structural aspects of organizations and understanding their implications for information processing.[51] Egelhoff also relied on the process dimensions that distinguish between routine and nonroutine information processing and between sequential and reciprocal information processing.[52]

CONTROL MODELS FOR MULTINATIONAL CORPORATIONS

The Baliga and Jaeger Model

As stated by Child, "Control is essentially concerned with regulating the activities within an organization so that they are in accord with the expectations established in policies, plans and targets."[53] The activities or phenomena that are assumed to be monitored and evaluated are behavior and output.[54] These are the two objects of control. At the same time, the instruments of control are either pure bureaucratic/formalized controls, relying predominantly on accounting control instruments such as budgets, variances, and performance reports, or cultural controls, relying on an informal socialization process better known as corporate culture. In their article, Baliga and Jaeger proposed that the type of control system that is chosen, whether cultural or bureaucratic, dictates a different level of delegation and is itself a notion of the type of interdependence, environmental uncertainty, and cultural proximity.[55]

The types of interdependence, as based on the work of J. D. Thompson, include (1) pooled interdependence, whereby the autonomous subsidiaries share common resources; (2) sequential interdependence, whereby the output of one system is fed into another part of the system; and (3) reciprocal interdependence, whereby segments of firms feed their work back and forth among themselves.[56]

The environmental uncertainty is either high or low. The greater uncertainty is created by a highly dynamic, complex, diverse, and hostile environment that leads the firm to adopt low levels of formalization and centralization.[57, 58] Finally, cultural proximity is defined as "the extent to which the host cultural ethos permits the adoption of the home organization culture";[59] it is either high or low.

The rationale for the model rests on (1) the maximum need for control, coordination, and consistency in decision making under reciprocal interdependence, which amounts to more centralization than under sequential interdependence, first, and pooled interdependence, second; and (2) the need for more decentralization under high environmental uncertainty than under low environmental uncertainty and under a high level of cultural proximity than under a low level of cultural proximity. As stated by Baliga and Jaeger:

Regardless of the type of interdependence, under conditions of high environmental uncertainty some degree of delegation should be provided to subsidiary management so that they may be more responsive to their local environment. Conversely, centralization could be extensive under conditions of low uncertainty. Under conditions of low cultural proximity, employment of cultural control systems would probably not be worth the expenditure. Where cultural proximity is high, socialization and indoctrination can be carried out more effectively, and use of cultural control would permit a higher level of delegation.[60]

Strategy and Structure for Multinational Firms

Based on resource flow considerations, Herbert developed an interesting model of strategy-structure configurations for the multinational firm.[61] First, he distinguished between four resource flow–based strategies: (a) volume expansion, intended to create greater market volume through exports in new international markets; (b) resource acquisition, to receive the availability of resources through foreign subsidiaries; (c) reciprocity, to create a two-way flow of resources between the parent company and the foreign subsidiaries; and (d) integration, to conduct full integrated operations in major world markets. Each of these resource strategies is assumed to be carried under compatible local structural configurations to assume a perfect fit. They are presented as perfect matches. However, mismatches can occur and will require corrective actions.

Strategies/Structures and Control

The multinational environment has been used to establish a relationship between strategy, on the one hand, and structure and control, on the other.

Two economic reasons sustaining most international diversifications are experience and risk spreading.[62] First, the experience curve favors a globally centralized power—an ethnocentric organization. Risk spreading favors the creation of a portfolio of unrelated, globally distributed subsidiaries—a polycentric organization.[63] In fact, these strategies are in evidence, leading to either ethnocentric organization, polycentric organization, or geocentric organization.

1. The ethnocentric organization is created to benefit from the experience curve effects, passing them from one location to another. It is product oriented, with divisions operating efficiently to produce products for the parent company market. Therefore, performance evaluation will be tightly controlled by the parent company.

2. The polycentric organization is created to favor, and benefit from, geographic diversification. It has a host country orientation with a unique product strategy for each market. The subsidiaries operate as independent strategic business markets (SBUs). As a result, performance evaluation is less controlled by the parent company.

3. The geocentric organization is created to favor both product and geographic divisions in order to handle changes in market preferences and products. It is best seen as a global matrix structure. As a result, performance evaluation is shared between the divisions and the parent company.

Another strategic consideration is related to the phenomenon of waxing and waning of performance evaluation. This was noticed by Robbins and Stobaugh, who found that the performance evaluation function for multinational operations depended mainly on the degree of foreign experience of the firm and the size of its foreign operations.[64] In fact, they noticed three phases of the evolutionary process of performance evaluation:

1. Given the small scale of foreign operations and the lack of foreign experience, relatively little control is exercised by the parent company and each subsidiary is practically left on its own to improve its performance, with the possible result of suboptimization. The performance evaluation system of the firm in general are far from being coordinated.

2. The foreign operations expand and top management starts gaining closer control in foreign operations. The result is a strong and coordinated performance evaluation system that is dominated by the parent company.

3. The scale of operations is so large and complex that the control exercised by headquarters begins to diminish in favor of a more decentralized performance evaluation system. Headquarters keeps a hand in the situation, however, by formulating guidelines for the foreign subsidiaries to follow.

Finally, the multinational corporation can be viewed as a network of transactions in knowledge, goods, and capital among subsidiaries in different countries. If a focus is placed on the knowledge flows, differences in the subsidiaries' contexts can be analyzed along two dimensions: (1) the extent to which the subsidiary is the user of knowledge from the rest of the corporation, and (2) the extent to which the subsidiary is the provider of such knowledge to the rest of the corporation.[65] Gupta and Govindarajan used the differences in knowledge flow patterns between focal and peer subsidiaries to distinguish between four types of subsidiaries.

1. The global innovation, which is high in the outflow and the inflow of knowledge.

2. The integrated player, which is high in the outflow but low inflow of knowledge.

3. The local innovation, which is low in both the outflow and inflow of knowledge.

4. The implementer, which is low in the outflow but high in the inflow of knowledge.[66]

Different control mechanisms are required for each of these forms, based on the differences in knowledge flow patterns. The differences in control mechanisms can also be changed early on by varying the product flow patterns.[67] The strategic importance of the local environment and the level of local resources and capabilities,[68] as well as the extent of change in the subsidiary's local environment,[69] are also important factors.

EVALUATING DIVISIONAL PERFORMANCE

Organization of a Decentralized Concern

Cost centers, profit centers, and investment centers are the types of segments used by a decentralized concern in creating the type of organization structure most suitable to the efficient conduct of its activities.

A cost center is the smallest segment of activity or area of responsibility for which costs can be accumulated. Responsibility in a cost center is restricted to cost. For planning purposes, the budget estimates are cost estimates; for control purposes, performance evaluation is guided by a cost variance equal to the difference between the actual and budgeted costs for a given period. In general, cost centers are associated with segments of the firm that provide either tangible or intangible services to line departments. For example, cost centers may include departments providing services such as legal advice and accounting, personnel, and data processing. Cost centers may also be found in producing or line departments. When a production process requires different types of machines and operations, cost centers are created to enhance the accumulation of costs by operation.

A profit center is a segment of activity or area of responsibility for which both revenues and costs are accumulated. The manager holds responsibility for both revenues and expenses. For planning purposes, the budget estimates include both revenues and expenses. For control purposes, performance is guided by both a revenue variance and a cost variance. In short, the objective function of a profit center's manager is to maximize the center's profit. Although the profit center concept is vital to the implementation of decentralization, it can be used in firms with centralization. In other words, the profit center concept leads essentially to a divisionalized firm, but not necessarily to a decentralized firm. Decentralization implies the relative freedom to make decisions.

An investment center is a segment of activity that is held responsible for both profits and investment. For planning purposes, the budget estimate is a measure of the rate of return on investment (ROI) estimate. For control purposes, performance evaluation is guided by an ROI variance. In short, the objective function of an investment center is to maximize the center's ROI. The merits of the ROI measure and the possible problems associated with such a measure are illustrated later in the chapter.

Rate of Return on Investment

Measurement of the Return on Investment. E.I. Du Pont de Nemours and Company is generally credited with the development of the ROI concept. The ROI is found by dividing the net income by the amount of investment. It relates the profit to invested capital, both of which are important areas of management responsibility. The rationale lies in the belief that there is an optimal investment level in each asset, leading to an optimal profit level. The ROI is the product of two components; profit margin and investment turnover. The profit margin equals net income divided by sales and indicates the segment's ability to transform sales into profit. The investment turnover equals sales dividend by investment capital. Thus, the ROI can be expressed as follows:

$$\text{ROI} = \frac{\text{Net income}}{\text{Invested capital}} = \frac{\text{Sales}}{\text{Invested capital}} \times \frac{\text{Net income}}{\text{Sales}}$$

This formula shows that the ROI can be increased by an increase in either the profit margin or the investment turnover and decreased by a decrease in either the profit margin or the investment turnover. These are not the only alternatives. Exhibit 5.1 shows the factors that can affect the final ROI outcome.

Rate of Return on Investment Issues. Although the ROI may qualify as a good management tool, some potential problems must be recognized. First, the net income figure used in calculating the ROI may require certain adjustments that do not conform with generally accepted accounting principles. Exhibit 5.2 illustrates the format and content of a divisional income statement. Distinctions are made between sales to outside customers and sales to other divisions, between controllable and uncontrollable costs, and between variable and fixed costs. This format allows for the possibility of distinguishing between the performance of the manager and the performance of the division. Two rates of return can be computed—the controllable ROI and net ROI—as follows:

Controllable ROI = Controllable income / Controllable capital investment
Net ROI = Net income after taxes / Total capital investment

Another problem with the ROI is that the investment figure used in calculating the ROI may lead to an "unrealistic" figure. Hence, the most obvious figure is the net book value of assets, which is the original cost minus depreciation to date. Such a measure has inherent weaknesses. For example, it enables the di-

Exhibit 5.1
Relationship of Factors Influencing the Rate of Return on Investment

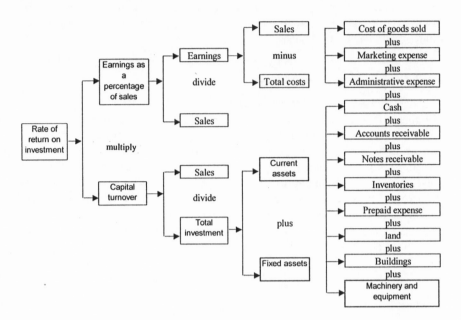

visions with the older assets to earn a higher rate of return than divisions with newer assets, given the low book value resulting from greater depreciation charges.

Several solutions can overcome this limitation of the ROI method. First, gross book value can be used. This approach, however, still enables a divisional manager to increase the ROI by scrapping nonprofitable assets that may be detrimental to the company. Second, four nonhistoric cost valuation methods can be used to determine the economic value: the replacement cost, the net realizable value, capitalized value, and the general price level–adjusted historical cost. The first three methods approximate the current value, whereas the last one merely adjusts the historical cost. The replacement cost represents the amount of cash or other consideration that would be required to obtain the same asset or its equivalent. The net realizable value represents the amount of cash for which an asset can be sold. The capitalized value refers to the present value of net cash flows expected to be received from the use of the asset. The three current values are relevant to different types of decisions. Although the capitalized value appears to be dominant, it is a subjective value based on the present value of expected cash flows. Replacement cost and net realizable value may be more easily available and constitute a better alternative to historical cost.

Third, the use of an increasing-charge depreciation (annuity depreciation), the

Exhibit 5.2
Format and Content of a Divisional Income Statement (in thousands)

Revenues		12,000
External sales	5,000	
Internal sales (transfer of price equal to market value)	6,000	
Internal sales (transfer price different from market value)	1,000	
Minus		
Variable costs		5,000
Variable cost of goods sold	2,000	
Variable selling and administrative divisional expense	3,000	
Total contribution margin		7,000
Add(Deduct)		
Fixed costs allocated to other divisions for transfers made at other		
than market value	500	
(Deduct)		
Controllable discretionary and committed fixed costs	200	
Equals		
Controllable operation income		6,300
(Deduct)		
Untrollable fixed costs	300	
Operating income before taxes		6,000
Income taxes	500	
Net income (after taxes)		5,500

compound-interest depreciation, can lead to a lower income being related to a smaller investment base. Sinking-fund depreciation is based on the financial concept that depreciation represents the return on investment. Suppose that a company is considering buying an asset with a two-year life and no salvage value. If the cost of the asset is estimated to be $8,680 and the yearly cash flow is estimated at $5,000, using a discounted cash flow method, the ROI can be obtained by solving the following equation for r:

$$\$8,680 = \sum_{t-1}^{2} \frac{\$5,000}{(1 + r)^t}$$
$$r = 10\%$$

Given the knowledge of the ROI, compound-interest depreciation assumes a capital recovery factor. Exhibit 5.3 presents the results of sinking-fund, depreciation, showing each cash payment to be equal to interest on investment plus principal. Exhibit 5.4 shows the superiority of compound-interest depreciation with the income statement and the ROI computations using either constant (increasing or decreasing depreciation). The compound-interest depreciation method results in a stable, constant ROI figure compared to the fluctuating

Exhibit 5.3
Example of Compound-Interest Depreciation

Year	Initial Investment (a)	Cash Earnings (b)	Return of 10% (c=10%a)	Depreciation (d=b-c)	Unrecovered Investment (e=a-d)
1	$8,680	$5,000	$868	$4,132	$4,548
2	4,548	5,000	454.8	4,542.20	2.8*

*Due to rounding

results obtained by the straight-line and accelerated methods. Therefore compound-interest depreciation is preferred by many companies as a measure of divisional profitability.

An appropriate allocation of assets to divisions makes the ROI more meaningful and contributes to goal congruence. Such an allocation differs from one company to another, given that companies elect to centralize certain activities and decentralize others. For instance, in most decentralized companies, the home office centralizes cash management billing or receivables collection.

As a general rule, the basis of allocation of assets to divisions should be controllability. That is, the amount of assets controllable by any given segment in its managerial activities should be the rate of return on divisional investment. To summarize, the ROI's limitations can be overcome if the investment base is at current value net of depreciation and a sinking-fund depreciation method is used.

Residual Income

Developed in the 1950s by General Electric Company, the concept of residual income (RI) is an accounting measure of income minus a required dollar return on an accounting measure of investment.

Residual Income = Income − (Required Rate of Return × Investment)

This concept directs the manager toward the maximization of income above a charge for assets used, or computed costs. Basically, the computed costs of the investment, computed as the required rate of return multiplied by investment, reflect the opportunity cost or return foregone by investing in the division rather than another investment of similar risk. For example, if divisional income were $50,000 for a budgeted investment of $200,000 with a required rate of return of 10 percent, the residual income would be computed as follows:

Exhibit 5.4
Depreciation Methods and Rate-of-Return Computations

	Methods of Depreciation					
	Straight-Line Depreciation		Accelerated Depreciation		Compound Interest	
Year	1	2	1	2	1	2
Cash earnings	$5,000	$5,000	$5,000	$5,000	$5,000	$5,000
Depreciation	4,340a	4,340a	5,786b	2,893b	4,132	4,545.2
Net income	$660	$660	($786)	$2,107	$868	$454.8
Investment base	$8,680	$4,340	$8,680	$2,894	$8,680	$4,548
Rate of return on investment	7.6%	15.2%	-9%	72%	10%	10%

Divisional net income	$50,000
minus	
Imputed costs at 10% of investment	$20,000
equals	
Residual income	$30,000

There are two main advantages to using the residual income method to measure divisional performance. First, the method enables the division to continue to expand as long as it meets the costs of capital of 10 percent, whereas the ROI was 25 percent ($50,000 / $200,000). In other words, using the ROI of 25 percent as an investment criterion would eliminate projects whose returns might exceed the costs of capital and, consequently, would eliminate projects that were acceptable from the point of view of the corporation as a whole. Second, the method requires setting a rate-of-return target for every type of asset, regardless of the division's profitability. The end result is a yardstick for comparisons between divisions. However, the adequate determination of the cost of capital and the rate of return of individual assets is a possible problem.

Economic Value Added (EVA®)

A trademarked variant of residual income, proposed by Stern Stuwart & Company, is economic value added (EVA®).[70] The new measure is supported to improve RI by adjusting the net operating profit after tax and capital from distortions in the accounting model of performance measurement.[71] It is computed as follows:

> EVA® = (Net operating income after tax + Accounting adjustments to operating profits) − weighted average cost of capital (Capital + Accounting adjustments to capital)

An approximation of EVA® is as follows:

> EVA® = Operating income after tax − (Weighted average cost of capital × [Total assets − Current liabilities])

Three main differences exit between RI and EVA®. They are as follows:

1. Income is equal to before-tax operating income under RI and after-tax operating income under EVA®.
2. The required rate of return is equal to the weighted average cost of capital under EVA®.
3. The investment is equal to to total assets minus current liabilities and can also be computed as: Total assets − Current liabilities = Long-term assets + Current assets − Current liabilities or Total assets − Current liabilities = Long-term assets + Working capital

Return on Sales

The income to revenues return, or the return on sales (ROS) ratio, is another frequent measure of divisional performance. It is equal to:

$$\text{ROS} = \frac{\text{Operating income}}{\text{Sales}}$$

Application of Divisional Performance Metrics

A fictional example is used to illustrated the application of the three main divisional performance metrics, namely ROI, RI, and EVA®. The Royal Plaza Hotels owns and operates three hotels, located in Chicago (United States), Tunis (Tunisia), and Ougadonzou (Burkina Faso). Exhibit 5.5 illustrates the relevant data for each of the three hotels for 19×9, assuming that Royal Plaza Hotels do not allocate total debt to each individual hotel.

A. The ROI is measured as:

$$\text{ROI} = \frac{\text{Income}}{\text{Investment}}$$

Exhibit 5.5
Relevant Data for the Evaluation of Royal Plaza Hotels for 19X9

	Chicago Royal Plaza Hotel (1)	Tunis Royal Plaza Hotel (2)	Ougedougou Royal Plaza Hotel (3)	Total (4) = (1) + (2) + (3)
1. Hotel Revenues (Sales)............	$2,245,000	$2,122,000	$1,325,000	$5,692,000
2. Hotel Variable Costs	$350,000	$220,000	$130,000	$700,000
3. Hotel Fixed Costs	$575,000	$628,000	$545,000	$1,748,000
4. Hotel Operating Income	$1,320,000	$1,274,000	$650,000	$3,244,000
5. Interest Costs on Long Term Debt at 12%				$864,000
6. Income Before Income Taxes.				$2,386,000
7. Income Taxes	$300,000	$300,000	$114,000	$714,000
8. Net Income (After Taxes).........	$1,070,000	$974,000	$536,000	$1,666,000
9. Average values for 19x9				
a. Current Assests	$1,356,000	$1,452,000	$1,225,000	$4,033,000
b. Long Term Assets	$1,875,000	$1,632,000	$1,542,000	$5,049,000
c. Total Assets	$3,231,000	$3,084,000	$2,767,000	$9,082,000
d. Current Liabilities	$65,000	$52,000	$32,000	$149,000
e. Long Term Debt				$7,200,000
f. Stockholders' Equity				$1,882,000
g. Total Liabilities and Stockholders' Equity				$9,231,000

In the case of the three Royal Plaza Hotels, ROI is captured as follows:

Hotel	Operating Income	÷	Total Assets	=	ROI
Chicago	$1,320,000		$3,231,000		40.85%
Tunis	$1,274,000		$3,084,000		41.35%
Ougadougou	$650,000		$2,767,000		23.49%

Using ROI as a measure of divisional performance, the Tunis Royal Plaza Hotel is making the best use of its assets.

B: The RI is measured as:

RI = Income − (Required rate of return × Investment)

If the required rate of return is 15% of the total assets of the hotel, the residual income for the three Royal Plaza Hotels is computed as follows:

Hotel	Operating Income	−	(Required rate of return x Investment)	=	RI
Chicago	$1,320,000		(15% x $3,231,000)		$835,350
Tunis	$1,274,000		(15% x $3,084,000)		$811,400
Ougadougou	$650,000		(15% x $2,757,000)		$234,950

Using RI as a measure of divisional performance the Chicago Royal Plaza Hotel has the best performance.

C. The return on sales is measured as:

ROS = Operating income / Sales

In the case of the three Royal Plaza Hotels, it is computed as follows:

Hotel	Operating Income	Sales	ROS
Chicago	$1,320,000	$2,245,000	58.79%
Tunis	$1,274,000	$2,122,000	60.03%
Ougadougou	$650,000	$1,325,000	49.06%

D. The EVA® is computed as follows:

EVA® = After-tax operating income − (Weighted average cost of capital × [Total assets × Current liabilities])

The market values of debt and equity are, respectively, $8,000,000 and $2,000,000. The cost of equity capital is 18 percent. The after-tax cost of debt is 0.084, or 8.4 percent. Therefore, the weighted-average cost of capital (WACC) is:

$$\begin{aligned}
\text{WACC} &= \frac{(0.084 \times \$8,000,000) + (0.18 \times \$2,000,000)}{\$8,000,000 + \$2,000,000} \\
&= \frac{\$672,000 + \$360,000}{\$10,000,000} \\
&= 0.1032 \text{ or } 10.32\%
\end{aligned}$$

The EVA® for the three Royal Plaza Hotels is computed as follows:

Hotel	$\text{After-Tax Operating Income} - \left[\text{Weighted-Average Cost of Capital} \times \left(\text{Total Assets} - \text{Current Liabilities} \right) \right] = \text{EVA®}$
Chicago	$1,020,000 [10.32% ($3,231,000 − $65,000)] = $693,268.8
Tunis	$974,000 [10.32% ($3,084,000 − $52,000)] = $661,097.6
Ougadougou	$536,000 [10.32% ($2,767,000 − $32,000)] = $253,748

Using EVA® as a measure of divisional performance, the Chicago Royal Plaza Hotel has the best performance. The result using the three measures are as follows:

Hotel	ROI (Rank)	RI (Rank)	EVA® (Rank)	ROS
Chicago	40.8% (2)	$835,350 (1)	$693,268.8 (1)	58.79% (1)
Tunis	412.5% (1)	$811,400 (2)	$661,097.6 (2)	60.03% (1)
Ougadougou	23.4% (3)	$234,950 (3)	$253,748 (3)	49.05% (3)

Both RI and EVA® rate the Chicago Royal Plaza Hotel as the most efficient. Given that both measures overcome some of the goal-congruence problems that ROI creates, the rating of the Chicago Royal Plaza Hotel is correct. In fact, when comparing these performance means, it becomes apparent that:

1. ROI, RI, and EVA® measures consider both the income earned and the investment made and are therefore more appropriate than ROS.
2. Even though ROI indicates the investment yielding the highest return, both RI and EVA® overcome some of the goal congruence problems created by ROI. Note again that some may prefer RI because it relies on pretax operating income whereas others will prefer EVA® because it relies on after-tax operating income.

Time Horizon of the Performance Measures

The previous computations of ROI, RI, EVA®, and ROS reflected the results of a single, one-time period. A multiple-year analysis with any of these measures will take into account the long-term interest of the firm and is highly recommended. What may appear as in a single year of these performance measures may be profitable as the long term.

The use of a multiple-year analysis proves the superiority of the RI measure. In fact, it may be shown that the net present value of all the cash flows over the life of an investment equals the net present value of RIs. To prove this result, let assume that a $600,000 investment in the Ougadougou hotel leads to an annual increase of the operating income by $100,000 for four years. Assuming a straight line depreciation is used, the operating annual cash flow will be equal to $250,000, namely, the $100,000 operating income plus the $150,000 depreciation. ($600,000 / 4). Assuming a required rate of return of 12 percent, the net present values of cash flows and residual incomes will be as follows:

Year	0	1	2	3	4	Net Real Value
(1) Cash Flow	-$600,000	$250,000	$250,000	$250,000	$250,000	
(2) Present Value of $1 discounted at 2%	1	0.89286	0.79719	0.71178	0.63552	
(3) Present Value (1) x (2)	-$600,000	$223,215	$199,297	$177,945	$158,880	$159,337
(4) Operating Income		$100,000	$100,000	$100,000	$100,000	
(5) Assets at the start of the year		$600,000	$450,000	$300,000	$150,000	
(6) Capital Change (5) x12%		$72,000	$54,000	$36,000	$18,000	
(7) Residual Income (4) - (6)		$28,000	$46,000	$64,000	$82,000	
(8) Present Value of RI: (7) x (2)		$25,000.08	$36,670.74	$45,553.92	$52,112.64	$159,337

Techniques Used for Performance Evaluation Internationally

As might be expected, multinational firms use a variety of techniques for international performance evaluation in order to adapt to different contexts. Various surveys have attempt to determine the nature of these techniques. Both financial and nonfinancial criteria have been used for the evaluation of the performance of overseas units and subsidiary managers.

In surveys, firms indicated that the primary purpose of a performance evaluation system is to ensure adequate profitability. Of the multiple criteria used, the budget compared to actual profit was indicated as being the most important financial criterion, followed by the return on investment, budget compared to actual sales, return on sales, return on assets, budget compared to actual return on investment, and operating cash flows. One noticeable result is that U.S.-based multinationals preferred cash flows to the parent company rather than cash flows to the subsidiary, indicating a more global perspective than the non–U.S.-based multinationals. Of the multiple nonfinancial criteria used, the market share was judged to be the most important, followed by productivity improvements, relationships with host governments, quality control, employee development, and safety. Other criteria included, by order of importance, the following:[72]

1. operating budget comparison
2. contribution to earnings per share

3. return on investment

4. contribution to corporate cash flow

5. return on sales

6. return on assets

7. asset/liability management

8. nonaccounting data such as market share, quality control, and labor turnover

9. long-term plan comparisons

10. return on investment—inflation adjusted

What is noticeable from the surveys is the dominant importance of operation budget comparisons and variance analysis in performance evaluation internationally. While no recent exhaustive survey has been done, it is believed that EVA® is gaining in use over the other dedicated measures. Finally, the Committee on International Accounting of the American Accounting Association provided the following list of performance evaluation approaches:

1. No formal evaluation of operations exists: the general manager's performance evaluation for salary, bonus, and promotion purposes is entirely subjective on the basis of personality and other personal traits. This approach cannot be considered desirable and typically is found in domestic operations; however, it is rather more frequently encountered in evaluation of foreign subsidiaries and their managers.

2. Operating results are evaluated in absolute terms, which are generally profit or return-on-investment (ROI). Here, a subjective evaluation is made about what is good performance and the general manager is regarded accordingly. This approach also includes a large subjective element and is found only where more sophisticated approaches have not been developed.

3. Operating results of the entity are compared to operating results of other entities in the same family; resource utilization and the entity general manager are both evaluated on this basis, as an entity is assumed to exist between the two for evaluation purposes. This approach is called "the comparison of entities" approach, and it has merit in cases where the most important environmental variables are much the same for the entities being compared.

4. Operating results are evaluated relative to operating results for the same entity in preceding periods, and an identity between the general manager and the entity is assumed. This approach is called the "temporal comparison." A major problem here is that an improvement over the preceding period's poor results still may not represent good performance in absolute terms.

5. Operating results are evaluated on the basis of how closely they conform to planned operating results. Although this is potentially an excellent evaluation approach, in practice the evaluation is less than satisfactory. For example, performance is often based on actual results compared to budget only for key factors such as profit and ROI, the constituents of which may not be entirely controllable by the general manager. Another common problem with this approach is that the plan becomes obsolete because of the factors beyond the manager's control but is not revised accordingly.

With this approach, too, an identity is generally assumed between operating results and the general manager's performance.[73]

There are, however, various factors that may affect the usefulness of currently used techniques of performance evaluation:

- The interaction of organizational structures and environmental factors in a complex network may cause profit indicators of performance evaluation to be misleading.[74]
- The reliance on a company-wide ROI measure may not portray important aspects of the subsidiary.
- Comparisons of ROI figures may be misleading, given the difficulties associated with the determination of an appropriate investment base for the computation of the ROI.[75]
- The fluctuations of the exchange rate of the different countries housing the subsidiaries must become the responsibility of the managers of the foreign subsidiaries. Assignment of such responsibility is difficult.[76]
- Wide variations in multinational corporations exist in order to approach and secure an overall balance between control and attention to local conditions.
- In comparing actual results with budgeted figures, there is a need to consider the explicit assumptions that are incorporated in the budget and the knowledge of how changes in these assumptions are likely to affect the budgeted numbers.[77]
- The purpose of evaluation—appraisal of an economic entity or of managerial performance—should dictate the selection of the information to be used and the choice of the basis of comparison.[78]

CURRENCY CONSIDERATIONS IN PERFORMANCE EVALUATION

Corporate Versus Subsidiary Emphasis

The control process of firms with foreign operations may be exercised as for domestic operations by a comparison between the actual profit performance and a budgeted profit performance based on forecast sales and expenses. Unlike the domestic operations, and because the basic operating budget of the subsidiary must be expressed in the parent company's currency for intercountry comparability, the future course of exchange rates and the choice of exchange rates in the control process have a definite impact on the performance evaluation of subsidiaries. Given this impact of the choice of exchange rates on performance evaluation, two decisions have to be made:

1. The first decision may be deciding who should set these exchange rates in the budgeting and control process. If, as suggested by various normative models, these exchange rates are set centrally, this may create negative behavioral patterns in subsidiaries where operating managers may think that their performances are being influenced by exchange risk policies over which they have no control. A more behaviorally sound solution is to give the subsidiaries' operating managers responsibility for fi-

nancial decisions in general and for setting foreign exchange rates in particular. If this decentralized solution is chosen, the problem is to control any attempt by the operating managers to "suboptimize," that is, to choose policies that may not be optimal from a corporate point of view as a result of an overreaction to exchange risks.

2. The second decision is whether to use the local currency and/or the home currency for the performance evaluation of foreign subsidiaries. Movements in exchange rates have an effect on the operating performance of foreign subsidiaries. There are also limitations in the use of either the home or local currency. As stated by Kirsch and Johnson:

Thus, when the *home currency* is used for evaluation purposes, it is necessary to have performance measures which accurately convert subsidiary foreign currency net worth into parent currency and also incorporate the effects of exchange rate movements on foreign subsidiary operating revenues and expenses. When the local currency is used, comparability of subsidiaries in different currency environments is difficult to achieve. If all subsidiaries are evaluated using the home currency, achieving performance evaluation which is equitable to subsidiaries operating in different currency environments is hindered. However, firms must use one or both, recognizing that there are the above mentioned limitations.[79]

Impact of Fluctuating Exchange Rates

The planning and control systems of a multinational corporation requires a choice of an exchange rate for both the budgeting phase and control phase of a foreign subsidiary. Research to date has considered four possible exchange rates that are usable in the setting of operations budgets and five possible exchange rates to be used in the comparison between actual and budgeted performance.[80, 81, 82]

The potential exchange rates that can be used in the budget-setting phase include the actual spot rate at the time the budget is prepared, a forecast average rate for the budget period, a forecast rate at the end of the budget period, and the ending rate obtained by continuously updating the budgeted rate to reflect changes in the exchange rates.

The five potential exchange rates that can be used in the performance evaluation include the actual rate at the time the budget was prepared, the forecast average rate for the budget period, the forecast rate at the end of the budget period, the actual average rate for the budget period, and the actual exchange rate at the end of the period.

Although in general, twenty different combinations can be used (see Exhibit 5.6), only nine combinations—*A1, A4, A5, B2, B4, B5, C3, C5,* and *D5*—can be used for the performance evaluation of foreign subsidiaries.

1. A_1: Actual exchange rate at the time of setting the budget for budgeting and actual exchange rate at the time of setting the budget for comparing results. The focus in this approach is on the local currency, leading managers to poten-

Exhibit 5.6
Combinations of Exchange Rates Used for Budgeting Cross-Tabulated with
Exchange Rates Used for Performance Evaluation

Rates Used for Performance Evaluation

Rates Used for Determining Budgets	Initial	Forecast (Average)	Forecast (End of Period)	Actual (Average)	Actual (Ending)
Initial	A1	A2	A3	A4	A5
Forecast (Average)	B1	B2	B3	B4	B5
Forecast (End of Period)	C1	C2	C3	C4	C5
Actual (Continuously Updated)	D1	D2	D3	D4	D5

tially ignore the impact of anticipated exchange rate changes in their operating results. Demirag gives the example of a sales manager in a weak currency who is evaluated on the basis of the actual spot rate at the time of sale, rather than the forecast rate prevailing at the time of receivables being collected, and who may well be motivated in uneconomical credit sales.[83]

2. A_4 and A_5: Actual exchange rate at the time of setting the budget for budgeting and actual exchange rate at the end of the period for comparing results. Under this approach, the local managers bear full responsibility for the exchange rate fluctuations, and some undesirable outcomes may result:

It is likely that this method could encourage managers to be risk-averse, perhaps by "engaging in hedging activities that are less than optimal from a corporate standpoint. This is because the risk preferences of individual foreign subsidiary managers are likely to be different and tend to have a narrower horizon on currency risk than those of corporate headquarters with a larger portfolio of assets. Hence operating decisions" made by foreign subsidiary managers, given their perceptions of risk preferences, may not be in the best interest of the corporation as a whole. Furthermore, this approach could lead local managers to pad their budgets in order to absorb some of the impact of exchange rate changes.[84]

3. D_5: Actual exchange rate at the end-of-period for budgeting (budgeted rates continuously updated) and actual exchange rate at the end-of-period for comparing results. Foreign subsidiary managers have a focus on local currency using the same rate.

4. B_2 and C_3: Forecast exchange rate for budgeting and forecast exchange rate for comparing results. Lessard and Lorange favor these combinations. The

forecast rates are viewed as "internal forward rates," because their use is analogous to the treasurer's acting as a backer and "buying forward" receipts in foreign currencies at a guaranteed rate. As a result, these combinations exclude unplanned exchange rate fluctuations but acknowledge expected fluctuations at the budgeting stage. The management control criteria used to support the choice of internal forward exchange rates as the basis to decision making and performance evaluation are goal congruence and fairness. As stated by Lessard and Lorange:

Goal congruence is restored because a corporate-wide point of view has been brought to bear on the currency exchange rates, eliminating decisions taken on the basis of the expectations and risk-preferences of local managers, who necessarily have a narrower horizon on the currency risk problem than the corporate headquarters. Fairness is restored, at least in regard to the exchange rate fluctuations, by the establishment of a standard under which the local decision maker gets no blame or credit for currency fluctuations outside of the division manager's control.[85]

5. B_4, B_5, and C_5: Forecast end-of-period or forecast average exchange rate for budgeting and actual end-of-period or actual average rate for comparing results. This approach allows the subsidiary manager to request an "internal forward rate" that best reflects the anticipation of exchange rate changes and adjust the operations of the subsidiary, during the budget period. A good evaluation of these combinations follows:

Under this approach, the performance of managers may depend on how well they have forecast the exchange rates rather than on their ability to cope with exchange rate changes. But the responsibility for the forecasting error would provide the incentive to adjust managerial decisions, such as changing currencies of denominations for export sales, preparing imported inputs etc. As long as the managers have significant opportunities to adjust to exchange rate changes, this approach appears supportable. If, however, the foreign subsidiary managers have very little flexibility for reacting to and lessening the impact of adverse exchange rate changes, then they may be encouraged to use speculative and redundant foreign exchange risk management policies.[86]

To illustrate the impact of these nine logical combinations upon performance evaluation against a budget, Kirsch and Johnson used a simple example.[87] The example as well as the outcome of performance evaluation are shown in Exhibit 5.7. The total variance in each is equal to a volume variance plus a foreign exchange-rate variance. Combinations (1), (2), (3), and (9) yield a positive volume variance and a foreign exchange-rate variance equal to zero. The responsibility of the foreign subsidiary manager is limited to the volume variance. Combinations (4), (6), (7), and (8) yield a positive volume variance and a positive foreign-exchange-rate variance due to the different rates used for budgeting and for control. These combinations are evaluated as follows:

Exhibit 5.7
Demirag's Logical Combinations of Foreign Exchange Rates (FXRs):
Variance Analysis Example

FACTS

Expected volume	1,000 units	Actual volume	800 units
Expected LC price	1 LC	Actual LC price	1 LC
Initial exchange rate	1 LC = $0.50	Actual exchange rates:	
Forecast exchange rates:		Average	1 LC = $0.35
Average	1 LC = $0.40	End of period	1 LC = $0.20
End of period	1 LC = $0.25		

Budget	Actual

(1) Initial by Initial

$$\frac{\text{Expected}}{\text{volume}} \times \frac{\text{Expected}}{\text{LC price}} \times \frac{\text{Initial}}{\text{FXR}} = \text{Budget} \qquad \frac{\text{Actual}}{\text{volume}} \times \frac{\text{Actual}}{\text{LC price}} \times \frac{\text{Initial}}{\text{FXR}} = \text{Performance}$$

$$1,000 \times 1 \times \$0.50 = \$500 \qquad\qquad 800 \times 1 \times \$0.50 = \$400$$

Total variance = Volume variance + FXR variance
[$500 - 400] = [200 units x ($0.50)] + 0
$100 = $100 + 0

(2) Forecast (avg.) by Forecast (avg.)

$$\frac{\text{Expected}}{\text{volume}} \times \frac{\text{Expected}}{\text{LC price}} \times \frac{\text{Forecast}}{\text{(avg.)FXR}} = \text{Budget} \qquad \frac{\text{Actual}}{\text{volume}} \times \frac{\text{Actual}}{\text{LC price}} \times \frac{\text{Forecast}}{\text{(avg.) FXR}} = \text{Performance}$$

$$1,000 \times 1 \times \$0.40 = \$400 \qquad\qquad 800 \times 1 \times \$0.40 = \$320$$

Total variance = Volume variance + FXR variance
[$400 - 320] = [200 units x ($0.40)] + [1,000 x ($0.40-0.40)]
$80 = $80 + 0

(3) Forecast [End of period (EOP)] by Forecast (end of period)

$$\frac{\text{Expected}}{\text{volume}} \times \frac{\text{Expected}}{\text{LC price}} \times \frac{\text{Initial}}{\text{FXR}} = \text{Budget} \qquad \frac{\text{Actual}}{\text{volume}} \times \frac{\text{Actual}}{\text{LC price}} \times \frac{\text{Forecast}}{\text{(avg.) FXR}} = \text{Performance}$$

$$1,000 \times 1 \times \$0.25 = \$250 \qquad\qquad 800 \times 1 \times \$0.25 = \$200$$

Total variance = Volume variance + FXR variance
[$250 - 200] = $30 + 0
$50 = $50 + 0

(Continued)

Source: Kirsch, Robert J., and Wayne Johnson, "The Impact of Fluctuating Exchange Rates on Budgeting for, and Performance Evaluation of, Foreign Subsidiaries," *International Journal of Accounting* 26, no. 3 (1991), p. 154–155.

Budget	Actual

(4) Initial by Actual (average)

$$\begin{array}{c}\text{Expected} \\ \text{volume}\end{array} \times \begin{array}{c}\text{Expected} \\ \text{LC price}\end{array} \times \begin{array}{c}\text{Forecast} \\ \text{(avg.)FXR}\end{array} = \text{Budget} \qquad \begin{array}{c}\text{Actual} \\ \text{volume} \\ \text{price}\end{array} \times \begin{array}{c}\text{Actual} \\ \text{LC price}\end{array} \times \begin{array}{c}\text{Forecast} \\ \text{(avg.) FXR}\end{array} = \text{Performance}$$

$$1,000 \times 1 \times \$0.50 = \$800 \qquad\qquad 800 \times 1 \times \$0.35 = \$280$$

Total variance = Volume variance + FXR variance
[$500 - 280] = [200 units x ($0.35)] + [1,000 x ($0.50-0.35)]
$220 = $70 + $150

(5) Forecast (avg.) by Actual (avg.)

$$\begin{array}{c}\text{Expected} \\ \text{volume}\end{array} \times \begin{array}{c}\text{Expected} \\ \text{LC price}\end{array} \times \begin{array}{c}\text{Initial} \\ \text{FXR}\end{array} = \text{Budget} \qquad \begin{array}{c}\text{Actual} \\ \text{volume}\end{array} \times \begin{array}{c}\text{Actual} \\ \text{LC price}\end{array} \times \begin{array}{c}\text{Forecast} \\ \text{(avg.) FXR}\end{array} = \text{Performance}$$

$$1,000 \times 1 \times \$0.40 = \$400 \qquad\qquad 800 \times 1 \times \$0.35 = \$280$$

Total variance = Volume variance + FXR variance
[$400 - 280] = [200 units x ($0.35)] + [1,000 x ($0.50-0.35)]
$120 = $70 + $50

(6) Initial by Actual (ending)

$$\begin{array}{c}\text{Expected} \\ \text{volume}\end{array} \times \begin{array}{c}\text{Expected} \\ \text{LC price}\end{array} \times \begin{array}{c}\text{Forecast} \\ \text{(avg.)FXR}\end{array} = \text{Budget} \qquad \begin{array}{c}\text{Actual} \\ \text{volume}\end{array} \times \begin{array}{c}\text{Actual} \\ \text{LC price}\end{array} \times \begin{array}{c}\text{Forecast} \\ \text{(avg.) FXR}\end{array} = \text{Performance}$$

$$1,000 \times 1 \times \$0.50 = \$500 \qquad\qquad 800 \times 1 \times \$0.20 = \$160$$

Total variance = Volume variance + FXR variance
[$500 - 160] = [200 units x ($0.20)] + [1,000 x ($0.50-0.20)]
$340 = $40 + 300

(7) Forecast (avg.) by Actual (EOP)

$$\begin{array}{c}\text{Expected} \\ \text{volume}\end{array} \times \begin{array}{c}\text{Expected} \\ \text{LC price}\end{array} \times \begin{array}{c}\text{Forecast} \\ \text{(avg.)FXR}\end{array} = \text{Budget} \qquad \begin{array}{c}\text{Actual} \\ \text{volume}\end{array} \times \begin{array}{c}\text{Actual} \\ \text{LC price}\end{array} \times \begin{array}{c}\text{Forecast} \\ \text{(avg.) FXR}\end{array} = \text{Performance}$$

$$1,000 \times 1 \times \$0.40 = \$400 \qquad\qquad 800 \times 1 \times \$0.20 = \$160$$

Total variance = Volume variance + FXR variance
[$400 - 160] = [200 units x ($0.20)] + [1,000 x ($0.40-0.20)]
$240 = $40 + 200

(Continued)

Budget	Actual

(8) Forecast (EOP) by Actual (EOP)

$$\underset{\text{volume}}{\text{Expected}} \times \underset{\text{LC price}}{\text{Expected}} \times \underset{\text{(avg.)FXR}}{\text{Forecast}} = \text{Budget} \qquad \underset{\text{volume}}{\text{Actual}} \times \underset{\text{LC price}}{\text{Actual}} \times \underset{\text{(avg.) FXR}}{\text{Forecast}} = \text{Performance}$$

$$1{,}000 \times 1 \times \$0.25 = \$250 \qquad\qquad 800 \times 1 \times \$0.20 = \$180$$

Total variance = Volume variance + FXR variance

$$[\$250 - 160] = [200 \text{ units} \times (\$0.20)] + [1{,}000 \times (\$0.25\text{-}0.20)]$$

$$\$90 = \$40 + 50$$

(9) Actual (updated continuously) by Actual (EOP)

$$\underset{\text{volume}}{\text{Expected}} \times \underset{\text{LC price}}{\text{Expected}} \times \underset{\text{(avg.)FXR}}{\text{Forecast}} = \text{Budget} \qquad \underset{\text{volume}}{\text{Actual}} \times \underset{\text{LC price}}{\text{Actual}} \times \underset{\text{(avg.) FXR}}{\text{Forecast}} = \text{Performance}$$

$$1{,}000 \times 1 \times \$0.20 = \$200 \qquad\qquad 800 \times 1 \times \$0.20 = \$160$$

Total variance = Volume variance + FXR variance

$$[\$200 - 160] = [200 \text{ units} \times (\$0.20)] + [1{,}000 \times (\$0.20\text{-}0.20)]$$

$$\$40 = \$40 + 0$$

Combinations (4) and (6) employ initial exchange rates for budgeting and actual exchange rates for evaluation, thus placing responsibility for currency movements upon the local operating managers, while combinations (7) and (8) employ forecast exchange rates for budgeting, thereby incorporating expected currency fluctuations at the budgeting stage, and actual exchange rates for evaluation; thus, unexpected foreign exchange rate variations are highlighted. Combination (5) smoothes the difference between the budget and performance evaluation exchange rates by averaging the fluctuations in actual exchange rates over the period. Thus, if the same foreign exchange rate is used for budgeting and performance evaluation, foreign subsidiary management is held accountable for volume variance only; foreign exchange fluctuations are lost. Use of *different exchange* rates for budgeting and performance evaluation highlight both volume variance and foreign exchange rate variance. The *magnitude of both variances*, volume and foreign exchange rate, depends upon the spread between the value *of the budgeting* exchange rate and the performance evaluation exchange rate.[88]

Hard Currencies versus Soft Currencies

Hard currencies tend to be less volatile than soft currencies, causing subsidiaries in hard currency countries to experience less adverse currency fluctuations than those in soft currency countries. Exhibit 5.8 shows the coefficients of exchange rate variations for industrialized and nonindustrialized countries for first quarter 1986 through third quarter 1989.[89] It shows the existence of both hard currency and soft currency countries and a significant difference in mean variation between the groups. On the basis of these results, Kirsch and Johnson suggested that multinational corporations should use different performance evaluation techniques in hard currency environments versus soft currency environments.[90] Exhibit 5.9 shows that multinationals in the United States used different performance evaluation techniques in hard and soft currency countries.

Hyperinflationary Versus Non-Hyperinflationary Countries

The preceding analysis has been found to be inadequate in evaluating affiliates located in countries experiencing hyperinflation and rapid exchange-rate devaluation, where it may yield distorted results.[91] Jacque and Lorange suggested that under these extreme operating conditions of monetary hyperinflation, multinational firms should upgrade, or "environmentalize," their control systems by removing from an affiliate's operating results any variance that is due to economic exposure and therefore uncontrollable.

Another improvement is the use of a purchasing power parity–normalized approach. Stewart suggested the use in performance evaluation of a "normalized" exchange rate, computed as the exchange rate that would exist if the market were properly adjusted for the purchasing power parity over the short run.[92] The rationale is that in the short run, the exchange rate fluctuates and, as a result of nonmarket factors, fails to return to the purchasing power parity conditions. The suggested adjustment of the exchange rate can correct for the

Exhibit 5.8

Coefficients of Exchange Rate Variation for Industrialized and Nonindustrialized Countries: First Quarter 1986 through Third Quarter 1989

Country group	Coefficient of variation	
	End of quarter national currency value of the SDR	End of quarter average market exchange rates of national currency (percentage variation)
Industriaized		
Pegged to other composite		
Austria	4.094	9.642
Finland	3.07	8.343
Norway	2.07	5.691
Sweden	0.97	6.374
Cooperative arrangements		
Belgium	3.717	9.104
Denmark	3.688	8.86
France	2.784	7.444
Germany	4.25	9.792
Italy	8.938	7.394
Luxembourg	3.717	9.104
Netherlands	4.308	9.879
Spain	3.179	8.453
Independently floating		
Canada	5.585	6.401
Japan	5.639	11.057
UK		-
US	5.751	-
Group means		
industrialized country currency values	4.117	8.395

(Continued)

Country group	Coefficient of variation	
	End of quarter national currency value of the SDR	End of quarter average market exchange rates of national currency (percentage variation)
Less industrialized		
pegged to US dollar		
Afghanistan	5.751	-
Antigua & Barbuda	5.751	-
Bahamas	10.871	-
Barbados	5.751	-
Belize	5.751	-
Dijbouti	5.751	-
Dominica	5.751	-
El Salvador	5.751	-
Ethiopia	5.751	-
Grenada	5.751	-
Guatemala	19.074	23.996
Guyana	77.399	78.612
Haiti	5.751	-
Honduras	5.751	-
Liberia	5.751	-
Nicaragua	224.7	225.313
Oman	5.751	-
Panama	5.751	-
Peru	203.55	174.757
St Lucia	5.751	-
St Vincent	5.751	-
Suriname	5.751	-
Syrian Arab Rep.	53.4	51.417
Trinidad & Tobago	10.607	8.31
Uganda	86.897	87.478
Yemem Arab Republic	10.6	18.444

(Continued)

Country group	Coefficient of variation	
	End of quarter national currency value of the SDR	End of quarter average market exchange rates of national currency (percentage variation)
Pegged to French franc		
Benin	2.784	7.445
Burkina Faso	2.784	7.445
Cameroon	2 .784	7.445
C.African Republic	2.784	7.445
Chad	2.784	7.445
Comoros	2.784	7.445
Congo	2 .784	7.445
Cote d'Ivoire	2 .784	7.445
Equatorial Guinea	2 .784	7.445
Gabon	2 .784	7.445
Mali	2 .784	7.445
Niger	2.784	7.445
Senegal	2.784	7.445
Togo	2.784	7.445
Pegged to SDR		
Brundi	16.445	14.196
Iran	-	5.736
Myanmar	-	5.704
Rwanda	5.662	5.953
Seychella	-	5.72
Pegged to other composite		
Algeria	22.684	21.551
Bangladesh	7.196	2.363
Fiji	16.18	12.238
Hungary	12.159	10.511
Iceland	17.567	17.233

(Continued)

Country group	Coefficient of variation	
	End of quarter national currency value of the SDR	End of quarter average market exchange rates of national currency (percentage variation)
Israel	12.036	10.216
Kenya	12.89	10.267
Malawi	17.884	15.281
Malaysia	6.053	3.121
Mauitius	8.357	7.486
Nepal	12.461	10.166
Poland	89.944	90.26
Romania	2.848	7.521
Solomon Islands	13.169	10.154
Somalia	63.606	62.063
Tanzania	48.59	47.615
Thailand	4.209	1.602
Vanuatu	6.001	5.822
More flexibility - other managed floating		
Argentina	268.209	267.682
China P.R.	9.41	4.933
Costa Rica	18.254	14.888
Dominican Rep.	36.732	34.568
Ecuador	58.295	57.865
Egypt	5.751	-
Greece	8.956	8.448
India	12.606	10.594
Indonesia	15.901	12.526
Jamaica	6.185	2.018
Korea	9.099	10.754
Mauritania	6.805	5.0198
Mexico	46.946	44.76
Morocco	1.324	4.669
Pakistan	10.794	8.256
Singapore	4.213	4.392
		(Continued)

Country group	Coefficient of variation	
	End of quarter national currency value of the SDR	End of quarter average market exchange rates of national currency (percentage variation)
Sri Lanka	13.277	10.528
Tunisia	10.05	7.917
Yugoslavia	182.425	183.502
More flexibility- independently floating		
Bolivia	16.385	13.513
Gambia	6.398	6.762
Ghana	39.715	38.216
Lebanon	71.298	70.013
Maldives	15.221	11.513
Nigeria	48.566	48.098
Paraguay	45.323	45.198
Philippines	6.729	2.358
Uruguay	52.701	52.156
Venezuela	59.704	56.577
Zaire	67.389	67.561
Flexibility limited - single currency		
Qatar	5.751	-
Saudi Arabia	6.105	0.691
United Arab Emirates	5.751	-
More flexible adjusted to set of indicators		
Brazil	187.972	189.116
Chili	15.741	12.207
Columbia	27.112	25.096
Madagascar	34.761	32.43
Portugal	5.589	5.828

(Continued)

Country group	Coefficient of variation	
	End of quarter national currency value of the SDR	End of quarter average market exchange rates of national currency (percentage variation)
Group mean less industrialized country currency values	26.68	25.113
Results of two tailed t-test of equality of means of Industrialized and less industrialized country groups of SDR & US dollar value of foreign exchange rates	-4.728	-3.559
Significance level	0.0001	0.0006

Source: Kirsch, Robert J., and Johnson, Wayne, "The Impact of Fluctuating Exchange Rates on Budgeting for, and Performance Evaluation of, Foreign Subsidiaries," *International Journal of Accounting* 26, no. 3 (1991), p. 169–172. Reprinted with permission.

distortions caused by the fluctuations. An illustration of such an adjustment follows:

	Period 1	Period 2
Jourdanian price index	100	140
US price index	100	120
Ratio: Jourdanian to US	JDO.600 / $	JDO.700 / $
Actual exchange rate	JDO.600 / $	JDO.7056 / $

The PPP normalized rate for the translation of assets and profits and the computation of the rate of return are judged the most appropriate measures of foreign operating performance for the following reasons:

• They reflect the underlying real performance of the local economy and of local operating managers.

• They reflect the cost of sustaining real holding losses on monetary assets that must be compensated for by a higher return in the business.

Exhibit 5.9
Combinations of Exchange Rates Used for Budgeting Cross-Tabulated with
Exchange Rates Used for Performance Evaluation: A Tabular Summary (%)

	Kirsch/ Johnson Study		Demirag Study
	Hard Currency Countries	Soft Currency Countries	
Initial by Initial	10.20%	5.41%	35.30%
Forecast (average and end of period) by Forecast (average and end of period)	26.53%	27.03%	31.70%
	6.12%	13.51%	0.00%
Actual (Continuously updated by Actual (ending)	6.12%	8.11%	1.10%
Actual (Continuously updated) by Actual (ending)	8.16%	0.00%	9.20%
Initial by Actual (average and ending)			
Forecast (average and end of period) by Actual (average and ending)	30.62%	29.73%	16.50%
Total	87.75%	83.79%	93.80%

Source: Kirsch, Robert J., and Johnson, Wayne, "The Impact of Fluctuating Exchange Rates on
Budgeting for, and Performance Evaluation of, Foreign Subsidiaries," *International Journal of
Accounting* 26, no. 3 (1991), p. 164. Reprinted with permission.

- They include holding gains that, after translation, would be commensurate with U.S. inflation, making it directly comparable to costs of capital experienced in dollars (which, of course, implicitly incorporates U.S. inflation).

- They are equally applicable for countries that experience appreciating exchange values realized by investors.

- The use of normalized exchange rates forces management, both local and corporate, to see through distortions caused by the temporary suspension of fundamental economic forces and to incorporate anticipated currency changes into forward planning.[93]

CONCLUSION

The organization and control of foreign operations reveal their complexity when multinational firms experiment to find the options that fit the specific characteristics of their operations. This chapter has identified various issues and questions in need of further research and investigation with the aim of better implementing management control systems internationally.

NOTES

1. Fligstein, Neil, "The Spread of the Multidivisional Firm among Large Firms," *American Sociological Review* 30 (June 1985), pp. 377–391.

2. Chandler, A. D., Jr., *Strategy and Structure* (Cambridge, MA: MIT Press, 1962).

3. Ibid., p. 13.

4. Williamson, O., *Markets and Hierarchies* (New York: Free Press, 1975).

5. Ibid., p. 133.

6. Hamman, M., and J. Freeman, "The Population Ecology of Organizations," *American Journal of Sociology* 92, (1977), pp. 929–964. See also Hamman and Freeman, "Structural Inertia and Organizational Change," *American Sociological Review* 49 (1984), pp. 149–164.

7. Fligstein, "The Spread of the Multidivisional Firm," p. 379.

8. Pfeffer, Jeffrey, *Power in Organizations* (Marshfield, MA: Pitman, 1981). See also *Organizations and Organization Theory* (Marshfield, MA: Pitman, 1982); Pfeffer, J, and G., Salanick, *The External Control of Organizations: A Resource Dependency Perspective* (New York: Harper and Row, 1978).

9. DiMaggio, Paul, and Walter Powell, "Institutional Isomorphism," *American Sociological Review* 48 (1983), pp. 147–160.

10. Fligstein, "The Spread of the Multidivisional Firm," p. 380.

11. Chandler, *Strategy and Structure.*

12. Williamson, *Markets and Hierarchies.*

13. Hoskisson, R. E. "Multidimensional Structure and Performance: The Contingency of Diversification Strategy," *Academy of Management Journal* 30, (1987), pp. 625–644.

14. Harrigan, K. R., "Vertical Integration and Corporate Strategy," *Academy of Management Journal* 28 (1985), pp. 397–425.

15. Kerr, J. L., "Diversification Strategy and Managerial Rewards: An Empirical Study," *Academy of Management Journal* 28 (1985), pp. 155–179.

16. Ackerman, R. W., "Influence of Integration and Diversity on the Investment Process," *Administrative Science Quarterly* 15 (1970), pp. 341–351.

17. Lorsch, J. W., and S. A., Allen, *Managing Diversity and Independence* (Boston: Harvard University, Graduate School of Business Administration, Division of Research, 1973).

18. Dundas, K. N. M., and P. R. Richardson, "Implementing the Unrelated Product Strategy," *Strategic Management Journal* 3 (1982), pp. 287–301.

19. Teece, D. J., "Economies of Scope and the Scope of the Enterprise," *Journal of Economic Behavior and Organization* 1 (1980), pp. 223–247.

20. Riahi-Belkaoui, A., "Multinational Structure and Productivity: The Contingency of Diversification Strategy," *Journal of Business Finance and Accounting* 15 (June 1999), pp. 615–628.

21. Porter, M. E., *Competitive Advantage: Creating and Sustaining Superior Performance* (New York: Free Press, 1985).

22. Kerr, "Diversification Strategy and Managerial Rewards."

23. Robinson, Richard D., *Internationalization of Business: An Introduction* (Hinsdale, IL: Dryden, 1984), p. 84.

24. Egelhoff, W. G., "Strategy and Structure in Multinational Corporations: An Information Processing Approach," *Administrative Science Quarterly* 27 (1982), pp. 435–

458; Daniels, J. D., R. A. Pitts, and M. J. Tretter, "Strategy and Structure of U.S. Multinationals: An Exploratory Study," *Academy of Management Journal* 27, no. 2 (June 1984), pp. 292–307.

25. Brooke, M. Z., and H. L. Remmers, *The Strategy of the Multinational Enterprise* (New York: Elsevier, 1970).

26. Davidson, W. H., and P. Hasjeslagh, "Shaping a Global Product Organization," *Harvard Business Review* 17 (March–April 1982), pp. 69–76.

27. Drake, Rodman, and Lee M. Caudill, "Management of the Large Multinational Trends and Future Challenges," *Business Horizons* 24, (May–June 1981), p. 85.

28. Ibid., p. 86.

29. Mintzberg, H., *The Structure of Organizations* (Englewood Cliffs, NJ: Prentice-Hall, 1978).

30. Egelhoff, "Strategy and Structure in Multinational Corporations," p. 440.

31. Drake, and Caudill, "Management of the Large Multinational," p. 7.

32. Naylor, Thomas H., "The International Strategy Matrix," *Columbia Journal of World Business* (Summer 1985), pp. 11–19.

33. Ibid., p. 11.

34. Ibid., p. 12.

35. Sheglitz, H., *Organizational Structures of International Companies*, Studies in Personnel Policy no. 198 (New York: National Industrial Conference Board, 1965), p. 5.

36. Committee on International Accounting, "Report," *The Accounting Review*, suppl. 48 (Summer 1973), p. 135.

37. Ibid., p. 136.

38. Chandler, *Strategy and Structure*.

39. Chandler, A. D. Jr., "The Multi-Unit Enterprise: A Historical and International Comparative Analysis and Summary," in H. F. Williamson, (ed.), *Evolution of International Management Structures* (Newark: University of Delaware Press, 1975), pp. 292–307.

40. Daniels, Pitts, and Tretter, "Strategy and Structure of U.S. Multinationals," pp. 292–307.

41. Stopford, J. M., and L. T. Wells, *Managing the International Enterprise* (New York: Basic Books, 1972).

42. Prabolad, C. K., "Strategic Choices in Diversified Multinational Corporations," *Harvard Business Review* 55 (1977), pp. 127–136.

43. Knickerbocker, F. T., *Oligopolistic Reaction and Multinational Enterprise* (Cambridge, MA: Harvard University, Graduate School of Business, Division of Research, 1974).

44. Egelhoff, "Strategy and Structure in Multinational Corporations," pp. 435–458.

45. Ibid., pp. 453–454.

46. Davis, Stanley M., "Trends in Organization of Multinational Organizations," *Columbia Journal of World Business* (Summer 1976), p. 59.

47. Robbins, Sidney M., and Robert B. Stobaugh, "Evolution of the Finance Function," in *Money in the Multinational Enterprise* (New York: Basic Books, 1973); reprinted as "Growth of the Financial Function," *Financial Executive*, July 1973, pp. 24–31.

48. Egelhoff, William G., "Information Processing Theory and the Multinational Enterprise," *Journal of International Business Studies* 27, no. 3 (1991), p. 346.

49. Thompson, James D., *Organizations in Action* (New York: McGraw-Hill, 1967), p. 13.

50. Galbraith, Jay R., *Organizational Design* (Reading, MA: Addison-Wesley, 1977).

51. Egelhoff, "Information Processing Theory and the Multinational Enterprise," p. 350.

52. Ibid., p. 351.

53. Child, J. T., "Strategy and Control and Organizational Behavior," *Administrative Science Quarterly*, March 1973, p. 117.

54. Ouchi, W. G., "The Relationship between Organizational Structure and Control," *Administrative Science Quarterly*, (March 1977), pp. 95–112.

55. Baliga, B. A., and A. M., Jaeger, "Multinational Corporations: Control Systems and Delegations Issues," *Journal of International Business Studies* (Fall 1984), pp. 25–40.

56. Thompson, J. D., *Organizations in Action* (New York: McGraw-Hill, 1967).

57. Lawrence, P. R., and J. W. Lorsch, *Organization and Environment* (Homewood, IL: Irwin, 1967).

58. Burns, T., and G. M. Stalker, *The Management of Innovation*, 2nd ed. (London: Tavistock, 1964).

59. Baliga and Jaeger, "Multinational Corporations," p. 33.

60. Ibid., p. 34.

61. Herbert, Theodore T., "Strategy and Multinational Organization Structure: An Interorganizational Relations Perspective," *Academy of Management Review* 9, no. 2 (1984), pp. 259–271.

62. Rutenberg, D. P., *Multinational Management* (Boston: Little Brown, 1982), p. 12.

63. Perimutter, Howard, "The Tortuous Evolution of the Multinational Corporation," *Columbia Journal of World Business* (January–February, 1969), pp. 9–18.

64. Robbins and Stobaugh, "Evolution of the Finance Function," p. 25.

65. Gupta, A. K., and V. Govindarayan, "Knowledge Flows and the Structure of Control within Multinational Corporations," *Academy of Management Review* 16, no. 4, (1991), pp. 768–792.

66. Ibid.

67. Doz, Y. L., "Managing Manufacturing Rationalization within Multinational Companies."

68. Lessard, D. R., "Transfer Price, Taxes, and Financial Markets: Implications of International Financial Transfers with the Multinational Firms;" in R. G. Hawkins (ed.), *The Economic Effects of Multinational Firms* (Greenwich, CT: JAI Press, 1979), pp. 101–125.

69. Bartbelt, C. A., and S. Ghoshel, *Managing across Borders: The Transnational Solution* (Boston, MA: Harvard University Press, 1989).

70. Egelhoff, W. G., *Organizing the Multinational Enterprise: An Information Processing Perspective* (Cambridge, MA: Ballinger, 1988).

71. Stewart, G. B., "EVA: Fact and Fantasy," *Journal of Applied Corporate Finance* 10 (Summer 1994), 15–21.

72. Ibid.

73. Steward, G. B., III *The Quest for Value* (New York: Harper Business, 1991).

74. Ibid.

75. Committee on International Accounting, "Report," *The Accounting Review*, suppl. 48 (Summer 1973), pp. 120–136.

188 International Financial and Managerial Accounting

76. Ibid., p. 92.

77. Spillar, Earl A., Jr., "Return on Investment: A Need for Special Purpose Information," *Accounting Horizons*, (June 1988), pp. 1–9.

78. Kirsch, Robert J., and Wayne Johnson, "The Impact of Fluctuating Exchange Rates in U.S. Multinational Corporate Budgeting for, and Performance Evaluation of, Foreign Subsidiaries," *The International Journal of Accounting* 26, no. 3 (1991), p. 151.

79. Demirag, Isteni S., "The Treatment of Exchange Rates in International Performance Evaluation," *Accounting and Business Research*, Spring 1986, pp. 157–164.

80. Lessard, Donald R. and Lorange, Peter, "Currency Changes and Management Control: Resolving the Centralization/Decentralization Dilemma," *The Accounting Review* (July 1977), pp. 628–637.

81. Kirsch and Johnson, "The Impact of Fluctuating Exchange Rates," pp. 149–173.

82. Demirag, "The Treatment of Exchange Rates in International Performance Evaluation," p. 158.

83. Ibid., p. 159.

84. Lessard and Lorange, "Currency Changes and Management Control."

85. Ibid., p. 634.

86. Demirag, "The Treatment of Exchange Rates in International Performance Evaluation," p. 160.

87. Kirsch and Johnson, "The Impact of Fluctuating Exchange Rates," p. 53.

88. Ibid., p. 153.

89. Ibid., pp. 169–172.

90. Ibid., p. 151.

91. Jacque, Laurent L., and Peter Lorange, "The International Control Conundrum: The Case of Hyperinflationary Subsidiaries," *Journal of International Business Studies* (Fall 1984), pp. 185–201.

92. Stewart, G. Bennet, "A Proposal for Measuring International Performance," *Midland Corporate Finance Journal* (Summer 1983), pp. 57–71.

93. Ibid., p. 71.

SELECTED READINGS

Abdullah, Wagdy. *Internal Accountability: An International Emphasis*. Ann Arbor, MI: UMI Research Press, 1984.

Chandler, A. D., Jr. *Strategy and Structure*. Garden City, NY: Anchor, 1966.

Choi, F. D. S., and I. J. Czechowicz. "Assessing Foreign Subsidiary Performance: A Multinational Comparison." *Management International Review*, 4 (1983), pp. 14–25.

Committee on International Accounting. "Report." *The Accounting Review*, suppl. 48 (Summer 1973), pp. 120–136.

Daniels, J. D., R. A. Pitts, and M. J., Tretter. "Strategy and Structure of U.S. Multinationals: An Exploratory Study," *Academy of Management Journal* 27, no. 2, (June 1984), pp. 292–307.

DiMaggio, Paul, and Walter Powell. "Institutional Isomorphism." *American Sociological Review* 48 (1983), pp. 147–160.

Egelhoff, W. G. "Strategy and Structure in Multinational Corporations: An Information Processing Approach." *Administrative Science Quarterly* 27 (1982), pp. 435–458.

Fligtein, Neil. "The Spread of the Multidivisional Firm among Large Firms" *American Sociological Review* (June 1985), pp. 377–391.

Hamman, M., and J. Freeman. "The Population Ecology of Organizations." *American Journal of Sociology* 92 (1977), pp. 929–964.

———. "Structural Inertia and Organizational Change," *American Sociological Review* 49 (1984), pp. 149–164.

Jacque, Laurent L., and Peter Lorange. "The International Control Conundrum: The Case of Hyperinflationary Subsidiaries." *Journal of International Business Studies* 15 (Fall 1984), pp. 185–201.

Lessard, Donald R., and Peter Lorange. "Currency Change and Management Control: Resolving the Centralization/Decentralization Dilemma." *The Accounting Review* (July 1977), pp. 628–637.

Naylor, Thomas H. "The International Strategy Matrix." *Columbia Journal of World Business* 10 (Summer 1985), pp. 11–19.

Perimutter, Howard. "The Tortuous Evolution of the Multinational Corporation." *Columbia Journal of World Business* 15 (January–February 1969), pp. 9–18.

Pfeffer, Jeffrey. *Organizations and Organization Theory.* Marshfield, MA: Pitman, 1982.

———. *Power in Organizations.* Marshfield, MA: Pitman, 1981.

Pfeffer, J., and G. Salanick. *The External Control of Organizations: A Resource Dependency Perspective.* New York, Harper and Row, 1978.

Spillar, Earl A., Jr. "Return on Investment: A Need for Special Purpose Information." *Accounting Horizons* (June 1988), pp. 1–9.

Williamson, O. *Markets and Hierarchies.* New York: Free Press, 1975.

6

Analyzing Foreign Financial Statements and Disclosure Innovativeness

INTRODUCTION

This chapter elaborates on the use and misuse of financial ratios in financial analysis in an international setting. The financial statements of multinational firms are shown to potentially contain information that (1) meets local standards, (2) meets international accounting standards, and (3) contains innovative information following the adoption of segmental reporting, employee reporting, and value-added reporting.

There are definitely known benefits to those foreign and U.S. investors who favor international portfolio diversification. The financial analysis of foreign financial statements demands, however, a special approach to account for the various problems and diversities that characterize the global economy. In addition, the financial information can be used and incorporated in special predictive models for the explanation and prediction of economic events taking place in foreign countries. Accordingly, this chapter evaluates the use and misuse of accounting information for analyzing foreign financial statements, as well as the innovative information that can be found in the financial statements of multinational firms. The chapter assumes that the analysis takes place in a strong public securities market.

Black[1] argues that there are two essential prerequisites for strong public securities markets. A country's laws and related institutions must give minority shareholders: (a) good information about the value of a company's business; and (b) confidence that the company's insiders will not cheat investors out of the value of their investment. He maintains that institutions necessary for the existence of capital markets include (a) extensive financial disclosure, including independent audits of public rules that address investors' need for reliable information; (b) a rule-writing institution with the competence and independence to write good accounting rules and an incentive to keep the rules up to date; (c) a sophisticated accounting profession with the skill and experience to catch at least some instances of false or misleading disclosure; and (d) securities or other laws that impose on accountants enough risk of liability to investors if the accountants have endorsed false or misleading financial statements so that the accountants will resist their clients' pressure for more favorable disclosure.[2]

Business Analysis

Business analysis rests on using data from financial statements and data based on the business context. The analysis tools of business include:[3]

a. a business strategy analysis: to produce performance expectations through industry analysis and competitive strategy analysis

b. an accounting analysis: to evaluate accounting quality by assessing accounting policies and estimates

c. a financial analysis: to evaluate performance using ratios and cash flow analysis

d. a prospective analysis: to make forecasts and value business

Business Strategy Analysis

The business strategy analysis is based on suggestions from the research on industrial organization on the influence of industry structure on profitability. It suggests that the average profitability is influenced by the following five forces:[4]

1. the rivalry of new entrants

2. the threat of new entrants

3. the threat of substitute products

4. the bargaining power of buyers

5. the bargaining power of suppliers

Two generic competitive strategies—(1) cost leadership, by supplying the same product or service at lower cost, or (2) differentiation by supplying a unique product or service at a lower cost than the price premium customers will pay— can potentially allow a multinational firm to build a sustainable competitive advantage.[5]

Accounting Analysis

Accounting analysis focuses on examining the three factors that may influence accounting quality and create noise and bias in accounting data: "(1) the noise and bias introduced by rigidity in accounting rules, (2) random forecast errors, and (3) systematic reporting choices made by corporate managers to achieve specific objectives."[6]

For example, management may make accounting choices:

a. to meet certain contractual obligations in the firm's debt covenants

b. to maximize management compensation

c. to trade off between financial reporting and tax considerations

d. to influence regulatory outcomes

e. to influence the perception of capital markets

f. to influence the perception of shareholders

g. for competitive considerations [7]

Accounting analysis therefore requires:

a. an analysis of the accounting policies

b. an assessment of accounting flexibility

c. an evaluation of the quality of disclosure

d. an undoing of accounting distortion.[8]

In the U.S. context, some consumer red flags are:

• "Unexplained changes in accounting, especially when performance is poor

• Unexplained transactions that boost profits

• Unusual increases in accounts receivable in relation to sales increases

• Unusual increases in inventories in relation to sales increases

• An increasing gap between a firm's reported income and its cash flow from operating activities

• A tendency to use financing mechanisms such as research and development partnerships and the sale of receivables with recourse.

• Unexpected large asset write-offs

• Large fourth-quarter adjustments

• Qualified audit opinions or changes in independent auditors that are not well justified.

• Related-party transactions or transactions between related entities"[9]

Financial Analysis

Financial analysis rests on the intelligent use of ratios for assisting users in the evaluation of the financial soundness of firms. In effect, financial analysis rests principally on the use of financial ratios. These ratios reflect "significant relationships" between various items in the financial statements. The ratios are generally compared to established standard ratios for the firm or for other firms in the same industry. If the comparison is with similar ratios of the firm over a certain number of years, the analysis is referred to as time-series analysis. If the comparison is with similar ratios of other firms over a certain number of years, the analysis is referred to as cross-sectional analysis. Whatever the type of analysis chosen, ratio analysis is used to evaluate important financial aspects of the firm that best depict its financial strengths. Examples include liquidity, leverage, profitability, and turnover dimensions. Some of the types of ratios used to measure these dimensions are presented next. They are classified into four major categories: (1) the firm's ability to meet its short-term obligations, (2) the capital structure of the firm and its ability to meet its long-term obligations, (3) the profitability and efficiency resulting from operational use of its assets, and (4) the inventory and receivables turnover. Some of the most popular ratios are summarized in Exhibit 6.1.

A comprehensive way of evaluating a firm's ratios is through the use of the concept of sustainable growth. A firm's sustainable growth is defined as the rate at which it can grow while keeping its profitability and financial policies unchanged. Basically,

$$\text{Sustainable growth rate} = \text{ROE} \times (1 - \text{Dividend payout ratio})$$

The dividend payout ratio (DPR) is defined as:

$$\text{DPR} = \frac{\text{Cash dividends}}{\text{Net income}}$$

The decomposition of sustainable growth rate proceeds as follows:

$$\text{ROE} = \frac{\text{Net income}}{\text{Shareholders' equity}} = \frac{\text{Net income}}{\text{Sales}} = \frac{\text{Net income}}{\text{Assets}}$$
$$\times \frac{\text{Assets}}{\text{Shareholders' equity}} = \text{ROA} \times \text{Financial leverage} \tag{1}$$

$$\text{ROA} = \frac{\text{Net income}}{\text{Assets}} = \frac{\text{Net income}}{\text{Sales}} \times \frac{\text{Sales}}{\text{Assets}}$$
$$= \text{Net profit margin or return in sales} \times \text{Asset turnover} \tag{2}$$

Exhibit 6.1
Summary of Main Financial Ratios

RATIOS	NUMERATOR	DENOMINATOR
A. Liquidity		
1. Current Ratio	-Current Assets	-Current liabilities
2. Quick Ratio	-Cash + short-term investments + accounts receivable	-Current liabilities
3. Cash Ratio	-Cash + short-term investments	-Current liabilities
4. Operating Cash flow Ratio	-Cash flow from operations	-Current liabilities
5. Defensive Internal Measure	-Total defensive assets	-Projected daily operating expenditures
B. Leverage		
1. Liabilities to equity	-Total liabilities	-Shareholders' equity
2. Debt to equity	-Short-term debt + long-term debt	-Shareholders' equity
3. Debt to capital	-Short-term debt + long-term debt	-Short-term debt + long-term debt + shareholders' equity
4. Interest coverage (earnings basis)	-Net income + interest expense + tax expense	-Interest expense
5. Interest coverage (cash basis)	-Cash flow from operations + interest paid + taxes paid	-Interest paid
6. Net-debt-to-equity ratio	-Short-term debt + long-term debt— cash and marketable securities	-Shareholders' equity
7. Net-debt-to-net capital ratio	-Interest-bearing liabilities—cash and marketable securities	-Interest-bearing liabilities— cash and marketable securities + shareholders' equity
C. Profitability		
1. Rate of return on assets (ROA)	-Net income	-Assets
2. Pre-interest ROA	-Net income + interest expense (1-tax ratio)	-Assets
3. Rate of return on net assets	-Net income + interest expense (1-tax ratio)	-Equity + debt
4. Operating ROA	-Net income + (interest expense – interest income) × (1-tax rate)	-Equity + debt – cash and short-term investments
5. Rate of return on equity (ROE)	-Income available for stockholders	-Stockholders' equity
6. Net profit margin or ratio of return on sales	-Sales	-Assets
7. Dividend pay-out ratio	-Cash dividends paid	-Net income
8. Gross profit margin	-Sales—cost of goods sold	-Sales
9. Net operating profit after taxes (NOPAT)	-Net income + net interest expense after tax	
10. NOPAT margin	-NOPAT	-Sales
11. EBITDA margin	-Earnings before interest, taxes, depreciation and amortization	-Sales

$$ROE = \text{Return in sales} \times \text{Asset turnover} \times \text{Financial leverage} \qquad (3)$$

$$\text{Sustainable Growth Rate} = (\text{Return on sales} \times \text{Asset turnover} \times \text{Financial leverage}) \times (1 - \text{Dividend payout ratio}) \qquad (4)$$

Therefore, the firm's sustainable growth rate is linked to most of the ratios identified in Exhibit 6.1 and the equations can be used as the benchmark against which a firm's growth rate can be evaluated.

Another possible decomposition of ROE proceeds as follows:

D. Turnover		
1. Current asset turnover	-Sales	-Current assets
2. Working capital turnover	-Sales	-Current assets – current liabilities
3. Accounts receivable turnover	-Sales	-Accounts receivable
4. Inventory turnover	-Cost of goods sold	-Inventory
5. Accounts payable turnover	-Cost of goods sold	-Accounts payable
6. Days' receivables	-Accounts receivable	-Average sales per day
7. Days' inventory	-Inventory	-Average cost of goods sold per day
8. Days' payables	-Accounts payable	-Average cost of goods sold per day
9. Property, plant and equipment turnover	-Sales	-Property, plant and equipment
10. Operating working capital	-(Current assets—cash and marketable securities) – (current liabilities – short-term and current portion of long-term debt)	
11. Operating working capital-to-sales ratio	-Operating working capital	-Sales
12. Operating working capital turnover	-Sales	-Operating working capital
13. Net long-term assets	-Total long-term assets—non-interest-bearing long-term liabilities	
14. Net long-term asset turnover	-Sales	-Net long-term assets
E. New Metrics		
1. Economic Value Added (EVA)	-(Net operating profit after tax) -(WAAC×Capital employed)	
2. Cash Flow Return on Investment (CFROI)	-Profit from continuing operations -cash taxes + depreciation	-Cash investments
F. Market Performance		
1. Total shareholder return	-Share price at end of the year -share price at the beginning of year + dividends	-Share price at the beginning of the year.

$$ROE = \frac{NOPAT}{Equity} - \frac{Net\ interest\ expense\ after\ tax}{Equity} \tag{5a}$$

where

Net interest expense after tax = (interest expense − interest income) × (1 − tax rate)

Net operating profit after taxes (NOPAT) = Net income + net interest expense after tax.

$$ROE = \frac{NOPAT}{Net\ assets} \times \frac{Net\ assets}{Equity} - \frac{Net\ interest\ expense\ after\ tax}{Net\ debt}$$
$$\times \frac{Net\ debt}{Equity} \tag{5b}$$

where

Net debt = Total interest-bearing liabilities—cash and marketable securities

Net assets = Operating working capital + Net long-term assets

Operating working capital = (Current assets − cash and marketable securities) − (Current Liabilities—short-term debt and current portion of long-term debt)

Net long-term assets = Total long-term assets—non-interest-bearing long-term liability

$$\text{ROE} = \frac{\text{NOPAT}}{\text{Net assets}} \times (1 + \frac{\text{Net Debt}}{\text{Equity}})$$
$$\qquad - \frac{\text{Net interest expense after tax}}{\text{Net debt}} \times \frac{\text{Net debt}}{\text{Equity}} \qquad (5c)$$

where

net capital = net debt + shareholders' equity

ROE = Operating ROA + (Operating ROA − Effective interst rate after   (5d)
      tax) × Net financial leverage

ROE = Operating ROA + Spread × Net financial leverage   (5e)

Accordingly, the sustainable growth may be computed in two ways, as follows:

Sustainable growth rate = (Operating ROA + Spread × Net financial   (5f)
leverage)(1 − dividend payout ratio)

Sustainable growth rate = ([Net Operating profit margin × operating asset (5g)
turnover] + [Spread × Net financial leverage] [1 − dividend payout ratio])

Valuation Analysis

Valuation analysis of foreign firms, like of domestic firms, can be made using any of the four following methods:

1. discounted dividends model, where by the value of the firm's equity is equal to the present value of forecasted future dividends
2. discounted abnormal earnings, where the value of the firm's equity is equal to the sum of its book value and discounted forecasts of "abnormal earnings"
3. *price multiples-based valuation model*, whereby a price-to-earnings ratio, price-to-book ratio or price-to-sales ratio is applied to either earnings, book value or sales to obtain the value of the firm's equity
4. *discounted cash flow analysis*, whereby the value of the firm's equity is equal to the present value of forecasts of cash flow at the firm's estimated cost of capital

In all these approaches, the equity of the firm can be computed directly. Another way is to value the assets of the firm first and then deduct the value of net debt to arrive at the value of equity estimate. Because of its complexity, the discounted abnormal earnings approach is presented here. Basically, the equity and asset valuation formulas will be as follows:

$$\text{Equity value} = BVE_0 + \frac{NI_1 - r_e \times BVE_0}{(1 + r_e)}$$
$$+ \frac{NI_2 - r_e \times BVE_1}{(1 + r_e)^2} + \frac{NI_3 - r_e \times BVE_2}{(1 + r_e)^3} \cdots \tag{1}$$

where

BVE_t = book value of equity at the end of year t

NI_t = net income available to common shareholders for year t

r_e = cost of equity capital

$$\text{Equity value to book value ratio} = 1 + \frac{ROE_1 - r_e}{(1 + r_e)} + \frac{(ROE_2 - r_e)(1 + gbve_1)}{(1 + r_e)^2}$$
$$+ \frac{(ROE_3 - r_e)(1 + gbve_1)(1 + gbve_2)}{(1 + r_e)^3} + \cdots \tag{2}$$

where

ROE_t = return on beginning book equity for year t

$gbve_t$ = growth in book equity from year $t - 1$ to year t, or $\dfrac{BVE_t - BVE_{t-1}}{BVE_{t-1}}$

r_e = cost of equity capital

$$\text{Asset value} = BVA_0 + \frac{NOPAT_1 - WACC \times BVA_0}{(1 + WACC)_e}$$
$$+ \frac{NOPAT_2 - WACC \times BVA_1}{(1 + WACC)^2} + \cdots \tag{3}$$

where

BVA_t = book value of assets at the end of year t

$NOPAT_t$ = net operating profit after tax for year t

$WACC$ = weighted-average cost of debt and equity capital

$$\text{Asset value-to-book ratio} = 1 + \frac{ROA_1 - WACC}{(1 + WACC)} + \frac{(ROA_2 - WACC)(1 + gbva_1)}{(1 + WACC)^2}$$
$$+ \frac{(ROA_2 - WACC)(1 + gbva_1)(1 + gbva_2)}{(1 + WACC)^3} \tag{4}$$

where

ROA_t = ratio of $NOPAT$ in year t to beginning-of-year operating assets

$gbva_t$ = growth in book assets from year $t - 1$ to year t, or $\dfrac{BVA_t - BVA_{t-1}}{BVA_{t-1}}$

$WACC$ = weighted-average cost of debt and equity capital

FINANCIAL AND VALUATION ANALYSIS APPLIED INTERNATIONALLY

The analysis of foreign financial statements and the use of financial ratios for such analysis are fraught with several problems, which are discussed in this section. It is generally agreed that the most important means of communication with stockholders is the annual report. The extent of disclosure adequacy in the annual report may be a major determinant of the quality of investment decision making in particular and economic resource allocation in general. There is, however, a marked difference in disclosure adequacy from one country to another.

Although the general situation in most developing countries is characterized by data availability and accessibility, various countries still suffer from the lack of either timely reliable accounting information and/or computerized databases. The timeliness of the information is best characterized by the time delay between the year-end date and the date of the auditor's report, averaging from 31 to 60 days, in countries such as Brazil, Canada, and the United States, to 121 days and over in countries such as Austria and Italy.

The usefulness of financial statement information seems to differ from one country to another. In the United Kingdom, the evidence supports the usefulness of financial statement information.[11] A comparison of international investors, individual investors, and financial analysts from the United States, New Zealand, and Europe, however, showed intercountry differences in the importance attached to some parts of the corporate annual report.[12]

Investment in foreign security markets is on the increase for investors eager to capitalize on higher rates of growth anywhere in the world and for corporations searching for distant markets where they can raise capital and reduce their cost of capital. There is, however, the fact that accounting principles, disclosure requirements, and auditing standards vary between countries. These differences can be real, in the sense of affecting after-tax corporate cash flows, or nominal, in the sense of affecting internally reported accounting values.[13] The following result is implied by the accounting diversity:

"Accounting diversity, therefore, holds the possibility of leading to a real economic difference by changing managerial decisions, corporate cash flows, or analysts' evaluation of the firm. But accounting diversity may have only a nominal impact (i.e., a change in accounting numbers but not a change in market values) if the accounting rules affect only non-cash flow items, do not affect the variables that managers use for decision making, or do not affect evaluation of the firm by external analysts.[14]

In the first case of real differences, reinstatement to common methods would obscure the real cash flow differences between the two firms. In the second case, the same market value should be achieved in spite of the different accounting methods and restatement should allow the user to "see through" the nominal differences.

Choi showed the connection between accounting diversity and economic environments. The following results are presented:

1. an ideal situation in which the economic situation of the firms and the accounting treatments are similar and where the accounting statements of the two firms can be used for comparative analysis

2. a situation in which the financial statements of the two firms are not (by themselves) suitable for comparative analysis because the economic situations of the two firms are dissimilar, even though the accounting treatments are similar

3. a situation in which the economic situation of two firms is similar but the accounting treatments are dissimilar. This is a situation in which the adoption of similar accounting treatments may or may not be a suitable response. Choi and Levich illustrate the point with the following example:

For example, an airline that depreciates aircraft over five years (because these aircraft make thousands of takeoffs and landings per year) is not similarly situated to an airline that flies long-haul routes and depreciates its aircraft over ten years. Use of the same accounting rule (in this case straight-line depreciation) allows this economic difference to be highlighted.

However, suppose that the dissimilarity between the two firms pertains to the definition of income, or the rules available for computing taxes, or the cultural accounting variables that influence managerial performance measures and compensation. In this case the adoption of similar accounting treatments would only obscure the dissimilarities between the two firms. As a result, when the economic situation of firms is dissimilar, the adoption of similar accounting treatments may or may not be a suitable response.[15]

4. a situation in which both the economic situations of the two firms and the accounting treatments are dissimilar and, therefore, direct comparison between the two firms may be difficult.[16]

There is definitely a need to translate the financial statements into the language of the potential analyst. In making the linguistic translation from one language to another, there has to be an awareness of the different worldviews that can be created by the newly translated financial statements (as expressed in the hypothesis of linguistic relativism), the different social classes or different professional affiliations (as expressed by the sociolinguistic thesis in accounting), and the special needs and capabilities of bilinguals (as expressed by the bilingual thesis in accounting).[17] One major difference between the U.S. GAAP and European GAAP is the use in Europe of various types of reserves to deal with inflation. Some European countries, such as France, Greece and Spain, require that companies revalue to current costs at the same time. The other countries allow their companies to revalue at their discretion. The other reserves include statutory reserves intended to profit creditors by retaining some profits permanently as assets, general reserves, and hidden reserves in the form of asset understatements or liability overstatements.

A standardization method of analysis and presentation of company accounts developed by the European Federation of Financial Analysts Societies (EFFAS) can be used to compute a figure that can be used as a basis for earnings forecasts and the computations of ratios. What has been done is an exclusion from the profit of various discretionary transfers to or from reserves and of any exceptional provisions. Gray used these figures for a sample of companies from France, West Germany, and the United Kingdom to compute a conservation index as follows:[18]

$$1 - \frac{Ra - Rd}{|Ra|}$$

where Ra = adjusted profit
   Rd = disclosed profit

A negative index implies a conservative approach in the measurement of profit. The results showed intensive conservatism in Germany and a similar conservatism in Germany and a similar conservatism in France. The following explanation is provided.

All of the foregoing suggests that the discretion is likely to be the preserve of the United Kingdom with its emphasis on flexibility. But although uniform accounting principles and forms of presentation are specified in France and Germany, there remains considerable scope for flexibility in application and for such discretion to manifest itself in a more conservative view of profits. The most significant areas of flexibility are indeed those identified by the analysts and concern transfers to and from reserves, and the creation and write-back of provisions for various risks and special purposes including those which are designed to gain tax advantages. These can be used to create hidden or secret reserves and to smooth out bias fluctuations in profits.[19]

Ratios can be misused when they do not take into account the specific institutional characteristics of each country. This misuse was best illustrated in a study that F. D. S. Choi et al.[20] undertook to compare firms from Japan, Korea, and the United States using ratio analysis. Before any adjustment, the ratios suggest that Japanese and Korean firms are less profitable and efficient and bear a higher financial risk than their U.S. counterparts. In fact, however, the high leverage of Japanese firms is acceptable in Japan because the Keiretsu network allows for interdependency between banks and their industrial borrowers. As stated by Choi et al.:

Interdependence was fostered among Keiretsu group companies through financial, commercial and personal ties. Under such arrangements, the relationships between the borrowing company, related companies, and their banks are very close. Cross shareholdings between borrower, related companies, and the bank are common. Today, their relationship has evolved to the point where a bank would seldom impose financial penalties on delayed interest payments nor call a delinquent loan from a related company; instead, the lending bank would typically postpone interest and principal repayments and, in some instances, even refinance the loan on more liberal terms. It is common practice for the lending bank to install a bank official as president or board member of the troubled company to provide it with helpful managerial assistance.[21]

Similarly, the high leverage of Korean firms is attributed to the larger role assumed by governments in corporate finance, which includes tax and trade privileges, special financing, foreign currency loans secured by bank guarantees, and subsidized interest rates. This role of government is more pronounced in firms belonging to the Korean *chaebol* which are giant conglomerates or financial cliques unique to the Korean corporate sector, characterized by concentrated family ownership and management. In fact, a study of corporate debt and dividend policies of Korean companies showed that, for a fixed level of growth opportunities, *chaebol* carry a higher level of debt.[22] The role of Korean banks is also different:

Another feature of Korean lending practice is that corporate borrowers are not classified into credit risk categories with interest rates scaled accordingly. Rather, the more bank debt a company has, the greater the bank's stake in the success of the enterprise, and the higher the probability that the bank views the debt with alarm. High debt ratios in Korea signify a company's close ties with its bank which, in turn, signify a company's favorable association with the government.[23]

The situation shows higher liquidity in the United States than in Japan and Korea. The Japanese situation is explained by (1) their preference for short-term debt, (2) the tendency to sell their accounts receivable without recourse, and (3) the potential understatement of marketable securities compared to market values. The Korean situation is due to their continuous use of short-term financing as a substitute for long-term financing. In the process, short-term debt is a misnomer in the Korean context and is, in fact, long term. The situation shows higher turnover ratios in the United States than in Japan and Korea. For example, the collection period is 86 days in Japan, 33 days in Korea, and 43 days in the United States. The reason may be related to the 60 to 120 additional days given in Korea to cope with the scarcity of capital and to the Japanese tradition of lifetime employment.

Another example relates to the high fixed asset turnover in the United States compared to Japan and Korea. The situation in Korea is due to the enormous investments made in plants and equipment and to the understatement of sales revenues caused by government price controls imposed on domestic goods to stem inflation and imposed on exports to penetrate overseas markets. Finally, the situation shows higher profit margins and return on total assets in the United States compared to Japan and Korea. The focus on long-term profits in Japan and low pricing and margins in Korea form the potential explanation.

The assumption of nonnormality for the distribution of ratios was also verified in the case of a British sample. In addition, the deletion of outliers had a stronger impact on the data, in terms of improving approximation of normality, than did square root and natural logarithm transformation.

Earnings Management and Financial Analysis for U.S. Multinational Firms

Financial reporting allows a distinction between well-performing firms and poor-performing firms and a better and more efficient resource allocation and financial analysis by stakeholders. The U.S. accounting standards permit managers to exercise judgment in financial reporting, allowing them to provide, not only timely and credible information, but also relevant information under the alternative standards. The situation creates opportunities, however, for "earnings management," in which managers select reporting methods and estimates that do not reflect the firm's true economic picture. This led the chairman of the U.S. Securities and Exchange Commission (SEC), Arthur Levitt, to warn about the threat to the credibility of financial reporting created by abuses of "big bath" restructuring changes, premature revenue recognition, "cookie jar" reserves, and write-offs of purchased in-process research and development (R&D).[25] A good definition of earnings management follows: "Earnings management occurs when managers use judgement in financial reporting and in structuring transactions to alter financial reports to either mislead some stakeholders about the underlying economic performance of the company or to influence contractual outcomes that depend on reported accounting numbers."[26]

The detection of earnings management can be accomplished by:[27]

a. the use of simple analytical procedures, which can reveal unusual relationships and significant changes in financial statement item relationships

b. the use of sophisticated models to assess the risk of earnings manipulation, such as the use of artificial neural network technology to assess fraud[28]

c. the use of a probit model, which can yield an earnings manipulation index as a linear combination of financial variables to be converted to a "probability of manipulation"

The third technique is of interest to international accounting and can best be illustrated by the Beneish probit model.[29] With the objective of differentiating between GAAP violators and control firms, Beneish uses a number of variables to proxy for (1) the probability of detection of the violation by the market through distortions in the financial statements and (2) the incentive ability to violate GAAP.

The six financial statement variables designed to capture distortions in financial a statement data to assess the probability of detection are as follows (see also Exhibit 6.2):

1. day's sales in receivables index—measuring whether changes in receivables are in line with changes in sales

2. gross margin index—assessing whether gross margins have deteriorated, a negative signal about a firm's prospects

3. asset quality index—measuring changes in the risk of asset realization, with an increase to be interpreted as indicating an increased prosperity to capitalize and therefore defer costs

4. depreciation index—measuring the change in the rate of depreciation

5. SG&A index—measuring sales, general and administrative expense (SG&A) relative to sales, with a disproportionate increase in SG&A relation to sales to be considered as a negative signal suggesting a loss of managerial cost control or unusual sales effort

6. total accruals to total assets—measuring the extent to which earnings are cash based, with higher increases in noncash working capital to reflect possible manipulation[30]

The five variables intended to measure a firm's incentives ability to isolate GAAP are as follows[31]

1. Capital structure as the incentive to violate GAAP increases with leverage

2. Prior market performance as the incentive to violate GAAP increases with declining stock prices.

3. Time listed, as few may violate GAAP and manipulate earnings at the time of initially going public or shortly thereafter.

4. Sales growth, as high growth firms may have an incentive to dispel the impression that their growth is decelerating following a stock price drop or the release of bad news.

5. Prior positive accruals' decisions as incentive to violate GAAP may increase if managers attempt to accrue reversals or cannot increase earnings.

The five proxies are operationalized by six variables: leverage, abnormal return, time listed, sales growth index, declining cash sales dummy, and positive accruals dummy. They are defined in Exhibit 6.2.

The earnings manipulation index, proposed by Beneish probit analysis, is expressed as the following linear combination.

Exhibit 6.2
Variables Used in the Beneish (1997) Probit Model

Variable	Definition	Hypothesized Relationship With Dependant Variable
Days sales in receivable index	$$\frac{\dfrac{\text{Receivables}_t[2]}{\text{Sales}_t[12]}}{\dfrac{\text{Receivables}_{t-1}[2]}{\text{Sales}_{t-1}[12]}}$$	+
Gross Margin Index	$$\frac{\dfrac{\text{Sales}_{t-1}[12] - \text{COGS}_{t-1}[41]}{\text{Sales}_{t-1}[12]}}{\dfrac{\text{Sales}_t[12] - \text{COGS}_{t-1}[41]}{\text{Sales}_t[12]}}$$	+
Asset Quality Index	$$\frac{\left(1 - \dfrac{\text{Current Assets}_t[4] + \text{PPE}_t[8]}{\text{Total Assets}_t[6]}\right)}{\left(1 - \dfrac{\text{Current Assets}_{t-1}[4] + \text{PPE}_{t-1}[8]}{\text{Total Assets}_{t-1}[6]}\right)}$$	+
Depreciation Index	$$\frac{\dfrac{\text{Depreciation}_{t-1}[14\text{-}65]}{\text{Depreciation}_t[14-65] + \text{PPE}_{t-1}[8]}}{\dfrac{\text{Depreciation}_t[189]}{\text{Depreciation}_{t-1}[2]}}$$	+
SG&A Index	$$\frac{\dfrac{\text{SG\&A expense}_t[189]}{\text{Sales}_t[2]}}{\dfrac{\text{SG\&A expense}[189]}{\text{Sales}_{t-1}[2]}}$$	+
Total Accruals to Total Assets	$$\frac{\left[\begin{array}{c}(\Delta\text{Current Ass.}_t[4] - \Delta\text{Cash}_t[1]) - \\ (\Delta\text{Current Liab.}_t - \Delta\text{Short-term Debt}_t[341]- \\ \text{Deprec.\&Amort.}_t[14] - \text{Deferred tax on Earnings}[50]+ \\ \text{Equity in earnings}[55]\end{array}\right]}{\text{Total Assets}_t[6]}$$	?
Sales Growth Index	$\text{Sales}_t[12] / \text{Sales}_{t-1}[12]$	+
Abnormal Return	Size-adjusted return for a 12-month period ending on the month prior to the release of the financial statements. Computed by subtracting from the firm's buy-and-hold return the buy-and-hold return on size-matched, value-weighted portfolio of the firms.	-
Time Listed	Distance in months between the fiscal year end and the date the company was first listed on either the New York, American or NASDAQ exchange.	-
Leverage	$$\frac{\text{LTD}_{t-1}[9] + \text{Current Liabilities}_{t-1}[5]}{\text{Total Assets}_{t-1}[6]}$$	+
Positive Accruals Dummy	1 if total accruals were positive in the current and prior year; 0 otherwise.	+
Declining Sales Dummy	1 if cash sales in the current year were lower than in previous year: 0 otherwise. Cash sales$_t$ = Sales$_t$ − (Δ Receivables$_t$)	?

Note: Annual Compustat data items are provided in brackets. Δ means the change in the account from the previous year. *t* refers to the year of interest.

$$\text{Manipulation Index} = -2.224 + 0.221* \text{ (Day's Sales in Receivables Index)}$$
$$+ 0.102* \text{ (Gross Margin Index)} + 0.007* \text{ (Asset Quality Index)}$$
$$+ 0.062* \text{ (Depreciation Index)} + 0.198* \text{ (SG\&A Index)}$$
$$- 2.415* \text{ (Total Accruals to Total Assets)} + 0.40* \text{ (Sales Growth Index)}$$
$$- 0.684* \text{ (Abnormal Return)} - 0.001* \text{ (Time Listed)}$$
$$+ 0.587* \text{ (Leverage Index)} + 0.421* \text{ (Positive Accruals Dummy)}$$
$$- 0.413* \text{ (Declining Cash Sales Dummy)}$$

The probability of manipulation is then computed by looking up the Manipulation Index in a standard normal distribution table, where $F(x)$ is the cumulative area under the standard normal distribution. That is:

Probability of earnings manipulation $= F$ (manipulation index)

Beneish derives cut-off values based on different relative costs of Type 1 vs. Type 2 errors. A Type 1 error occurs when a GAAP violation is incorrectly classified as a control firm. Conversely, a Type 2 error occurs when a control firm is incorrectly classified as a GAAP violator.

The Beneish model relies on various cutoff values that can deliberate different levels of risk of earnings manipulation. A cutoff value of 11.72% results in only 45% of GAAP violators being correctly classified as being violators and only 3.6% of the control firm being incorrectly classified as violators. A cutoff value of 5.99% results in 67% of GAAP violators being correctly classified and 13.5% of control firms being incorrectly classified as violators. A cutoff value of 4.3% results in 76% of GAAP violators being incorrectly classified and 20.4% of control firms being incorrectly classified as violators. Finally, a cutoff value of 2.94% results in 83% of GAAP violators being incorrectly classified as violators and 28.6% of control firms being classified as violators. Selection of the appropriate cutoff depends on different decision values and different levels of risk.

Employee Reporting

Although the question of the final identity of users of financial reports continues to plague the accounting world, it is a well accepted fact in the literature and in practice that employees deserve to be considered as important users of financial reports during their recruitment.

Unions, as representatives of employees, also qualifiy as important users of accounting information, especially with the purpose of finding convincing arguments for their collective-bargaining positions. With the emergence of employees and unions as potential users of accounting information, it also appears, and for a good many reasons, that the annual report to shareholders is not the all-inclusive document suitable for all unions. The solution lies in the production of a special report to employees and unions. This solution has been accepted in many of country members of the OECD, including the United States, Germany, Canada, France, Denmark, Norway, Sweden, and the United Kingdom. The idea has been accepted, not only conceptually, but also operationally. For example, in the United Kingdom, the Corporate Report identifies employees as a user group of published company annual reports.[32] Therefore, the objective of this chapter is to review the literature on employee reporting with the purpose of providing answers on the factors influencing the phenomenon, the information needs of employees and unions, the content of this special report, and the role of the accountant. A sample employment report, included as an appendix to the Corporate Report, showed quantitative data under the following headlines:

1. number employed (analyzed in various ways)
2. location of employment
3. age distribution of permanent workforce
4. hours worked during the year (analyzed)
5. employee costs
6. pension information
7. education and training (including costs)
8. recognized trade unions
9. additional information (race relations, health and safety statistics, etc.)
10. employment ratios

In Canada, the Canadian Institute of Chartered Accountants published report in June 1980 entitled *Corporate Reporting: Its Future Evolution*.[33] The report explicitly identifies employees (past, present and future) as users of corporate reports. In Europe, the OECD called for the disclosure of the average number of employee in each geographical area as part of its guidelines for multinational enterprises. Similarly the EC's Fourth Council Directive, Article 43.1.9, called for disclosure in the annual reports of limited companies of the average number of persons employed during the past year, broken down by categories.

In France, following use of the recommendations of the Sudreau report, all enterprises employing more than 750 employees are required to supply their works councils, a committee of employee and management, the union representatives and the *inspector du travail* (an official of the French labor administration) with an annual social report (*le bilan social*) that reports on such matters as employment, wages, social costs, working conditions, and training and industrial relations. The International Confederation of Free Trade Unions (ICEI-U) calls for the disclosure of employee-related data in its list of public accountability requirements.[34]

The content of the report to employees has not been standardized yet. Consequently, the available alternatives vary in the level of qualification and sophistication. A survey of the relevant literature reveal the following report contents: (1) employee relationships, (2) future prospects (firm and employee), (3) statement of value-added, (4) corporate-government relationships, (5) corporate objectives, (6) cash flow, (7) where money came from and where it went, (8) profit and loss, (9) balance sheet, (10) social balance sheet, (11) break-even chart, (12) role of profits, (13) personnel-related information, (14) chairman's address, and (15) competitions to encourage readership.[35]

Similarly, the dissemination of the information varied. The same survey identified the following techniques used: (1) mailed directly to employees, (2) report issued plus a management meeting, (3) letter format, (4) newspaper, (5) slides and films, (6) radio, (7) notice boards, (8) video tapes, (9) pay packets, (10) a request, (11) supervisors, (12) financial training, and (13) integration with the total communication network.[36]

VALUE ADDED REPORTING

The Move toward Value-Added Reporting

Conventional reporting as it exists in most countries of the world includes a measurement and disclosure for (1) the financial position of the firm, through the balance sheet, (2) the financial performance of the firm, through the income statement, and (3) the financial conduct of the firm, through the statement of changes in cash flows. While the usefulness of the statements is testified to by their extensive use over time, they fail to give important information on the total productivity of the firm and the share of the team of members involved in management resources—namely, shareholders, bondholders, workers, and the government. The value-added statement is assumed to fill that crucial role.

Value-added refers to the increase in wealth generated by productive use of the firm's resources before its allocation among shareholders, bondholders, workers, and the government. Thus, the value-added may be obtained by adding pretax profit to payroll costs and interest charges. Another way of computing value-added is to deduct bought-in costs from sales revenue, where bought-in costs represent all costs and expenses incurred in buying goods and services from other firms.

The value-added statement can be traced back to the U.S. treasury in the eighteenth century.[37] It has remained a subject of debate, with attempts and/or suggestions made at various times for having it included in financial accounting practice.[38] The emergence and introduction of value-added taxation in the European countries gave impetus to value-added reporting, although the new type of tax did not require the computation of a value-added statement.

The value-added concept was given serious attention during the late 1970s in various European countries and achieved greater prominence in the United Kingdom with the publication of the *Corporate Report*, a discussion paper prepared by a working party drawn from the accounting bodies, which was published by the Accounting Standards Steering Committee (now the Accounting Standards Committee) in August 1975.[39] This report recommended, among other things, a statement of value-added, showing how the benefits of the efforts of an enterprise are shared between employees, providers of capital, the state, and reinvestment. The rationale for the value-added statement appears to be contained in paragraphs 6.7 and 6.10:

6.7 The simplest and most immediate way of putting profit into proper perspective vis-à-vis the whole enterprise as a collective effort by capital, management and employees is by presentation of a statement of value added (that is, sales income less materials and services purchased). Value added . . . is the wealth the reporting entity has been able to create by its own and its employees' efforts. This statement would show how value added has been used to pay those contributing to its creation. It usefully elaborates on the profit and loss account and in time may come to be regarded as a preferable way of describing performance. . . .

6.10 The statement of value added provides a useful measure to help in gauging performance and activity. The figure of value can be a pointer to the net output of the firm; and by relating other key figures (for example, capital employee costs) significant indicators of performance may be obtained.[40]

The recommendation was obviously accepted when one of the legislative proposals contained in a British government report, *The Future of Company Reports*, included a legislative proposal for a statement of value-added.[41] There, then followed an increasing number of companies each year producing value-added statements. One survey reported that one-fifth of the largest British companies disclosed value-added statements.[42] The growth of value-added reporting was helped by the trade unions' support of the concept. For example, a document produced by one of the trade unions stated the following: "The Federation therefore aims to encourage the use of the added value as a discipline, so that all managers, with or without experience of accounting practice, will appreciate the financial environment within which decisions affecting manpower are taken.[43]

To the labor movement the value-added report was deemed a good vehicle for information disclosure and a basis for determining wages and rewards, namely, what is termed the value-added incentive payment scheme (VAIPS).[44] In addition to these uses, Stuart Burchell, Colin Clubb, and Anthony Hopwood[45] mention its occasional use in the context of the performance of British industry,[46] in reforming company-wide profit sharing schemes,[47] and in facilitating financial performance analysis.[48] Aware of these developments, the various British accounting bodies produced research reports on the value-added concept, namely, the Institute of Chartered Accounting in England and Wales,[49] The Institute of Chartered Accountants Of Scotland,[50] the Institute of Cost and Management Accountants,[51] and the Association of Certified Accountants.[52]

The Structure of the Value-Added Statement

The value-added statement may be conceived as a modified version of the income statement. Consequently, it can be derived from the income statement as follows:

Step 1: The income statement computes retained earnings as a difference between sales revenues on one hand and costs, taxes and dividends on the other hand, thus:

$$R = S - B - DP - W - I - DD - T \tag{1}$$

where

R = retained earnings

S = sales revenue

B = brought-in materials and services

DP = depreciation

W = wages

I = interest

DD = dividends

T = taxes

Step 2: The value-added equation can be obtained by rearranging the profit equation as follows:

$$S - B = W + I + DP + DD + T + R \tag{2}$$

$$S - B - DP = W + I + DD + T - R \tag{3}$$

Equation (2) expresses the gross value-added method. Equation (3) expresses the net value-added method. Note that in either case, the left-hand part of the equation shows the value-added (gross or net) and the right-hand part shows the allocation of the value-added groups involved in the managerial production team, namely the workers, the shareholders, the bondholders, and the government. The right-hand side is known as the additive method and the left-hand side as the subtractive method.

Exhibit 6.3 shows how the value-added statement can be derived from a regular income statement. It shows how a company deducted bought-in material, services and depreciation from sales to arrive at a value-added of $2,120,000. The second part shows how the $2,120,000 was divided among the team of workers ($400,000) shareholders, ($100,000), bondholders ($120,000) and the government ($300,000), leaving $1,200,000 for retained earnings.

Exhibit 6.3
Deriving the Value-Added Statement

A. The conventional income statement of a company for 19×8 was:

			$
Sales:			3,000,000
Less:	materials used	200,000	
	Wages	400,000	
	Services purchased	600,000	
	Interest paid	120,000	
	depreciation	80,000	
Profit before tax			1,600,000
Income tax			300,000
Profit after tax			1,300,000
Less Dividend payable		100,000	
Retained earning for one year			1,200,000

B. A value added statement for the same year would be:

		$
Sales		3,000,000
Less: bought-in materials	880,000	
& services and depreciation		
Value added available for		2,120,000
distribution or retention		
Applies as follows:		
To employees:		400,000
To providers of capital		
Interest	120,000	
Dividends	100,000	220,000
To government		300,000
Retained earnings		1,200,000
Value added		2,120,000

Value Added-Based Financial Statement Analysis

Role of Value Added-Based Financial Analysis. The role of value added-based financial analysis is similar to that of conventional financial analysis, but with two notable differences. First, the ratios in the value-added–based financial analysis include net value-added or gross value-added as either a numerator or a denominator of the ratios. Second, the ratios in the value-added–based financial analysis are assumed to be better predictors of economic events affecting the firm than to conventional ratios. The value-added represents the total return of the firm and serves as a better basis if the computation of ratios is done to express relationships to total return rather than a less informative concept such as net income.

Managerial Efficiencies. Various value-added–based ratios have been proposed as indexes of managerial efficiency:

- Net value-added/total assets is considered a better expression of return on assets than the conventional profit/total assets ratio.
- Net value added/shareholders' equity is considered a better expression of return on equity than the conventional profit/shareholders' equity ratio.
- Net value added/common stock is considered a better expression of return on common stock than the conventional profit/common stock ratio.

In each of these ratios, net value-added expresses the total return to the firm compared to profit, which is only the return accruing to the shareholders. A value-added–based index as a measure of managerial efficiency is computed as follows:

$$\frac{\text{Value added or net output of the firm}}{\text{Costs of the inputs of labor and capital}}$$

Ball put forward the following argument for using a value-added–based measure of efficiency in preference to return on capital:

Efficiency measures are concerned with the interrelationship between inputs and outputs. Efficiency measurement consists in relating inputs to work done. But the work done by the firm is not measured by its profit or by its sales. Neither of these figures can be brought into relation with the resources employed by management.[53]

Contribution to Total Return. Value-added is the result of a team effort. The contribution of each member of a team can be assessed as well:

- Wages/net value-added is a good measure of labor's share of, and contribution to, the total return.
- Net profit/net value-added is a measure of the shareholders' share in the return pool.
- Taxation/net value-added is a measure of the government's share in the return pool.
- Interest expense/net value-added is a measure of the bondholders' share in the return pool.

These four ratios can be compared both for the same firm and across firms as well as for the same year and across years to indicate changes in the relative share in the return pool held by the shareholders, bondholders, workers, and government.

Measures of Vertical Integration. Value-added/sales has been suggested as a measure of vertical integration, with a fully integrated company having a ratio equal to one. Morley provides the following explanation:

For example, if a company owned forest plantation and felled its own timber and matured it and made wood products then its ratio of value added to sales would be high as the bought-in costs would be fairly low. However, a company which restricted itself to the manufacturing of wood products would have all its timber costs appearing as bought-ins and this would give a lower ratio of value added to sales.[54]

Value-added/sales can also be used as an index of vulnerability to disruptive actions affecting the supply of materials and services. Morley stated, "If the ratio is high, and bought-in costs are trivial, the company is safe from its suppliers who then have little commercial leverage or monopoly power over it."[55]

Immediate Benefit to Shareholders. Dividends payable/net value-added may be considered a good measure of wealth creation that is of immediate benefit to shareholders. It is superior to the conventional dividends payable/net profit ratio.

Firm's Flexibility. Depreciation plus retention/gross value-added may be considered a good measure of a firm's flexibility or ability to change. Similarly, investment (fixed assets and stock building) gross value-added may be considered a good measure of the extent to which the flexibility is exploited.

Research Intensity of the Firm. Research and development/net value-added may be used as an indicator of the research intensity of a firm. A high ratio reflects a managerial policy favorable to the research and development effort. It is clearly superior to the conventional ratio of research and development/profit, which shows only the proportion of research and development coming out of profit rather than the proportion deriving from the total return of the firm.

Productivity Measures. Productivity can be measured at various levels including (1) national economy, (2) industry, (3) intercompany, and (4) intracompany. It has been explained as follows:

"(1) National Economy Level: National Income (NI), Gross Domestic Product (GDP), National Economy Welfare Index, National Economy Productivity, etc.

(2) Industry-Level Productivity: Productivity by Industry and by Business.

(3) Intercompany-Level Productivity: Productivity within Specific Business Categories and According to Business Scale.

(4) Intracompany-Level Productivity: Management Planning and Value Added, Physical Productivity by Division and Production Process, etc."[56]

The focus in this book is on value-added as the basis of measurement of intracompany-level of productivity. Value-added can be used for the computation of the following value-added productivity indexes.[57]

Value-added productivity can be computed as:

Value-added/Number of employees

It can be broken down into the two factors of value-added ratio and sales per employee, as follows:

$$\text{Value-added productivity: } \frac{\text{Value-added}}{\text{Net sales}} \times \frac{\text{Net sales}}{\text{Number of employees}}$$

where Value-added ratio = Value-added/Sales, and Sales per employee = Net sales/Number of Employees

Similarly, the sales per employee may be broken down into the two factors of capital intensity and operating capital turnover rate, as follows:

$$\text{Sales per employee} = \frac{\text{Operating capital}}{\text{Number of employees}} \times \frac{\text{Net sales}}{\text{Operating capital}}$$
$$= \text{Capital intensity} \times \text{Capital turnover rate}$$

Operating capital is generally defined as follows:

Operating capital = (Total in assets balance sheet)—(Construction program payments and construction advance payments)—(Investments plus other assets)—(Stock issue costs, margin on bond issues, bond issue costs, interest during construction, extraordinary bonds)

Given that net value-added can be computed as the sum of interest, dividend, wages, taxes, and retained earnings, the value-added productivity may be then broken down into:

1. interest component as interest/number of employees, plus
2. dividends components as dividends/number of employees, plus
3. labor component as wages/number of employees, plus
4. tax components as tax/number of employees, plus
5. retained earnings competent as retained earnings/number of employees

Labor productivity can be computed as:

$$\text{Labor productivity} = \frac{\text{Value-added}}{\text{Manpower}}$$

where manpower can be measured by personnel cost, number of hours worked, other production factors, or the average number of employees.

The labor productivity can be broken down into production (sales) per employee and a value-added rate as follows:

$$\frac{\text{Value-added}}{\text{Manpower}} = \frac{\text{Production}}{\text{Manpower}} \times \frac{\text{Value-added}}{\text{Production}}$$

It follows that:

Labor productivity = Production per employee × Value-added ratio

Therefore, increasing labor productivity can be achieved by increasing one or both of the production per employee and the value-added ratios. Production per employee can be broken down into a labor equipment ratio and equipment utilization ratio as follows:

$$\frac{\text{Production}}{\text{Manpower}} = \frac{\text{Equipment}}{\text{Manpower}} \times \frac{\text{Production}}{\text{Equipment}}$$
$$= \text{Labor equipment ratio} \times \text{Equipment utilization ratio}$$

As a result, the production per employee will increase if one or both of the labor equipment and the equipment utilization ratios increases.
Capital productivity can be computed as follows:

Capital productivity = Value-added/Invested capital

Various measures may be used for invested capital, as follows:
The choice of total capital as a measure of invested capital leads to the following formula for total capital productivity:

Total capital productivity = Value-added/Average total capital

The choice of working capital as a measure of invested capital leads to the following formula for working capital productivity:

Working capital productivity = Value-added/Average working capital

The choice of tangible fixed assets as a measure of invested capital leads to the following formula for equipment capital productivity:

Equipment capital productivity = Value-added/Average tangible fixed assets

The capital productivity ratio can be broken down into a value added ratio and a capital utilization ratio as follows:

$$\frac{\text{Value-added}}{\text{Invested capital}} = \frac{\text{Value-added}}{\text{Production}} \times \frac{\text{Production}}{\text{Invested capital}}$$
$$= \text{Value-added ratio} \times \text{Capital utilization ratio}$$

The capital productivity can be linked to productivity by breaking productivity into capital productivity and capital's share as follows:

$$\frac{\text{Profit}}{\text{Invested capital}} = \frac{\text{Value-added}}{\text{Invested capital}} \times \frac{\text{Profit}}{\text{Value-added}}$$
$$= \text{Capital productivity} \times \text{Capital's share}$$

A more complete relation between productivity and profitability goes as follows. First,

$$\text{Wage level} = \frac{\text{Personnel cost}}{\text{Manpower}}$$

Second, wage level can be decomposed into labor productivity and labor's share, as follows:

$$\text{Wage level} = \frac{\text{Value-added}}{\text{Manpower}} \times \frac{\text{Personnel cost}}{\text{manpower}}$$
$$= \text{Labor productivity} \times \text{Labor's share}$$

Third, labor productivity can be decomposed into capital productivity and capital intensity, as follows:

$$\text{Labor intensity} = \frac{\text{Value-added}}{\text{Total capital}} \times \frac{\text{Total capital}}{\text{Manpower}}$$
$$= \text{Capital productivity} \times \text{Capital intensity}$$

Fourth, capital productivity can be decomposed into the value-added and capital utilization ratios as follows:

$$\text{Capital productivity} = \frac{\text{Value-added}}{\text{Production}} \times \frac{\text{Production}}{\text{Total capital ratio}}$$

Fifth, productivity was earlier decomposed into capital productivity and capital share. Given this decomposition of capital productivity, we may state profitability as the product of the value-added ratio, capital utilization ratio, and capital's share in two ways, as follows:

$$\frac{\text{Profit}}{\text{Total capital}} = \frac{\text{Value added}}{\text{production}} \times \frac{\text{Production}}{\text{Total capital}} \times \frac{\text{Profit}}{\text{Value-added}} \tag{1}$$

$$\text{Productivity} = \text{Value added ratio} \times \text{Capital utilization} \times \text{Capital's share} \tag{2}$$

Other Ratios and Indexes. Other ratios based on the value-added concept can also be proposed:

- Gross value-added or net value-added may be used as a good surrogate of size.
- Net value-added/annual interest payments may be used as a better measure of debt coverage than the conventional times interest earned.
- Cash plus marketable securities/net value-added may be used as measure of the relative cash position of a firm.
- Working capital from operation/net value-added and cash flow from operations may be used as measures of cash-generating abilities of firms.
- Net value-added/accounts receivable may be used as a measure of accounts receivable turnover.
- Net value-added/plan assets may be used as a measure of plant assets turnover.

Evaluation of Value Added Reporting

Although the concept has not yet reached the level of expansion experienced by more conventional modes of reporting, various authors have already examined some of the benefits and limitations associated with value-added reporting.

Advantages of Value-Added Reporting. The advantages of value-added reporting stem basically from the multidimential scope of the technique when compared to the conventional mode of reporting the financial affairs of a going concern. Among the most cited advantages are the following.

Value-added reporting generates a good organizational climate for the workers by highlighting their importance to the final results of the firm. What is expected from the disclosure of the value-added statement is a more favorable and positive attitude on the part of the employees toward their employing companies. Considering the employees as major participants in the making of the firm may act as good motivation for better work, more cooperation, and closer identification with the company.

Value-added reporting may provide a more practical way of introducing productivity bonus increases through linking rewards to changes in the value-added accounts.[58] A claim is also made that value added ratios may act as good diagnostic and predictive cues. In other words, they may be more useful than traditional measures in detecting or predicting economic events of importance to the firm.

Compared to traditional techniques, value-added reporting is more congruent with the concepts used to measure national income and may create a more useful link to the macroeconomic data bases and techniques used by economists. It is also useful to governments in measurement of national income, which involves aggregating (among other things) the value-added (net output) of firms.

The reason why value added rather than sales or the sales value of production (both measures of gross output) is used is to avoid "double counting" in the aggregation process, since the cost of materials and services which would be included in the gross output measures of one firm will probably already have been included in the gross output measures of its suppliers. Hence national income, if it involved aggregating gross outputs, would be a function of the degree of vertical integration in the economy. Thus, value added information from firms forms a useful function in macroeconomic measurement and forecasting from government's point of view. In line with this, therefore, it will presumably be useful to individual economists in constructing and testing explanatory models of the economy.[59]

There are, however, qualifications to the general rules equating the sum of the value-added by all companies to national income. Morley lists them as follows:

1. National income includes value added by government and by other public bodies. For example, the value-added by defense expenditure is assumed to be equal to its costs.
2. The value-added of a company may arise partly in foreign territories. Similarly, value may be added in the domestic country by a foreign concern.
3. Economic measures of national income concentrate on production rather than on sales. Differences arise, therefore, in the valuation of increases or decreases in inventory.
4. National income conventions involve several major simplifying assumptions which are not used by financial accountants. For example, the output of durable consumer goods is assumed to have been consumed in the year of manufacture. In effect, the economist depreciates a car by 100 percent in the first year, while the accountant would write off the company's fleet of vehicles at, say, 25 percent of cost in each year.[60]

Value added reporting may act as a measure of the size and importance of companies. It is a better measure of the net creation of wealth a company has achieved. Both sales and capital, generally used as surrogate for size, may be misleading. This case is argued as follows:

When an accountant is asked "Is BP bigger than ICI," his first reaction is to decide which is the best measure of size for the purpose in question. For some purposes Sales might be appropriate, but that figure can give a false impression if a large proportion of a company's turnover is merely representing the passing on to customers of costs incurred in buying-in from other companies. For some purposes, net capital employed may be appropriate, but this can overstate the company's importance if the industry is a very capital intensive one.[61]

Value-added reporting may be useful to the employee group because it could affect its aspirations and those of their negotiating representatives. Value-added reporting may be used as a measure of "relative equity," in relation to other stockholder groups. The same argument is made by Maunders:

This is because such a statement reveals (or should reveal) the comparative shares of each of the stockholder groups in the firm's net output for a given period. For this purpose compared with, say, the profit and loss account, it has the advantage that it shows explicitly what relative share each group takes. It should be noted, however, that its usefulness in this respect will be dependent on both its coverage and classification of group rewards.[62]

The rules may also be used as a measure of "ability to pay" and a measure of total productivity in the bargaining process.

Value-added reporting may be useful to the equity investor group. The argument has validity in that the value-added information could be related to the prediction of either the systematic risk of a firm's securities or the expected return and total risk of those securities, dependent on which view of the efficiency of the market is considered relevant. The link can be made by the possible indirect impact of value added in the earning of a firm. Maunders offers the following rationale:

Value added information can affect the conduct of collective bargaining and hence the company's future labor costs. Unless such changes in labor costs are exactly cancelled by increases in the value of output (an unlikely coincidence), company earnings will also change. So, on the presumption that we are able to show . . . that value added information may affect collective bargaining, we can also deduce that it is potentially useful to investors for forecasting a company's earning and, hence, the expected returns and total risk associated with securities.[63]

Disadvantages of Value Added Reporting. It is naturally expected that while some see advantages to the adoption of value added reporting, others will only see disadvantages. Among the disadvantages, we may cite the following:

Value-added reporting relies on the erroneous assumption that a company is a team of cooperating groups. The facts may show that in general, such groups have a basic conflict relationship as to the allocation of the firm's resources, the firm's increase in wealth, and the best way of managing the firm. Besides, some may question the legitimacy of including the government as a cooperating, or even invited, member. Another point raised is that some legitimate member of the cooperating team may not be included. The case in point is the specialist supplier to a sole customer, who would be excluded from the team even though the supplier had no other outlet for the production."[64]

The value-added statement can lead to confusion, especially in those cases where the value-added is increasing while earnings are decreasing. If the shareholders understand that the value-added statement is not a report to shareholders, the problem could be resolved. Some would then argue that there is still a need to use the earnings statement as a special report to shareholders and the value-added statement as a special report on the welfare of a more broadly defined team. Needless to say, this argument would certainly lead to cries of information overload and information redundancy.

The inclusion of the value-added statement might lead management to wrongly seek to maximize the firm's value-added. This unwise objective has already been unfortunately advocated in some publications; the impact of such unsound objectives has been demonstrated as follows:[65]

Suppose a company is buying a component for $5 and the question is asked, "Should we make it ourselves?" An investigation reveals that the cost of a self-made component would be $4 for direct materials plus $10 for direct labor (we shall ignore the overhead for simplicity). Assume that the labor costs are all variable and therefore the company's management does not need to incur losses as the price of keeping together the workforce. In these circumstances, any sensible manager would be grateful for the outside supplier and forget about the idea of in-house manufacture of the component. But not so for the value added maximizer. They would cancel the order to buy at $5 from outside and manufacture the component themselves for $14. They would make this inefficient and wasteful decision because it would raise their value by $9. The amount to be shared out among the company team (value added) would have risen by $1 per component, but the workers would require $10 extra per component for the additional hours worked and the $9 difference represents the loss to the shareholders. Here, the attempt to maximize value added resulted in a disastrous decision.[66]

FINANCIAL REPORTING OF A SEGMENT OF BUSINESS ENTERPRISE

Evaluation of Segmental Reporting

The growth of conglomerate multinational corporations, international accounting, and international trade has led to a need for segmental reporting. Rather than being limited to reporting financial position, performance, and conduct of the whole firm, segmental reporting adds specific information concerning the activities of identifiable and reportable segments of the firm. In addition, there was an international call for such reporting as firms expanded beyond their domestic activities to generate revenues and perform operations outside the borders of their parent countries. Diversification, added to the internationalization of firms, presented an opportunity for a change in the framework of accountability and disclosure toward a combination form of aggregate and segmental reporting. Also, users of accounting information in general, and shareholders in particular, are interested in segmental information as it may affect cash flows. As stated by Roberts and Gray:

They are therefore interested in the performance of the company as a whole rather than the performance of any specific part of a company. However, this does not mean that only consolidated information is of value to them. Both the size and uncertainty of cash flows are likely to be affected by many factors including those that are related to the industries and countries that a company operates in. Different industries and different countries have various profit potentials, degrees and types of risk, and growth opportunities. Different rates of return on investment and different capital needs are also likely to occur across the various segments of a business.[67]

Various arguments have been made in favor of segmental reporting ever since business concerns began to grow and acquire multisegmental characteristics. The usefulness of segmental reporting has been linked to (1) the content of the information in terms of the profitability, risk, and growth of the different segments of a firm and (2) the relevance to users in their assessments of the earnings potential and risk of the company as a whole, to governments in their development of public policy positions concerning multinational or other large companies, and to management encouraging a corporate strategy.

Various other reasons are given in favor of segmental reporting, including the following:

"1. Segmental information is needed by the investor to make an intelligent investment decision regarding a diversified company.

    a. Sales and earning of individual segments are needed to forecast consolidated profits because of the differences between segments in growth rate, risk, and profitability.

    b. Segmental reports disclose the nature of a company's businesses and the relative size of the components as an aid in evaluating the company's investment work.

2. The absence of segmented reporting by a diversified company may put its unsegmented, single product-line competitors at a competitive disadvantage because the conglomerate may obscure information that its competitors must disclose."[68]

Naturally, as in all accounting issues, not all arguments are in favor of segmental reporting. Not only is the usefulness of segmental reporting questioned when compared to the role of consolidated data, but the costs of disclosure are also raised as a subject of concern. The question is whether the costs of segmental disclosure could serve to offset the theoretical benefits of "finer" information systems. Undoubtedly, there is limited evidence with regard to the cost aspects of segmental disclosures, in addition to the lack of evidence on information-processing issues, data-reliability consideration, and externality costs. There is also the problem of the lack of comparability when apparently similar segments in different firms can be identified differently, there is a difference in the treatment of intersegment transfers, and the common costs are allocated over different bases."[69]

Various other reasons against segmental reporting are advocated, including these provided by Kieso et al.:

"1. Without the thorough knowledge of the business and an understanding of such important factors as the competitive environment and capital investment requirements, the investor may find the segmented information meaningless or even draw improper conclusions about the reported earnings of the segment.

2. Additional disclosure may harm reporting firms because it may be helpful to competitors, labor unions, suppliers, and certain government regulatory agencies.

3. Additional disclosure may discourage management from taking intelligent business risks because segments reporting losses or unsatisfactory earnings may cause shareholder dissatisfaction with management.

4. The wide variation among firms in the choice of segments, cost allocation, and other accounting problems limits the usefulness of segmented information.

5. The investor is investing in the company as a whole and not in the particular segments, and it should not matter how any segment is performing if the overall performance is dissatisfactory.

6. Certain technical problems, such as classification of segments and allocation of segment revenues and cost (especially 'common costs') are formidable."[70]

Needless to say, the advocates of segmental reporting are winning their case, given that segmental reporting is mandated internationally.

The U.S. Position: SFAS 14

The U.S. position on reporting financial information by segment is mainly FASB Statement of Financial Accounting Standards No. 14 (SFAS 14), *Financial Reporting for Segments of a Business Enterprise*.[71] Other applicable authoritative statements include Statements 18, 21, 24, 30, and 69[72] and technical bulletins 79–4, 79–5, and 79–8.[73] SFAS 14 requires public companies whose securities are publicly traded or that are required to file financial statements with the Securities and Exchange Commission (SEC) to include disaggregated information about operations in various industries, foreign operations export sales, and sales to major customers. SFAS 21, *Suspension of the Reporting of Earnings per Share and Segment Information by Nonpublic Enterprises*, exempts nonpublic enterprises from the provision of SFAS 14. Similarly, SFAS 24, *Reporting Segment Information in Financial Statements That Are Presented in Another Enterprise's Financial Report*, exempts the reporting entity with consolidated financial statements containing separable financial statements in any of the following circumstances:

1. The separable financial statements are also consolidated or combined in a complete set of financial statements and both sets of financial statements are included in the same financial reports.

2. The separable financial statements are those of a foreign investee (not a subsidiary) of the primary reporting unit and the separable financial statements do not follow the provisions of SFAS No. 14.

3. The separable financial statements are those of an investee accounted for using the cost or equity method.[74]

Therefore, SFAS 21 and SFAS 24 limit the applicability of SFAS 14. Because SFAS 14 differentiates between domestic and foreign operations, the following section delineates this differentiation.

Domestic Operations. In SFAS 14, an "industry segment" is defined as a component of an enterprise engaged in providing a product or service, or a group of related products and services, primarily to unaffiliated customers for a profit. The first requirement of SFAS 14 is the determination, by a three-step procedure, of the industry segments that need to be reported separately.

In the first step, the company identifies its sources of revenue (by product or service rendered) on a worldwide basis. In the second step, the company groups related products and services into industry segments. Three factors are to be considered in determining industry segments:

1. The nature of the product: Related products have similar purposes or end uses. Thus, they may be expected to have similar rates of profitability, similar degrees of risk, and similar opportunities for growth.

2. The nature of the production process: The sharing of common or interchangeable production or sales facilities, equipment, labor force, or service group or use of the same or similar basic raw materials may suggest that products or services are related. Likewise, similar degrees of labor or capital intensiveness may indicate a relationship among products or services.

3. Markets and marketing methods: Similarity of geographic marketing areas, types of customers, or marketing methods may indicate a relationship among products or services. The sensitivity of the market to price changes in general economic conditions may indicate whether products and services are related or unrelated.[75]

In the third step, the company should determine the reporting segments. Six tests are suggested to facilitate the decision, namely, the revenue, profitability, asset, comparability, dominance, and explanation tests.

The revenue test requires that the segment revenue be 10 percent or more of the combined revenue of all the enterprise's industry segments (this includes sales to unaffiliated customers and intersegment sales or transfers). Segment revenue is calculated as follows:

$$SR = S + IS + INTO + INTR$$

where

SR = segment revenue

S = sales to unaffiliated customers

IS = intersegment sales and transfers

$INTO$ = interest income from sources outside the form

$INTR$ = interest income for intersegment notes receivable.

The profitability test requires that the absolute of the segment's operating profit or loss be 10 percent or more, in absolute amount, of the greater of either the combined operating profits of all industry segments that did not incur an operating loss or the combined operating losses of all industry segments that did incur an operating loss. The operating profit or loss is equal to segment revenue less operating expenses, except for the following items:

a. any revenue earned at the corporate level and not related to any segment

b. general corporate expenses

c. interest expenses, except if segment operations are primarily financial in nature

d. domestic and foreign income taxes

e. equity in earnings of unconsolidated subsidiaries or investees

f. extraordinary items

g. gains and losses on discontinued operations

h. minority interest

i. cumulative effect of changes in accounting principles

If the segment fails both the revenue and profitability tests, the asset test requires that the identifiable assets of the segments be 10 percent or more of the combined segments' identifiable assets. Identifiable assets include tangible and intangible assets, net of valuation allowances used by the industry segments. Assets that are intended for general purposes are excluded.

The comparability test requires that the segment be reported separately if management feels such a treatment is needed to achieve interperiod comparability.

The test of dominance requires that the segment not be reported separately if it can be classified as dominant. A dominant segment should represent 90 percent or more of the combined assets; in addition, no other segment can meet any of the 10 percent tests.

The explanation test determines whether a substantial portion of an enterprise's operation is explained by its segment information. The combined total of the revenue for reportable segments must be 75 percent or more of all revenue from sales to unaffiliated customers. If combined revenues do not meet this test, additional segments must be added until the test is met.

Following the choice of the reportable segments, SFAS 14 suggests specific disclosure requirements for segmental reporting that appear in one of three places: (1) in the financial statements, with reference to related footnote disclosures; (2) in the footnotes to the financial statements; (3) in a supplementary schedule that is not part of the four financial statements. The following information to be reported in the reportable segments includes the following items:

1. revenue information, including sales to unaffiliated customers, intersegment sales or transfers (along with the basis of accounting for such sales or transfers), and a reconciliation of sales to unaffiliated customers and intersegments sales or transfers on the consolidated income statement

2. profitability information

3. identifiable assets information

4. other disclosures, including the aggregate amount of depreciation, depletion, and a-mortization; the amount of capital expenditures; equity in unconsolidated but verti-

cally integrated subsidiaries and their geographic locations; the effect of a change in accounting principle on segment income; the type of products and services produced by each segment; specific accounting policies; the basis used to price intersegment transfers; the method used to allocate common costs; and the nature and amount of any unusual or infrequent items added to or deducted from segment profit

Foreign Operations. SFAS 14 requires separate disclosure of domestic and foreign activities. Foreign operations are those revenue-generating activities that are located outside the enterprise's home country and generate revenues either from sales to unaffiliated customers or from intraenterprise sales or transfers between geographic areas.

Two tests may be used to determine if foreign operation activities are to be reported separately: (1) revenue from sales to unaffiliated customers is 10 percent or more of consolidated revenue as reported in the firm's income statement and (2) identifiable assets of the firm's foreign operations are 10 percent or more of consolidated total assets as reported in the firms' balance sheet. After an individual foreign operation has been determined to be reportable, its activities must be added to activities from foreign operations in the same geographic area. Geographic areas are defined as individual countries or groups of countries as determined to be appropriate according to a firm's circumstances. The following factors are to be considered in grouping foreign operations: proximity, economic affinity, similarities in business environment, and nature, scale, and degree of interrelationship of the firm's operations in various countries. The disclosure requirements for foreign operations are similar to those for domestic operations.

Export sales are those sales made by a domestic segment to unaffiliated customers in foreign countries. If export sales amount to 10 percent or more of the total sales to unaffiliated customers, they should be separately disclosed in the aggregate statements by such geographic areas as are considered appropriate.

Similarly, if 10 percent or more of the revenue of a firm is derived from a single customer, a separate disclosure is required, along with indications of the segments making the sale. SFAS 30 *Disclosure of Information about Major Customers* identifies either a group of entities under common control, the federal government, a state government, a local government, or a foreign government as a single customer for purpose of compliance with the 10 percent test.

The U.S. Position: SFAS 131

The June 1997, FASB Statement 131, "Disclosures about Segments of an Enterprise and Related Information," was approved. It brought a significant change in how reportable segments are determined, as well as in the amount and types of information to be provided.

A. It called for a management approach to the determination of segments by requiring firms to report disaggregated information about reportable segments based on management's organization of the firm and consistent with the way in which management organizes the business internally. This differs drastically from SFAS 16, in which the firms were required to disclose segment information by both line-of-business and geographical area, with no specific link to the internal organization of the company or the measurements that were used for internal decision making.

B. The required disclosures under SFAS 131 include:

1. general information about the operating segment (factors used to identify the operating segments as well as types of products and services from which each operating segment derives its revenues

2. segment profit or loss, including:

   a. revenues from external customers

   b. revenues from transactions with other operating segments

   c. interest revenue and interest expense (reported separately); net interest revenue to be reported for finance segments if this measure is used internally for evaluation

   d. depreciation, depletion, and amortization expense

   e. other significant noncash items included in segment profit and loss

   f. unusual items (discontinued operations and extraordinary items)

   g. income tax expense or benefit.

3. Total segment assets, including

   a. Investment in equity method affiliates

   b. Expenditures for additions to long-lived assets

C. The enterprise-wide disclosures included data about

1. information about products and services if operating segments have not been determined based on differences in products and services

2. information about geographical areas, including data about

   a. revenues from external customers attributed to the country of domicile and attributed to all countries in total, with separate disclosure of any revenues from an individual country that are material

   b. long-lived assets located in the country of domicile and located in all other countries, with separate disclosure of any assets in an individual country that are material

3. Whenever 10 percent or more of a company's revenues are derived from a single customer, information about major customers and the identity of the segment(s) reporting the revenue

D. FSAF 131 retained the three tests introduced in SFAS 14 for identifying operating segments for which separate disclosure is required:

- a revenue test

- a profit and loss test

- an asset test

NOTES

1. Black, B., "The Legal and Institutional Preconditions for Strong Stock Markets," Working Paper (Stanford Law School, John M. Olin Program in Law and Economics, 2000).

2. Bushman, Robert, Qi Chen, Ellen Engel, and Abbie Smith, "The Sensitivity of Corporate Governance Systems to the Timeliness of Accounting Earnings," Working Paper (University of Chicago, 2000).

3. Palepu, K. G., V. L. Bernard, and P. M. Healy, *Business Analysis and Valuation* (Cincinatti, Ohio: South Western Publishing Co., 1996).

4. Porter, Michael E., *Competitive Strategy* (New York: The Free Press, 1980).

5. Palepu, Bernard, and Healy, *Business Analysis and Valuation*, pp. 2-10.

6. Ibid., pp. 3–5.

7. Ibid., pp. 3–6, 3–7.

8. Ibid., pp. 3–13.

9. Ibid., pp. 3–11, 3–12.

10. Nissim, Doron and Stephen Pennan, "Ratio Analysis and Valuation," unpublished manuscript, March 1999.

11. Day, J. F. S., "The Use of Annual Reports by the UK Investment Analysts," *Accounting and Business Research* 15 (Autumn 1986), pp. 295–307.

12. Belkaoui, A., A. Kahl, and P. Peyrard, "Information Needs of Financial Analysis: An International Comparison," *Journal of International Education and Research in Accounting* 13 (Fall 1977), pp. 19–27.

13. Choi, Frederick D. S., and Richard M. Levich, "International Accounting Diversity and Capital Markets Decisions," in Frederick D. S. Choi (ed.), *Handbook of International Accounting* (New York: John Wiley and Sons, 1991), 16–21.

14. Ibid., p. 74.

15. Ibid, pp. 74–75.

16. Ibid.

17. Belkaoui, Ahmed, "Accounting and Language," *Journal of Accounting Literature* 8 (1989), pp. 281–292.

18. Gray, S. J., "The Impact of International Accounting Differences from a Security-Analysis Perspective: Some European Evidence," *Journal of Accounting Research* 18 (Spring 1980), pp. 69–76.

19. Ibid., pp. 72–73.

20. Choi, F. D. S., H. Huio, S. K. Miu, S. O. Nam, J. Ujie, and A. I. Stonehill, "Analyzing Foreign Financial Statements: The Use and Misuse of International Radio Analysis," *Journal of International Business Studies* 15 (Spring/Summer 1983), pp. 113–131.

21. Ibid., p. 121.

22. Gul, Ferdinand A., and Burch T. Kealey, "Chaebol, Investment Opportunity Set and Corporate Debt and Dividend Policies of Korean Companies," *Review of Quantitative Finance and Accounting* 13, no. 4 (December 1999), pp. 401–416.

23. Choi, Huio, Miu, Nam, Ujie, and Stonehill, "Foreign Financial Statements."

24. Ezzammel, Mahmoud, and Cecilio Mar-Molinero, "The Distributional Properties of Financial Ratios in UK Manufacturing Companies," *Journal of Business Finance and Accounting* 25 (Spring 1990), pp. 1–32.

25. See Chairman Levitt's remarks in a speech entitled "The Numbers Game," delivered at New York University on September 28, 1998.

26. Healy, Paul M., and James M. Wahlen, "A Review of the Earnings Management Literature and Its Implications for Standard Setting," *Accounting Horizons* 10 (December 1999), p. 368.

27. Wiedman, Christine I., "Instructional Case: Detecting Earnings Manipulation," *Issues in Accounting Education*, 14, no. 1, (February 1999), pp. 157–158.

28. Green, B. P., and J. H. Choi, "Assessing the Risk of Management Fraud through Neural Network Technology," *Auditing: A Journal of Practice and Theory* 16, no. 5 (1997), pp. 14–28.

29. Beneish, M. D., "Detecting GAAP Violation: Implications for Assessing Earnings Management among Firms with Extreme Financial Performance," *Journal of Accounting and Public Policy* 16, no. 3 (1997), pp. 271–309.

30. Wiedman, "Instructional Case," p. 160.

31. Ibid., p. 161.

32. Accounting Standards Steering Committee, *The Corporate Report* (London: Accounting Standards Steering Committee, 1975), p. 200.

33. Stamp, Edward, *Corporate Reporting: Its Future Evolution* (Toronto: Canadian Institute of Chartered Accountants, 1980).

34. International Confederation of Free Trade Unions (ICFTU), *Multinational Charter of Trade Unions Demands for the Legislative Control of Multinational Companies* (Brussels: ICFTU, November 1975), pp. 34–36.

35. Lewis, N. R., L. D. Parker, and P. Sutcliffe, "Financial Reporting to Employees: The Pattern of Development 1919 to 1979," *Accounting Organizations and Society* (June 1984), p. 278.

36. Ibid., p. 279.

37. Cox, B., *Value Added: An Application for the Accountant Concerned with Industry* (London: Heinemann and the Institute of Cost and Management Accountants, 1978).

38. Suojanen, W. W., "Accounting Theory and the Large Corporation," *Accounting Review* (July 1954), pp. 391–398.

39. Accounting Standards Steering Committee, *The Corporate Report*, p. 48.

40. Ibid.

41. British Department of Trade, *The Future of Company Reports* (London: HMSO, 1977), pp. 7–8.

42. Gray, S. J., and K. T. Maunders, *Value Added Reporting: Uses and Measurement* (London: Association of Certified Accountants, 1980).

43. Engineering Employers Federation, *Business Performance and Industrial Relations* (London: Kogan Page, 1977).

44. Woodmansay, M., *Added Value: An Introduction to Productivity Schemes* (London: British Institute of Management, 1978).

45. Burchell, Stuart, Colin Chubb, and Anthony G. Hopwood, "Accounting and Its Social Context: Towards a History of Value Added in the United Kingdom," *Accounting, Organizations and Society* 10, no. 4 (1985), p. 387.

46. Siones, F. C., *The Economic Ingredients of Industrial Success* (London: James Clayton Lecture, Institution of Mechanical Engineers, 1976); Jones, F. C., "Our Manufacturing Industry: The Missing $100,000 Million," *National Westminster Bank Quarterly Review*, May 1978, pp. 8–17; New, C., "Factors in Productivity That Should Not Be Overlooked," *The Times*, February 1, 1978.

47. Cameron, S., "Added Value Plan for Distributing ICI's Wealth," *Financial Times*, January 7, 1977.

48. Vickers da Costa, *"Testing for Success"* (mimeo, London, 1979).

49. Rensahll, M., R. Allan, and K. Nicholson, *Added Value in External Financial Reporting* (London: Institute of Chartered Accountants in England and Wales, 1979).

50. Morley, Michael F., *The Value Added Statement* (London: Gee, 1978), p. 131.

51. Cox, *Value Added*.

52. Gray and Maunders, *Added Value Reporting*.

53. Ball, R. J. "The Use of Value Added in Measuring Managerial Efficiency," *Business Ratios* (Summer 1968), p. 6.

54. Morley, *The Value Added Statement*, p. 131.

55. Ibid., p. 132.

56. Shimizu, Masayoshi, Kiyoshi Wainai, and Kazuo Nagai, *Value Added Productivity Measurement and Practiced Approach to Management Improvement* (Tokyo: Asian Productivity Organization, 1991), p. 3.

57. Ibid., pp. 21–36.

58. Morely, *The Value Added Statement*, p. 621.

59. Maunders, K. T., "The Decision Relevance of Value Added Reports," in Fredrick D. Choi and Gerhard G. Mueller (eds.), *Frontiers of International Accounting: An Anthology* (Ann Arbor: UMI Research Press, 1985), p. 241.

60. Morley, *The Value Added Statement*, p. 623.

61. Morley, M. F., "Value Added Reporting," in Thomas A. Lee (ed.), *Developments in Financial Reporting* (London: Phillip Allan, 1981), p. 259.

62. Maunders, "The Decision Relevance of Value Added Reports," p. 225–245.

63. Ibid., p. 229.

64. Morley, *The Value Added Statement*, p. 624.

65. Cilchrist, R. R., *Managing for Profit: The Value Added Concept* (London: Allen and Unwin, 1971).

66. Morley, *The Value Added Statement*, p. 30.

67. Roberts, C. B., and S. Gray, "Segmental Reporting," in C. Nobes and R. Parker (eds.), *Issues in International Accounting* (Oxford: Philip Allan, 1988), p. 106.

68. Keiso, D. F., D. E. Weygandt, J. J. Irvine, V. B. Silvester, and W. H. Silvester, *Intermediate Accounting* 2nd ed. (Toronto: John Wiley and Sons Canada, 1986), p. 1296.

69. Ibid., p. 33.

70. Keiso, Weygandt, Irvine, Silvester, & Silvester, *Intermediate Accounting*, p. 1296.

71. Financial Accounting Standards Board (FASB), *Financial Reporting for Segments of a Business Enterprise*. Statement of Financial Accounting Standards No. 14 (Stamford, CT: FASB, 1976), par. 10.

72. Financial Accounting Standards Board, (FASB), *Financial Reporting for Segments of a Business Enterprise—Interim Financial Statements*, Statement of Financial Accounting Standards No. 18 (Stamford, CT: FASB, November 1977); Financial Accounting Standards Board, *Suspension of the Reporting of Earnings per Share and Segment Information by Nonpublic Enterprises*, Statement of Financial Accounting Standard No. 21 (Stamford, CT: FASB, April 1978), par. 10; Financial Accounting Standards Board, *Reporting Segment Information in Financial Statements That Are Presented in Another Enterprise's Financial Report*, Statement of Financial Accounting Standard No. 24 (Stamford, CT: FASB, December 1987), par. 9; Financial Accounting Standards Board, *Disclosure of Information about Major Customers*, Statement of Financial Accounting

Standard No. 30 (Stamford, CT: FASB, August 1979), par. 20. Financial Accounting Standards Board, *Disclosures about Oil and Gas Activities*, Statement of Financial Accounting Standard No. 69 (Stamford, CT: FASB, November 1982), par. 11.

73. Financial Accounting Standards Board (FASB), *Technical Bulletin 79–4* (Stamford, CT: FASB); Financial Accounting Standards Board, *Technical Bulletin 79–5* (Stamford, CT: FASB); Financial Accounting Standards Board, *Technical Bulletin 79–8* (Stamford, CT: FASB).

74. FASB, *Reporting Segment Information in Financial Statements*, SFAS 24, par. 22.

75. FASB, *Financial Reporting for Segments of a Business Enterprise*, SFAS 14, par. 100.

SELECTED READINGS

Beneish, M. D. "Detecting GAAP Violation: Implications for Assessing Earnings Management among Firms with Extreme Financial Performance," *Journal of Accounting and Public Policy* 16, no. 3 (1997), pp. 271–309.

Copeland, T., T. Koller, and J. Murrin. *Valuation: Measuring and Managing the Value of Companies*. 2nd Ed. New York: John Wiley and Sons, 1994. (See especially Chapter 12, "Valuing Foreign Subsidiaries," and Chapter 13, "Valuation Outside of the United States.")

Gul, Ferdinand A., and Burch T. Kealy. "Chaebol, Investment Opportunity Set and Corporate Debt and Dividend Policies of Korean Companies," *Review of Quantitative Finance and Accounting* 13, no. 4 (December 1999), pp. 401–416.

Palepu, Krishna G., Paul M. Healy, and Victor L. Bernard. *Business Analysis and Valuation: Using Financial Statements*. 2nd Ed. Cincinatti, OH: Southwestern College Publishing, 2000.

Wiedman, Christine I. "Instructional Case: Detecting Earnings Manipulation," *Issues in Accounting Education* 14, no. 2 (February 1999), pp. 145–176.

APPENDIX: INTERNATIONAL ACCOUNTING STANDARDS

IAS1, *Disclosure of Accounting Policies*, requires the disclosure of all the significant accounting policies that have been used in the preparation of financial statements.

IAS2, *Valuation and Presentation of Inventories in the Context of the Historical Cost System*, requires that inventories be valued at the lower of historical cost and net realizable value when presented in financial statements.

IAS3, *Consolidated Financial Statements*, requires the presentation of consolidated financial statements for a group of related companies under the central control of one parent firm. It provides for the use of the equity method of accounting for certain kinds of long-term investments. Superseded by IAS27.

IAS4, *Depreciation Accounting*, requires that fixed assets be depreciated on some systematic basis over their useful lives.

IAS5, *Information to be Disclosed in Financial Statements*, specifies minimum disclosures of information in the annual report. A balance sheet, income statement, notes, and other statements must be clear and understandable.

IAS6, *Accounting Responses to Changing Prices*, requires that financial statements disclose how they reflect the impact of changing prices. Superseded by IAS15.

IAS7, *Statement of Changes in Financial Position*, requires the presentation of a statement of changes in financial position as a part of the financial statements.

IAS8, *Unusual and Prior Period Items and Changes in Accounting Policies*, requires disclosure of prior period items and adjustments resulting from changes in accounting policies.

IAS9, *Accounting for Research and Development Activities*, requires development costs to be charged to expense in the period in which they were incurred. Deferral is permitted in special circumstances.

IAS10, *Contingencies and Events Occurring after the Balance Sheet Date*, defines the circumstances in which a contingency loss should be accrued for by a charge against current income and distinguishes between those post–financial statement events that require disclosure.

IAS11, *Accounting for Construction Contracts*, requires that accounting for construction contracts follow either the completed contract method or the percentage of completion.

IAS12, *Income Accounting for Taxes*, requires that the tax expenses for an accounting period be determined by using "tax effect" accounting, employing either the deferral or the liability methods.

IAS13, *Presentation of Current Assets and Current Liabilities*, defines current assets and liabilities.

IAS14, *Preparing Financial Information by Segment*, requires the presentation of segment information on the basis of industrial and geographical segments in the financial statements of publicly traded firms.

IAS15, *Information Reflecting the Effects of Changing Prices*, requires that firms that prepare consolidated financial statements indicate which method they use to adjust for changes in the price level, in both the balance sheet and the income statement (the items to be reported include the effect of price changes on depreciation, the cost of goods sold, and the effect on net monetary liabilities position). Withdrawn in late 1989.

IAS16, *Accounting for Property, Plant, and Equipment*, defines the measurement base for property, plant, and equipment and gives guidelines for the presentation of these items in the balance sheet under the historical cost approach and when this basis has been revalued.

IAS17, *Accounting for Leases*, requires that the asset and liability created for a firm under a finance lease be reflected in the firm's balance sheet and that information regarding the terms of the lease and the amount of assets that are the subject of finance leases be disclosed.

IAS18, *Revenue Recognition*, concerns the basis for revenue recognition and provides guidelines to be followed in the recognition of revenue from sales of goods and the rendering of services.

IAS19, *Accounting for Retirement Benefits in Financial Statement of Employers*, defines various types of employee pension plans and establishes the accounting guidelines and related disclosure requirements to be followed for each.

IAS20, *Accounting for Government Grants and Disclosure of Government Assistance*, requires that government grants and other forms of financial assistance be recognized in firms' income statements and systematically matched against the costs which they are intended to compensate.

IAS21, *Accounting for the Effects of Changes in Foreign Exchange Rates*, requires that firms generally use the closing rate method for translating the financial statements of foreign subsidiaries for consolidation purposes.

IAS22, *Accounting for Business Combinations*, requires business combinations to be accounted for by the purchase method and allows any resulting goodwill to either be recorded as an asset and amortized or adjusted against shareholders' interests in the period of acquisition. The pooling-of-interests method may only be used if a combination qualifies as a uniting of interests.

IAS23, *Capitalization of Borrowing Costs*, requires an enterprise to consistently apply a policy of either capitalization or noncapitalization of borrowing costs for assets that take a substantial period of time to make ready for their intended use. Guidelines for capitalization and disclosure requirements are outlined for companies opting to capitalize.

IAS24, *Disclosure of Related Party Transactions*, defines related parties, requires any related party relationships involving control to be disclosed, and requires the elements and types of any transaction between any related parties to be disclosed.

IAS25, *Accounting for Investments*, applies to all investments other than interest in joint ventures, subsidiaries, and associates. It requires short-term investments to be carried at market value or the lower of cost and market value and long-term investments to be carried at a cost revalued amount, applied on a portfolio basis.

IAS26, *Accounting and Reporting of Retirement Benefit Plans*, defines the contents of retirement benefit reports to all participants as a group, requires the investments to be carried at fair value, and requires the actuarial present value of the benefits to be disclosed.

IAS27, *Consolidated Financial Statement and Accounting for Investments in Subsidiaries*, defines subsidiary ownership on the basis of control, requires consolidated financial statements from all groups except all wholly owned, foreign and domestic subsidiaries, and provides guidelines for line-by-line consolidation and disclosure in a parent's separate financial statements of its investment in a subsidiary.

IAS28, *Accounting for Investments in Associates*, defines an associate as an entity in which an investor has significant influence although it is neither a subsidiary nor a joint venture. Such investments are generally required to be carried under the equity method unless the investment is exclusively acquired with the intention of disposal in the near future, in which case the cost method must be utilized.

IAS29, *Financial Reporting in Hyperinflationary Economies*, requires the financial statements of enterprises reporting in the currency of a hyperinflationary economy to be stated in terms of the measuring unit current at the balance sheet date, by applying the change in the general price index. It applies whether the financial statements are based on the current cost or historical cost method.

IAS30, *Disclosure in the Financial Statements of Banks and Similar Financial Institutions*, requires such institutions to include specific items in the income statement and balance sheet. An analysis of assets and liabilities divided into maturity groups is required and significant concentrations of assets, liabilities, and off-balance sheet items must be disclosed. Other required disclosures include losses on loans and advances, assets pledged as security, and amounts accrued for general banking risks.

IAS31, *Financial Reporting of Interests in Joint Ventures*, requires a venturer to report any interest in jointly controlled assets, operations, and entities in the financial statements. Transactions between the venturer and the joint venture must be reported to reflect the substance of the transaction.

7

Capital Budgeting for Multinational Firms and Political Risk

INTRODUCTION

Exhibit 7.1 shows the 1999 gross domestic products of selected countries and U.S. companies whose market capitalization are about equal to them. This provides an idea of the size of those companies and their potential direct foreign investment projects. Multinational companies rely on capital budgeting for the evaluation of their direct foreign investment projects. The use of capital budgeting techniques is a direct consequence of their adoption of the stockholders' wealth maximization model as their objective function.[1] The maximization of the owners' wealth dictates the application of capital budgeting techniques in both the domestic and international contexts. There are specific problems, however, that may complicate capital budgeting for the multinational corporation. Accordingly, this chapter examines the specific uses of capital budgeting techniques by multinational corporations in analyzing the financial benefits and costs of a potential investment. It also examines the problems associated with the management of political risks that can be encountered when investing internationally.

FOREIGN DIRECT INVESTMENT

Multinational capital budgeting is a direct consequence of a foreign direct investment decision. Motives for direct foreign investment include: (1) strategic motives, (2) behavioral motives, and (3) economic motives.[2]

Strategic motives for foreign investment include the five following categories:[3]

Exhibit 7.1
1999 Gross Domestic Products of Selected Countries and Companies Whose Market Capitalizations Are Roughly Equal to Them

Countries	GNP	Companies
Cuba	$16 Billion	Juniper Naturals
Jamaica	$8 Billion	Phone.Com
Columbia	$201 Billion	IBM
Chile	$121 Billion	Oracle
Argentina	$296 Billion	Wal-Mart Stores
Poland	$246 Billion	Intel
Latvia	$9 Billion	VA Linux Systems
Ukraine	$161 Billion	Merck
Spain	$ 593 Billion	Microsoft
Tunisia	$43 Billion	Sprint PCS
Greece	$107 Billion	Hewlett-Packard
Egypt	$184 Billion	Citigroup
South Africa	$227 Billion	Lucent Technologies
Tanzania	$19 Billion	Sycamore Networks
Kuwait	$33 Billion	Internet Capital
Iran	$344 Billion	Cisco Systems
Bangladesh	$155 Billion	Home Depot
Singapore	$72 Billion	Qualcomm
Thailand	$496 Billion	General Electric
Vietnam	$109 Billion	Dell Computer
Philippines	$149 Billion	America On Line
Papua New Guinea	$11 Billion	Free Markets
New Zealand	$66 Billion	America Express

1. market seekers, who produce in foreign markets either to satisfy local demand or to export to markets other than their home market

2. raw material seekers, who extract raw materials wherever they can be found, either for exports or for further processing and sale in the host country

3. production efficiency seekers, who produce in countries where one or more of the factors of production are underpriced relative to their productivity

4. knowledge seekers, who invest in foreign countries to gain access to technology or managerial expertise

5. political safety seekers, who invest in countries that are considered unlikely to expropriate or interfere with their business[4]

Behavioral motives consist of those arising from external stimuli and some auxiliary motives.[5] The four motives arising from external stimuli are:

"1. An outside proposal, provided it comes from a source that cannot be easily ignored. The most frequent sources of such proposals are foreign governments, the distributors of the company's products, and its clients.

2. Fear of losing a market.

3. The "bandwagon" effect: very successful activities abroad of a competing firm in the same line of business, or general belief that investment in some area is "a must."

4. Strong competition from abroad in the home market."[6]

The four auxiliary motives are:

"1. Creation of a market for components and other products.

2. Utilization of old machinery.

3. Capitalization of know-how; spreading of research and development and other fixed costs.

4. Indirect return to a lost market through investment in a country that has commercial agreements with these lost territories."[7]

Economic motives for direct foreign investment are generally based on the theory of imperfections in individual natural markets for products, factors of production and financial ones. As argued by Eiteman, Stonehill, and Moffelt, [8]

a. Product and factor market imperfections provide an opportunity for multinational firms to outcompete local firms, particularly in industries characterized by worldwide oligopolistic competition, because the multinational firms have superiority in economies of scale, managerial expertise, technology, differentiated products and financial strength.

b. Oligopolistic competition also motivates firms to make defensive investments abroad to save both export and home markets from foreign competition.

c. As suggested by the product cycle theory, large firms in advanced countries are able to introduce new product in their local market before exporting them. As foreign competitors enter the home market with lower-priced, similar products, the large firms switch their production abroad to take advantage of the lower costs of production.

d. Considerations such as "follow the leader," establishing checklists, "grow-to-success," acquiring factor-endowed firms, and following the customer may explain some of the defensive direct foreign investment.

e. As suggested by the internalization theory, multinational firms capitalize on their "proprietary" information to penetrate foreign markets.

RISK ANALYSIS

Direct capital investment is not without specific risks that can affect the value and the feasibility of the project. The following list includes some of the risks that can be faced when investing in the global economy.

1. A distortion of the value of the project may arise with the failure to distinguish between project and parent cash flows. A decision has to be made whether to analyze the capital budgeting decision from a project or a parent perspective.
2. Fluctuating exchange rates can also distort the value of the cash flows and the desirability of the project. Accurate forecasting of the exchange rates over the life of the project may be necessary for an accurate and reliable analysis of the capital budgeting decision.
3. Changes in the general price or specific price levels in the foreign country can also create a distortion in the capital budgeting decision if they are not accounted for. The inflation factor has to be incorporated in the analysis.
4. Various obstacles may be created by the foreign country to hinder the remittance of earnings to the parent firm. Examples of obstacles include fund blockages, exchange control appropriation, and various forms of foreign currency controls.
5. Other factors that can affect the remittance of funds to the parent company include tax laws and institutional factors as well as political factors.

Each of these risks need to be accounted for in the analysis of a capital budgeting decision by multinational firms, and the following questions need to be addressed:

- What level of confidence is present in the various elements of the cash flow forecast?
- For the elements involving the greatest degree of uncertainty, what will be the result of a large forecasting error?
- How sensitive is the value of the investment to the foreseeable risks?[9]

PROJECT VERSUS PARENT CASH FLOWS: THE ISSUES

Project cash flows and parent cash flows differ as a result of the various tax requirements and exchange controls that can affect the final amounts remitted to the parent company. Two schools of thought are instrumental in the choice of cash flows. One school of thought that discounts the effect of restriction on repatriation favors the use of the project cash flows in the capital budgeting analysis. Following this precept, the list of elements of projected return from an overseas industrial investment includes the following:

"1. All income, operating and nonoperating, from overseas operating unit, based on its demonstrated capacity to supply existing markets with its present management and excluding any impact of the merger of resources with those of the investing company.

2. Additional operating income of the overseas unit resulting from the merger of its own capabilities with those of the investing corporation.

3. Additional income from increased export sale resulting from the proposed investment action, including (a) additional export income at each U.S. operating unit that manufactures products related to those that will be produced overseas and (b) additional earnings from new export activity at the overseas operating unit resulting from its increased capabilities to sell beyond the boundaries of its traditional national markets.

4. Additional income from increased licensing opportunities shown both in the books of the affected U.S. units and the books of the overseas unit.

5. Additional income from importing technology, product design, or hardware from the overseas operating unit to U.S. operating units.

6. Income presently accruing from the investment but seriously and genuinely threatened by economic, political, or social change in an overseas region."[10]

A second position, derived from economic theory, is that the value of a project is determined by the net present value of future cash flows back to the investor. Therefore, the project cash flows that are or can be repatriated are included, "since only accessible funds can be used to pay dividends and interest, amortize the firm's debt, and be reinvested."[11] In spite of the strong theoretical argument in favor of analyzing foreign projects from the viewpoint of the parent company, empirical evidence from surveys of multinationals shows that firms are using project flows and rates of return as well as parent flows and rates of return.[12] In fact, a more recent survey shows that multinationals were almost evenly split among those that looked at cash flow solely from the subsidiaries' perspective, and from both perspectives.[13] Those who viewed cash flow from the point of view of the subsidiary felt that the subsidiaries were separate businesses and should be viewed as such. Those who took the parent company's view argued that the investment was ultimately made from the company's stockholders. Finally, those who adopted both perspectives considered this the safest approach, providing two ways of making a final decision. One of the respondent treasures put it as follows:

The project must first be evaluated on its chances of success locally. It must be profitable from the subsidiary's point of view. Then you step back and look at it from the parent's point of view. What cash flows are available to be remitted or otherwise used in another country? What's going to come back to the parent is the real issue. The project has to meet both tests to be acceptable.[14]

What appears from this discussion is that the use of the parent company's view is compatible with the traditional view of net present value in capital budgeting, whereas the use of the project's view leads to a closer approximation of the effect on consolidated earnings per share.[15]

An operational differentiation between project cash flows and present cash flows is as follows:

Cash flows generated by subsidiary
− Corporate taxes paid to host government

= After-tax cash flows to subsidiary
− Retained earnings by subsidiary

= Cash flows remitted by subsidiary
− Withholding tax paid to host government

= After-tax Cash flows remitted by subsidiary
× Exchange rate

= Cash flows received by parent
− Corporate taxes paid to local government

Cash flows available to parent

PROJECT VERSUS PARENT CASH FLOWS: AN EXAMPLE

To illustrate the differences between the subsidiary perspective and the parent company perspectives in multinational budgeting, consider an example of a Jordanian subsidiary of a U.S.-based multinational corporation considering the decision to invest in new equipment, on the basis of the following information:

- The cost of investment is JD39,100. The exchange rate is $2/JD.
- The cash flows for an estimated useful life of six years are respectively, JD20,000, JD14,000, JD10,000, JD6,000, JD5,000 and JD4,000.
- The required rate of return is 10 percent.
- The Jordanian government does not tax the earnings of the subsidiary but does require a withholding tax of 10 percent on funds remitted to the parent company.
- The U.S. tax rate on foreign earnings of the subsidiary is 25 percent.
- The exchange rate of the Jordanian dinar is estimated to be $2.00 at the end of years 1 and 2, $1.80 at the end of years 3 and 4, and $1.50 at the end of years 5 and 6.

The capital budgeting from the project or subsidiary perspective is shown in Exhibit 7.2. The cumulative net present value (NPV) is JD7,633; therefore, the project is acceptable from the subsidiary's point of view. The capital budgeting from the parent's perspective is shown in Exhibit 7.3. The project appears profitable from the subsidiary's perspective but unprofitable from the parent's perspective.

COST OF CAPITAL FOR THE MULTINATIONAL FIRM

In both the internal rate-of-return method and the net present value method, a cost of capital, or a 'hurdle rate,' is needed. The two rules of thumb are as follows: (1) the internal rate of return must be superior to the hurdle rate to be

Exhibit 7.2
Subsidiary Views of Foreign Investment

	Year 1	Year 2	Year 3	Year 4	Year 5	Year 6
Cost of Investment						
JD 39,100						
Cash Flows	JD20,000	JD14,000	JD10,000	JD6,000	JD5,000	JD4,000
Discount Factor 10%	0.909	0.826	0.7530	0.683	0.621	0.564
PV of Cash Flows	JD18,180	JD11,564	JD7,530	JD4,098	JD3,105	JD2,256
Cumulative NPV	- JD20,920	-JD9,356	-JD1,826	JD2,272	JD5,377	JD7,633

Exhibit 7.3
Capital Budgeting: Parent Company's Perspective

	Year 1	Year 2	Year 3	Year 4	Year 5	Year 6
Cost of Investment						
$78,200						
Cash Flows	JD20,000	JD14,000	JD10,000	JD6,000	JD5,000	JD4,000
Withholding Tax (10%)	JD2,000	JD1,400	JD1,000	JD600	JD500	JD400
Funds Remitted	JD18,000	JD12,600	JD9,000	JD5,400	JD4,500	JD3,600
Exchange Rate	$2	$2	$1.80	$1.80	$1.50	$1.50
Funds to be Received	$36,000	$25,200	$16,200	$9,720	$6,750	$5,400
US Taxes Paid (25%)	$9,000	$6,300	$4,050	$2,430	$1,687.50	$1,350
After Tax Funds	$27,000	$18,900	$12,150	$7,290	$5,062.50	$4,050
Discount Factor	0.909	0.826	0.753	0.683	0.621	0.564
PV of Cash Flows	$24,543	$15,611.40	$9,148.95	$4,979.07	$3,143.81	$2,284.20
Cumulative NPV	($53,657)	($38,045.60)	($28,896.65)	($23,917.58)	($20,773.77)	($18,489.57)

acceptable; and (2) the present value, obtained by discounting cash flows at the hurdle rate, must be positive for a project to be acceptable. For a multinational corporation, the overall cost of capital is the sum of the costs of each financing source, weighted by the proportion of that financing source in the firm's total capital structure. The weighted average cost of capital is therefore:

$$K = \frac{E}{V} \times K_e + \frac{D}{V} K_d(1 - t)$$

where

K = weighted average cost of capital

K_d = cost of debt

K_e = cost of equity

t = tax rate

D = value of the firm's debt

E = value of the firm's equity

$V = D + E$ = total value of the firm

The cost of capital of a multinational corporation is assumed to be affected by a host of factors, including size of the firm, access to international capital markets, international diversification, tax concession, exchange risk and country risk.[16] The larger the firm, the greater its international diversification, the more it capitalizes on tax concessions, the lower its exchange rate exposure, the lower the country risk and the lower the cost of capital to the multinational corporation (MNC).

A MULTINATIONAL CAPITAL BUDGETING EXAMPLE

Theoretically, the capital budgeting process for an MNC involves the following phases:

1. identification of cash flows generated by the proposed project
2. identification of cash flows available for repatriation to the MNC
3. conversion of cash flows by means of exchange rates
4. adjustments to compensate for financial risks, including sensibility analysis
5. selection of a minimum rate of return
6. calculation of investment profitability, including sensitivity analysis
7. acceptance or rejection of the proposed investment[17]

The input for a multinational capital budgeting decisions are:

a. initial investment
b. price

c. variable cost

d. fixed cost

e. project lifetime

f. salvage (liquidation) value

g. fund-transfer restrictions

h. tax laws

i. exchange rates

j. required rate of return.[18]

The net present value (NPV) method is based on the following formula:

$$NPV = -IC + \sum_{t=1}^{n} \frac{CF_t}{(1 + K)^t} + \frac{SV_n}{(1 + K)^n}$$

where

IC = initial cost of the investment

CF_t = cash flow in period t

SV_n = salvage value

K = required rate of return on the project

n = lifetime of the project (number of periods)

If the internal rate of return is used, the equation will be:

$$0 = -IC + \sum_{t=1}^{n} \frac{CF_t}{(1 + r)^t} + \frac{SV_n}{(1 + r)^n}$$

where

r = internal rate of return

The following example concerns the case of Computer Inc., a U.S.-based manufacturer of personal computers (PCs), which is considering exporting their PCs to Denmark. The decision was made to create a Danish subsidiary to manufacture and sell the PCs in Europe. The following information is collected.

1. Revenue information: The forecast price and sales of the PCs were as follows:

Year	Price per PC	Sales in Denmark and Europe
1	Krone 600	5,000,000 units
2	Krone 700	6,000,000 units
3	Krone 800	8,000,000 units

2. Initial investment: The parent company intends to invest a total of $200,000,000.

3. Variable costs per units: These costs are estimated as follows:

Year	Variable Cost per Unit
1	Krone 100
2	Krone 120
3	Krone 150

4. Fixed expenses are estimated to be KR1,100,000,000 per year for the first three years.

5. Noncash expenses including depreciation expenses are estimated to be KR200,000,000 per year.

6. Most government taxes include a 20 percent tax on earnings and a 10 percent tax on the remittances to parent. The subsidiary intends to remit 50 percent of net cash flow to the parent company.

7. Exchange rates are estimated to be as follows:

Year	Exchange Rates of Krone
1	$0.15
2	$0.17
3	$0.20

8. The required rate of return for the project is 10 percent.

The capital budgeting analysis is shown in Exhibit 7.4, which shows that for the first three years considered, the project has a cumulative positive cash flow in year 3 of $219,010,516.00. Therefore, the decision should be made to accept the project.

CAPITAL BUDGETING ISSUES FOR MULTINATIONALS

Capital Budgeting under Inflation

Changes in the general price level can create a distortion in the capital-budgeting analysis of multinationals. A specific consideration of the impact of inflation or the analysis is warranted. The correct approach includes either using a money discount rate to discount money cash flows, or using a real discount rate to discount real cash flows. Money cash flows are measured in dollars from various periods having different purchasing power. Real cash flows are cash flows measured in dollars having the same purchasing power. The real cash flow for a given year t expressed in terms of dollars of year 0

Exhibit 7.4
Capital Budgeting Analysis: Computer Inc.

	Year 0	Year 1	Year 2	Year 3
1. Sales in Units		5,000,000	6,000,000	8,000,000
2. Price per Unit		KR600	KR700	KR800
3. Total Sale= (1) x (2)		KR3,000,000,000	KR4,200,000,000	KR6,400,000,000
4. Variable Cost		KR100	KR120	KR150
5. Total Variable Cost Per Unit		KR500,000,000	KR720,000,000	KR1,200,000,000
6. Fixed Cost		KR1,100,000,000	KR1,100,000,000	KR1,100,000,000
7. Noncash Expense		KR200,000,000	KR200,000,000	KR200,000,000
8. Total Expense = (5) + (6) + (7)		KR1,800,000,000	KR2,020,000,000	KR2,500,000,000
9. Before Tax Subsidiary Earnings = (3) - (8)		KR1,200,000,000	KR2,180,000,000	KR3,900,000,000
10. Danish Government Tax (20%)		KR240,000,000	KR436,000,000	KR780,000,000
11. After Tax Subsidiary Earnings		KR960,000,000	KR1,744,000,000	KR3,120,000,000
12. Net Cash Flow to Subsidiary (11) + (7)		KR1,160,000,000	KR1,944,000,000	KR3,320,000,000
13. Remittance by Subsidiary		KR580,000,000	KR972,000,000	KR166,000,000
14. Withholding Tax (10%)		KR58,000,000	KR97,200,000	KRKR166,000,000
15. Net Remittance by Subsidiary		KR522,000,000	KR874,800,000	KR1,494,000,000
16. Exchange Rate of Danish Krone		$0.15	$0.17	$0.20
17. Cash Flow to Parent		$78,300,000.00	$148,716,000.00	KR1,494,000,000
18. PV of Parent Cash Flows at (10%)		$71,174,700.00	$122,839,416.00	$224,996,400.00
19. Initial Investment	$200,000,000			
20. Cumulative NPV of Cash Flows		($128,825,300.00)	($5,985,884.00)	$219,010,516.00

(the base year) is equal to the money cash flow for that year t multiplied by the following ratio:

$$\frac{\text{Price level index in year}_0}{\text{Price level index in year}_1}$$

For example, if an investment promised a money return of $100 for three years and the price indexes for years 0 through 3 are 100.0, 110.0, 121.0, and 133.1, respectively, the real cash flows are as follows:

Year 1: $100 $\times$ 100/110 = 90.90

Year 2: $100 $\times$ 100/121 = 82.64

Year 3: $100 $\times$ 100/133.1 = 75.13

The money discount rate r can also be computed. Assuming that f is the annual rate of inflation, i is the real discount rate, and the decision maker is in the zero bracket, then

$$r = (1 + f)(1 + i) - 1$$

or

$$r = i + f + if$$

For example, if the real return before taxes is 3 percent and the rate of inflation is 10 percent, the nominal discount rate is:

$$0.03 + 0.10 + 0.003 = 0.133$$

To illustrate the correct analysis under inflation, assume the same data as in the previous example. The correct analysis can be made using either of two procedures. The first analysis discounts the money cash flows using a money discount rate. The present value of the investment will be computed as follows:

Period	Money cash flow	Nominal present factor at 13.3%	Present value
1	100	0.8226	88.26
2	100	0.7792	77.92
3	100	0.6874	68.74
			234.92

The second analysis discounts the real cash flows using a real discount rate. The present value of the investment will give the same present value, as follows:

Period	Real cash flow	Real present value at 3%	Present value
1	90.90	0.9709	88.254
2	82.64	0.9426	77.896
3	75.13	0.9151	68.751
			234.901

Assuming a marginal tax rate t on nominal income, the nominal discount rate will be computed as follows:

$$1 + (1 - t)r = (1 + f) + 1 + (1 - t)$$

or

$$r = i + if + f/(1 - t)$$

Assuming the tax rate to be 30 percent, the nominal rate is then computed as follows:

$$0.03 + (0.03 \times 0.10) + 0.10/(1 - 0.30) = 0.1758$$

In other words, a nominal rate of 17.58 percent is needed for an investor in a 30 percent tax bracket and facing an inflation rate of 10 percent to earn a real discount rate of 3 percent.

Impact of Exchange Rate Changes

Capital budgeting for multinational corporations can lead to different results depending on the nature of the expectation of the levels of exchange rates. In general, three scenarios are possible: (1) a stable exchange rate, (2) a strong exchange rate characterized by increasing values over the life of the project, and (3) a weak exchange rate characterized by decreasing values over the life of the project. Exhibits 7.5, 7.6, and 7.7 illustrate the impact of each of these three scenarios on the cumulative NPV of cash flows of a capital project by the Jordanian subsidiary of an American multinational corporation. The NPVs of the project are $43,610 under a strong rate scenario, $24,210 under a stable rate scenario, and −$14,500 under a weak rate scenario. The large difference between these scenarios points to the importance of exchange rate fluctuations in multinational capital budgeting and also the importance of accurate exchange rate forecasting.

Exhibit 7.5
Capital Budgeting Analysis under a Strong Rate Scenario

	Year 1	Year 2	Year 3	Year 4	Year 5	Year 6
Funds Remitted After Withholding Taxes	JD 20,000	JD 20,000	JD 20,000	JD 20,000	JD 20,000	JD 20,000
Exchange Rate	$2.00	$2.10	$2.20	$2.30	$2.40	$2.50
Cash Flow to the Parent	$40,000	$42,000	$44,000	$46,000	$48,000	$50,000
Discount Factor	0.909	0.826	0.753	0.683	0.621	0.564
PV of Cash Flows	$36,360	$34,692	$33,132	$31,418	$29,808	$28,200
Cumulative NPV of Cash Flows	($113,640)	($78,948)	($45,816)	($14,398)	$15,410	$43,610

Note: Initial investment by the parent = $150,000.

Exhibit 7.6
Capital Budgeting Analysis under a Stable Rate Scenario

	Year 1	Year 2	Year 3	Year 4	Year 5	Year 6
Funds Remitted After Withholding Taxes	JD 20,000	JD 20,000	JD 20,000	JD 20,000	JD 20,000	JD 20,000
Exchange Rate	$2	$2	$2	$2	$2	$2
Cash Flow to the Parent	$40,000	$40,000	$40,000	$40,000	$40,000	$40,000
Discount Factor	0.909	0.826	0.753	0.683	0.621	0.564
PV of Cash Flows	$36,360	$33,040	$30,120	$27,320	$24,840	$22,560
Cumulative NPV of Cash Flows	($113,640)	($80,600)	($50,480)	($23,160)	$1,680	$24,240

Note: Initial investment by the parent = $150,000.

Exhibit 7.7

Capital Budgeting Analysis under a Weak Rate Scenario

	Year 1	Year 2	Year 3	Year 4	Year 5	Year 6
Funds Remitted After Withholding Taxes	JD 20,000	JD 20,000	JD 20,000	JD 20,000	JD 20,000	JD 20,000
Exchange Rate	$2.0	$1.8	$1.6	$1.4	$1.2	$1.0
Cash Flow to the Parent	$40,000	$36,000	$32,000	$28,000	$24,000	$20,000
Discount Factor	0.909	0.826	0.753	0.683	0.621	0.564
PV of Cash Flows	$36,360	$29,736	$24,096	$19,124	$14,904	$11,280
Cumulative NPV of Cash Flows	($113,640)	($83,904)	($59,808)	($40,684)	($95,780)	($14,500)

Note: Initial investment by the parent = $150,000.

251

Foreign Tax Regulations

The tax regulations in the country where the project is planned are extremely important to the capital budgeting analysis. The first reason concerns the requirements of using after tax cash flows for the capital budgeting decisions as well as a tax-adjusted project cost of the capital. The second reason is that countries levy different income tax rates on the earnings of subsidiaries as well as remittance taxes when they are finally remitted to the parent company. The percentage of the profit that can be remitted can also be the subject of regulations that attempt to limit the amount of funds leaving the country, especially in the case of the developing countries. Some countries, in fact, may require that a certain percentage of the profit be reinvested in specific areas of importance to the economic and social growth of the country.

Political and Economic Risk

Multinational companies face the risks created by political, exchange, and economic changes. This chapter covers some of the techniques used to manage economic risks. In a capital budgeting context, various ways may be used to account for political risks. One is to adjust each year's cash flows by the cost of an exchange risk adjustment. Other ways include shortening the minimum payback period, raising the discount rate or required rate of return without adjusting cash flows, and adjusting cash flows and raising the discount rate. A consensus seems to suggest that multinationals should use either the risk-adjusted discount rate or the certainty-equivalent approach to adjust proper estimates for political risk.[19]

A scenario approach to risk analysis, generally used to forecast expected cash flow domestically, can be applied to political risk evaluation. Hypothetical cash flow scenarios for political risk evaluation include (a) plant not nationalized, (b) plant nationalized with adequate compensation, (c) plant nationalized with inadequate compensation, and (d) plant nationalized with no compensation. The expected cash flow number for each scenario can be evaluated year by year and discount back to the present. The discounted values obtained can then be multiplied by the probability of cash outcome to yield and expected value.

Risk-Adjusted Discount Rate Method

One of the techniques for incorporating risk in the evaluation process is the discount rate, which involves manipulating the discount rate applied to the cash flow to reflect the amount of risk inherent in a project. The higher the risk associated with a project, the higher the discount rate applied to cash flows. If a given project is perceived to be twice as risky as most projects acceptable to the firm and the cost of capital is 12 percent, the correct adjusted discount rate is 24 percent.

Certainty-Equivalent Method

Another technique for incorporating risk in the evaluation process is the equivalent method, which involves adjusting the future cash flows so that a project can be evaluated on a riskless basis. The adjustment is formulated as follows:

$$NPV = \sum_{t=0}^{n} \frac{\alpha_t CF_t}{(1 + R_F)^t} - I_0$$

where

α = risk coefficient applied to the cash flow of period $t(CF_t)$

I_0 = initial cost of the project

R_f = risk-free rate

As this formula shows, the method multiplies the future cash flows by certainty equivalents to obtain a riskless cash flow. Note also that the discount rate used is R_f, which is a risk-free rate of interest.

To illustrate the certainty:

I_0 = initial cost = $30,000

CF_1 = cash flow, year 1 = $10,000

CF_2 = cash flow, year 2 = $20,000

CF_3 = cash flow, year 3 = $30,000

α_1 = certainty equivalent, year 1 = 0.9

α_2 = certainty equivalent, year 2 = 0.8

α_3 = certainty equivalent, year 3 = 0.6

The NPV of the investment using a risk-free discount rate of 6 percent is computed as in Exhibit 7.8. Because the NPV is positive, the investment should be considered acceptable. The main advantage of the certainty-equivalent method is that it allows the assignment for a different risk factor to each cash flow, given that risk can be concentrated in one more periods.

The certainty-equivalent method and the risk-adjusted discount rate method are comparable methods of evaluating risk. To produce similar ranking, the following equation must hold:

$$\frac{\alpha_t CF_t}{(1 + R_F)^t} = \frac{CF_t}{(1 + R_A)^t}$$

where

Exhibit 7.8
Certainty Equivalent Method

Period	Cash Flow (CF₁)	Risk Coefficient (α)	Certainty Equivalent	Risk Free Rate	Present Value
				(R_f)	
1	$10,000	0.9	$9,000	0.943	$8,487
2	$20,000	0.8	$16,000	0.890	$14,420
3	$30,000	0.6	$18,000	0.840	$15,120
Present value of cash flows					$37, 847
Initial investment					$30,000
Net present value					$7,847

α_t = risk coefficient used in the certainty-equivalent method

R_F = risk free discount rate

R_A = discount rate used in the risk adjusted discount method

CF_t = future cash flow

Solving for t yields:

$$\alpha_t = \frac{(1 + R_F)^t}{(1 + R_A)^t}$$

Given that R_A and R_F are constant and $R_A < R_F$, then α_t decreases over time, which means that risk increases over time. To illustrate, assume that in the previous example, $R_A = 15$ percent. Then

$$\alpha_1 = \frac{(1 + R_F)^1}{(1 + R_A)^1} = \frac{(1 + 0.006)^1}{(1 + 0.15)^1} = 0.921$$

$$\alpha_2 = \frac{(1 + R_F)^2}{(1 + R_A)^2} = \frac{(1 + 0.006)^2}{(1 + 0.15)^2} = 0.848$$

$$\alpha_3 = \frac{(1 + R_F)^3}{(1 + R_A)^3} = \frac{(1 + 0.006)^3}{(1 + 0.15)^3} = 0.783$$

In many cases, however, this assumption of increasing risk may not be realistic.

Expropriation

Multinational companies sometimes face the extreme outcome of risk expropriation. One way to account for expropriation is to charge a premium for political risk insurance to each year's cash flow, whether or not such insurance is purchased. Another way, suggested by Shapiro, is to examine the impact of expropriation on the project's present value to the parent company. As a result:

$$\text{old present value} = -C_0 + \sum_{t=1}^{n} \frac{X_t}{(1 + k)^t}$$

$$\text{new present value} = -C_0 + \sum_{t=1}^{h-1} \frac{X_t}{(1 + k)^t} + \frac{G_h}{(1 + k)^t}$$

where

C_0 = initial investment outlay

X_t = parent's expected after-tax cash flow from the project in year t

n = life of the project

k = project cost of capital

h = year in which expropriation takes place

G_h = expected value of the net compensation provided

The compensation (G_h) is supposed to come from one of the following sources:

1. direct compensation paid to the firm by the local government
2. indirect compensation, such as other business contracts to the firm expropriated (an example would be the management contracts received by oil companies after the Venezuelan government nationalized their properties)
3. payment received from political insurance
4. tax deductions received after the parent declares the expropriation as an extraordinary loss
5. a reduction in the amount of capital that must be repaid by the project equal to the unamortized portion of any local borrowing

Blocked Funds

Multinationals sometimes face the situation in which funds are blocked for various reasons, including forms of exchange control. Again, Shapiro suggested raising the present value expression to include the impact of blocked funds on the project's cash flows. As a result:

$$\text{old present value} = -C_0 + \sum_{t=1}^{n} \frac{X_t}{(1+k)^t}$$

$$\text{new present value} = -C_0 + \sum_{t=1}^{j=1} \frac{X_t}{(1+k)^t} + \sum_{t=j}^{n} \frac{Y_t}{(1+k)^t}$$
$$+ (1 - \alpha_j) \sum_{t=j}^{n} \frac{(X-Y_t)}{(1+k)^t} + \alpha_j \sum_{t=j}^{n} \frac{(X-Y_t)}{(1+r)^{n-1}}$$

where the symbols C_0, X_t, n, and k are the same as in the formulas used for expropriation. The new symbols are:

j = year in which funds become blocked

n = year in which exchange controls are removed

α_j = probability of exchange controls in year 1 and 0 in other years

Y_t = units of currency that can be repatriated if exchange costs exist

Uncertain Salvage Value

When the salvage value may be uncertain, Madura suggested the estimation of a breakeven salvage value or break-even terminal value, the salvage value for which $NPV = 0$. The breakeven salvage value is estimated by setting the net present value equal to zero, as follows:

$$NPV = -OI + \sum_{t=1}^{n} \frac{CF_t}{(1 + r)^t} + \frac{SV_n}{(1 + z)^n}$$

$$0 = -OI + \sum_{t=1}^{n} \frac{CF_t}{(1 + r)^t} + \frac{SV_n}{(1 + z)^n}$$

$$SV_n = \left[OI - \sum_{t=1}^{n} \frac{CF_t}{(1 + z)^t} \right] (1 + z)^n$$

where

NPV = net present value
0 = zero
SV_n = salvage value
OI = original investment
CF_t = cash flow at time t
r = desired rate of return[20]

EVALUATION OF INTERNATIONAL ACQUISITIONS

Foreign mergers and acquisitions are on the increase, particularly in the United States, due to the resulting wealth effects. The reasons for foreign investment in the United States include:[21]

1. dollar devaluation effect expressed as a documented inverse relation between the exchange rate of the U.S. dollar and the level of foreign investment in the United States[22]

2. favorable tax treatment for foreign buyers because overseas firms that acquire American companies may have the ability to deduct interest on acquisition debt both in the United States and their home countries, through, for example, the creation of a third subsidiary to finance the deal in cases where this tax treatment of such units is favorable.[23] A description of a typical plan follows: "A typical plan would have the foreign acquire; borrow 100 percent of acquisition cost and establish two subsidiaries, a U.S. acquisition subsidiary and a finance subsidiary in a third country. The foreign acquirer injects a fraction of borrowed funds as equity into its third-country finance subsidiary. The third-country finance subsidiary then would loan all of its funds to its brother/sister company, the U.S. acquisition subsidiary. The foreign acquirer deducts

interest expense on acquisition debt and receives an income tax benefit on its own operation from its home country. Meanwhile, the bulk of the borrowed funds are loaned by the third-country finance subsidiary, which deducts the interest expense on the debt against the income of the acquired operations and receives a U.S. tax benefit. If the interest income that the third country finance subsidiary receives from the U.S. acquisition subsidiary does not trigger significant taxation in the form of U.S. with-holding tax, income taxation by the host country of the finance subsidiary or income taxation for the foreign parent, an extra tax benefit for the acquisition interest expense has been achieved."[24]

3. goodwill accounting treatment because foreign companies create acquired goodwill through their choice of acquisition accounting: "In deciding how high to bid, foreign companies do not have to worry about penalizing future profits. They can write off goodwill immediately against their balance sheet reserves; this shrinks the balance sheet but profits are unaffected. If acquired goodwill is left on the balance sheet as is done in United States (and Canada), companies must then amortize it from profit over forty years; reported profits are reduced by the amortization charge each year for as many years as it takes to eliminate the acquired goodwill from the balance sheet altogether."[25]

The evaluation of international acquisition is similar to a capital budgeting problem. The decision is to determine if the net present value of a company from the acquiring firm's perspective (NPV_a) is positive. It may be computed as follows:

$$NPV_a = - (IO_f)SP_{-t} + \sum_{t=1}^{n} \frac{(CF_{f,t})(SP_t)}{(1 + r)^t} + \frac{SV_f SP_n}{(1 + r)^n}$$

where

NPV_a = net present value of a foreign takeover prospect

IO_f = acquisition price in foreign currency

SP = spot rate of the foreign currency

$CF_{f,t}$ = foreign currency cash flows per period to be remitted

r = required rate of return on the acquisition of the company

SV_t = salvage value in foreign-currency units

n = time at which the company will be sold[26]

MANAGING POLITICAL RISK

Capital budgeting decisions, as well as other operating, financing and distri-bution decisions taken by multinational firms, need to take into account the impact of politics on the potential outcomes of these decisions. There is an objective need for a definition of the nature of political risk, methods for fore-casting it, and a role for management accounting in managing it.

Nature of Political Risk

Political risk is a phenomenon that characterizes an unfriendly human climate in both developed and developing countries. A high crime rate or an upsurge of violent unrest, even in highly developed countries, qualifies such countries for the dubious label of "political risk." Political risk essentially refers to the potential economic losses arising as a result of governmental measures or special situations that may either limit or prohibit the multinational activities of a firm. Examples of these situations include those when (1) discontinuities occur in the business environment, (2) they are difficult to anticipate, or (3) they result from political change.

Political risk can affect all foreign firms; in such a case it is macropolitical risk. It may, however, affect only selected foreign firms or industries or only certain foreign firm characteristics. In such a case, it is micropolitical risk. In both cases, the risk refers to "that uncertainty stemming from unanticipated and unexpected acts of governments or other organizations which may cause a loss to the business firm."[27] It is manifest through a climate of uncertainty dominated by a probable loss to the business enterprise. It may arise from different sources. Green noted that a wide spectrum of political risks may be generated "by the attitudes, policies and overt behavior of those governments and other local power centers such as rival political parties, labor unions, and nationalistic groups."[28] A study prepared for the Financial Executives Research Foundation identified the following twelve political risk factors:

- radical change in government composition or policy
- expropriation
- nationalization
- attitude of opposition groups
- probability of opposition-group takeover
- attitude toward foreign investment
- quality of government management
- ownership requirements
- anti-private-sector influence
- labor instability
- relationship with the company's home government
- relationship with neighboring countries[29]

Political risk may lead to various outcomes, namely, expropriation/nationalization, compulsory local equity participation, operational restrictions, discrimination, price controls, blockage of remittances, or breach of government contracts. Given the negative impacts of the outcomes of political risk on foreign operations, especially in the extreme case in which a government takes over a business activity through confiscation and expropriation, there is a strong need to be able to forecast political risk.

Forecasting Political Risk

It would not be surprising to learn that various proposals have been made about how to forecast political risks; Robock and Simmonds suggested an evaluation of the vulnerability of a company to political risk by an analysis of its operations, with the following questions in mind:

- Are periodic external inputs of new technology required?
- Will the project be competing strongly with local nationals who are in, or trying to enter, the same field?
- Is the operation dependent on natural resources, particularly minerals or oil?
- Does the investment put pressure on the country's balance of payments?
- Does the enterprise have a strong monopoly position in the local market?
- Is the product socially essential and acceptable?[30]

Robert Stobaugh noticed that a number of U.S.-based multinational enterprises had developed scales with which to rate countries on the basis of their investment climates.[31] An *Argus Capital Market Report* offered for country risk analysis a laundry list of economic indicators to "educate the decision-maker and force him to think in terms of the relevant economic fundamental."[32] These indicators are monetary base, domestic base, foreign reserves, purchasing power parity index, currency/deposit ratio, consumer prices as a percentage change, balance of payments, goods and services as a percentage of foreign reserves, percentage change exports/percentage change imports, exports as a percentage of the gross national product (GNP), imports as a percentage of the GNP, foreign factor income payments as a percentage of the GNP, average tax rate, government deficit as a percentage of the GNP, government expenditures, real GNP as a percentage change, and real per capita GNP as a percentage change.

Shapiro offered the following common characteristics of country risk:

1. a large government deficit relative to GDP
2. a high rate of money expansion if it is combined with a relatively fixed exchange rate
3. high leverage combined with highly variable terms of trade
4. substantial government expenditures yielding low rates of return
5. price controls, interest rate ceilings, trade restriction, and other government-imposed barriers to the smooth adjustment of the economy to changing relative price
6. a citizenry that demands, and a political system that accepts, government responsibility for maintaining and expanding the nation's standard of living through public sector spending

The less stable the political system, the more important this factor is likely to be.[33] More recently, Rummel and Heenan provided a four-way classification of attempts to forecast political interference: "grand tours," "old hands," Delphi techniques, and quantitative methods.[34] A "grand tour" involves a visit of the potential host country by an executive or a team of people for an inspection tour and later a visit to the home office. Superficiality and overdose of selective information have marred the grand tour technique.

The "old hands" technique involves acquiring area expertise from seasoned educators, diplomats, journalists, or businesspeople. Evidently, too much implicit faith is put in the judgment of these so-called experts.

The Delphi techniques may be used to survey a knowledgeable group. First, selective elements influencing the political climate are chosen. Next, experts are asked to rank these factors toward the development of an overall measure or index of political risk. Finally, countries are ranked on the basis of the index. As stated by Rummel and Heenan, "the strength of the Delphi technique rests on the posing of relevant questions. When they are defective, the entire structure crumbles."[35]

The quantitative methods technique involves developing elaborate models using multivariate analysis to either explain and describe underlying relationships affecting a nation-state or predict future political events. Two such political risk models using this technique may be identified in the literature and are examined next.

The Knudsen "Ecological" Approach

Harald Knudsen's model involves gathering socioeconomic data depicting the "ecological structures" or investment climate of a particular foreign environment to be used to predict political behavior in general and national propensity to expropriate in particular. (The model is shown in Exhibit 7.9.) The model maintains that the national propensity to expropriate may be explained by "a national frustration" factor and "scapegoat function of foreign investment."[36] Basically, if the level of national frustration is high and, at the same time, the level of foreign investment presence is also high, these foreign investments become a scapegoat, leading to a high propensity to expropriate. The level of frustration is envisaged as the difference between the level of aspirations and the level of welfare and expectations. The scapegoat of foreign investment is determined by the perceived general and special roles of foreign investment.

The variables are measured as follows. First, national aspirations may be expressed in terms of six proxy variables, namely, degree of urbanization, literacy rate, number of newspapers, number of radios, degree of labor unionization, and national endowment of national resources. Second, the welfare of people may be measured by proxy variables, namely, infant survival rate, caloric consumption, number of doctors per population size, number of hospital beds per population size, percentage of housing with piped water supply, and per

Exhibit 7.9
National Propensity to Expropriate Model

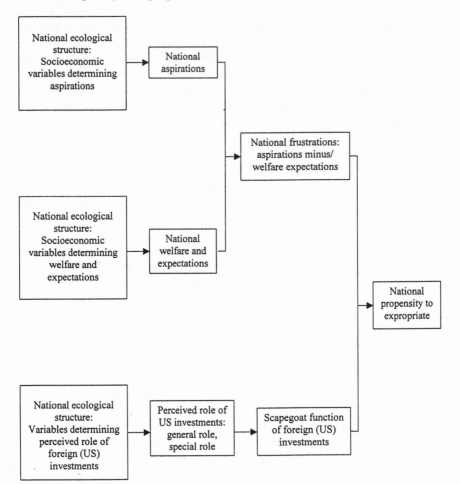

capita GNP. Third, national expectations may be measured by the percentage of GNP being invested. These are surrogate measures of the underlying factors in Knudsen's model. The models reliability may be improved by a search for more relevant measures by subjecting a bigger selection of these surrogate measures to factor analysis. Such an analysis, if used in a confirmatory way, may reduce their number to only the salient measure. However, more research, especially in the management accounting field, may be needed to improve and test Knudsen's model or similar "components-based" models of predicting political risk.

The Haendel-West-Meadow "Political System Stability Index"

Another components approach to the forecasting of political risk was provided by Haendel, West, and Meadow in an empirical, indicator-based measure of political system stability, the Political System Stability Index (PSSI), in sixty-five developing countries.[37] It is composed of three equally weighted indices: the socioeconomic index, the governmental process index, and the societal conflict index (which itself is derived from three subindices: public unrest, internal violence, and coercion potential). All of these indices are derived from fifteen indirect measures of the political system that evaluate stability and adaptability. Basically, the higher the PSSI score, the greater the stability of the political system. The index was based on data from the 1961–1966 period. There is a need to test the validity of the index with more recent data before using it as a forecasting tool. In any case, the model demonstrates again the feasibility of a components approach to the study of political risk. As stated by Haendel, the Political System Stability Index derives its importance from the role the political system plays in establishing power relationship and norms for resolving conflicts in society. It assumes that the degree of political stability in a country may indicate the society's capacity to cope with new demands.[38]

Belkaoui and Belkaoui's Determinants of Political Risk

Belkaoui and Belkaoui developed a model for the explanation and prediction of political risk. The dependent variable used is political risk (PR).[39] The dependent variable used is political risk as evaluated by the *International Country Risk Guide (ICRG)*. The independent variables are:

1. United Nations human development index (HDI)
2. gross domestic savings as a percentage of gross domestic product (GDSP)
3. labor force as a percentage of total population (LFTP)
4. terms of trade (TOT)
5. total expenditures on education and health as a percentage of gross domestic product (TEEHG)
6. military expenditures as a percentage of gross national product (MEG)

The model is as follows:

$$PR = -10.281 + 63.103\ HDI + 0.561\ GDSP + 0.435\ LFTP - 0.154\ TOT + 1.105\ TEEHG - 1.120\ MEG$$

Basically, the higher the political risk, the lower will be the human development index, the labor force as a percentage of the total population, the gross domestic savings as a percentage of gross domestic product, and the total expenditures on education and health as a percentage of gross domestic product. Similarly, the higher the political risk, the higher will be the terms of trade and military expenditures as a percentage of gross national product.

Coping with Political Risk

Forecasting political risk is not enough; the problem is how to cope with or minimize it. Various techniques have been proposed for minimizing political risk. Eiteman and Stonehill suggested the following three categories of techniques for dealing with political risk:

1. negotiating the environment before investment by concluding concession agreements, adaptation to host country goals, planned investment, and investment guarantees

2. implementing specific operating strategies after the investment decision in production, logistics, marketing, finance, organization, and personnel, for example, local zoning, a safe location of facilities, and control of transportation and of patents and processes are examples of operating strategies in production and logistics that may reduce the likelihood of political interference or expropriation

3. resorting to specific compensation strategies after expropriation, including rational negotiation, application of power tactics to bargaining legal remedies, use of the International Center for Settlement of Investment Disputes, and surrenders in the interest of seeking salvage[40]

Another way of coping with political risk is to negotiate a tight investment agreement that spells out the specific rights and responsibilities of both the foreign firm and the host government. Eiteman and Stonehill suggested that the investment agreement spell out, among other things, the following policies on financial and managerial issues:

- the basis on which fund flows, such as dividends, management fees and loan repayments, may be remitted
- the basis for setting any applicable transfer prices
- the right to export to third-country markets
- obligations to build, or fund, social and economic overhead projects, such as schools, hospitals, and retirement systems
- methods of taxation, including the rate and type of taxation and how the rate base is determined
- access to host country capital markets, particularly for long-term borrowing
- permission for 100 percent foreign ownership versus required local ownership (joint venture) participation
- price controls, if any, applicable to sales in the host country markets
- requirements for local sourcing versus import of raw materials and components

- permission to use expatriate managerial and technical personnel
- provision for arbitration of disputes[41]

Haendel classified, appropriately, the traditional tools of risk management into five general categories:

1. avoidance, whereby the risk manager may recommend not investing or diversifying, or else impose a ceiling on the exposure a firm allows a country
2. transfer, whereby the risk manager may recommend including local individuals, either investors or managers
3. diversification and loss prevention, whereby the risk manager may recommend diversifying to reduce the reliance on a production facility of natural resource supply in any one country
4. insurance, whereby the risk manager may recommend that the firm secures insurance against political risk as a way of shielding the firm's assets from unexpected losses, possibly even including self-insurance in the form of a separate fund
5. retention, whereby the risk manager may recommend that not all political risks can be avoided, transferred, diversified, or insured against, in which case the firm should include political risk analysis in its decision-making process.[42]

There remains the question of what the multinationals actually do to cope with risk. A study prepared for the Financial Executives Research Foundation researched multinationals and found a number of techniques that could be used both for investment and when operating overseas.[43] The techniques found to be most useful by participant firms in their preinvestment negotiations with local business, once the investment had been made and the firms were committed, were maximizing the use of local debt and local funding, adapting to changing governmental priorities, sourcing locally to stimulate the economy and reduce dependence on imports, and increasing exports. Besides using those techniques, the respondent firms admitted to insuring against the losses that might be caused by expropriation/confiscation, nationalization, foreign exchange inconvertibility, war, revolution or insurrection damages, kidnapping and ransom, long-term currency losses, and even inflation. The insurance was provided by the Overseas Private Investment Corporation (OPIC), a credit insurance program administered by the Export/Import Bank of the United States (Eximbank) jointly with Foreign Credit Insurance Association (FCIA), and private political risk insurance organizations such as the American International Group (AIG) and Lloyd's of London.

OPIC is a little known U.S. government agency that mixes private capital with government guarantees to promote American foreign policy goals. OPIC is present in more than 140 emerging economies. It uses the promise of very high returns and the protection of government guarantees to attract American investors to all parts of the globe. OPIC has even sponsored emerging market funds that buy stocks in emerging market business. These funds are structured so that private investors—typically, large corporations and pension funds—can invest with limited exposure to downside risk and, if their investments are successful, reap huge gains. A portrait of such a fund is shown in Exhibit 7.10.

Accounting for Political Risk

Accounting for political risk calls for a systematic approach to the assignment of a risk premium to a return on investment (ROI) budget. One approach consists of adjusting the corporate ROI by a numerical risk index developed for each country of operation. For example, assume that the Mantis Company owns three wholly affiliated in countries A, B, C. For the first year, the actual divisional income and investment of each affiliate are as follows:

Division	Total Investment	Divisional Income
A	$1,000,000	$ 200,000
B	$5,000,000	$1,550,000
C	$2,200,000	$ 550,000

The Mantis company requires an 8 percent return on its investments locally. In evaluating its foreign affiliates, the Mantis company relied on a political risk instrument containing forty risk attributes. The scores for countries A, B, and C are as follows:

Country	Political Risk Index
A	20
B	10
C	12

The adjusted ROIs are computed as follows:

Division	Nominal ROI	Country Risk Coefficient	Risk Adjusted ROI	Actual ROI
A	8%	20/40 = 0.50	0.08/0.50 = 0.16	0.20
B	8%	10/40 = 0.25	0.08/0.25 = 0.32	0.31
C	8%	12/40 = 0.30	0.08/0.30 = 0.26	0.25

Other things being equal, the best performance is obtained by the affiliate in country B.

CONCLUSIONS

Capital budgeting for multinationals relies on the same evaluation techniques as for domestic operations. There are, however, many adjustments to be made

Exhibit 7.10
The Africa Growth Fund, 1999

Started in 1987, the fund made its first investment in 1991 and is a 20-year, limited partnership. Its mission is to take equity and debt positions in a small number of high-quality African businesses. The fund's objective is a compounded return to investors of 12 to 15 percent or more.

Capital

- *Equity*

$5 million, $1 million from each of five institutional investors

- *Debt*

$20 million in U.S. Government-guaranteed interest-bearing notes

Equity Investors

- Citicorp Sub-Saharan Investments
- Coca-Cola Export Corporation (a subsidiary of Coca-Cola)
- Kellogg Development (a subsidiary of Dresser Industries)
- Lommus Development
- Rockefeller & Company

Investments

- Continental Acceptance a merchant bank in Ghana.
- Gaberone International Hotel, a Botswana hotel company.
- Eden Roc Somiaf, a gold mine in Ivory Coast.
- Fidelity Resources, a vehicle leasing company in Ghana
- Africa Air Products, which refills oxygen cylinders and makes acetylene in Cameroon.
- Central Glass Industries, a Kenyan bottler of beer and Coca-Cola.
- Societe Ivorienne de Torrefaction de Café, a coffee grinder, roaster and exporter in Ivory Coast.
- Ghana Prawn Farm, an aquaculture farm.

to account for project cash flows, the impact of inflation, the impact of changes in the exchange rate, foreign tax regulations, political and economic risk, expropriation, blocked funds, and uncertain salvage value. These issues and their corresponding solutions have been examined in this chapter. When investing abroad, political risk must be accounted for and managed.

NOTES

1. Riahi-Belkaoui, Ahmed, *Evaluating Capital Projects* (Westport, CT: Greenwood Publishing, 2001).

2. Evans, Thomas G., Martin E. Taylor, and Oscar J. Holzmann, *International Accounting and Reporting* (Cincinnati, OH: South-Western Publishing Co., 1994), p. 322.

3. Eiteman, David K., Arthur I. Stonehill, and Michael H. Moffelt, *Multinational Business Finance* (Reading, MA: 1992), p. 436.

4. Ibid.

5. Aharoni, Yair, *The Foreign Investment Decision Process* (Boston: Harvard Graduate School of Business Administration, Division of Research, 1966).

6. Ibid., pp. 54–55.

7. Ibid., pp. 70–71.

8. Eiteman, Stonehill, and Moffelt, *Multinational Business Finance*, p. 459.

9. Czinkota, Michael R., Rietra Rivoli, and Illsea A. Ronkainen, *International Business* (Chicago: Dryden Press, 1989), p. 529.

10. Graddis, Paul O., "Analyzing Overseas Investments," *Harvard Business Review* 10 (May–June 1966), p. 119.

11. Shapiro, A. C., "Capital Budgeting and Long-Term Financing," *Financial Management*, (Spring, 1978), p. 8.

12. Bavishi, U. B., "Capital Budgeting Practices of Multinationals," *Management Accounting*, (August 1981), pp. 32–35.

13. Newman, Charles M., II, and I. James Czechowica, *International Risk Management* (Morristown, NJ: Financial Executives Research Foundation, 1983), p. 88.

14. Ibid., p. 89.

15. The weighted cost of capital concept can be extended to include debt denominated in foreign currencies, debt issued by foreign subsidiaries, and retained earnings of foreign subsidiaries.

16. Stonehill, Arthur, and Lessard Nathanson, "Capital Budgeting Techniques and the Multinational Corporation," *Journal of International Business Studies* (Spring 1975), p. 67.

17. Clark, John J., Thomas J. Hindelang, and Robert E. Pritchard, *Capital Budgeting: Planning and Control of Capital Expenditures*, 2nd Ed. (Englewood Cliffs, NJ: Prentice-Hall, 1984), pp. 419–426.

18. Madura, Jeff, *International Financial Management* (St. Paul, MN: West, 1995), p. 504.

19. Shapiro, Alan C., "Capital Budgeting for the Multinational Corporation," *Financial Management*, (Spring 1978), p. 10.

20. Madura, *International Financial Management*, p. 457.

21. Calkici, Nusret, Chris Hessel, and Kishore Tandon, "Foreign Acquisitions in the

United States and the Effect on Shareholder's Wealth," *Journal of International Financial Management and Accounting* (March 1, 1991), pp. 38–60.

22. Caves, R., "Corporate Mergers in International Economic Integration," Working Paper (Harvard University, Center for Economic Policy Research, 1990).

23. Haas, R. and J. Karls, "How Foreign Buyers Can Get Double Tax Deductions," *Mergers and Acquisitions* (July/August), 1989, pp. 16–33.

24. Ibid., p. 20.

25. Calkici, Hessel, and Tandon, "Foreign Acquisitions in the United States and the Effects on Shareholder's Wealth," p. 46.

26. Madura, *International Financial Management*, p. 518.

27. Greene, Fred, "Management of Political Risk," *Best's Review* (July 1974), p. 15.

28. Ibid., p. 73.

29. Newman, and Czechowicz, *International Risk Management*, pp. 15–16.

30. Robock, S. H., and K. Simmonds, *International Business and Multinational Enterprises* (Homewood, IL: Irwin, 1973), p. 371.

31. Stobaugh, Robert, Jr., "How to Analyze Foreign Investment Climates," *Harvard Business Review* (September–October 1969), pp. 101–102.

32. "A Primer on Country Risk," *Argus Capital Market Report* (June 4, 1975), pp. 15–25.

33. Shapiro, Alan C., "Currency Risk and Country Risk in International Banking," *The Journal of Finance* (July 1985), p. 891.

34. Rummel, R. J., and David A. Heenan, "How Multinationals Analyze Political Risk," *Harvard Business Review* (January–February 1978), pp. 51–71.

35. Ibid., p. 70.

36. Knudsen, Harald, "Explaining the National Propensity to Expropriate: An Ecological Approach," *Journal of International Business Studies* (Spring 1974), pp. 51–71.

37. Haendel, Dan, and Gerald T. West, with Robert Meadow, *Overseas Investment and Political Risk*, Monograph Series no. 21 (Philadelphia, PA: Foreign Policy Research Institute, 1957).

38. Haendel, Dan, *Foreign Investments and the Management of Political Risk* (Boulder, COL: Westview Press, 1979), pp. 106–107.

39. Monti-Belkaoui, Janice, and Ahmed Riahi-Belkaoui, *The Nature, Estimation and Management of Political Risk* (Westport, CT: Greenwood Publishing, 1999).

40. Eiteman, D. K., and A. I. Stonehill, *Multinational Business Finance* (Reading, MA: Addison-Wesley, 1989), pp. 203–223.

41. Ibid., p. 503.

42. Haendel, *Foreign Investments*, pp. 139–146.

43. Newman and Czechowicz, *International Risk Management*, p. 81.

SELECTED READINGS

Booth, Laurence D. "Capital Budgeting Frameworks for the Multinational Corporation." *Journal of International Business Studies* 15 (Fall 1982), pp. 114–123.

Collins, J. Markham, and William S. Sekely. "The Relationship of Headquarters and Industry Classification to Financial Structure." *Financial Management* (Autumn 1983), pp. 45–51.

Doukas, John, and Nickolaos G. Travlos. "The Effect of Corporate Multinationalism on

Shareholders' Wealth: Evidence from International Acquisitions." *Journal of Finance* 13 (December 1988), pp. 1161–1175.

Kester, W. Carl. "Capital and Ownership Structure: A Comparison of United States and Japanese Manufacturing Corporations." *Financial Management*, Spring 1986, pp. 5–16.

Kim, Suk H., Edward J. Farragher, and Trevor Crick. "Foreign Capital Budgeting Practices Used by the U.S. and Non-U.S. Multinational Companies." *The Engineering Economist* 10 (Spring 1984), pp. 207–215.

Monti-Belkaoui, Janice, and Ahmed Riahi-Belkaoui. *The Nature, Estimation and Management of Political Risk* (Westport, CT: Greenwood Publishing, 1999).

Oblak, David J., and Roy J. Helm, Jr. "Survey and Analysis of Capital Budgeting Methods Used by Multinationals." *Financial Management* (Winter 1981), pp. 34–41.

Riahi-Belkaoui, Ahmed. *Handbook of Cost Accounting: Theory and Techniques* (Westport, CT: Greenwood Publishing, 1991).

———. *The New Foundation of Management Accounting* (Westport, CT: Greenwood Publishing, 1992).

Shapiro, A. C. "Capital Budgeting and Long-Term Financing." *Financial Management* (Spring 1978), pp. 5–25.

Srinivasan, Venkat, and Yong H. Kim. "Integrating Corporate Strategy and Multinational Capital Budgeting: An Analytical Framework." *Recent Developments in International Banking and Finance* 15 (1988), pp. 381–397.

Stanley, Marjorie T. "Capital Structure and Cost of Capital for the Multinational Firm." *Journal of International Business Studies* (Spring–Summer 1981), pp. 103–120.

Stanley, Marjorie T., and Stanley B. Block. "A Survey of Multinational Capital Budgeting." *Financial Review* (March 1984), pp. 36–54.

8

Accounting for Foreign Currency Transactions, Translation, Derivative Instruments, and Hedging Activities

INTRODUCTION

Multinational firms engage mostly in transactions that are denominated in a foreign currency. The value of these transactions is affected by the changes in exchange rates. Accounting for foreign-currency transactions needs to take account of these changes in values. The consolidation of the financial statements of foreign subsidiaries requires that both the parent's and the subsidiaries' financial statement to be denominated in the same currency. Therefore, a translation of the financial statement of the subsidiaries is required before consolidation.

This chapter examines the accounting treatments associated with both of the two phenomena affecting the activities of multinational firms, namely, accounting for foreign-currency transactions (1) and the translation of foreign financial statements.

ACCOUNTING FOR FOREIGN-CURRENCY TRANSACTIONS

Foreign currency transactions require settlement in a currency other than the functional currency of the reporting entity. The functional currency of an entity is the currency used in the economic environment in which that entity operates. Statement of Financial Accounting Standards No. 52 covers the accounting treatments required for accounting for foreign currency transactions.

For those foreign currency transactions not involving forward-exchange contracts, the following treatments apply.

1. At the time of the transaction, the asset, liability, revenue, or expense is recorded in the functional currency of the recording entity by use of the current exchange rate on the transaction.

2. At the balance-sheet date and at the date of the settlement of the foreign-currency translation, recorded balances in the foreign-currency transaction accounts are adjusted to reflect the current exchange rate.

3. With two exceptions, gains and losses resulting from the restatement are reflected in the current period's income statement.

4. The two exceptions are foreign-currency transactions that are the result of an economic hedge of a net investment in a foreign entity and long-term, intercompany foreign-currency transactions when the entities to the transaction are consolidated, combined, or accounted for by the equity method in the reporting enterprise's financial statements. In both cases, the gains and losses are reported as translation adjustments in a separate component of the stockholders' equity account.

The two examples that follow illustrate these treatments. In Example 1, the treatment of transaction gains and losses in current net income is discussed in relation to the export and import of goods. Example 2 uses an intercompany foreign-currency transaction to illustrate the treatment of transaction gains and losses as translation adjustments to stockholders' equity.

Example 1: Foreign-Exchange Transaction Involving Imports or Exports of Goods

The American National Company, a domestic entity with a December 31, 19X3 year end, sold merchandise to a foreign company on December 15, 19X3 for FC500,000, at 'net 30' terms. The following exchange rates are in effect on the following dates:

December 15, 19X3: FCI = $0.50
December 31, 19X3: FCI = $0.60
January 15, 19X3: FCI = $0.80

The accounting entries for this transaction follow:
1. At the date of the foreign-exchange transaction, December 15 19X3:

Accounts Receivable = $250,000
Sales = $250,000

to record the sale of goods for $250,000 (FC500,000 × $0.50).
2. At the balance-sheet date, December 31, 19X3:

Accounts Receivable = $50,000
Exchange Gain = $50,000

to record the exchange gain of $50,000 (FC500,000)($0.60 − $0.50). This exchange gain will be included in the 19X3 income statement of the American National Company, as a nonoperative item.

3. At the date of the settlement, January 15, 19X4:

Cash = $400,000
Exchange Gain = $100,000
Account Receivable = $300,000

to record the amount received on settlement, equal to $400,000 (FC500,000 × $0.8) and the exchange gain of $100,000 (FC500,000 × ($0.80 − $0.60)).

Example 2: Foreign-Exchange Transactions involving Intercompany Items

On November 20, 19X3, the American National Company made an advance of FC800,000 to the Other National Company, which is a subsidiary of the American National Company. The advance is long-term in nature and is not expected to be repaid this year. Information about the exchange rates between the U.S. dollar and the foreign currency of the subsidiary is as follows:

November 20, 19X3: FCI = $0.80
December 31, 19X3: FCI = $0.95

The entries for this foreign-exchange transaction follow:

1. At the date of the foreign-exchange transaction, November 20, 19X3:

Investment in Other National Company = $640,000
Cash = $640,000

2. At the balance sheet date, no exchange gains and losses are recognized in the current net income, so instead we enter into the determination of the translation adjustment as a component of stockholders' equity, as determined by the following:

Amount used in translation adjustment = FC800,000 ($0.95 − $80) = $40,000.

TRANSLATION METHODS

The translation of financial statements denominated in a foreign currency relies on exchange rates. Because these exchange rates fluctuate, the translation process raises two important questions:

1. Should current or historical exchange rates be used?
2. How should changes in the values of monetary items resulting in gains or losses be reported?

Various solutions have been proposed. Statement of Financial Accounting Standards (SFAS) No. 52 (par. 59) recognized that satisfactory resolution of these questions would not be easy:

for enterprises conducting activities in more than a single currency, the practical necessities of financial reporting in a single currency require that the changing prices between two units of currency be accommodated in some fashion. People generally agree on this practical necessity but disagree on concepts and details of implementation. As a result, there is significant disagreement among informed observers regarding the basic nature, information content, and meaning of results produced by various methods of translating amounts from foreign currencies into the reporting currency. Each method has strong proponents and severe critics.

Four methods have been used: (1) the current-noncurrent translation method, (2) monetary-nonmonetary translation method, (3) the current-rate translation method, and (4) the temporal translation method.

Current-Noncurrent Translation Method

Under the current-noncurrent method of translation, current assets and liabilities are translated at the current exchange rate (the actual exchange rate in effect at the balance-sheet date) and noncurrent assets and liabilities are translated at historical exchange rates (rates in effect when the assets were acquired and liabilities were incurred). Income statement items are translated at the average exchange rate, except for depreciation and amortization charges, which are translated at the historical rates in effect when the assets were acquired.

The current-noncurrent method suffers from a basic limitation: the assumptions that accounts should be grouped first according to maturity and then translated according to maturity lacks conceptual justification. Balance-sheet presentation according to maturity does not justify it as a choice of a translation rate.

Monetary-Nonmonetary Translation Method

Under the monetary-nonmonetary method of translation, monetary assets and liabilities are translated at current rates, while nonmonetary assets and liabilities are translated at historical rates. Income statement items are translated in the same manner as in the current-noncurrent method. Basically, monetary assets and liabilities are those representing rights to receive obligations to pay a fixed number of foreign currency units. Examples of monetary assets and liabilities include cash, receivables, payables, and long-term debt. Examples of nonmonetary assets and liabilities include fixed assets, long-term investment, and inventories.

The monetary-nonmonetary method was introduced as a way of correcting some of the limitations of the current-noncurrent method. The rationale behind the method was that monetary assets and liabilities represent fixed amounts of money, the parent-currency equivalent of which changes each time the exchange rate changes.

The monetary-nonmonetary method suffers from the same conceptual limitation as the current-noncurrent method. In effect, the monetary-nonmonetary classification scheme does not present any conceptual ground for the choice of the translation rates.

Current-Rate Translation Method

Under the current-rate translation method, all assets and liabilities are translated at the current exchange rate. The principal advantage of the current-rate method is that in the translation of accounts, it reflects the economic situation and perspective of the local country. Basically, the ratios and relationships existing in a local currency do not change after translation to the parent currency. Maintenance of the local perspective after translation is seen as a positive factor.

A problem arising from the use of the current-rate method is in the choice between the market exchange rate and the official exchange rate. The problem is aggravated by the degree of fluctuation in currency values in a world of floating exchange rates.

A better choice for translation would be the market exchange rate quoted for spot transactions in the country where the accounts to be translated originate, given that it is readily available and that it gives a better measure of the economic value of the local currency. A second problem that may arise from the use of the current-rate method is the possibility of having "abnormal" exchange gains and losses when the foreign currency is subjected to strong fluctuations.

A third problem arises from the use of foreign currency rather than the parent currency as the unit of measure. The parent firm may object to the situation, while the subsidiary may argue that the local perspective allows it to see the same relationships in parent-currency units as seen in the local currency. The situation is basically a plus from the point of view of the subsidiary and a minus from the parent's point of view.

Finally, the current-rate method may be considered a partial departure from the cost principle. In effect, it becomes a revaluation of assets expressed in foreign currencies, while those assets expressed in local currencies are kept at cost.

Temporal Translation Method

The purpose of the method is to use translation as a measurement process that does not change the attribute of the item being measured, but changes only the unit of measurement. Basically, accounts carried at past exchange rates are translated at historical rates, while accounts carried at current purchase prices, sale exchange prices, or future exchange prices are translated at current rates. Thus, under the temporal method, both current and non-current cash, receivables and payables are translated at current rates.

Other assets and liabilities are translated at either the current rate or their historical rates, depending upon whether they are carried at current values or historical values. In other words, the temporal method retains the accounting valuation basis used to measure the foreign currency items. It should be noted that similar results may be obtained under both the monetary-nonmonetary and the temporal methods if the historical cost-valuation basis is applied to all accounts. It should also be noted that the temporal method may be adapted to all other forms of asset-valuation bases, such as replacement cost, net realizable value, or discounted cash flows. Finally, the temporal method appears to avoid most of the limitations of the other translation methods.

A comprehensive tabulation of the rates for the translation of balance-sheet items under the current method, the current-noncurrent method, the monetary-nonmonetary method, and the temporal method is presented in Exhibit 8.1.

Financial Statement Effects

Exhibits 8.2–8.4 depict the financial statement effects of a hypothetical company under each of the translation methods depicted in the previous sections: (1) current-rate method, (2) current-noncurrent method, (3) monetary-nonmonetary method, and (4) temporal method. A simple balance-sheet example of year-end balance for a foreign subsidiary of a U.S. firm is shown in Exhibit 8.2. The values of the foreign currency have suffered a 20 percent depreciation, going from FC1 = \$2.00 the previous year to FC1 = \$1.60 this year.

The accounting exposure and the translation gain and loss under each of the four translation methods is shown in Exhibit 8.3. The balance sheet of the foreign subsidiary, using each of the translation methods is shown in Exhibit 8.4.

The wide array of results and exposures resulting from the different translation methods may call for a choice of one of the methods, based on conceptual reasons and in order to provide some uniformity in the translation process for multinational companies. This choice has been made repeatedly over the years and has included each of the translation methods. More recently, official pronouncements in the United States, the United Kingdom, and Canada have selected either the temporal method or the current-rate method for various conceptual and practical reasons.

Exhibit 8.1
Rates Used to Translate Assets and Liabilities

Balance Sheet Account	Current-Rate Method	Current-Nonccurent Method	Monetary-nonmonetary method	Temporal Method
Asset				
Cash	c	C	h	c
Marketable equity securities:				
Carried at Cost	c	C	h	h
Carried at current Market Price	c	C	h	h
Accounts and Notes Receivable	c	C	c	c
Inventories:				
Carried at cost	c	C	h	h
Carried at market	c	C	h	C
Prepaid Expenses	c	C	h	h
Property, plant and equipment	c	H	h	h
Accumulated depreciation	c	H	h	h
Other intangible assets	c	H	h	h
Liabilities and				
Equities				
Accounts and notes payable	c	C	c	c
Bonds payable or other long-term debt	c	H	c	c
Common Stock	h	H	h	h
Retained Earnings	Amount used to balance the balance sheet			

Note: h = historical; c = current.

Let us illustrate the financial statement effects with another example. Wellington Corporation, the New Zealand affiliate of a U.S. manufacturer, has the balance sheet shown in Exhibit 8.5. The relevant exchange rates applicable to the translation of the balance sheet are shown in Exhibit 8.6. The balance sheet expense and the translated balance sheet are in Exhibits 8.7 and 8.8, respectively.

Defining and Managing Translation Exposure

A translation exposure results from the periodic necessity of consolidating or aggregating the financial statements of parent companies and their subsidiaries.

Exhibit 8.2
Year-End Balance Sheet, Foreign Subsidiary of a U.S. Firm

Assets	
Cash	FC10,000
Account Receivables	20,000
Inventories [a]	30,000
Fixed asset (net)	40,000
Total	FC100,000

Liabilities and Owner's Equity	
Short-term payables	FC30,000
Long-term debt	40,000
Stockholder's equity	30,000
Total	FC100,000

[a]Inventories are carried at lower cost or market.

Before being consolidated with their parent's financial statements, the subsidiaries' financial statements have to be translated into the parent's currency. Translation exposure results from the possibility that a change in exchange rates will create an exchange gain or loss and, therefore, depends on the translation method and the exchange rate used for the translation of individual items in the balance sheet and income statement. The accounting for translation exposure, translated at the current exchange rate, may be stated in the following manner:

Translation exposure = (Foreign assets − Foreign liabilities)

Under the current-rate method, all accounts are translated at the exchange rate prevailing at the time of consolidation. In such cases, the translation exposure is equal to the net worth of the subsidiary as expressed in its local currency.

Under the current-noncurrent method, current assets and liabilities are translated at historical rates. In such cases, the translation exposure is equal to the difference between current assets and current liabilities, that is, the working capital.

Under the monetary-nonmonetary method, monetary assets and liabilities are translated at the current rate while nonmonetary assets and liabilities are translated at historical rates. In such cases, the translation exposure is equal to the difference between the monetary assets and the monetary liabilities.

Under the temporal method, assets and liabilities are translated in a manner

Exhibit 8.3
Balance Sheet Exposure to Foreign Exchange Rate

	Current Rate method	Current-Noncurrent Method	Monetary-Nonmonetary Method	Temporal Method
Assets				
Cash	FC10,000	FC10,000	FC10,000	FC10,000
Accounts Receivables	20,000	20,000	20,000	20,000
Inventories	30,000	30,000		30,000
Fixed Assets (net)	40,000			
Total	FC100,000	FC60,000	FC30,000	FC60,000
Liabilities and Owner's				
Equity				
Short-term payables	FC30,000	FC30,000	FC30,000	FC30,000
Long-term debt Shareholders' equity	40,000		FC40,000	FC40,000
Total	FC70,000	FC70,000	FC70,000	FC70,000
Accounting Exposure	FC30,000	FC30,000	FC(40,000)	FC(10,000)
Translation Gains	(12,000)	(12,000)	16,000	4,000

that retains their original measurement bases. Basically, cash, receivables, and payables are translated at the current rate. Assets carried at historical cost are translated at the historical rate, while assets carried at the current costs are translated at the current rate.

One way of minimizing translation exposure is to try to reach a "monetary balance," where exposed assets are equal to exposed liabilities. This may be achieved by the early declaration of dividends, prepayments of debits in foreign currencies, and settlement of other liabilities denominated in strong currencies. The objective is to reach a zero net translation exposure, where change in the exchange rate will affect the value of exposed assets in an equal, but opposite direction, to the change in value of exposed liabilities. If a firm uses the monetary-nonmonetary translation method, a monetary balance is reached when the exposed monetary assets are equal to the exposed monetary liabilities, which, under SFAS 52, is possible for a firm using the monetary-nonmonetary method of translation and that has the dollar as its functional currency.

Firms may elect to reduce translation exposure with a hedge in the forward, money, or option markets. The firm hedges the potential translation loss by selling local currency forward in an amount determined by the following formula:

Exhibit 8.4
Balance Sheet from Exhibit 8.2 Expressed in U.S. Currency

		US Dollars before FC Devaluation FC1=$2.00	US Dollars After FC Devaluation FC1=$1.60			
			Current rate	Current-non-current rate	Monetary-Non-monetary Rate	Temporal
Assets						
Cash	FC 10,000	$ 20,000	$ 16,000	$16,000	$16,000	$16,000
Accounts Receivable	FC 20,000	$ 40,000	$32,000	$32,000	$32,000	$32,000
Inventories (market)	FC 30,000	$ 60,000	$48,000	$48,000	$60,000	$48,000
Fixed Assets (net)	FC 40,000	$ 80,000	$80,000	$80,000	$80,000	$80,000
Total FC	$100,000	$200,000	$160,000	$176,000	$188,000	$176,000
Liabilities and Owners' Equity						
Short-term payables	FC30,000	$48,000	$48,000	$48,000	$48,000	$48,000
Long-term debt	FC40,000	$80,000	$64,000	$80,000	$64,000	$64,000
Stockholders' Equity	FC30,000	$60,000	$48,000	$48,000	$76,000	$64,000
Total FC	$100,000	$200,000	$160,000	$176,000	$188,000	$176,000

$$\text{Forward contract size} = \frac{\text{Expected transaction loss in reporting currency}}{\begin{array}{cc}\text{(Forward rate in} & \text{(Expected future spot}\\ \text{reporting currency units} - \text{rate in reporting currency}\\ \text{per local currency units} & \text{units per local currency units)}\end{array}}$$

Basically, the amount of foreign currency that may be sold forward is equal to the potential translation loss divided by the difference between the forward rate and the expected future spot rate, where the difference indicates the expected foreign-exchange profit per unit of the parent's reporting currency.

For example, assume that the exchange rate has changed from $0.30/peso (Ps) to $0.15/Ps, and the forward-exchange rate is $0.20/Ps. Then, for an expected translation loss of $300,000 where the dollar is the reporting currency, the size of the forward contract is represented as

$$\text{Forward Contract Size} = \frac{\$300,000}{0.20 - 0.15} = \text{Ps6,000,000}$$

Exhibit 8.5
Year-End Balance Sheet, Foreign Subsidiary of a U.S. Firm

Assets		Liability and Owner's Equity	
Cash	FC2,000	Accounts Payable	FC3,000
Accounts receivable	FC3,000	Long-term debt	FC6,000
Marketable securities at cost	FC8,000	Common stock	FC9,000
Inventories (at market)	FC7,000	Retained earnings	FC7,000
Fixed assets (net)	FC5,000		
	FC25,000		FC25,000

Assuming that the subsidiary is correct about its expectations and that it sold Ps6,000,000 forward, the transactions appear as follows:

1. At the time of sale: Sell pesos forward at $0.20/Ps, which amounts to Ps6,000,000 × 0.20 = $1,200,000 to be received at maturity.

2. At maturity: Buy pesos at a spot rate of $0.15/Ps, which amounts to Ps6.000 × 0.15 = $900,000 to pay out at maturity.

3. Profit: $1,200,000 − $900,000 = $300,000, which exactly offsets the translation loss of $300,000 before taxes.

The U.S. Position in FASB 52

In December 1982 the FASB issued SFAS 52. According to this statement, foreign-currency financial statements must be in conformity with GAAP before being translated to the reporting currency. Foreign-currency financial statements must be expressed and, if necessary, remeasured in the functional currency before being translated to the reporting currency. SFAS 52 provides some guidelines to be used in determining the functional currency. These guidelines are based on indicators of cash flow, sales price, sales market expense, financing, and intercompany transactions and arrangements.

SPAS 52 specifies six "salient economic factors" to guide management in the determination of the functional currency. These are:

1. cash flow direction

   a. denomination of cash flows

   b. impact on parent's cash flows

2. sales price indicators

Exhibit 8.6
Relevant Exchange Rates for Translating the Balance Sheet

Current exchange rate (end of previous year)	FC1 = $ 2.00
Current exchange rate (end of year)	FC1 = $1.60
Historical exchange rate for the marketable equity securities	FC1 = $1.80
Historical exchange rate for inventories	FC1 = $2.40
Historical exchange rate for property, plant and equipment	FC1 = $2.30
Historical exchange rate for long-term debt	FC1 = $2.30
Historical exchange rate for common stock	FC1 = $2.30
Average current exchange rate	FC1 = $2.00

    a. responsiveness of sales price to changes in exchange rates
    b. the market where the price is determined
3. sales market indicator

    a. location of primary sales market
4. expense indicator

    a. location of primary input market
5. financial indicators

    a. denomination of financing

    b. sufficiency of cash flows to meet obligations
6. intercompany transactions and arrangement indicators

    a. volume

    b. extent of interrelationships

These indicators, as indicated in paragraph 42 of SFAF 52, are listed in Exhibit 8.9.

Paragraph 80 of SFAS 52 represents the following characteristics as indicative of a foreign currency functional currency entity; it must: (1) be relatively self-contained and integrated in the local economy; (2) not be dependent on the day-to-day economic environment of the parent's currency; and (3) primarily generate and expand the local currency; moreover, it (4) may reinvest or convert to the parent local net cash flows and (5) must experience a low volume of intercompany transactions.

Paragraph 81 presents the following characteristics as indicative of a U.S. dollar functional currency: (1) it must be a direct and integral part of a parent's operations; (2) its assets must be acquired from the parent or through dollar spending; (3) financing must be obtained primarily from the parent or from dollar sources; (4) it must be dependent day-to-day upon the economic environment of the parent's functional currency; (5) cash flows related to individual

Exhibit 8.7
Balance-Sheet Exposure to a Foreign-Exchange Risk

	Current Rate Method		Current-Non-current Method	
Cash	FC	2,000	FC	2,000
Accounts Receivable		3,000		3,000
Marketable Equity				
Securities (cost)		8,000		8,000
Inventories (market)		7,000		7,000
Property, plant and equipment		5,000		---
Total	FC	25,000	FC	20,000
Accounts payable	FC	3,000	FC	3,000
Long-term debt		6,000		---
Common stock		9,000		---
Total		18,000		3,000
Accounting exposure	FC	7,000	FC	17,000

	Monetary Non-monetary Method		Temporal Method	
Cash	FC	2,000	FC	2,000
Accounts Receivable		3,000		3,000
Marketable Equity				
Securities (cost)		---		
Inventories (market)		---		7,000
Property, plant and equipment		---		---
Total	FC	5,000	FC	12,000
Accounts Payable	FC	3,000	FC	3,000
Long-term Debt		6,000		6,000
Common Stock		---		---
Total	FC	9,000	FC	9,000
Accounting Exposure	FC	(4,000)	FC	3,000

assets and liabilities must impact directly on the parent's cash flows in the parent's currency and must be relatively freely available for remittance to the parent; and (6) it must have a high volume of intercompany transaction.

The translation process may be divided into two categories. In the first category, the U.S. dollar is the functional currency and the temporal process is used. The translation gains and losses are reported in the income statements as a nonoperating item. In the second category, the foreign currency is the functional currency and the current method is used. In addition, the translation gains

Exhibit 8.8
Balance Sheet Expressed in U.S. Currency

Balance Sheet Items	Current Rate Method		Current Non-current Method	
	Rate	$	Rate	$
Assets				
Cash	$ 1.60	$32,000	$1.60	$32,000
Accounts Receivable	1.60	4,800	1.60	4,800
Marketable Equity Securities (cost)	1.60	12,800	1.60	12,800
Inventories (market)	1.60	11,200	1.60	11,200
Property, Plant and Equipment	1.60	14,400	2.30	20,700
Total		$40,000		$43,500
Liabilities				
Accounts Payable	1.60	4,800	1.60	$4,800
Long-Term Debt	1.60	9,600	2.30	13,800
Common Stock	1.60	14,400	2.30	20,700
Retained Earnings	1.60	11,200*		4,200
Total		$40,000		$43,500

	Monetary Non-monetary Method		Temporal Method	
Assets	Rate	$	Rate	$
Accounts Receivable	1.60	4,800	1.60	4,800
Marketable Equity Securities (cost)	1.80	14,400	1.80	14,400
Inventories (market)	2.40	16,800	1.60	11,200
Property, Plant and Equipment	2.30	11,500	2.30	11,500
Total		$50,000		$45,100
Liabilities				
Accounts Payable	1.60	$4,800	1.60	$4,800
Long-Term Debt	1.60	9,600	1.60	9,600
Common Stock	2.30	20,700	2.30	20,700
Retained Earnings		15,600*		10,000*
Total		$50,000		$45,100

*Exchange gains and losses are included in the income figure.

Exhibit 8.9
Functional Currency Indicators

Economic Indicator	Indicators Pointing to Local Currency as Functional Currency	Indicators Pointing to US Dollar as Functional Currency
Cash Flows	Primarily in the local currency and do not directly affect parents's cash flows.	Directly affect the parent's cash flows on a current basis and are readily available for remittance to the parent
Sales Price	Are not primarily responsive in the short-term to exchange rate changes; determined primarily by local conditions.	Are primarily responsive in the short-term to exchange rate changes determined primarily by worldwide competition
Sales Market	Active local market, although there may be significant amounts of exports.	Sales are mostly in the US, or sales contracts are denominated in dollars.
Expenses	Production costs and operating expenses are determined primarily by local conditions.	Production costs and operating expenses are obtained primarily US sources.
Financing	Primarily denominated in the local currency, and foreign entity's cash flow from operation is sufficient to service existing and normally expected obligations.	Primarily from parent or other dollar-denominated obligations, or parent company is expected to service the debt.
Intercompany Transactions	Low volume of intercompany transactions and there is not an extensive interrelationship between operations of the foreign entity and those of the parent. However, foreign entity may rely on parents or affiliates' competitive advantages such as patents and trademarks.	High volume of intercompany transactions; there is an extensive interrelationship between operations of the parent an those of foreign entity, or the foreign entity is an investment or financing device for the parent.

or losses are reported in the stockholders' equity section of the balance sheet as a translation adjustment. The translation rates for both categories given by SFAS 52 appear in Exhibit 8.10.

The only exception to these translation prices relates to the financial statements of a foreign entity in a country that has had cumulative inflation of approximately 100 percent or more over a three-year period (high inflation). In this case, the reporting currency is the functional currency. A summary of the translation process and dispositions of translation gains and losses under FASB 52 is shown in Exhibit 8.11.

Exhibit 8.10
Rates Used in the Translation Balance Sheet Items under SFAS 52

	US Dollar is Functional Currency Translation		Foreign Currency is Functional Currency Translation	
	Rates		Rates	
	Current	Historical	Current	Historical
ASSETS				
Cash on hand and demand and time deposits	X		X	
Marketable equity securities:				
Carried at cost		X	X	
Carried at current market price	X		X	
Accounts and notes receivable and related unearned discounts	X		X	
Allowance for doubtful accounts and notes receivable	X		X	
Inventories				
Carried at cost:		X	X	
Carried at current replacement price (produced under fixed price contracts)	X		X	
Prepaid insurance, advertising and rent		X	X	
Refundable deposits	X		X	
Advances to unconsolidated subsidiaries	X		X	
Property, plant, and equipment		X	X	
Accumulated depreciation of property, plant, and equipment		X	X	
Cash surrender value of life insurance	X		X	
Patents, trademarks, licenses, and formulas		X	X	
Goodwill		X	X	
Other intangible assets		X	X	
LIABILITIES				
Accounts and notes payable and overdrafts	X		X	
Accrued expenses payable	X		X	
Accrued losses on firm purchase commitments	X		X	
Refundable deposits	X		X	
Deferred income		X		
Bonds payable on other long-term debt	X	X		
Unamortized premium or discount on bonds of notes payable	X		X	
Convertible bonds payable	X		X	
Accrued pension obligations	X		X	
Obligations under Warranties	X		X	

Exhibit 8.11
Summary of Translation Process and Disposition of Translation Gain or Loss

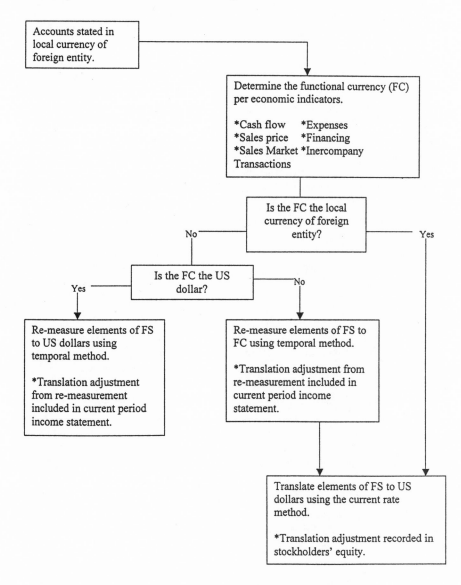

Illustration of the Translation Process under SFAS 52

The rates used under SFAS 52 to translate assets and liabilities depend on whether the U.S. dollar or the foreign currency is the functional currency. To illustrate the translation process under SFAS 52, it is desirable to examine both cases.

Let us assume that the first financial statement of a subsidiary, named the Foreign Company, for the period ending December 31, 19X1, are as shown in Exhibits 8.12, 8.13, and 8.14 and have been prepared in accordance with GAAP of the United States. To facilitate the translation process, selected foreign-exchange rates are provided in Exhibit 8.15. The translation process is examined first with the assumption that the foreign currency is the functional currency.

Translation Process when the U.S. Dollar Is the Functional Currency. Exhibit 8.10 indicates when to use historical or current exchange rates when the U.S. dollar is the functional currency. When the exchange rates provided in Exhibit 8.10 are applied to the balance-sheet items of Exhibit 8.12, they result in the balance sheet of the Foreign Company shown in Exhibit 8.16. Although the translation of the balance-sheet items is straightforward, it is important to note that the retained-earnings figure is determined as a "plug" figure. The computation of retained earnings is made in the following manner:

Total dollar value of assets translated	$206,170.22
Total dollar value of liabilities and equities translated (other than retained earnings)	$202,869.11
Retained earning balance	$ 3,301.11

The translation of the income statement proceeds in three phases: the first phase determines the net income translated before finding the translation gains or losses, the second phase determines the translation gains or losses, and the third phase combines the first two results. The first phase of the income statement translation of the Foreign Company is shown in Exhibit 8.17. The second phase includes the determination of the translation gains or losses as a "plug" figure. Using the previous results of the computation for retained earnings for December 31, 19X1, the computation of the translation gains or losses is accomplished in the following manner:

Retained earnings—January 1, 19X1 $0.0000

Add net income 2,765.5298

Minus retained earnings, December 31, 19X0 3,301.1100

Translation gains 544.5802

Translation Process When the Foreign Currency Is the Functional Currency. When the foreign currency is the functional currency, SFAS 52 advises the use of the current method of translation. Basically, most balance-sheet accounts are translated using the current exchange rate and most revenues and expenses are translated using the average rate for the period; thus, the translation

Exhibit 8.12
Balance Sheet Expressed in Foreign, Functional Currency Based on U.S. Dollars,
Foreign Company, December 31, 19X1 (in thousands)

	19X1
Current Assets	
Cash	FC 478.15
Account receivable-trade	FC1,221.85
Notes-receivable-intercompany	0
Notes receivable	FC500.00
Inventories	FC3,920.25
Prepaid expenses	FC 0.00
Accrued interest on notes receivable	FC 5.70
Total current assets	FC 6,155.95
Long-term notes receivable	FC 3,000.00
Property, plant, and equipment	FC 8,500.00
Land	
Buildings	FC 74,905.50
Equipment	FC16,313.00
Total property, plant, equipment	FC 99,718.50
Accumulated depreciation	FC 5,632.60
Net property, plant, and equipment	$ 94,085.90
Total assets	FC103,241,85
Current Liabilities	
Accounts payable	$1,814.00
Accrued interest on long-term debt	$225.00
Income tax payable	$383.25
Dividends payable	$125.00
Current portion of long-term debt	$1,250.00
Total current liabilities	FC 3,797.25
Long-term debt	FC 33,750.00
Deferred income taxes	FC 548.10
Stockholders' equity	FC 65,000.00
Common stock	FC 38,591.20
Contributed capital in excess of par	FC 38,591.20
Retained earnings	FC 1,555.30
Stockholders' equity	FC 65,146.50
Total liabilities and stockholders' equity	FC 103,241.85

process is more straightforward. Exhibit 8.18 provides the income statement of
the Foreign Company in U.S. dollars and is based on the use of foreign currency
as the functional currency. All income statement items have been translated
using the average exchange rate of 1.964. Translation gains and losses do not

Exhibit 8.13
**Income Statement Expressed in Foreign Currency, Functional Currency Based on
U.S. Dollars, Foreign Company, December 31, 19X1 (in thousands)**

		19X1
Sales		FC 36,638.00
Costs and expenses		
Cost of goods sold:		
Inventory (January 1)	0.00	
Production costs	FC 24,982.00	
Goods available for sale	FC 24,982.00	
Inventory (December 31)	(FC 3,950.00)	
Cost of good sold		FC 21,032.55
General administrative		FC 4,122.50
Advertising and selling		FC 2,335.75
Depreciation		FC 5,632.60
Total cost and expenses		FC 33,123.40
Net income from operations		FC 3,514.60
Other income (expenses)		(FC 339.00)
Net income before taxes		FC 3,175.50
Income taxes		
Current		FC 572.10
Deferred		FC 548.10
Total taxes		FC 1,120.20
Net income		FC 2,055.30

appear in the income statement of Exhibit 8.19, but they are shown in the
stockholders' equity section of the balance sheet provided in Exhibit 8.20. With
the exception of common stock and the contributed capital in excess of par, all
balance-sheet items have been translated using the current exchange rate of
$1.92. The common stock and the contributed capital are translated at the his-
torical rate of $2.04. The translation adjustment of ($7,698.8698) appears as a
"plug" figure in Exhibit 8.20. For the sake of reconciling the figures and checking on the accuracy of the computation, the determination of the translation
adjustment is shown in Exhibit 8.21.

Exhibit 8.14
**Statement of Retained Earnings Expressed in Foreign Currency, Functional
Currency Based on U.S. Dollar, Foreign Company, Years Ended December 31,
19X1, and December 31, 19X2 (in thousands)**

	19X2	19X1
Retained earnings – January 1	FC 1,555.30	FC 0.00
Add net income for the year	FC 1,429.60	FC 2,055.30
Deduct dividends for the year	(FC 1,000.00)	(FC 500.00)
Retained earnings – December 31	FC 1,984.90	FC 1,555.30

ACCOUNTING FOR DERIVATIVE INSTRUMENTS AND HEDGING ACTIVITIES

Summary of FAS 133

SFAS No. 133, *Accounting for Derivative Instruments and Hedging Activities*,[1] which became effective in June 1999, provides the accounting and reporting requirements for derivative instruments, including certain derivative instruments embedded in other contracts and for hedging activities. The main requirement is that all derivatives are recognized as either assets or liabilities in the statement of financial position at their fair market value.

A. If the derivative is not used as a hedging instrument, the changes in the fair value of the derivative is recognized in earnings in the period of change, namely, as a component of income from continuous operation.

B. If the derivative is used as a hedging instrument, three general types of derivative hedges are possible:[2] (a) a fair values hedge, namely, a hedge of the exposure to changes in fair value of a recognized asset or liability or an unrecognized firm commitment; (b) a cash flow hedge, namely, a hedge of the exposure to variable cash flow of a forecasted transaction; and (c) a foreign currency hedge, namely the hedge of the foreign currency exposure of a net investment in a foreign operation, an unrecognized firm investment, an available-for-sale security, or a foreign-currency–denominated forecasted transaction.

C. If the derivative is a fair value hedge (designated as hedging the fair value of a recognized asset or liability or a firm commitment), both of the derivative instruments and the hedged item are reported at fair value and the changes in value of both derivative and hedged items are recognized in earnings as components of income from continuing operations.

D. If the derivative is a cash flow hedge (designated as hedging the variable cash flows of a forecasted transaction), the derivative instrument is reported at

Exhibit 8.15
Foreign-Currency Rates

	US Dollar is Functional Currency	Foreign Currency is Functional Currency
	FC 1	FC 1
	19X1	19X1
Rates		
1. Current rate at March 31	$ 2.00	NA
2. Current rate at September 30	$ 1.98	NA
3. Current rate at June 30	$ 1.96	NA
4. Current rate at December 31	$ 1.92	$
5. Average rate for the year	$ 1.964	$
6. Historical rate when stock was issued and land purchased	$ 2.04	$
7. Historical rate when property, plant and equipment were purchased	$ 2.00	NA
8. Average historical rate applicable to inventories on hand at December	$ 1.94	NA

fair value and the changes in the value of the derivative is reported as a component of other comprehensive income for the effective portion of the derivative's gain or loss and as a component of income from continuing operations for the ineffective portion of the gain or loss. Note that FAS 133 does not require the hedged item in a cash flow hedge to be reported at fair value.

E. If the derivative is a foreign currency hedge, it is either unrecognized firm commitments, available-for-sale securities, foreign currency transactions, or net investments in foreign operations. Both hedges related to unrecognized firm commitments and available-for-sale securities are considered to be fair value hedges and accounting rules for fair value hedges apply to them. Hedges related to foreign currency transactions are classified as cash flow hedges and accounting for cash flow hedges apply to them. Finally, for a derivative that is a hedge of foreign currency exposure of a net investment in foreign operations, the gain and losses are reported as a component of other comprehensive income as part of the cumulative translation adjustment.

F. By fair value it means the amount a willing buyer and a willing seller agree on for an asset to be bought or sold and a liability to be incurred or settled. Fair value can be estimated by quoted market prices of similar derivative instruments or contracts or by valuation techniques such as present value of estimated expected future cash flows using discount rates commensurate with the risks in-

Exhibit 8.16
Balance Sheet Expressed in U.S. Dollars, Functional Currency Based on U.S. Dollar, Foreign Company, December 31, 19X1 (in thousands)

	FC	Translation Rate	$
Current Assets			
Cash	FC 478.15	1.92	$918.048
Accounts receivable-trade	1,221.85	1.92	$2,345.952
Accounts receivable-intercompany	0.00	1.92	$0.000
Notes receivable	500.00	1.92	$960.00
Inventories	3950.25	1.94	$7,663.485
Prepaid expenses	0.00	1.92	$0.00
Accrued interest on notes receivable	5.70	1.92	$10.944
Total current assets	6,155.95		$11,898.429
Long-term notes receivable	3,000.00	1.92	$5,760.000
Property, plant and equipment			
Land	8,500.00	2.04	$17,340.000
Buildings	74,905.50	2.00	$149,811.000
Equipment	16,313.00	2.00	$32,626.000
Total property, plant and equipment	99,718.50		$199,777.000
Accumulated depreciation	(5,632.60)	2.00	(11,265.000)
Net property, plant and equipment	94,085.90		$188,511.800
Total Assets	FC 103,241.85		$3,482.880
Current liabilities			
Accounts payable	FC 1,814.00	1.92	$3,482.880
Accrued interest on long-term debt	225.00	1.92	$432.000
Income tax payable	383.25	1.92	$735.840
Dividends payable	125.00	1.92	$240.000
Current portion of long-term debt	1,250.00	1.92	$2,400.000
Total current liabilities	FC 3,797.25		$7,290.720
Long-term debt	FC 33,750.00	1.92	$64,800.000
Deferred income taxes	FC 548.10	1.92	$1,052.352
Stockholders' equity			
Common stock	25,000	2.04	$51,000.000
Contributed capital in excess of par	38,591.20	2.04	$78,726.048
Retained earnings	1,555.30		$3,301.110
Total stockholders' equity	65,146.50		$133,027.150
Total liabilities and stockholders' equity	103,241.85		$206,170.220

Exhibit 8.17
Income Statement Translation before Gains and Losses, Expressed in U.S.
Dollars, Functional Currency Based on U.S. Dollar, Foreign Company, December
31, 19X1 (in thousands)

	FC	Rate	$
Sales	36,638.00	1.964	71,957.032
Costs and expenses			
Costs of goods sold			
Inventory – January 1	0.00		0.000
Production costs	24,982.80	1.964	49,066.219
Goods available for sale	24,982.80		49,066.219
Inventory (December 31)	(3,950.25)	1.94	(7,663.485)
Cost of goods sold	21,032.55		41,402.734
General and administrative	4,122.50	1.964	8,096.590
Advertising and selling	2,335.75	1.964	4,578.413
Depreciation	5,632.60	2	11,265.200
Total costs and expenses	33,123.40		65,351.937
Net income from operations	3,514.60		6,605.095
Other income (expenses)	(339.10)	1.964	(665.9924)
Net income before taxes	3,175.50		5,939.1026
Income taxes			
Current	572.10	1.964	1,123.6044
Deferred	548.10	1.964	1,076.4684
Total taxes	1,120.20		2,200.0780
Net income before dividends	2,055.30		3,739.0289
Dividends			
1st quarter	125	2	250.00
2nd quarter	125	1.98	247.00
3rd quarter	125	1.96	245.00
4th quarter	125	1.92	240.00
Total Dividends	500		982.50
	1,555.3		2,756.5298

Exhibit 8.18
Income Statement Expressed in U.S. Dollars, Functional Currency Based on U.S. Dollar, Foreign Company, December 31, 19X1 (in thousands)

Sales		$71,957.032
Costs and expenses		
Cost of goods sold		
Inventory	$0.000	
Production costs	$49,066.219	
Goods available for sale	$49,066.219	
Inventory (December 31)	($7,663.485)	
Costs of goods sold		$41,402.734
General and Administrative		$8,096.590
Advertising and Selling		$4,587.413
Depreciation		$11,265.200
Total costs and expenses		$65,351.937
Net income from operations		$6,605.095
Non-operating items		
Other income (expenses)		($665.9924)
Translation gains		$554.5802
Net income before taxes		$6,493.6828
Income Taxes		
Current		$1,123.6044
Deferred		$1,076.4684
Net income		$4,293.610
Add Retained Earnings- January 1, 19X1		$0.000
Deduct dividends for the year		$982.500
Retained earnings- December 31, 19X1		$3,301.110

volved, option-pricing models, matrix pricing, option-adjusted spread models, and fundamental analysis.

What Is a Derivative Instrument?

A derivative instrument is defined as cash, ownership interest, or contractual right or obligation to receive (with case of a contractual right), deliver (in the case of a contractual obligation) cash or another financial instrument, or exchange (under either contract) other financial instruments or potentially unfavorable terms with the other firm.

Exhibit 8.19
Income Statement Expressed in U.S. Dollars, Functional Currency Based on
Foreign Currency, Foreign Company, December 31, 19X1 (in thousands)

	FC	Rate	$
Sales	36,638.00	1.964	$71,957.032
Costs and Expenses			
Inventory (January 1)	0.00	1.964	$0.000
Production costs	24,982.80	1.964	$49,066.219
Goods available for sale	24,982.80		$49,066.219
Inventory (December 31)	(3,950.25)	1.964	($7,758.291)
Costs of goods sold	21,032.55		$41,307.928
General and Administrative	4,122.50	1.964	$8,096.590
Advertising and Selling	2,335.75	1.964	$4,587.413
Depreciation	5,632.60	1.964	$11,062.429
Total costs and expenses	33,123.40		$65,054.357
Net income from operations	3,514.60		$6,902.675
Other income expenses	(339.10)	1.964	$(665.992)
Net income before taxes	3,175.50		$36,236.683
Income taxes			
Current	572.10	1.964	$1,123.604
Deferred	548.10	1.964	$11,076.468
Total taxes	1,120.20		$2,200.073
Net income before dividends	2,055.30		$4,036.610
Deduct dividends	500.00		$982.500
Retained Earnings– December 31	1,553.30		$3,054.110

A derivative instrument is then defined as a financial instrument or other contract if it meets the following three characteristics:

1. It has one or more underlyings, one or more notational amounts, and one or more payments or settlement provisions. The underlyings that may cause the fair value or the cash flow to change include one or a combination of the following variables: interest rate, security prices, commodity price, foreign exchange rate, index of prices or rates, or another variable. The interaction of the notional account with the underlyings determines the settlement of the de-

Exhibit 8.20

Balance Sheet Expressed in U.S. Dollars, Functional Currency Based on Foreign Currency, Foreign Company, December 31, 19X1 (in thousands)

	FC	Rate	$
Current Assets			
Cash	478.15	1.92	$918.048
Accounts receivable—trade	1,221.85	1.92	$2,345.592
Intercompany	0.00	1.92	$0.000
Notes receivable	500.00	1.92	$960.000
Inventories	3,950.25	1.92	$7,584.480
Prepaid expenses	0.00	1.92	$0.000
Accrued interest on notes receivable	5.70	1.92	$10.944
Total current assets	6,155.90		$11,819.424
Long-term notes receivable	3,000.00	1.92	$5,760.000
Property, plant and equipment			
Land	8,500.00	1.92	$16,320.000
Buildings	74,905.50	1.92	$143,818.560
Equipment	16,313.00	1.92	$31,320.960
Total property, plant and equipment	99,718.50	1.92	$191,459.520
Accumulated depreciation	(5,632.60)		($10,814.592)
Net property, plant and equipment	94,085.90		$180,644.930
Total assets	103,241.85		$198,224.350
Current liabilities			
Accounts payable	1,814.00	1.92	$3,482.880
Accrued interest on long-term debt	225.00	1.92	$432.000
Income tax payable	383.25	1.92	$735.840
Dividends payable	125	1.92	$240.00
Current portion of long-term debt	1,250.00	1.92	$2,400.000
Total current liabilities	3,797.25		$7,290.720
Long-term debt	33,750.00	1.92	$64,800.000
Deferred income taxes	548.10	1.92	$1,052.352
Stockholders' equity			
Common stock	25,000.000	2.04	$51,000.000
Contributed capital in excess of par	38,591.20	2.04	$78,726.048
Retained earnings	1,555.30		$3,054.110[a]
Translation adjustment			($7,698.870)[b]
Total stockholders' equity	65,146.50		$125,081.280
Total liabilities and stockholders' equity	103,241.85		$198,224.350

[a]See Exhibit 8.19. [b]See Exhibit 8.21 for reconciliation of this result.

rivative, where the notional amount is the amount or quantity specified in the agreement. Notional amounts can be expressed in dollars, shares, bushes, pounds or other units.

2. It has no initial net investment or else it has one that is lower than what is required in similar contracts.

Exhibit 8.21
Reconciliation of Translation Adjustment

Total assets—foreign currency		FC 130,241.85
Total liabilities—foreign currency		
Current	FC 3,797.25	
Long-term debt	FC 33,750.00	
Deferred income taxes	FC 548.10	
Total liabilities—foreign currency	FC 38,095.35	FC 38,095.35
Net assets—foreign currency	FC 65,146.50	
End of the period exchange rate		$1.92
Net assets in dollars		$125,081.28
Stockholders' equity in dollars		
Common stock	$51,000.00	
Contributed capital in excess of par	$78,726.05	
Retained earnings	$3,054.11	
Total stockholders' equity in dollars	$132,780.16	$132,780.16
Translation adjustment		$7,698.9698

3. It requires net settlement of the contract if the settlement provisions meet one of the following conditions:

a. There is no requirement for the delivery of an asset equal to the notional amount related to the underlying.

b. A market mechanism exists for facilitating the net settlement.

c. The asset that is delivered is readily convertible to cash or is itself a derivative instrument.

FAS 133 excludes from this definition the following contracts:

a. "regular-way" security trades

b. normal purchases and normal sales

c. certain insurance contracts

d. certain financial guarantee contracts

e. derivatives that serve as impediments to sales accounting

f. contracts which are not traded in an exchange

g. contracts related to stock compensation

h. contracts issued by the entity as a contingent consideration in a business combination

i. contracts issued by the reporting entity that are included in stockholders' equity and indexed to its own stock

The FASB also considered the special case of embedded derivative instruments where a hybrid contract consists of a host contract and an embedded derivative. After a firm decides to separate the host contract from the embedded derivative, the embedded derivative is accounted for using the requirements of FAS 133 if all the following requirements apply:

1. Fair value changes in the hybrid instrument are not reported in the financial statements under applicable accounting principle.
2. The embedded derivative instrument would be accounted for as a derivative in accordance with FAS 133 if it were a separate instrument.
3. There is no clear and close relation between the economic characteristics and risks of the embedded derivative instrument and host contract.

The host contract without the embedded derivative is to be accounted for based on principles that apply to instruments of that type without embedded derivative instruments.

What Is an Effective Hedge?

If the derivative instrument is not designed as a hedge, it is reported at fair value and the changes in fair value are reported as part of income from continuing operations. Similarly if a derivative or part of a derivative is qualified as ineffective as a hedge, the changes in fair value of the part of the derivative considered ineffective as a hedge is also reported as a component of income, with one exception existing in a specific situation related to cash flow hedges. The way of assessing whether a hedge is expected to be highly effective is deemed to depend on the nature of the risk being hedged and the type of hedging instrument used and is left to the judgment of the entity making the determination. FAS 133 allows the entity to exclude all or part of the derivative in the assessment process in the following three cases:

a. change in the time value of an option contract when the effectiveness is assessed using changes in the option's intrinsic value
b. change in the difference between the spot price and the forward or futures price when the effectiveness of a hedge with a forward or futures contract is based on changes in spot prices
c. change in the volatility value of an option contract when effectiveness is assessed using the changes in the option's minimum value, that is, its intrinsic value plus the effects of discounting

Fair Value Hedge

After meeting the highly effective assessment process, the derivative is classified in one of three basic types: (1) fair value hedge, (2) cash flow hedge and (3) foreign currency hedge. The fair value hedge is discussed next.

A fair value hedge is used when the derivative instrument hedges risk resulting from potential changes in the fair value of asset or liability as a result of fixed provisions such as interest rates or prices. It can be a hedge of an existent asset, an existing liability, or a firm commitment. The following requirements are needed before a derivative instrument can be classified as a fair value hedge:

1. At the inception of the hedge, there should be a formal documentation of the hedging situation that includes the objective and strategy for undertaking the hedge.

2. The firm must have a reasonable basis for assessing the hedging instrument's effectiveness.

3. The combination of the hedged item and the hedge provide as much potential for gains as exposure to losses from changes in their combined fair value.

4. The hedging relationship is expected to be highly effective, both at the inception of the hedge and on an ongoing basis.

5. The hedged item is all or part of an existing asset or liability, all or part of a portfolio of similar assets or liabilities, or all or part of a firm commitment.

6. Reported earnings may be affected by the exposure to changes in fair value attributable to the hedged risk.

7. The hedged item is not excluded by FAS 133.

8. The designated risk being hedged of a held-to-maturity security relates to changes in the obligor's creditworthiness.

9. The designated risk of an option in a held-to-maturity security that is being hedged relates to entire fair value of the option.

10. The designated risk of a nonfinancial asset or liability that is being hedged relates to the total asset or liability.

11. The risk exposure of a hedged item that is a financial asset or liability, a recognized loan servicing right, or a nonfinancial commitment with financial components relates to: (a) the risk of changes in the overall fair value of the entire hedged item, (b) the risk of changes in its fair value due to changes in market interest rates, (c) the risk of changes in its fair value due to changes in the related foreign currency exchange rates, or (d) the risk of changes in the fair value due to changes in credit rating.

If the derivative instrument meets the requirements for a fair value hedge as outlined here and the hedge is considered highly effective, the derivative is reported at fair value and changes in the fair value of the derivative are recognized currently in earnings, as a component of income. Similarly, the changes in fair value on the hedged item are used to both adjust the carrying amount of the hedged item and be recognized as a component of income. In addition, the change in value related to the ineffective part of the derivative is recognized currently in earnings. For some hedged items, such as available-for-sale securities, which were measured using fair value with changes in fair value reported in comprehensive income, the change in value following hedging is no longer reported in other comprehensive income but as a component of income.

The accounting for a fair value hedge should be discontinued if:

a. the requirements for a fair value hedge are no longer met

b. the derivative is sold, terminated, or exercised

c. the firm removes the fair value designation

Cash Flow Hedge

A cash flow hedge is used when the derivative instrument is used to hedge the exposure to variability in expected cash flows due to a particular risk. Cash flow hedges are hedges of existing assets, existing liabilities, or forecasted transactions. To distinguish between a cash flow hedge and a fair value hedge, consider a firm with an inventory whose value and future selling prices are subject to change. Entering a future contract that is designated as a hedge of the expected sale of the inventory is a cash flow hedge, whereas entering a future contract that is designated as a hedge of the value of the inventory is a fair value hedge. For an example of a cash flow hedge of a liability, a firm facing a variable interest rate can enter into an interest swap of the variable rate stream for a fixed rate stream. Forecasted transactions include (a) the expected purchase or sale of a nonfinancial asset, and (b) the expected insurance of debt. To qualify as a cash flow hedge, the following requirements must be met:

1. At the inception of the hedge, there should be a formal documentation of the hedging situation that includes the objective and strategy for undertaking the hedge.

2. The firm must have a reasonable basis for assessing the hedging instrument's effectiveness.

3. The hedging relationship must be expected to be highly effective, both at the inception of the hedge and on an ongoing basis.

4. The combination of the hedge item and the hedge must provide as much potential for favorable cash flows as exposure to unfavorable cash flows.

5. A hedging instrument used to modify a variable interest payment or interest receipt to another variable interest payment or interest receipt must be a link between a designated asset with variable flows and designated liability with variable flows.

The following requirements must be met for the hedging of a forecasted transaction:

a. The forecasted transaction is designated as either an individual transaction or a group of individual transactions.

b. The forecasted transaction is likely to occur.

c. The forecasted transaction is made with an external entity and creates an exposure to variations in cash flows that affect earnings (except as permitted by paragraph 40).

d. The forecasted transaction does not involve the acquisition of an asset or the incurrence of a liability that will later be remeasured for changes in fair value due to the hedge risk reported currently in earnings.

e. For a held-to-maturity debt, the risk being hedged is due to default or changes in credit worthiness.

f. The designated risk being hedged for a forecasted purchase or sale of a non-financial asset is (1) the risk of change in the functional-currency equivalent cash flows due to changes in the related foreign currency changes rates or (2) the risk of changes in cash flows due to the changes in the purchase or sale price of the asset.

g. The designated risk being hedged for a forecasted purchase of a financial asset or liability or the variable cash inflow or outflow of an existing financial asset or liability is (1) the risk of changes in cash flows of the entire asset or liability, (2) the risk of changes in its cash flows due to changes in market interest rates, (3) the risk of changes in the foreign-currency-equivalent cash flows due to changes in the related foreign currency exchange rates, or (4) the risk of changes in its cash flows due to defaults or changes in credit rating.[3]

If the derivative instrument meets the cash flow hedge requirements, then it is reported at fair value and the changes in fair value are reported in other comprehensive income for the effective part of the hedge and as a component of income for the ineffective part of the hedge. In addition:

1. Any gain or loss excluded from the assessment of the hedge effectiveness is reported as a component of income.

2. The balance in accumulated other comprehensive income should be adjusted for gains and losses from the hedged transaction to reflect the lesser of the following (in absolute amounts):

   a. the cumulative gain or loss on the derivative from inception less (i) the gain or loss excluded from the hedge effectiveness assessment process and (ii) the gains or losses previously reclassified from accumulated other comprehensive income into earnings

   b. the portion of the cumulative gain or loss on the derivative that is necessary to offset the cumulative change in expected future cash flows or the hedged transaction from inception of the hedge less the derivative's gains of losses previously reclassified from accumulated other comprehensive income into earnings.[4]

3. Other comprehensive income is adjusted to the balance specified in (2).

4. Any gain or loss required as a result of the treatment prescribed in (2) and any required adjustments to other comprehensive income are included as a component of income.

To illustrate point (2) take the information included in Exhibit 8.22. The exhibit includes different situations from two periods. In situation 1 and period 1, the balance that should be in accumulated other comprehensive income is the smaller of the first two columns or 4,000,000. Given that the beginning balance

Exhibit 8.22
Illustration of Income Recognition Requirements for Cash Flow Hedges

Situation	1 Cumulative Change in Fair Value of Derivative	2 Cumulative Change in Cash Flows of Hedged Transaction	3 Balance that Should be in Accumulated Other Comprehensive Income	4 Existing Balance in Accumulated Other Comprehensive Income	5 Amount of Gain/(Loss) Included in Other Comprehensive Income	6 Gain/Loss Included in Income
1-Period 1	$4,500,000	$4,000,000	$4,000,000	$0	$4,000,000	$6,000,000
1-Period 2	$6,000,000	$5,100,000	$5,100,000	$4,000,000	$1,100,000	$3,000,000
2-Period 1	$4,000,000	$4,500,000	$4,000,000	$0	$4,000,000	$0
2-Period 2	$6,000,000	$6,500,000	$6,000,000	$4,000,000	$2,000,000	$0

is assumed to be zero, the amount of gain to be included in other comprehensive income is $4,000,000. The last column shows $600,000 to be included as income as result of the difference between the cumulative change in fair value of the derivative and the cumulative change in cash flows of hedged transactions. In situation 1 and period 2, the balance that should be in the accumulated other comprehensive income is again the lesser of the first two columns or $5,100,000 and the amount to be included in other comprehensive income is $1,100,000 (the difference between $100,000 ($5,100,00 − 4,000,000). The last column shows $300,000 to be included as income, computed as: $6,000,000 − $5,1000,000 − 600,000 = $300,000.

In situation 2, period 2, the amount in the third column should be $4,000,000 (the lesser of the two amounts in columns 1 and 2). Given a beginning balance of $0 in column 4, the amount in column 5 will be $4,000,000. Since column 1 is less than column 2, no gain or loss is reported in column 6. Similarly, in situation 2, period 2, the amount in the third column should be $66,000,000 (the lesser of the two amounts in columns 1 and 2). Given a beginning balance of $4,000,000 in column 4, the amount of gain or loss in column 5 will be $2,000,000, and nothing is reported in column 6.

FAS 133 requires that if the hedged transaction results in the acquisition of an asset or the incurrence of a liability, the gains and losses in accumulated other comprehensive income are reclassified into earnings in the same period or periods during which the asset acquired or liability incurred affects earnings (much as in the periods that depreciation expense, interest expenses, or cost of sales are recognized).[5]

Foreign Currency Hedge

Foreign currency hedges are derivative instruments aimed at hedging risk resulting from exposure to possible changes in foreign currency exchange rates. Four possible types of foreign currency hedge are:

1. a fair value hedge of an unrecognized firm commitment or an available-for-sale security

2. a cash-flow hedge of a forecasted foreign-currency–denominated transaction

3. a cash-flow hedge of a forecasted intercompany foreign-currency–denominated transaction

4. a hedge of a net investment in a foreign operation

Therefore, both foreign currency hedges of an unrecognized firm commitments and available-for-sale securities are classified and accounted for as fair-value hedges, whereas the hedges of foreign-currency–forecasted transactions are classified and accounted for as cash-flow hedges. The hedge of a foreign currency exposure of a net investment of a foreign operation denominated in a foreign currency is not considered a fair value or cash flow hedge. Basically, the gains and losses for remeasuring the assets or liabilities denominated in a foreign currency and the gains and losses from the derivative used are both classified as a component of income and offset each other.

CONCLUSION

This chapter has elaborated on the accounting treatment associated with accounting for foreign currency transaction and translation, and accounting for future contracts. Each of the accounting treatments is the result of a Statement of Financial Accounting Standards issued by the Financial Accounting Standards Committee suggesting such accounting treatments.

NOTES

1. Financial Accounting Standards Board (FASB), *SFAS No. 133: Accounting for Derivative Instruments and Hedging Activities* (Norwalk, CT: FASB, 1999).

2. Ibid., p. 2.

3. Ibid., para. 29h.

4. Ibid., para. 30(b).

5. Ibid., p. 19, para. 31.

SELECTED READINGS

Adler, M., and T. S. Harris. "Inflation, Translation and Conflicts in Statements of Financial Accounting Standards," *Journal of International Financial Management and Accounting* (Summer 1989), pp. 152–170.

Arnold, J. L. and W. W. Holder, *Impact of Statement 52 on Decisions, Financial Reports and Attitudes* (Morristown, NJ: Financial Executives Research Foundation, 1987).

Brankovic, M., and J. Madura, "Effect of FASB Statement No. 52 on Profitability Ratios," *International Journal of Accounting* 25, no. 1 (1990), pp. 19–28.

Callaghan, J. H., and Mohammad Sadegh Bazaz, "Comprehensive Measurement of Foreign Income: The Case of SFAS No. 52," *The International Journal of Accounting* 27, no. 1 (1991), pp. 80–87.

Choi, F. S., "Price-level Adjustments and Foreign Currency Translation: Are They Compatible?" *The International Journal of Accounting Research* (Fall 1975), pp. 121–143.

Choi, F. S., and A. Sondhi, "Accounting for Floating Currencies: An International Perspective," *Journal of Accounting, Auditing and Finance* (Summer 1985), pp. 335–340.

Evans, T. C., and T. S. Doupnik, *Determining the Functional Currency under Statement 52* (Stamford, CT: Financial Accounting Standards Board, 1986).

Fekrat, M. A., "Accounting for Forward Exchange Contracts," *Advances in International Accounting* 3 (1990), pp. 249–262.

Financial Accounting Standards Board (FASB), *Accounting for the Translation of Foreign Currency Transactions and Foreign Currency Financial Statements*, Statement of Financial Accounting Standard No. 8 (Stamford, CT: FASB, October 1975).

———. *Foreign Currency Translations*, Statement of Financial Accounting Standard No. 52 (Stamford, CT: FASB, December 1981).

Gray, D., "Corporate Preferences for Foreign Currency Accounting Standards," *Journal of Accounting Research* (Autumn 1984), pp. 760–764.

Hamer, J. G., and M. H. Kistler, "The Statement of Cash Flows—An Analysis of Translation and Remeasurement Techniques for Foreign Subsidiaries," *The International Journal of Accounting* 25, no. 1 (1990), pp. 29–42.

Hooper, P., and L. Li-Thin, "Foreign Currency Accounting: A Review and Critique of Major Empirical Studies," *The International Journal of Accounting* 25, no. 2 (1990), pp. 113–126.

Hosseni, A., and Z. Rezaee, "Impact of SFAS No. 52 on Performance Resources of Multinationals," *The International Journal of Accounting* 25, No. 1 (1990), pp. 43–52.

Institute of Chartered Accountants in England and Wales, *Member's Handbook*, Statement No. 25. (London: Institute of Chartered Accountants in England and Wales, 1968).

Kirsch, R. J., T. G. Evans, and T. S. Doupnik, "FASB Statement 52, an Accounting Policy Intervention: US-Based Multinational Corporate Reenactment Lobbying Behavior," *Advances in International Accounting* 3 (1990), pp. 155–172.

Kligman, J. M., "Foreign Currency Translation: From Exposure Draft to Standard," *Chartered Accountant Magazine*, June 1983, pp. 25–32, 57.

Mehta, D. R., and S. B. Thapa, "FAS-52, Functional Currency, and the Non-Compatibility of Financial Reports," *The International Journal of Accounting* 26, no. 2 (1991), pp. 71–84.

Ndubizu, G. A., "Earnings Volatility and the Corporate Adoption Decision on FASB Statement No. 52: An Empirical Evaluation," *Advances in International Accounting* 3 (1990), pp. 186–188.

Parkinson, M. R., *Translation of Foreign Currencies* (Toronto: CICA, 1972).

Rezaee, Z., "The Impact of New Accounting Rules on the Consolidation of Financial

Statements of Multinational Companies," *The International Journal of Accounting* 26 no. 3 (1991), pp. 206–219.

Resvine, L., "The Rationale Underlying the Functional Currency Choice," *Accounting Review* (July 1984), pp. 505–514.

Rosenfield, P., "Accounting for Foreign Operations," *Journal of Accountancy* (August 1987), pp. 103–112.

Shalchi, H., and Hosseini, A., "The Impact of FASB No. 52 on Foreign Exchange Contracts: An Empirical Evaluation," *Advances in International Accounting* 3 (1990), pp. 189–204.

Stewart, J. E., "The Challenge of Hedge Accounting," *Journal of Accounting* (November 1989), pp. 48–56.

Taussig, R. A., "Import of SFAS No. 52 on the Translation of Foreign Financial Statements of Companies in Highly Inflationary Economies," *Journal of Accounting Auditing and Finance* (Winter 1983), pp. 142–156.

Tearney, M. G., and Z. Baridwan. "The Effects of Translation Accounting Requirements and Exchange Rates on Foreign Operations Financial Performance—The Case of Indonesia," *The International Journal of Accounting* 24, no. 3, (1989), pp. 251–266.

Troberg, P., "Foreign Currency Translation: A Comparative Analysis of Approaches," *Advances in International Accounting*, 3 (1990), pp. 317–356.

Wojciehowski, S. R., "Dupont Evaluates FAS 52," *Management Accounting*, July 1982, pp. 31–35.

Ziebart, D. A., and D. Kim, "An Examination of the Market Reactions Associated with SFAS No. 8 and SFAS No. 52," *Accounting Review*, April 1987, pp. 343–357.

9
Pricing Strategies and Transfer Pricing for Multinational Firms

INTRODUCTION

Multinational firms face a more complex and demanding market than domestic firms. Their pricing and transfer pricing strategies need to adapt to this international context and incorporate innovative approaches that can further the long-term economic objectives of the firm. This chapter outlines the main issues that characterize the product pricing and transfer pricing strategies of multinational firms.

PRICING UNDER THE ROBINSON-PATMAN ACT

Before presenting product pricing internationally, it is very important to have an appreciation of U.S. law concerning price discrimination. The Robinson-Patman Act of 1936 prohibits certain kinds of price discrimination. Its purpose is:

To make it unlawful for any person engaged in commerce to discriminate in price or terms of sale between purchasers of commodities of like grade and quality; to prohibit the payment of brokerage or commission under certain conditions, to suppress pseudo advertising allowances; to provide a presumptive measure of damages in certain cases; and to protect the independent merchant, the public whom he serves; and the manufacturer from whom he buys, from exploitation by unfair competitors.[1]

The legislation, however, does not prohibit price discrimination when it is justified by differences in costs of manufacturing, sales, or delivery. The act states:

"that nothing herein contained shall prevent differentials which make only due allowances for differences in cost of manufacture, sale, or delivery resulting from the different methods or quantities in which such commodities are to such purchasers sold or delivered."[2] Because the act rests on the interpretation of cost, Patman defined cost as including all costs of manufacture and sale, excluding the return on invested capital by including a prorated share of all overhead costs. The courts and the Federal Trade Commission base their decisions accordingly on the full cost, rather than on the direct or differential cost.

PRODUCT PRICING INTERNATIONALLY

In an international context, the pricing decision is complicated by a host of factors.

Product-Pricing Policies

Multinational companies face different environments. They need to adapt their product pricing policies to these environments. As a result, these firms may be faced with different pricing policies needed to maximize the total profit. Examples of these strategies include:

1. Presentation pricing, which is equivalent to lowering prices to penetrate a market or gain a dominant position.
2. Market skimming, which is equivalent to setting a specific high price to target one decision, is complicated by a host of factors.
3. Market holding, which is equivalent to adapting prices to local conditions to hold a certain market share.

Impact of Fluctuating Exchange and Inflation Rates

Fluctuating exchange rates demand different price and export strategies from multinational corporations. If the domestic currency is weak, requiring few units of the foreign buyer's currency to buy one unit of the domestic currency, firms need to exploit the favorable situation by appropriate pricing and export strategies. In matters of pricing, a full-costing approach should be favored. If the domestic currency is strong, requiring more units of the foreign buyer's currency to buy one unit of domestic currency, firms need to adapt and remain competitive through the appropriate pricing and export strategies.

In addition to fluctuating exchange rates, multinational firms face inflation rates that can undermine their most careful and elaborate pricing policies. They need to deal with those exchange and inflation gains and losses in their pricing policies by either passing on the increase in price to customers; cutting expenses to be able to maintain the price at its present level; or negotiating to bill in strong currency.

Dumping

Dumping, as defined by Congress, is equivalent to unfair trade practices—unfair price cutting having as its objective the injury, destruction, or prevention of the establishment of American industry. The General Agreement on Tariffs and Trade (GATT) refers to dumping as the difference between the normal domestic price and the export price.[3] Each country has its own international dumping regulations as an attempt to either protect the industry or limit foreign competition. Dumping has been categorized as:

1. Sporadic dumping, when the company wants to dispose of excess or distressed inventories.
2. Predatory dumping, when the company decreases its prices to get rid of the competition and acquire a monopoly position.
3. Persistent dumping, when the company consistently lowers the price in one market identified as being different in terms of overhead costs and demand characteristics.
4. Reverse dumping, when the company increases its price because the foreign demand is less elastic and the foreign market can tolerate higher prices.[4]

Dumping can be avoided by differentiating the exported item from the item being sold in the home market, or by moving the manufacturing of the product to the foreign country.

The antidumping process works as follows:

1. The American company claims that a foreign competitor is selling a product in the United States at less than fair market value, which is usually a lower price than what the product sells for in its home market. As a result the American company feels that its prices are being undercut unfairly and files a petition with the U.S. Department of Commerce, charging dumping.
2. The Commerce Department takes twenty days to examine the petition and decide if there is enough evidence to justify further investigation.
3. The Commerce Department sends the complaint to the International Trade Commission, an independent federal agency, which examines the Commerce Department findings with the objective of determining whether the American company is being hurt by the imports.
4. The commission's findings are sent to the Commerce Department to make a preliminary determination of whether the foreign competitor is selling its products at less than full value. Both companies are then informed of this preliminary finding.
5. The Commerce Department stays on the case by requesting detailed financial, production, and sales information from the foreign company and sending auditors to the home country to investigate the production costs. A final determination of guilt or innocence is then made and the case is sent back to the commission.

6. The commission determines the extent of any injury caused to the American company and other companies in the industry. An antidumping tariff may then be imposed to increase the price of the foreign competitor's product.

Parallel Imports

Parallel importing is the practice whereby importers buy products from distribution in one country and sell them to distributors from another country who are not part of the manufacturer's regular distribution system. Price differentials between country markets create a strong incentive for parallel imports. A case in point is the practice of Japanese firms charging a higher price for their products to customers in Japan than in other countries. It thus became beneficial for Japanese customers to buy these items outside Japan, as they could get cheaper prices than those charged in the Japanese market. The parallel import is a direct result of price differential, as in the case of the gray market. Witness the following comment on the gray market:

Purposefully restricting the supply of a product in a market is another practice that can cause abnormally high prices and thus make a parallel market lucrative. Such was the case with Mercedes-Benz automobiles, whose supply was limited in the United States. Americans could buy a Mercedes-Benz in Germany for $12,000 when it sold in the United States for $24,000. The gray market that evolved in Mercedes-Benz automobiles was partially supplied by Americans returning to the United States with cars they could sell for double the price they paid in Germany. This situation persisted until the relative value of the dollar to the mark weakened and the price differential created by limited distribution evaporated.[5]

Price Escalation

Prices of goods from a given country are sometimes priced extremely highly in other countries. The higher prices result from the additional shipping costs, tariffs, longer channels of distribution, larger middleman margins, special taxes, and exchange rate fluctuation.[6] Multinational firms need to apply specific strategies to lessen this phenomenon of price escalation. Some of these strategies include the following:[7]

* Firms may need to lower the net prices for goods in the foreign markets to offset the additional costs.
* Firms may need to produce the goods overseas to reduce the cost of production and distribution.
* Firms may need to resort to shorter channels and thereby reduce the value-added tax levied on goods as they pass through several channels.
* Firms may elect to reduce the quality of the product or redesign a cheaper product, which will lead to a cost and price reduction.

- Firms may elect to ask for a tariff reclassification, which will reduce the tariff rate and the cost of production.
- Firms may elect to modify the product to qualify for a tariff classification with a lower tariff rate.
- Firms may elect to ship in bulk and repackage in foreign trade zones (FTZ), to reduce tariffs and production costs. Costs could be lowered by shipping unassembled goods to an FTZ in the following ways:
  1. Tariffs may be lower because duties are typically assessed at a lower rate for unassembled than assembled goods.
  2. If labor costs are lower in the importing country, substantial savings may be realized in the final product cost.
  3. Ocean transportation rates are affected by weight and volume, thus, unassembled goods may qualify for lower freight rates.
  4. If local content, such as packaging or component parts, can be used in the final assembly, there may be a further reduction of tariffs.[8]

Administered Pricing and Government-Influenced Pricing

Administered pricing involves attempts to price products for an entire market through the participation of competitors, through national, state, or local governments and through international agreement. Mechanisms for administered pricing include:

- pricing agreements
- arrangements
- combines
- conspiracies
- cartels
- communities of profit
- profit pools
- patent licensing
- trade associations
- price leadership
- customary pricing
- informal interfirm agreements[9]

Government can also try to influence prices by resorting to any of the following mechanisms:

- establishing margins
- setting prices and floors or ceilings

- restricting price changes
- competing in the market
- granting subsidies
- acting as a purchasing or selling monopoly[10]

Countertrade

The tradition of trading without any money exchanged is not a new phenomenon. It is, however, appearing more frequently as an alternative market-pricing tool for multinational firms. Barter, countertrade, buybacks, and offsets are gaining popularity in the global economy.[11] Barter involves the simple exchange of goods between two parties in a transaction. Countertrade is similar, except that one of the parties is offered a larger menu of products from which to choose those items to be taken in exchange. If the payment by one of the parties involve both goods and cash, it is referred to as a compensation deal. Sometimes the parties agree on two contracts: one in which the first party pays for the goods in cash to the second party and a second contract whereby the second party agrees to buy goods from the first party for the total amount of the first contract or for a set percentage of that amount. This countertrade is referred to as a counterpurchase. Buybacks involve the sale of goods and services that produce other goods or services; the first seller agrees to take the latter as a partial amount and/or to buy back a certain portion of the output. Finally, offset trade involves the seller of a product in a country agreeing to assist or invest in an economically weak country. These descriptions seem to have influenced the following comment: "Countertrade deals are elaborate, inventive, and extremely diverse. No two deals are identical. Each is created to circumvent an obstacle, or to slalom through a set of obstacles. The tighter the situation, the more original the deal."[12]

TRANSFER PRICING

Nature of Transfer Pricing

Transfer pricing is a major issue confronting decentralized organizations that expect divisional managers to operate their divisions as a semiautonomous business. These organizations face the problem of what price to charge for goods and services sold by one organizational unit to another in the same company. This situation prevails within vertically integrated organizations, where transactions often occur between divisions; the revenue of the supplying unit becomes the cost of the purchasing unit. These intracompany charges ultimately will be reflected in the profit and loss statements of the respective divisions. Because divisional performance is evaluated by a profit-based criterion such as ROI or residual income, the profit center managers will attempt to maximize their own center's profit. A conflict occurs when improved divisional performance is achieved at the expense of overall company profits.

In theory, to optimize an organization's profits, the transfer price should be selected so that it motivates and guides managers to choose their inputs and outputs in coordination with the other subunits. Ideally, any intracompany pricing method should be consistent with the goals of maximizing both company and divisional profits. Transfer pricing should ensure goal congruence between units.

Because of the potential conflicts that can arise in transfer price determination, the primary objectives can be used to establish a proper transfer price:

1. to assist top management in evaluating and guiding divisional performance by providing adequate information on divisional revenues and expenses
2. to help the division manager in running the division
3. to ensure divisional autonomy and allow each profit center to act as an independent agent

In theory, the design of a transfer-pricing scheme ultimately must point each division manager toward top management's goals. The scheme must reward divisional external economies and prevent and penalize diseconomies. Furthermore, a firm's transfer pricing divisions must acknowledge domestic and foreign legal and tax requirements, as well as antitrust and financial reporting constraints.

Developing a set of transfer pricing rules that can integrate the complex dimensions of organization, ensure divisional autonomy, and at the same time achieve overall goals is a very difficult task. Consequently, a transfer-pricing system must be designed with an awareness of these difficulties.

The main positive characteristics of a transfer-pricing system include ensuring goal congruence, being fair to all concerned parties, and minimizing conflicts between divisions. Some corporations set guidelines to ensure an effective pricing system.

A transfer price is the price agreed upon between two divisions—for instance, a selling division I and a buying division II—for a product or service A supplied by the selling division to the buying division. The buying division uses the product or service for further processing toward a final product B. Product A is termed an intermediate product and product B may be either another intermediate product, if it is sold to another division, or a final product of the firm, if it is sold to an external market. In most situations, the buying division II may have the option of buying the product A from an external market rather than internally from division I, and the selling division may have the option of selling outside. If the firm is perfectly decentralized, the option of buying and selling outside is available to both divisions. Exhibit 9.1 depicts the relationship.

Exhibit 9.1
Operation of Divisional External and Internal Markets

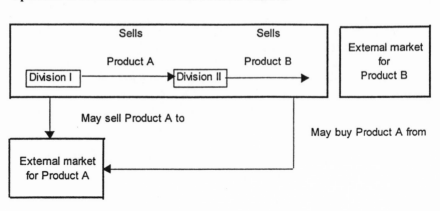

Example of Transfer Pricing

Backwoods Lumber is decentralized, with three divisions operating as profit centers:

1. The Raw Lumber Division manages the cutting of raw lumber from a large forest owned by the company.
2. The Transportation Division is in charge of carrying the raw lumber from the forest area to a nearby harbor city.
3. The Finished Lumber Division, located in the harbor city, is in charge of turning the raw lumber into finished lumber to be sold to outside markets. One hundred board feet of raw lumber are needed to produce ninety board feet of finished lumber.

The total annual finished lumber production of 9,000 board feet resulting from the processing of 10,000 board feet of raw lumber is sold entirely to the outside market.

The cost and price information for each of the three divisions is shown in Exhibit 9.2. Three pricing methods are considered:

• Method A: Transfer price is set at 120 percent of variable costs.

• Method B: Transfer price is set at 110 percent of absorption costs.

• Method C: Transfer price is set at market prices.

The transfer prices per 100 board feet of finished lumber under each method are as follows:

Method A: 120 percent of variable costs

Exhibit 9.2
Information on Backwoods Lumber's Three Divisions

Raw Lumber Division

Variable costs per 100 feet of raw lumber   = $120

Fixed costs per 100 feet of raw lumber   = $150   Market price per

Absorption costs per 100 feet of raw lumber = $270   100 feet of
                                                            raw lumber

Transportation Division   = $300

Variable costs per 100 feet of raw lumber   = $21

Fixed costs per 100 feet of raw lumber   =$40

Absorption costs per 100 feet of raw lumber = $61

Finished Lumber Division   Market price per

Variable costs per 100 feet of raw lumber   = $140   100 feet of raw lumbe

Fixed costs per 100 feet of raw lumber   = $60   delivered to the Finished

Absorption costs per 100 feet of raw lumber = $200   Lumber Division by
                                                            the intermediate market = $400

External Sale

Market price per 100 feet of finished lumber sold to external market = $600

Raw Lumber Division to Transportation Division 1.2($120) = $144

Transportation Division to Finished Lumber Division = 1.2($144 + $21) = $198

Method B: 110 percent of absorption costs

Raw Lumber Division to Transportation Division = 1.1 ($270) = $297

Transportation Division to Finished Lumber Division = 1.1 ($297 + 61) = $393.80.

Method C: Market Price

Raw Lumber Division to Transportation Division = $300

Transportation Division to Finished Lumber Division = $400

Exhibit 9.3 illustrates the impact of the use of each of the transfer prices on the incomes of the three divisions and on the total income of the firm. Two points are worth considering:

1. The transfer price used has no impact on the total income of the firm. The total is equal to $1,290,000 under either method.

2. The transfer price method used has a definite impact on the operating income of each of the three divisions, fluctuating from huge losses to material profits for the Raw

Exhibit 9.3

Operating Income of Backwood's Raw Lumber Division per 10,000 Board Feet of Lumber

	Transfer Price Set at 120% of Variable Costs	Transfer Price Set at 110% of Absorption Costs	Transfer Price Set at Market Price
1 Raw Lumber Division			
Revenue			
$144, $297, $300 x 10,000 feet			
of raw lumber	$1,440,000	$2,970,000	$3,000,000
Division Variable Costs			
$120 x 10,000 feet of raw lumber	$1,200,000	$1,200,000	$1,200,000
Division Fixed Costs			
$50 x 10,000 feet of raw lumber	$500,000	$500,000	$500,000
Division Operating Income	($260,000)	$1,270,000	$1,300,000
2 Transportation Division			
Revenue			
$198, $393.8, $400 x 10,000 feet			
of raw lumber	$1,980,000	$3,938,000	$4,000,000
Division Variable Costs			
$21 x 10,000 feet of raw lumber	$210,000	$210,000	$210,000
Division Fixed Costs			
$40 x 10,000 feet of raw lumber	$400,000	$400,000	$400,000
Transferred-in Costs			
$144, $297, $300 x 10,000 feet			
of raw lumber	$1,440,000	$2,970,000	$3,000,000
Division Operating Income	($70,000)	$358,000	$390,000
3 Finished Lumber Division			
Revenues			
$600 x 9,000 feet of finished lumber	$5,400,000	$5,400,000	$5,400,000
Division Variable Costs			
$140 x 9,000 feet of finished lumber	$1,260,000	$1,260,000	$1,260,000
Division Fixed Costs			
$60 x 9,000 feet of finished lumber	$540,000	$540,000	$540,000
Transferred-in Costs			
$198, $393.8, $400 x 10,000 feet			
of raw lumber	$1,980,000	$3,938,000	$4,000,000
Division Operating Income	$1,620,000	($338,000)	($400,000)
4 Total Company Income	$1,290,000	$1,290,000	$1,290,000

Lumber Division and the Transportation Division. What this result implies is that the divisions whose managers are compensated on the basis of divisional incomes will strive to choose the transfer price that will generate positive divisional incomes. That may lead to divisional transfer pricing policies that differ from one division to another and that may result in a conflict situation. Those transfer pricing policies and their implications are reviewed next.

Transfer-Pricing Methods

Market Price. A market price is the price at which the producing and selling division would sell the product externally. In other words, the producing division charges the same price to its divisions as it would charge to outside customers in open market transactions. The market price has the advantage of providing an objective measure of value for goods or services exchanged, and it may result in the best information for use in performance evaluation of the profit centers. A transfer-pricing system based on market prices requires a competitive market, minimal interdependencies of the profit centers, and the availability of dependable market quotations.

There are also serious drawbacks to using a transfer price based on market price:

1. In today's regulated economy, perfectly competitive markets are very rare. In an imperfect market, one seller or buyer, alone, can affect the market price, rendering it inapplicable as an effective price.
2. Even if the intermediate market is perfect, there is no guarantee that the market price is for a product strictly comparable in terms of grade and other relevant characteristics.
3. A situation may arise in which the market price is a distress price. Should the transfer price be the distress price, or should it be a long-run average, or "normal," market price? Both prices are defensible. On the one hand, the use of a distress price may lead managers of the supplying division to dispose of productive facilities to affect positively the short-run ROI. This may reduce the activities of the buying division, however, which would be disadvantageous to the company as a whole. On the other hand, the use of the long-run average market price may penalize the buying division by forcing it to buy at a price higher than the market price. If the objective is to preserve the spirit of decentralization and if safeguards exist to prevent the supplying division from disposing of productive facilities, the distress price should be chosen.
4. There may be problems if the goods or services that are transferred do not have a real market price.

In spite of these limitations, the market price is considered the most effective transfer price because (1) it ensures divisional autonomy, (2) it provides a good performance indicator for use in performance evaluation, and (3) it creates a climate conducive to goal congruence.

Negotiated Price. A negotiated transfer price is the price set after bargaining between the buying and selling divisions. This system requires that these divisions deal with one another in the same way that they deal with external suppliers and buyers. Thus, one basic requirement for the success of the bargaining process is the freedom of the divisions, not only to bargain with one another, but also to deal with external markets if they are unsatisfied with the internal offers. This freedom will avoid the bilateral monopoly that exists if the divisions are allowed to deal with only themselves. In fact, the negotiated transfer system works best when an intermediate market exists for the product or service being transferred, providing the divisions with objective and reliable information for successful negotiations.

The literature contains several recommendations for the use of negotiated prices.[13] The writers maintain that prices negotiated in arm's-length bargaining by divisional managers help accomplish goal congruence. They view these prices as compatible with profit decentralization through ensuring the divisional managers' freedom of action and increasing their accountability for profits. A survey conducted by Mautz indicated that about 24 percent of the participating diversified companies revealed negotiation as the basis for setting transfer prices between divisions.[14]

The negotiated transfer price system also may have a negative behavioral impact when personality conflicts arise between the bargainers; succeeding in the negotiation may become a more important goal than the company's profitability. Another drawback of the negotiated price system is that it can be time-consuming. Divisional managers may lose an coverall company perspective and direct their efforts to improving their divisional profit performance. In their attempts to obtain the best possible price, managers may find themselves in very lengthy argumentation.

When these conflicts arise, a transfer price should be set arbitrarily by a central decision of top management. This arbitrary or imposed price is the price believed to serve the overall company interests. However, the arbitrary price contradicts the spirit of decentralization, given the possible loss of divisional autonomy. Some authors in the accounting literature have fundamental objections to negotiation. Some have viewed the organization as a coalition of interests and suggested that the negotiation and renegotiation of transfer pricing can be expected to create conflict among the subunits constituting the coalition.[15] Others have suggested that the negotiated price implies an evaluation of the power to negotiate rather than an evaluation of performance itself.[16]

Actual Cost. A transfer price based on actual absorption cost is a price based on the historical full cost of the product or service being exchanged. It has the obvious advantage of being measurable, verifiable, and readily available.

When the actual costs are accepted for the determination of transfer prices, the problem remains of motivating the selling division to sell internally at a price other than the market price. One way of motivating it is to set the transfer price at full actual cost plus some markup, as a way of approximating the market price. The resulting synthetic market price may be better than the actual market price when the product existing in the intermediate market differs in terms of quality, grade, and other relevant characteristics from the product transferred.

The full-cost-plus, or synthetic market, price has been found to be the most popular approach under the following conditions:

- an absence of competitive prices
- the presence of an interest in saving the cost of negotiating prices
- the presence of a need to implement a policy of pricing the final product[17]

There are several limitations inherent in the implementation of a transfer pricing model based on actual cost:

1. A transfer price based on actual cost is actually based on absorption cost, in that it includes all direct and indirect expenses (variable and allocated joint and fixed costs). As a result, this type of transfer price may transfer the inefficiencies of the selling division to the buying division, making it unwise to use divisional profit for divisional performance evaluation.
2. A transfer price based on actual cost may lessen the selling division's incentive to control costs.
3. Cost-plus pricing of transfer goods can impede the search for technological progress by the manufacturing division.[18]

Standard Cost. We have seen that a transfer price based on actual cost can reinforce the inefficiencies of the selling division and lessen its motivation to control costs. A transfer price based on standard cost can correct for these problems. It reflects a normative position by expressing what costs would be under certain circumstances. As a result, a transfer price based on standard cost eliminates the inefficiencies of the selling division; when compared with actual cost, it may create an incentive to control cost.

Marginal or Variable Cost. A company using a transfer price based on either the full actual cost or the full standard cost may face at least two situations:

1. The full actual cost and full standard cost may be higher than the market price.
2. The full actual cost and the full standard cost include both direct and indirect costs (variable and fixed).

The indirect costs can result from arbitrary allocation procedures. The fixed costs can be committed costs that are incurred whether the selling division operates at full or at less-than-full capacity. Thus, the buying division may feel that either the indirect costs or the fixed costs should not be included in the determination of the transfer price. When this situation arises, it may be more motivating and important to maintain the spirit of decentralization and resort to a transfer price based on partial cost, which charges only a portion of the full actual or, preferably, full standard cost. Conceptually, this partial cost includes values between full cost and zero cost and refers to either the marginal cost or the variable cost.

The marginal cost is the incremental cost of producing additional units. In general, the buying division will be willing to buy as long as the marginal revenue is superior to the marginal cost. Although conceptually appealing, a transfer price based on marginal cost requires available information on all production levels. Because such figures are not always available, a surrogate for the marginal cost may have to be used—the variable cost.

The variable cost or the variable cost plus a lump sum can be used either as a surrogate marginal cost or as a way of encouraging the use of some facilities' services. First, the variable cost can be used when marginal cost cannot easily be computed because of the absence of adequate information. Second, the use of the variable cost can encourage divisions to use the services of facilities with excess capacity until it becomes more profitable or advantageous to the selling division to switch to a full cost (actual or standard).

Dual Price. From the preceding discussion of transfer pricing alternatives, it can be seen that: the best motivation transfer price for the selling division is the market price, and the most acceptable price for the buying division is the variable cost.

One way of meeting both of these optimal situations is to use a dual transfer price rather than a single transfer price. The dual price system allows the selling division to sell either at a market price or at a synthetic market price, hence creating a profit and motivating the selling division to sell. This system allows the buying division to buy inside the company at variable cost, which prevents the selling division from having excess capacity when the buying division buys outside at market prices equal to or lower than the variable cost. In short, the dual price system motivates both the buying and selling divisions to operate in the best interests of the company as a whole. One possible drawback of this system is the possibility that the division may no longer be motivated to control costs.

General Guideline for Computing Transfer Prices

The various methods discussed in the preceding sections illustrate the general infeasibility of one given method for all circumstances. There is, however, a general guideline that can be used as a benchmark in setting a transfer price. The guideline can be expressed as follows. The minimum transfer price is the sum of the additional outlay cost per unit incurred to the point of transfer (these costs may sometimes be approximated by the variable costs) plus the opportunity costs per unit to the firm as a whole (contribution margin per unit on outside sales). Following this guideline, the transfer price would be equal to the variable costs in those cases in which no alternative uses of the resources existed and to the market price where there was a strong external market for the product.

To illustrate the use of the guideline, assume that a multidivisional electronics company has a monitor division aimed at the external market. The monitor requires $400 in variable costs and sells for $700. The monitor division has a production capacity of 4,000 monitors. Another division, the computer division, needs a different monitor from an outside supplier at a price of $650 per monitor based on an order of 4,000 monitors. The monitor division has advised, however, that it would devote all of its capacity to the production of the new monitor required by the computer division. The variable cost of the new monitor would be $300 per unit.

Applying the guideline to this data, the transfer price for the monitor division would be:

Transfer price = $300 (variable cost of the new monitor) + $300 (the contribution margin lost to the monitor division as a result of giving up outside monitor sales: $700 selling price − $400 variable costs = $300)

Transfer price = $600

The decision should be to authorize the computer division to buy the new monitor from the monitor division at $600 per unit rather than from an outside supplier at $650 per unit, given the prevailing market conditions.

It is important to be cautious in the application of the general guideline for computing transfer price in the impact of capacity. If there is a surplus capacity, the transfer price should be the incremental cost (a variable cost). If the firm is producing and selling externally at maximum capacity, the transfer price should then be variable cost plus the per unit contribution margin cost from normal external sales given up. To illustrate the case of the surplus capacity and maximum capacity for the selling division, assume the following background information:

- Buying Division
  - The division makes and sells student desks.
  - A component part of a desk is a reading lamp.
  - Reading lamps can be purchased from an outside supplier at a cost of $15.00 each.
- Selling Division
  - This division makes and sells reading lamps.
  - Maximum capacity = 25,000 lamps annually.
  - Current year budgeted external sales = 15,000 lamps.
  - Lamps are sold for $16.00 each.
  - Lamps' variable costs = $12.00 each.
  - Of the variable costs (e.g., shipping costs), $2.00 can be saved if lamps are sold to the buying division, rather than to the normal external customers. (Thus, variable costs if transferred = $10.00 each.)

A. Assuming a surplus capacity for the selling division, the range of mutually accepted transfer prices is shown in Exhibit 9.4. The ceiling as determined in the buying division is $15.00 (the external purchase cost), whereas the floor as determined by the selling division (variable cost plus differential fixed cost plus

Exhibit 9.4
The Transfer Pricing Matrix in Simple Situations

Range of Mutually Acceptable Transfer Prices:		Selling Division "Condition:"	
		Surplus Capacity	Maximum Capacity
Ceiling -- determined by the Buying Division (market price)		External Purchase Cost = $15.00	External Purchase Cost = $15.00
Floor-- Determined by the Selling Division [variable cost (VC) + differential fixed cost per unit (DFC) + lost contribution margin per unit (LCM)]		VC + DFC + LCM ($10+ $0 +$0) $10.00	VC + DFC + LCM ($10 + $0 + $4) $14.00
Corporate Profit Effect			
(Differential cost savings per lamp. Which can be shared through negotiating a transfer price.)		Ceiling - Floor $5.00	Ceiling - Floor $1.00

contribution margin) is $10.00, creating a differential cost savings per lamp of $5.00, which can be showed though negotiating a transfer price.

B. Assuming a maximum capacity for the selling division, Exhibit 9.5 shows a differential cost savings of $1.00, which can be shared through negotiating a transfer price.

C. Assuming the buying division wants 16,000 lamps, resulting in an inadequate surplus capacity for the selling division. Assume also that the external purchase price is now $13.00 per lamp. Exhibit 9.6 shows the range of mutually accepted transfer prices. The $24,000 differential profit averages $1.50 per lamp. Thus, there is a $1.50 range of mutually accepted transfer prices, with a ceiling of $13.00 and a floor of $11.50.

FACTORS AFFECTING MULTINATIONAL TRANSFER PRICING

The following three criteria are used for setting transfer prices: goal congruence, divisional autonomy, and performance evaluation. These criteria are most dominant for domestic transfer pricing. Other factors stated by executives to be important in domestic transfer pricing include the following (by order of importance):

Exhibit 9.5
The Transfer Pricing Matrix with Limited Surplus Capacity

Range of Mutually Acceptable Transfer prices:	Selling Division "Condition"		Average (16,000 units)
	Surplus Capacity (for 10,000 units)	Maximum capacity (for 6,000 units)	
Ceiling --- Determined by the Buying Division (market price)	External Purchase Cost = $13.00	External Purchase Cost = $13.00	$13.00
Floor --- Determined by the Selling Division [variable cost (VC) =+ differential fixed cost per unit (DFC) =+ lost contribution margin per unit (LCM)]	VC + DFC + LCM ($10 +$0 + $0) $10	VC + DFC + LCM ($10 + $0 +$4) $14.00	Average (see a) $11.50
Corporate Profit Effect (Differential cost savings per lamp which can be shared through negotiating a transfer price)	Ceiling --- Floor $3.00	Ceiling --- Floor $1.00	C --- F (see b) $1.50

Calculation of averages:
(a) Average floor price: ([10,000 units × $10.00] + [6,000 units × $14.00]) / 16,000 units = $11.50 per unit.
(b) Average profit: (10,000 units × $3.00) + (6,000 units × $1.00) = $24.00; $24,000 / 16,000 units = $1.50 / unit.

"1. Performance evaluation—to measure the results of each operating unit;

2. Managerial motivation—to provide the company with a "profit-making" orientation throughout each organizational entity;

3. Pricing driven goals—to better reflect costs and "margins" that must be received from customers; and

4. Market driven goals—to maintain an internal competitiveness so that the company stays in balance with outside market forces."[19]

In the case of multinational transfer pricing, there are other "external" conditions that may exert an influence in establishing procedures and policies for a firm's transfer-pricing mechanism. Factors stated by executives to be important in international transfer pricing include the following (by order of importance):

Exhibit 9.6
A Summary of Transfer Pricing Methods Allowable by Section 482 and Related Regulations

---

For transfer of tangible property --- select one of the following six methods according to the best method rule (see reg. Section 1.482-1):

  1. The comparable uncontrolled price method (reg. section 1.482-3[b]);
  2. The resale price method (reg. section 1.482-3[c]);
  3. The cost plus method (reg. section 1.482-3[d]);
  4. The comparable profit method (reg. section 1.482-5);
  5. The profit split method (reg. section 1.482-6); and
  6. Unspecified methods (reg. section 1.482-3[e])

For transfer and use of intangible property – select one of the following four methods according to the best method rule (reg. section 1.482-1):

  1. The comparable uncontrolled transaction method (reg. section 1.482-5);
  2. The comparable profit method (reg. section 1.482-5);
  3. The profit split method (reg. section 1.482-6); and
  4. Unspecified methods (reg. section 1.482-4[d}).

---

1. overall income to the company

2. the competitive position of subsidiaries in foreign countries

3. performance evaluation of foreign subsidiaries

4. restrictions imposed by foreign countries on repatriation of profits or dividends

5. the need to maintain adequate cash flows in foreign subsidiaries

6. maintaining good relationships with host governments.[20]

Research in accounting has identified several factors that determine international transfer pricing. The general belief is that each multinational corporation (MNC) develops its own differential optimal set of accounting and management practices that are situation specific and contingent on the organizational and environmental characteristics of the MNC's operating milieu.[21] Based on this belief, Borkowski adapted a contingency theory-based managerial accounting model,[22] and a cognitive psychology model of perception and attention to information in the environment[23] to develop a model of international transfer-pricing choices within the firm.[24] The model indicates that organizational and international environment variables will vary among multinational firms, leading to different, yet appropriate, transfer-pricing decisions for each multinational firm.

TAX CONSIDERATIONS

Although the previous discussion reflects the positions stated by executives, a book written on behalf of the European Center for Study and Information on Multinational Corporations stated that "transfer price" has acquired a negative connotation because it "evokes the idea of systematic manipulation of prices in order to reduce profits artificially, cause losses, avoid taxes or duties."[25] The resulting situation can be summarized as the parent company dictating what the transfer price should be. However, the complexities of the situation may transform the transfer price problem into a major hurdle, as noted by Irwin Fantl:

The first hurdle involves personal relations with foreign management: it is easier to explain the need for arbitrary pricing to a domestic executive and to discount its effects in evaluating its performance. The foreign manager starts from a basis of suspicion of the motives by the U.S. parent. Any system that would make him feel unappreciated or misunderstood can undermine the success of the foreign venture. For internal measurement purposes, transfer pricing becomes more crucial than in domestic relations.[26]

The whole situation is, in fact, created by one of the goals of multinational corporations: the maximization of global after-tax profits. This is accomplished by minimizing the global income tax liability. Other factors being equal, profits are increased by setting high transfer prices to take out profits from subsidiaries located in high-tax countries and setting low transfer prices to move profits to subsidiaries domiciled in low-tax countries.

To illustrate the situation that can motivate multinational firms to use tax consideration in the selling of transfer prices, consider the following example: USX, a domestic U.S. firm, manufactures and sells machines both in the United States and abroad. Wholly owned firm FORX is used to execute the foreign sales. The machines purchased by USX cost $300 to manufacture and $50 to market and are sold abroad for $500. The following situations are worth considering:

Situation A: Regardless of the transfer price used, the combined income is $150 ($500 final sales price − $300 production costs − $50 selling expense)

Situation B: If the transfer price is $300, it will allocate the total profit to FORX, as follows:

Transaction	Effects on USX	Effects on FORX
Purchase Machine	$300 production cost	
Controlled Sales	$300 sales revenue	$300 cost of sales
Foreign Selling Activities		$50 selling expenses
Sales to Foreign Customers		$500 sales revenue
	$0 Net Profit	$150 Net Profit

Situation C: If the transfer price is $450, it will allocate the total profit to USX, as follows:

Transaction	Effects on USX	Effects on FORX
Purchase Machine	$300 production cost	
Controlled Sales	$450 sales revenue	$450 cost of sales
Foreign Selling Activities		$50 selling expenses
Sales to Foreign Customers		$500 sales revenue
	$150 Net Profit	$0 Net Profit

Now assume that the U.S. tax rate is 35 percent and the applicable foreign tax rate is 40 percent. The tax situation for USX depends on the choice of the transfer price, as follows:

a. If situation B is chosen, with a $300 transfer price and a $150 net profit allocated to FORX, then the total tax on that profit equals the foreign tax of $60 ($150 of income × 40% foreign tax rate).

b. If situation C is chosen, with a $450 transfer price and a $150 net profit allocated to USX, then the total tax on that profit equals the total tax of $52.50 ($150 of income × 35% U.S. tax rate).

From this simple example, it appears that a U.S. multinational firms have an incentive to shift income from a high-tax subsidiary to a low-tax subsidiary by using lower transfer prices on controlled inventory sales. Although the technique simply defers the tax until the foreign subsidiary negotiates the earnings through a dividend distribution, it allows the firm to temporarily avoid the residual U.S. tax on the minimally taxed foreign earnings.

This arbitrary shifting of profits purely for tax avoidance is being challenged by most governments in the developing and developed countries through the enactment of appropriate legislation. In the United States, the main legislation restricting the internal pricing policies of multinational corporations is contained within the 1954 Internal Revenue Code, Section 482 and the 1977 Regulation 861. A sum of the transfer pricing methods allowable by Section 482 and related results is shown in Exhibit 9.6.

INTERCORPORATE TRANSFER PRICING AND SECTION 482: TANGIBLES

Basic Principles

Objectives of intercorporate transfer pricing abound. Bradley grouped the key objectives of corporate transfer policies as follows:

moving funds internationally

minimizing taxes

minimizing tariffs

avoiding exchange controls and quotas

minimizing exchange risks

increasing share of profits from joint ventures

optimizing managerial incentives and performance evaluation.[27]

Abdallah proposes the following five criteria as necessary for an efficient international transfer-pricing system:

1. provision of an adequate measurement for the evaluation of foreign subsidiaries and their managers in terms of their controllable division contributions to global profit

2. provision of adequate information to top management to facilitate decision making

3. contribution to an increase in the overall profit of the multinational firms

4. motivation of foreign subsidiary managers to increase their efficiency and their divisional profits to meet the objectives of top management

5. minimization of the international transaction costs of the firms by minimizing border and income tax liabilities, foreign exchange risks, currency manipulation losses, and conflicts with the foreign government's policies.[28]

The objectives and criteria cited alone refer to both the objectives and criteria of minimizing taxes. This fad has naturally been met with the IRS drive to implement regulations that base transfer prices internationally on the arm's-length principle. These regulations, contained in Section 482 of the U.S. Internal Revenue Code, give the secretary of the treasury the authority to reallocate gross income, deductions, credits, or allowances between related corporations in order to prevent tax evasion:

In any case of two or more organizations, trades, or businesses (whether or not incorporated, whether or not organized in the United States, and whether or not affiliated) owned or controlled directly or indirectly by the same interests, the secretary, or his delegate, may distribute, apportion, or allocate gross income, deductions, credits, or allowances between or among such organizations, trades, or businesses, if he determines that such distribution, appointment, or allocation is necessary to prevent evasion of taxes or to reflect clearly the income of the organizations, trades or businesses.[29]

The purpose of Section 482 is to place a controlled taxpayer on a tax parity with an uncontrollable taxpayer by determining, according to the standards of an uncontrolled taxpayer, the true taxable income from the property and business of a controlled taxpayer. The IRS is allowed to disallow an existing transfer-pricing system and to reallocate income to reflect the true taxable income. The "true taxable income" is described as the income resulting if each member were acting "at arm's length" with the others. Detailed regulations were issued under this section based on the principle that transactions between related parties should take place on an arm's-length basis. These regulations set forth six methods to be used in determining the arm's length price—namely, in order of preference:

1. the comparable uncontrolled price method
2. the resale price method
3. the cost-plus method
4. the comparable profits method
5. the profit split method
6. unspecified methods

Any of these listed methods or any other method that can provide the most reliable estimate of an arm's-length price should be selected by the taxpayer.

Section 482 is intended to allocate the proper taxable income to the parent firm at arm's length, and Section 861 is intended to allocate corporate expenses to the foreign-source income. It allocates and apportions all of a firm's expenses, losses, and other deductions to specific sources of income (sales, royalties, dividends) and then apportions the expenses between domestic and foreign source incomes.

In spite of Sections 482 and 681, the U.S. situation is puzzling. Although foreign-owned assets have tripled in the past decade, to $1.8 trillion, the gross income of foreign-owned companies merely doubled and the taxes they paid hardly changed. Such was the finding of a 1986 IRS study of the returns of 36,800 foreign-owned companies. The job of the IRS is very difficult, given that most records of these companies are kept abroad and in different languages. In 1986, this situation allowed foreign companies to take tax deductions of $544.0 billion against total receipts of $543.0 billion, which, in late 1989, led the U.S. government and Congress to enact a law giving Draconian powers to the IRS in investigating foreign-company operations in the United States. This process led to the examination of transactions between foreign parent firms and their U.S. affiliates becoming an important part of IRS enforcement duties and gave the IRS the power to make an arbitrary assessment of taxes if its agents concluded that a foreign-owned company had not complied with a request for information.

The Comparable Uncontrolled Price Method

The comparable uncontrolled price method determines the transfer price as the basis of "uncontrolled sales" made to buyers that are not part of the same controlled group. Guidelines for what constitutes a "comparable uncontrolled price" are provided in the regulations as follows: uncontrolled sales are considered comparable to controlled sales if the physical property and circumstances involved in the uncontrolled sales are so nearly identical that any differences either have no effect on the price of property or can be reflected by a reasonable number of adjustments to the price of uncontrolled sales. Some of the differences that may affect the price of property are differences in the quality of the product, terms of sale, intangible property associated with the sale, time of sales, and level of the market and the geographic market in which the sale takes place.

Uncontrolled sales are defined to include sales made by the seller to an unrelated party, to the buyer by an unrelated party, or when neither party is a member of a controlled group. If there are no comparable uncontrolled sales, the regulations prescribe the use of the resale price method. For example, the U.S. company, a domestic corporation, sells equipment costing $300 to an unrelated foreign distributor for a sale price of $500. It also sells the same equipment to Tunis Co., a Tunisian company that it owns completely, which resells the equipment for $950. From the IRS's point of view, the sale to the unrelated foreign distributor is similar to the sale to Tunis Co. and constitutes comparable uncontrolled sales. Therefore, under the comparable uncontrolled price method, the transfer price that provides an estimate of the arm's-length price is $500.

The Resale Price Method

The resale price method is applicable if the buyer does not add significant value to the product, that is, simply serves as a distributor. In such a case, the transfer price is equal to the resale price to unrelated parties, less an appropriate markup, plus or minus certain adjustments. The resale price method establishes the arm's-length price by working back from a third-party selling price. The arm's-length price is equal to:

1. the applicable resale price: the price at which property purchased in the controlled sale is resold by the buyer, or ultimately resold by some later buyer, in an uncontrollable sale

2. adjusted by the appropriate markup percentage: equal to the percentage of gross profit earned by the reseller or another party on the resale of property that is both purchased and resold in an uncontrolled transaction similar to the controlled sale and

3. property adjusted for any differences: the functions or circumstances that have a definite and readily measurable effect on price, such as warranty or advertising contributions[30]

For instance, a U.S. company that owns 100% of Alger Co., an Algerian corporation, produces equipment at a cost of $800 each, to be sold to the Alger Co., which resells it at $1,000 each to unrelated foreign customers. The IRS has determined that other independent foreign distributors charge a 10 percent commission on the purchase and sale of similar products. Therefore, under the resale price method, the transfer price that provides the best estimate of the arm's-length price is $900 ($1,000 − [10% of 1,000]).

The Cost-Plus Method

The cost-plus method is prescribed in those situations when both the comparable price and the resale price methods are inapplicable. The cost-plus price is equal to full cost (actual or standard) plus an appropriate profit percentage similar to that earned by the division or other companies in similar transactions with unrelated parties. In this case, the arm's-length price is equal to:

1. the cost of production: computed in a consistent manner in accordance with sound accounting practices for allocating or appropriating costs that neither favor nor burden controlled sales in comparison with uncontrolled sales

2. plus an appropriate gross profit percentage: equal to the gross profit percentage earned by the seller or another party on uncontrolled sales that are most similar to the controlled sales in question and

3. property adjusted for any difference: differences that have a definite and readily measurable effect on price that would warrant an adjustment of price in uncontrolled transactions.[31]

For example, the U.S. company, a domestic corporation, sells equipment costing $100 both to an unrelated foreign corporation and to Morocco Co., a Moroccan corporation of which the U.S. company owns 100% of capital. The equipment is sold in the United States to unrelated customers for $150. The IRS has determined that similar equipment produced by an independent foreign manufacturer earns a gross profit markup of 10%. Therefore, under the cost-plus method, the transfer price that provides an estimate of the arm's-length price is $110 ($100 + [10% of $100]).

The Comparable Profit Method and the Profit Split Method

Both the comparable profit method and the profit split method consider the profits of uncontrolled corporations as the basis of determining an arm's-length allocation of profit between two related entities. The methods require that if there are no uncontrolled transfers that meet the standard of either matching transactions or comparable adjustable transactions, then an arm's-length consideration for the controlled transfer of an intangible must be determined by reference to the comparable profit interval of the tested party. If the reported operating income of the tested party is outside the comparable profit interval, an adjustment is required to bring the operating income within the comparable profit interval.

The comparable profit interval is composed of various amounts of profits that a firm would have earned if objective measures of its profit ability ("profit level indicators") had been equivalent to those of various uncontrolled taxpayers that performed similar functions. More precisely, profit level indicators derived from financial data of uncontrolled taxpayers are applied to the firm to recalculate its operating income. Each recalculated amount is labeled "constructive operative income." The comparable profit interval is then derived from those constructive operating incomes with that convergence. The following six steps are used in the development of the comparable profit level:

1. The firm is selected as the party to a controlled transaction to be tested.

2. The applicable business classification of the firm is determined, because the constructive operating incomes that are used to establish the comparable profit interval are derived from the operations of uncontrolled parties that are similar to the operations of the firm.

3. The constructive operating incomes are computed by applying profit-level indicators derived from uncontrolled taxpayers to the financial data of the firm. Profit-level indicators that provide a reliable basis for comparing profits may include the following:

a. Rate of return on assets: this is computed as the ratio of the operating income of the uncontrolled taxpayer by the assets of that taxpayer

b. Margins, meaning ratios that are determined by the relationships between income and costs: reliable margins include the ratios of operating income to sales, gross income to operating expenses, operating income to labor costs, and operating incomes to all expenses other than those included in the cost of goods sold.

c. Comparable profit split, derived from the combined operating income of controlled taxpayers that earned transactions and performed similar functions to those of the members of the controlled taxpayers. It may be computed as a residual profit split or an overall profit split. Under the residual profit split, income attributable to assets is determined by applying a rate of return to the value of assets held by the uncontrolled taxpayers. This amount is then subtracted from the operating income of each such uncontrolled taxpayer to yield the residual income. The sum of the uncontrolled taxpayer's residual income is the residual combined income. The profit split is the percentage of the residual income earned by each uncontrolled taxpayer. This profit split is then applied to the tested firm to determine its constructive operating income. The same rates of return that were applied to the uncontrolled taxpayers are applied to the assets of the group of controlled taxpayers and the combined operating income of the group of controlled taxpayers. The residual combined income is then allocated among the group of controlled taxpayers in the same percentages that were determined for the uncontrolled taxpayers. Under the overall profit split, the group of controlled taxpayers' profit split is determined in the same manner as under the residual profit split, but without first providing a return to assets.

4. The comparable profit interval is computed by selecting amounts of constructive operating income that converge to form an interval that is reasonably restricted in size. Two types of convergence are considered in constructing the comparable profit interval.

a. The first type of convergence is the convergence of constructive operating incomes derived from one or more profit-level indicators obtained from multiple uncontrolled taxpayers.

b. The second type of convergence is convergence of constructive operating incomes derived from one or more profit-level indicators obtained from a single uncontrolled taxpayer.

5. The most appropriate point in the comparable profit interval is determined. Statistical measures of central tendency may be used for the determination.

6. The transfer price for the controlled transaction is determined. Basically, it is determined by adjusting the actual charge for the controlled transaction to product and operating income for the firm that is equal to the constructive operating income corresponding to the most appropriate point.

TRANSFER PRICING OF INTANGIBLES

Basic Principles

In the case of transfers of intangibles, three methods can be used to determine the amount of an arm's-length transaction: the comparable uncontrolled transaction method, the profit split method, and the comparable profit method. An arm's-length consideration for an intangible is the amount of consideration that an uncontrolled taxpayer would have paid for the same intangible under the same circumstances. In deciding on the priority of methods to determine an arm's-length consideration, the comparable uncontrollable transaction method is considered first if the standards for its applications are met, given that the method requires the fewest adjustments and relies on the most complete and accurate data. In a case where the comparable uncontrollable transaction is found inapplicable because its standards are not met, an arm's-length consideration must be determined under the comparable profit method or the profit split method. (Both were examined earlier for the case of tangibles.)

Comparable Uncontrolled Transaction Method

This is similar to the comparable uncontrolled price method applicable to transfers of tangible property. However, the uncontrolled transfer must involve an identical intangible—an "exact" matching transaction is required. The matching transaction method requires that an arm's-length consideration for a controlled transfer of an intangible is determined by reference to the consideration charged in an uncontrolled transfer of the same intangible under the same or substantially similar economic conditions and contractual terms (a "matching transaction"). The determination of whether economic conditions in the controlled and uncontrolled transfers are substantially similar requires a comparison of economic factors that could affect the amount of consideration in the two transfers, such as:

1. the similarity of geographic markets, including (a)the relative size of the markets, (b) the extent of overall economic development in each market, and (c) the extent of competition in each market with regard to the uses to which the intangible is applied.

2. the extent to which the products or services to which the intangibles relate have been accepted within each market

3. the existence and extent of any collateral transactions or ongoing business relationships between the parties of each transfer

4. the functions performed by the parties and the economic risks associated with those functions

For example, suppose the XYZ firm licenses one of its software programs to an uncontrolled country A corporation, AF. At the same time the XYZ firm sells its software in country B through one of its wholly owned foreign subsidiary, BF. AF and BF have identical license agreements, allowing them to be exclusive distributors of the product in their respective countries, in exchange for a royalty of 10 percent of net selling price. In this case, assuming the economic conditions between countries A and B are similar, the matching transaction method is applicable, and the royalty of 10 percent in the controlled transfer to BF is considered to be an arm's-length amount of consideration.

Because information regarding a comparable uncontrolled transaction may be difficult to find for certain intangible assets such as patents and trademarks, another IRS requirement, Section 482, requires that the transfer prices for sales or licenses of intangibles must be "commensurate with the income attributable to the intangible." The idea is to make sure that the transfer price is adjusted to reflect any new profit experience and any unanticipated changes in the income actually generated by the intangibles. The only exceptions to this ruling are (a) the *de minimis* exception, if the profits realized are between 80 percent and 120 percent of the profits foreseeable when the agreement was initiated, (b) the extraordinary exception, if the new profit is due to extraordinary events, and (c) the same intangible exception. Another way to avoid the transfer-pricing problem associated with intangibles is to enter into a cost-sharing arrangement whereby the parent firm owns the right to manufacture and sell the product in the United States while the subsidiary owns the right to manufacture and sell the product overseas, thus negating the need for the subsidiary to pay a royalty to the parent firm.

Application of the Comparable Profit Interval

Assume that a domestic U.S. corporation licenses the right to use a patented manufacturing process for the production of a product P to a subsidiary CE in a foreign country in exchange for royalty payments of 5 percent of CE's net sales of P. CE is considered a controlled taxpayer. Assume also that an uncontrolled taxpayer, UE, operates in the same market and performs functions similar to those of CE. UE licenses rights to manufacturing a product Q from an uncontrolled taxpayer X in exchange for a royalty of 25 percent of its sales. The review of the financial data yields the following results:

	Data from CE	Data from UE
Sales	1,200	1,000
Cost of Goods Sold	(650)	(550)
Gross Income	550	450
Operating Expenses		
Royalty Payments	60	(250)
Other	(90)	(75)
Operating Income	400	125
Assets	570	440

	Data from U.S. Crop	Data from X
Operating Income	170	400
Assets	1,000	1,100

The first step is to compute the operating income under potential comparable adjustable transactions. If we apply the UE license agreement, the royalty from CE would have been $300 ($1,200 × 25%) rather than $60, and the operating income would have been $160 (400 − $240). The profit-level indicators are then computed:

1. Using the return as assets, the UE rate of return is 28.4 percent ($125 / $440). Using the same rate of return, the constructive operating income of CE would have been $162 ($570 × 28.4%).

2. Using the ratio of gross income to operating expenses, the ratio of UE is 138.5 percent ($450 / $325). Applying the same ratio, the operating expenses of CE are $397 ($550 / 135.5%). If CE made royalty payments of $307 ($397 / $90), then its gross income would have been $240 and its constructive operating income would have been $153 ($550 gross income minus $397) operating income).

3. The ratio of operating income to sales is 12.5 percent for UE ($125 / $1,000). Applying the same rate to CE yields a constructive operating income of $100 ($2,200 × 12.5%).

4. Using the profit split, the following analysis is relied on as follows: the combined rate of return on assets earned by CE and the U.S. corporation of 36.3 percent (400 + 170) / (570 + 1,000) does not differ significantly from the rate of return as assets earned by UE and X of 34.1 percent (125 + 400) / (440 + 1,100). The district director determines that an appropriate return for UE's

measurable assets is 15 percent and that an appropriate return for X's measurable assets is 10 percent. Subtracting these amounts from the operating income of each leaves a residual combined income of $349 (125 − [0.15 × 440] + 400 − [0.10 × 1100]). UE's residual income of $59 ($125 − [0.15 × 440]) represents 16.9 percent of the residual combined operating income. If CE had earned 15 percent of its measurable assets of 570 and the U.S. corporation had earned 10 percent of its measurable assets of 1,000, their residual combined operating income would be $384 ($570 − [0.15 × 570] − [0.10 × 1,000]). If CE had earned 16.9 % of this residual operating income, then CE's constructive operating income would have been $151 ([0.15 × 570] + [0.169 × 384.])

5. The summary of the profit-level indicators (PLI) from UE is as follows:

	PLI from UE	Constructive Operating Income for CE
Return on assets	28.4%	$162
Gloss Income to operating expenses	138.5%	$153
Operating income to sales	12.5%	$150
Profit split	16.9%	$151

Based on the review of UE, it can be determined that the royalty rate of 25 percent derived from the license between UE and X, which resulted in $160 of operating income for CE, should serve as a comparable adjustable transaction. The royalty to be received by a U.S. corporation should be 25 percent of CE's sales.

COMPLYING WITH TAX REGULATIONS

To allow the IRS to be able to assess the adequacy of a transfer-pricing mechanism used by a corporation or an individual, corporations and individuals are required to file Form 5471, "Information Return of U.S. Persons with Respect To Certain Foreign Corporations," and /or Form 5472, "Information Return of a 25% Foreign-Owned U.S. Corporation or a Foreign Corporation Engaged in a U.S. Trade or Business." To file Form 5472, a domestic or foreign corporation must have 25 percent or more of its stock owned, directly or indirectly, by one foreign person. In addition to Form 5472, the same corporation needs to maintain records adequate for a verification of the corporation's U.S. tax liability and its transactions with related parties.

Form 5471 is filed by any U.S. citizen who owns 50 percent or more of the stock of a foreign corporation. Failure to comply with the IRS requirements can result in one of the two special transfer-pricing penalties: the transaction penalty and the net adjustment penalty. The principal documents required of a taxpayer must accurately and completely describe the basic transfer-pricing analysis conducted by the taxpayer. They are as follows:

1. an overview of the taxpayer's business, including an analysis of the economic and legal factors that affect the pricing of its property or services

2. a description of the taxpayer's organizational structure (including an organization chart) covering all related parties engaged in transactions potentially relevant under Section 482, including foreign affiliates whose transactions directly or indirectly affect the pricing of property or services in the United States

3. any documentation explicitly required by the regulations under Section 482

4. a description of the method selected and an explanation of why that method was selected

5. a description of the alternative methods that were considered and an explanation of why they were not selected

6. a description of the controlled transactions (including the terms of sale) and any internal data used to analyze those transaction, for example, if a profit split method is applied, the documentation must include a schedule providing the total income, costs, and assets (with adjustments for different accounting practices and currencies) for each controlled taxpayer participating in the relevant business activity and detailing the allocations of such items to that activity

7. a description of the comparable measures that were used, how comparability was evaluated, and what (if any) adjustments were made

8. an explanation of the economic analysis and projections relied on in developing the method, for example, if a profit split method is applied, the taxpayer must provide an explanation of the analysis undertaken to determine how the profits would be split.

9. a description or summary of any relevant data that the taxpayer obtains after the end of the tax year and before filing a tax return and that would help determine if a taxpayer selected and applied a specified method in a reasonable manner.

10. a general index of the principal and background documents and a description of the record-keeping system used for cataloging and accessing those documents.[32]

Given these requirements and the potential penalties for noncompliance, corporations need to develop a transfer-pricing strategy in the form of a formal transfer-pricing study prepared internally or externally by an expert such as an attorney, an accountant, or even an economist. The study itself could be presented to the IRS to justify any transfer-pricing position. Another strategy was made possible when the IRS developed a process for granting advance price agreements (APAs) or certain international pricing arrangements under the APA. The taxpayer can apply for a specific APA for a given pricing, with assurance from the IRS that no adjustments would be proposed under Section 482.

EXCHANGE RATE PASS-THROUGH AND INTERNATIONAL PRICING STRATEGY

Transfer pricing can be complicated by the fact that costs and revenues may be accruing in different fluctuating currencies. International pricing is barely influenced by exporter reactions to exchange rate changes. The notion of exchange rate pass-though is central in international pricing.[33] Exchange rate pass-through can be defined as the extent to which exporters pass along exchange rate-induced margin increases (decreases) by lowering (raising) prices in export market currency terms.[34] The extent of pass-through has been found to be related to:[35]

1. the size of export market economy—which is greater for smaller countries[36]
2. the level of industry concentration in target country—which decreases with concentration[37]
3. wether the exchange rate in the export market is an appreciation or depreciation—which is greater for appreciating than depreciating rates[38, 39]
4. the proportion of foreign exporters to domestic firms—which becomes greater as the amount of export competition in a market increases[40, 41]
5. the type and height of nontariff barriers in the export market—with import quotes discouraging pass-through[42]
6. country-of-origin of exporter—with European exporters generally passing through exchange rate changes more than U.S. exporters[43]
7. across industries—with pass-through greater in final goods as compared to raw material and intermediary goods industries[44]
8. product size—with pass-through more pronounced for small as opposed to large German auto exports.[45]

A conceptual framework of export pricing and exchange rate pass-through is provided by Clark et al.[46] The model shows six responses: exchange rate uncertainty, sourcing strategy, distribution policy, brand equity, competitive symmetry, and firm orientation toward profit. The following interesting hypotheses are proposed:[47]

P1: The extent of exchange rate pass-through is highest for firms using cost-plus pricing, followed by those using incremental cost pricing, and then by those using profit contribution pricing.

P2: For firms using profit contribution pricing, the extent of exchange rate pass-through increases as the extent of gray market activity between the two markets increases.

P3: For firms using incremental cost export pricing to price below their home country levels, the extent of exchange rate pass-through is negatively related to the level of local competitive pressure and positively related to the level of local political pressure.

P4: When exporter's country currency appreciates, market share-oriented firms tend to pass through less of the cost increase in the export market than do financial performance-oriented firms.

P5: When exporter's country currency depreciates, market share-oriented firms tend to pass through more of the cost decrease in the export market than financial performance-oriented firms do.

P6: Firms using international suppliers on a long-term basis tend to pass through less of the exchange rate fluctuations than those relying on spot purchases of supplies.

P7: Firms with many alternative sources of supplies tend to pass through less of the exchange rate fluctuations than those with few such suppliers.

P8: In an export market currency appreciation, the extent of exchange rate pass-through is positively related to the firm's intensity of distribution in the export market.

P9: The extent of exchange rate pass-through is inversely related to channel length, as moderated by the degree of channel integration.

P10: Extent of pass-through decreases as exchange rate uncertainty increases.

P11: In an export market currency appreciation (depreciation), the greater the brand equity, the lesser (greater) the extent of exchange rate pass-through.

P12: In an export market currency depreciation (appreciation) where the firm's strategic competitor gains a comparative advantage (disadvantage). Extent of pass-though will be small (large).

P13: In an export market currency depreciation (appreciation) where the firm's strategic complement gains a comparative disadvantage (advantage), the extent of pass-through will be large (small).

CONCLUSIONS

Given the monetary consequences of noncompliance with IRS regulation in matters of transfer pricing, multinational corporations need to develop explicit, detailed strategies for the tax implications of transfer pricing. The various concepts and regulations presented in this chapter should be helpful in the enactment of such a strategy.

NOTES

1. Patman, Wright, *The Robinson Patman Act* (New York: Ronald Press, 1938), p. 3
2. Ibid., p. 7.
3. Belkaoui, Ahmed, *Cost Accounting: Theory and Practice* (Westport, CT: Quorum Books, 1990).
4. Onkvisit/Sak, and John J. Shaw, *International Marketing: Analysis and Strategy* (Columbus, OH: Merrill, 1989), pp. 677–678.
5. Cateora, P. R. *International Marketing* 7th Ed. (Homewood, IL: Irwin, 1990), p. 530.
6. Ibid., p. 541.
7. Ibid., pp. 543–545.
8. Ibid., p. 54.
9. Ibid., p. 550.
10. Ibid., pp. 553–554.
11. Cohen, S. S., and J. Zysman, "Countertrade, Offsets, Barter and Buybacks," *California Management Review* (Winter 1981), pp. 41–56.
12. Ibid., p. 43.

13. Dean, J., "Decentralizing and Intracompany Pricing," *Harvard Business Review* (July–August 1955), pp. 65–74.

14. Li, David H., "Interdivisional Transfer Planning," *Management Accounting* (June 1965), p. 51.

15. Haidinger, Timothy P., "Negotiate for Profits," *Management Accounting* (December 1970), pp. 25–31; Shaub, H. James, "Transfer Pricing in a Decentralized Organization," *Management Accounting* (April 1978), pp. 33–36, 42.

16. Mautz, R. K., *Financial Reporting by Diversified Companies* (New York: Financial Executives Research Foundation, 1968), p. 36.

17. Ibid.

18. Ibid.

19. Price Waterhouse, *Transfer Pricing Practices of American Industry* (New York: Price Waterhouse, 1984).

20. Ibid.

21. Susan C. Borkowski, "Organizational and International Factors Affecting Multinational Transfer Pricing," *Advances in International Accounting* 5 (1992), pp. 173–192.

22. J. Schweikart, "Contingency Theory as a Framework for Research in International Accounting," *International Journal of Accounting* (Fall 1985), pp. 89–98.

23. J. Birnberg, and M. Shields, "The Role of Attention and Memory in Accounting Decisions," *Accounting Organizations and Society* 9 (1984), pp. 365–382.

24. Borkowski, "Organizational and International Factors Affecting Multinational Transfer Pricing," p. 183.

25. T. R. Tang, "Environmental Variables of Multinational Transfer Pricing: A UK Perspective," *Journal of Business Finance and Accounting* (Summer 1982), p. 182.

26. Irwin, Fantl "Transfer Pricing—Treat Carefully," *The CPA Journal* (December 1972), p. 44.

27. Finnbarr Bradley, "International Transfer Pricing," in F.D.S. Choi (ed.), *Handbook of International Accounting* (New York: John Wiley and Sons, 1991), pp. 29–33.

28. W. M. Abdallah, *International Transfer Pricing Policies* (Westport, CT: Quorum Books, 1989.

29. U.S. Internal Revenue Code (1954), Section 482.

30. Michael P. Casey, "International Transfer Pricing," *Management Accounting* (October 1985), p. 33.

31. Ibid., p. 34.

32. Internal Revenue Code. Reg. Subjection 1.6662–6t(d)(2)(iii)(B), 1996.

33. Menon, Jayant, "Exchange Rate Pass-Through," *Journal of Economic Surveys* 9, no. 2 (1995), pp. 197–235.

34. Clark, Terry, "Exchange Rate Pass-Through and International Pricing Strategy: A Conceptual Framework and Research Proposition," *Journal of International Business Studies* 30, no. 2 (1999), p. 251.

35. Ibid., pp. 250–251.

36. Khosha, A., and J. Teranishi, "Exchange Rate Pass-Through in Export Prices: An International Comparison," *Hitotsubashi Journal of Economics* (June 1989), pp. 31–48.

37. Feinberg, R. M., "The Effects of Foreign Exchange Movements in U.S. Domestic Prices," *Review of Economics and Statistics* 71 (1989), pp. 505–511.

38. Kreinin, S. Martin, and E. J. Sheehey, "Differential Responses of U.S. Import Prices and Quantities to Exchange Rate Adjustments," *Weltwirschaftliches Archiv* 123, no. 3 (1987), pp. 449–462.

39. Marston, R. C., "Pricing to Market in Japanese Manufacturing," *Journal of International Economics* 29 (1990), pp. 217–236.

40. Dornfusch, R., "Exchange Rates and Prices," *American Economic Review* 77, (1987), pp. 93–106.

41. Feinburg, A. M., "The Interaction of Foreign Exchange and Market Power Effects on German Domestic Prices," *Journal of Industrial Economics* 35 (1986), pp. 61–70.

42. Bhagwati, J. N., "The Pass-Through Puzzle: The Missing Price for Hamlet," Mimeo, Columbia University, December 1988.

43. Athuleorara, P., and J. Menon, "Exchange Rates and Strategic Pricing in Swedish Machinery Exports," *Oxford Bulletin of Economics and Statistics* 87 (1999), pp. 533–546.

44. Khosha and Teranishi, "Exchange Rate Pass-Through in Export Prices."

45. Gagnon, J. E., and M. M. Krelter, "Market Adjustment and Exchange Rate Fluctuations: Evidence from Panel Data on Automobile Exports," *Journal of International Money and Finance* 14, no. 2 (1995), pp. 15–22.

46. Clark, "Exchange Rate Pass-Through and International Pricing Strategy," p. 253.

47. Ibid., pp. 253–261.

SELECTED READINGS

Bisat, T. *An Evaluation of International Intercompany Transactions.* Washington, DC: American University, 1966.

Burns, J. "How IRS Applies the Intercompany Pricing Rules of Section 482: A Corporate Survey." *The Journal of Taxation* 52 (May 1980), pp. 308–314.

Business International Corporation (BIC). *Solving International Pricing Problems.* New York: BIC, 1965.

———. *Setting Intra-Corporate Pricing.* New York: BIC, 1973.

Eccles, R. *The Transfer Pricing Problem.* Lexington, MA: D.C. Health, 1985.

Greene, J., and M. Duerr. *Intercompany Transactions in the Multinational Firm.* New York: The Conference Board, 1970.

Halperin, R., and B. Srindhi. "The Effects of the U.S. Income Tax Regulations Transfer Pricing Rules on Allocative Efficiency." *The Accounting Review* 62 (October 1987), pp. 687–706.

Milburn, A. *International Transfer Pricing in a Financial Accounting Context.* Champaign: University of Illinois, 1977.

Price Waterhouse. *Transfer Pricing Practices of American Industry.* New York: Price Waterhouse, 1984.

Rushinek, A., and S. Rushinek. "Multinational Transfer-Pricing Factors: Tax, Custom Duties, Antitrust/Dumping Legislation, Inflation, Interest, Competition, Profit/Dividend, and Financial Reporting." *The International Journal of Accounting* 23 (Spring 1988), pp. 95–111.

Schindler, G. "Intercorporate Transfer Pricing." *The Tax Adviser* (May 1988), pp. 378–384.

Schindler, G., and D. Henderson. "Intercorporate Transfer: 1985 Survey of Section 482 Audits." *Tax Notes* 29 (December 16, 1985), pp. 1171–1179.

U.S. Department of the Treasury and Internal Revenue Service. *A Study of Intercompany Pricing.* White Paper. Washington, DC: Commerce Clearing House, 1988.

10

Accounting for Inflation Internationally

INTRODUCTION

How to measure well-being at the more macro level and/or prosperity at the micro level is an important problem in international accounting. At both the macro and micro levels, different statistics abound, giving rise to different interpretations unless the necessary adjustments are made. Witness the following comment made to show that international statistical comparisons are invalid: "But part of what's unnecessarily stoking Americans' anxiety is a handful of false comparisons based on faulty ways of calculating the economic scorecard. Much of the trouble arises in converting other nations' output, consumption or investment from yen, mark or lira into dollars of comparable buying power."[1]

The same problem exists at the micro level, where an accounting method for dealing with inflation needs to be chosen and various countries opt for different methods. Accordingly, this chapter is intended to examine the problems associated with the measurement of well-being at the macro level and prosperity at the micro level.

MEASUREMENT OF WELL-BEING AT THE MACRO LEVEL

Various statistics are used to make international comparisons about living standards internationally. One common measure used is the per person gross domestic product, which is the sum of what is produced in a country divided by its population. To facilitate the comparison between countries, the per person gross domestic product may be computed, based on either (1) purchasing power parity exchange rates or (2) market exchange rates. The per person gross domestic product is, however, only an economic measure and does not make any adjustment for quality of life considerations. To compensate for this limitation, the United Nations (UN) produces a Human Development Index that combines gross domestic products with other indicators of well-being. This index may be adjusted (1) for life expectancy and literacy, (2) for life expectancy, literacy, and income distribution, and (3) for life expectancy, literacy, and sexual equality. Reliance on either measures of per person gross domestic product or the Human Development Index can provide different rankings of countries' living standards. The 1990 statistics for the top nineteen countries in the world are shown in Exhibit 10.1.

Exhibit 10.1 provides some surprising results. Although the United States was number one in terms of per person gross domestic product in 1990 according to purchasing power parity exchange rates, it was number seven according to market exchange rate. Using the 1990 UN Human Development Index adjusted for life expectancy and literacy, Japan was first, although its per capita income was less than two-thirds that of the United States. This is due to the fact that Japanese citizens tend to live three years longer than their U.S. counterparts. The 1990 ranking of the United States using the UN Human Development Index adjusted for life expectancy, literacy and income distribution sinks to ninth, given the disparities in income distribution. Finally, the 1990 UN Human Development Index adjusted for life expectancy, literacy and sexual equality shows Finland in the first position and the United States in the tenth position, due to the high disparities existing between men and women in the United States. Indeed, Czechoslovakia ranked higher than the United States on this dimension.

Does this mean that it is better for a woman to live in Czechoslovakia than in the United States? That depends on one's perception of what is important for quality of life. In fact, a better measure of quality of life is one that addresses the economic and basic needs of a society. One such measure is known in the literature as the "welfare of man."[2] The welfare of the common person is operationally computed as the difference between the ranking of the basic welfare and the ranking of the economic welfare. If the difference in the ranking is positive, the common person is not being treated as well as elsewhere. If it is negative, the country is assumed to be efficiently employing its resources to satisfy the welfare needs of its population. To determine the economic ranking, countries are ordered on the basis of their per capita gross national product. To determine the basic welfare standing, the following methodology is generally used: namely, by calculating a standardized value of each measure of need (health, life expectancy and education), adding the standardized value, and ranking the countries on the basis of the new variable.

Exhibit 10.1
The Top Nineteen Countries in the World

	Per Person Gross Domestic Product in 1990, using Purchasing Power Parity Exchange Rate	Per Person Gross National Product in 1990, using Market Exchange Rate	1990 UN Human Development Index Adjusted for Life Expectancy and Literacy Distribution	1990 UN Human Development Index Adjusted for Life Expectancy and Income Equality	1990 UN Human Development Index Adjusted for Life Expectancy and Sexual Equality
1 United States	$21,449 (1)	21,790 (7)	0.976(7)	0.994(9)	0.809 (10)
2 Switzerland	20,997 (2)	32,680 (1)	0,981(6)	0.961(4)	-
3 Luxembourg	19,340 (3)	-	-	-	-
4 Canada	19,120 (4)	20,470 (8)	0.983(1)	0.948(7)	0.813(9)
5 Germany	18,291 (5)	22,320 (6)	0.971 (10)	-	-
6 Japan	17,634 (6)	25,430 (3)	0.993(1)	0.990(1)	-
7 France	17,431 (7)	19,490 (10)	-	-	0.849(4)
8 Sweden	16,867 (8)	23,660 (4)	0.982(4)	0.963(3)	0.886 (2)
9 Denmark	16,765 (9)	-	-	-	0.878(3)
10 Finland	16,453 (10)	26,040 (2)	-	0.941 (10)	0.902(1)
11 Norway	-	23,120 (5)	0.978(6)	0.956(5)	0.845(5)
12 United Arab Emirates	-	19,860 (9)	-	-	-
13 Iceland	-	-	0.983(3)	-	-
14 Netherlands	-	-	0.976(8)	0.972 (2)	-
15 Australia	-	-	0.973(9)	-	0.843(6)
16 Belgium	-	-	-	0.951	-
17 Britain	-	-	-	0.948(8)	-
18 Austria	-	-	-	-	0.832(7)
19 Czechoslovakia	-	-	-	-	0.830(8)

MEASUREMENT OF WELL-BEING AT THE MICRO LEVEL

Income School of Thought

At the micro or firm level, the concern is with the profit of a firm, or business income. Although the measurement of business income differs all over the world, it is generally derived from the following school of thoughts: (1) classical school, (2) neoclassical school, and (3) radical school.

The classical school is characterized primarily by the adherence to unit of measure postulate and the historical-cost principle. Generally, known as "historical cost accounting" or "conventional accounting," the classical school considers accounting income as business income.

The neoclassical school is characterized primarily by its abandonment of the unit-of-measure postulate, recognition of changes in the general price level and adherence to the historical cost principle. Usually known as "general, price-level-adjusted historical cost-accounting," the neoclassical school's concept of business income is the general price-level-adjusted accounting income.

The radical school is characterized primarily by its reliance on current values for the valuation base. This school is composed of two categories. In the first category, the current-value-based financial statements are not adjusted for changes in the general price level. Generally known as "current value accounting," this school's concept of business income is current income. In the second category of the radical school, the current-value-based financial statements are adjusted for changes in the general price level. Usually known as "general, price-level-adjusted current-value accounting," this school's concept of business income is the adjusted current income.

The Income Concept and Capital Maintenance

The generally known concept of income is accounting income. It can be defined as the difference between the realized revenue arising from the transactions of the period and the corresponding historical costs. Accordingly accounting income rests on adherence to (1) the period postulate, (2) the revenue principle, (3) the realization principle, (4) the historical cost principle, and (5) the matching principle.

The adherence to those principles make the computation of accounting income practical, but its usefulness and meaning rather suspect. It is, however, the failure of accounting income to measure economic income that is the most serious problem. Hicks developed a general theory of economic income, which defined a person's personal income as the "maximum amount he can consume during a week and still expect to be as well-off at the end of the week as he was at the beginning."[3] The description implies a connection between the enjoyment of income and "well-offness." Basically the Hicksian concept of income is the maximum amount that may be consumed in a given period and still maintain the capital intact. It follows that to measure the economic income, we need to be able to measure capital maintenance. Four concepts of capital maintenance may be used:

1. Money maintenance, whereby financial capital is measured in units of money: it implies that the financial capital invested or reinvested by the owners is maintained. Conventional accounting, because it relies on historical cost for the valuation of assets and liabilities, conforms to the money-maintenance concept.

2. General purchasing-power money maintenance, whereby financial capital is measured units of the same purchasing power: it implies that the purchasing power of financial capital invested or reinvested by the owner is maintained. General price-level-adjusted historical-test accounting conforms to the general-purchasing-power money-maintenance concept.

3. Productive-capacity maintenance, whereby physical capital is measured in units money: it implies that the physical productive capacity of the firm is maintained. Productive capacity maintenance is the concept of capital maintenance used in current-value accounting, in which assets and liabilities are measured by their current values.

4. General purchasing-power, productive-capacity maintenance, whereby physical capital is measured in units of the same purchasing power: it implies that the physical productive capacity of the firm measured in units of the same purchasing power is maintained.

These four concepts of capital maintenance can be illustrated by the following example. Suppose a given firm has $10,000 of net assets of the beginning of a period and $30,000 of net assets at the end of a period. It is found that $15,000 of net assets is required to maintain the actual physical productivity of the firm at a time when the general level has increased by 10 percent. The income obtained under the four concepts of capital maintenance follow:

1. Money maintenance: $30,000 − $10,000 = $20,000

2. General purchasing-power money maintenance: $30,000 − ($10,000) + (0.01 × 10,000) = $19,000

3. Productive-capacity maintenance: $30,000 − $15,000 = $15,000

4. General purchasing-power productive-capacity maintenance: $30,000 − ($15,000) + (0.1 + $15,000) = $13,500

In other words, the accounting income is $20,000; the general price-level–adjusted accounting income is $19,000; the current-value–based income is $15,000; and the general price-level-adjusted current-value–based income is $13,500.

ALTERNATIVE ASSET VALUATION AND INCOME DETERMINATION MODELS

Description of the Different Accounting Models

Each of the capital maintenance concepts justifies the use of asset valuation and income determination models. Money maintenance suggests the use of historical cost accounting; general purchasing-power money maintenance suggests the use of general-price–level adjusted historical accounting; and productive capacity maintenance suggests the use of some forms of current value accounting—examples include replacement accounting or net realizable value accounting. General purchasing-power productive-capacity maintenance suggests the use of some forms of adjusted current value accounting, such as adjusted replacement accounting or adjusted net realizable value accounting. The difference between all these methods rests on either the choice of the attributes to be measured, or the units of measure. More precisely, three attributes are considered:[4]

1. historical cost, referring to the amount of cash or cash-equivalent paid to acquire an asset, or the amount of cash-equivalent liability

2. replacement cost, referring to the amount of cash or cash-equivalent that would be paid to acquire an equivalent or the same asset currently, or that would be received to incur the same liability currently

3. net realizable value, referring to the amount of cash or cash-equivalent that would be obtained by selling the asset currently, or that would be paid to redeem the liability currently

The units of measure refer to either units of money or units of general purchasing power.

Basically, the attributes can be distinguished as those that do not recognize changes in the specific price level (as in the case of historical costs) and those that do (such as replacement cost and net realizable value). The units of measurement can also be distinguished as those that do not recognize changes in the general price level, as with units of money, and those that do, as with units of purchasing power. It follows that:

1. Historical cost accounting does not recognize either general or specific price-level changes.

2. General price-level-adjusted historical accounting does not recognize changes in specific price levels, but recognizes changes in the general price level.

3. Replacement cost accounting recognizes changes in specific price levels but does not recognize changes in the general price level.

4. Adjusted replacement cost accounting recognizes both changes in the general and specific price levels.

5. Net realizable value accounting recognizes changes in specific price levels but does not recognize changes in general price levels. In addition, the realization principle is abandoned.

6. Adjusted net realizable value accounting recognizes both changes in the general and specific price levels. In addition, the realization principle is abandoned.

Illustration of the Different Accounting Models

A simplified example will be used to illustrate the preparation of financial statements under the different accounting models. For example, assume that the Ahla Wa Sahla company was formed on January 1, 19X3, to distribute a new product called "Baraka." Its capital is composed of $8,000 equity and $8,000 liabilities carrying an interest of 10 percent. On January 1, the company purchased 700 units of Baraka at $20 per unit. On June 1, the company sold 500 units at $30 per unit. Changes in general and specific price levels for the year 19X3 are as follows:

	January 1	June 1	December 31
Replacement cost	$ 20	$ 22	$ 26
Net realizable value	—	$ 30	$ 35
General price-level index	$100	$120	$144

In what follows, this example will be used to illustrate the six accounting models outlined earlier.

Historical Cost Accounting

Historical cost accounting, or conventional accounting, rests on the adoption of strict principles for both asset valuation and income determination. These principles include the use of historical cost as the attribute of the elements of financial statements, the assumption of a stable monetary unit, the matching principle, and the realization principle.

All that results from the adoption of these principles is that historical cost income, or accounting income, becomes the difference between realized revenues and their corresponding historical costs. The financial statements resulting from the use of historical cost accounting are shown in Exhibits 10.2 and 10.3.

Exhibit 10.2 shows accounting income to be equal to $4,200. To the Ahla Wa Sahla Company, this $4,200 figure represents an acceptable basis for the determination of taxes and dividends and the evaluation of performance. For general taxation purposes worldwide, accounting income is an acceptable measure because it is objective, verifiable, practical, and easy to understand. It is however, a known and empirical fact that accounting income includes both timing and measuring unit errors that are reflected in the $4,200 figure. First, accounting income contains timing errors because it includes operating income and holding gains and losses that are recognized in the current period and that occurred in a previous period while it omits the operating profit and holding gains and losses that occurred in the current period but that are recognizable in future periods. Second, the accounting income contains measuring-unit errors because (1) it does not take into account changes in the general price level that would have resulted in amounts expressed in units of general purchasing power, and it does not take into account changes in the specific price level, because it relies on historical cost (rather than replacement cost net realizable value) as the attribute of the elements of financial statements.

How, then, should we evaluate historical cost financial statements? First, they

Exhibit 10.2
Ahla Wa Sahla Company, Income Statements, for the Year Ended December 31, 19X3

	Historical Cost	Replacement Cost	Net Realizable Value
Revenues Cost of goods sold	$15,000[a] 10,000[c]	$15,000 11,000[d]	$22,000[b] 16,200[e]
Gross Margin	$5,000	$4,000	$5,800
Interest (10%)	800	800	800
Operating income	$4,200	$3,200	$5,000
Realized holding Gains and losses	(included above)	$1,000[f]	$1,000
Unrealized holding Gains and losses	(included above)	1,200[g]	1,200
General price level Gains and losses	(not applicable)	(not applicable)	
Net Income	$4,200	$5,400	$7,200

[a]$500 \times \$30 = \$15,000$
[b]$\$15,000 + (200 \times 35)$
[c]$500 \times \$20 = \$10,000$
[d]$500 \times \$22 = \$11,000$
[e]$11,000 + (\$26 \times 200) = \$16,200$
[f]$500 \times (\$22 - \$20) = \$1000$
[g]$200 \times (\$26 - \$20) = \$1,200$

are interpretable. Historical cost financial statements are based on the concept of money maintenance, and the attribute being expressed is the number of dollars (NOD). The balance sheet reports the stocks in NOD as of December 31, 19X3, and the income statement reports the change in NOD during the year.

Second, historical cost financial statements are not relevant because the command of goods (COG) is not measured. A measure of COG reflects changes in both the specific price level and the general price level, and, as such, represents the ability to buy the amount of goods necessary for capital maintenance.

In summary, historical cost financial statements measuring-unit errors, are interpretable and not relevant.

Exhibit 10.3
Ahla Wa Sahla Company, Balance Sheets for the Year Ended December 31, 19X3

	Historical Cost	Replacement Cost	Net Realizable Value
Assets			
Cash	$16,200[a]	$16,200	$16,200
Inventory	4,000	5,200[b]	7,000[d]
Total Assets	$20,200	$21,400	$23,200
Equities			
Bonds (10%)	$8,000	$8,000	$8,000
Capital	$8,000	$8,000	$8,000
Retained Earning			
Realized	4,200	4,200[c]	4,200
Unrealized	(not applicable)	1,200	3,000[e]
Total Equities	$20,200	$21,400	$23,200

[a](8,000 + 58,000 − 814,000 + $15,000 − $800) = $16,200
[b](200 × $26) = $52,000
[c]$3,200 + $1,000 = $4,200
[d](200 × $35) = $7,000
[e]Unrealized operating gain $1,800 ($7,000 − $5,200) + unrealized holding gain $1,200

In addition, the understatement of assets values, using historical costs, results in understated expenses and overstated income. The overstated income may in turn lead to the following results:

• "Increases in proportionate taxation.
• Requests by shareholder for more dividends.
• Demands for higher wages by labor or their representatives.
• Disadvantageous actions by host governments (e.g., imposition of excess profit taxes.)"[5]

Replacement Cost Accounting

Replacement cost accounting, as a particular case of current-entry price-based accounting, is characterized primarily by the use of replacement cost as the attribute of the elements of financial statements, the assumption of a stable monetary unit, the realization principle, the dichotomization of operating income and holding gains and losses, and the dichotomization of realized and unrealized holding gains and losses.

Accordingly, replacement-cost net income is equal to the sum of replacement-cost operating income and holding gains and losses. Replacement-cost operating income is equal to the difference between realized revenues and their corresponding replacement costs. From Exhibit 10.2, the Ahla Wa Sahla company's replacement-cost net income of $5,400 is composed of (1) replacement-cost net income of $3,200, (2) realized holding gains and losses of $1,000 and (3) unrealized holding gains and losses of $1,200.

What do these figures represent for Ahla Wa Sahla? The replacement-cost operating income of $3,200 represents the "distributable" income, or the maximum amount of dividends that Ahla Wa Sahla can pay while still maintaining its productive capacity. The realized holding gains and losses of $1,000 are an indicator of the efficiency of holding resources up to the point of sale. The realized holding gains and losses are an indicator of the efficiency of holding resources after the point of sale and may act as a predictor of future operating and holding performances.

In addition to these practical advantages, replacement-cost net income contains timing errors only on operating profit. It does, however, contain measuring-unit errors. First, the replacement-cost net income contains timing errors because (1) it omits the operating profit that occurred in the current period but that is realizable in future periods, (2) it includes the operating profit that is recognized in the current period but that occurred in previous periods, and (3) it includes holding gains and losses in the same period in which they occur. Second, the replacement-cost net income contains measuring-unit errors because (1) it does not take into account changes in the general price level that would have resulted in the amount expressed in units of general purchasing power, and (2) it does take into account changes in the specific price level because it relies on replacement as the attribute of the elements of financial statements.

We may evaluate replacement-cost financial statements as follows. First, they are interpretable. Replacement-cost financial statements are based on the concept of productive-capacity maintenance, and the attribute being expressed is the NOD in the income statement. The asset figures, however, are interpretable measures of the command of goods. The asset figures shown in Exhibit 10.3 are expressed in terms of the purchasing power of the dollar at the end of the year. They reflect changes in both the specific price level and the general price level and therefore represent the COG required for capital maintenance. Second, because COG is the relevant attribute, replacement-cost net income is not relevant, even though the asset figures are relevant.

In summary, replacement-cost financial statements contain timing errors in operating profit, contain measuring-unit errors, are interpretable as NOD for income-statement figures and as COG for asset figures, and provide relevant measures of COG only for asset figures.

Net Realizable Value Accounting

Net realizable value accounting, as a particular case of current exit price-based accounting, is characterized primarily by the use of net realizable value as the attribute of the elements of financial statements, the assumption of a stable monetary unit, the abandonment of the realization principle, and the dichotomization of operating income and holding gains and losses.

Accordingly, net realizable value net income is equal to the sum of net realizable value operating income and holding gains and losses. Net realizable value operating income is equal to the operating income on sales, and the net operating income on inventory on operating income on sales is equal to the difference between realized revenues and the corresponding replacement costs of the items sold. In Exhibit 10.2, the Ahla Wa Sahla Company's net realizable value net income of $7,200 is composed of (1) net realizable value operating income of $5,000, (2) realized holding gains and losses of $1,000, and (3) unrealized holding gains and losses of $1,200.

Note that the net realizable value operating income of $5,000 is composed of operating income on sales of $3,200 and operating income on inventory of $1,800. Thus, in Exhibit 10.3, unrealized retained earnings equal the sum of unrealized holding gains and losses of $1,200 and operating income on inventory of $1,800.

What do these figures represent for the Ahla Wa Sahla Company? They are similar to the figures obtained with replacement cost accounting except for the operating income in inventory, which results from the abandonment of the realization principle and the recognition of revenues at the time of production and at the time of sale. Net realizable value net income is an indicator of the ability of the firm to liquidate and to adapt to new economic situations.

To these practical advantages, we may add that net realizable value net income contains no timing errors, but it does contain measuring-unit errors. First, the net realizable, value net income does not contain any timing errors because (1) it reports all operating profit and holding gains and losses in the same period in which they occur, and (2) it excludes all operating and holding gains and losses that occurred in previous periods.

Second, the net realizable value net income contains measuring-unit errors because (1) it does not take into account changes in the general price level (if it had, it would have resulted in amounts expressed in units of general price level), because it relies on net realizable value as the attribute of the elements of financial statements.

We may evaluate net realizable value financial statements as follows. First, they are interpretable. Net realizable value financial statements are based on the concept of productive-capacity maintenance, the attribute being measured is expressed in NOD on the income statement and in COG on the balance sheet. Unlike replacement-cost accounting, under net realizable value accounting asset figures are expressed as measures of COG in the output market rather than in the input market. Second, because COG is the relevant attribute, net realizable value income is not relevant, although the asset figures are relevant.

In summary, net realizable value financial statements contain no timing errors, contain measuring unit errors, interpretable as NOD for net income and as COG for asset figures, and provide relevant measures of COG only for asset figures.

Alternative Accounting Models Expressed in Units of General Purchasing Power

To illustrate both timing and measuring-unit errors in this section, we will present accounting models that reflect changes in the general price level. These models are (1) general price-level-adjusted, historical-cost accounting, (2) general price-level-adjusted, replacement-cost accounting, and (3) general price-level-adjusted, net realizable value accounting. Continuing with our example of the Ahla Wa Sahla Company, the income statement and the balance sheet for 19×3, under the three accounting models, appear in Exhibits 10.4 and 10.5, respectively. The general price-level gain or loss is shown in Exhibit 10.6. It is equal to $360.

General Price-Level-Adjusted, Historical-Cost Accounting

General price-level-adjusted, historical-cost accounting is characterized primarily by the use of historic cost as the attribute of the elements of financial statements, the use of general purchasing power as the unit of measure, the matching principle, and the realization principle.

Accordingly, general price-level-adjusted, historical cost income is the difference between realized revenues and their corresponding historical costs, both expressed in units of general purchasing power. In Exhibit 10.4, general price-level-adjusted, historical cost income is equal to $2,440. Included in the $2,440 historical cost income figure is a ($360) general price level loss, computed as shown in Exhibit 10.6. Again, what does the $2,440 figure represent to the Ahla Wa Sahla Company? It represents accounting income expressed in dollars that have the purchasing power of dollars at the end of 19×3. In addition to the practical advantages listed for accounting income, general price-level-adjusted, historical cost income is expressed in units of general purchasing power. For these reasons, the use of such an accounting model may constitute a less radical change for those used to historical cost income than any current-value accounting model.

Despite these practical advantages, the general price-level-adjusted, historical cost income of $2,400 contains the same timing errors that historical cost income contains. However, general price-level-adjusted, historical cost income contains no measuring-unit errors, because it takes into account changes in the general price level. It does not, however, take into account changes in the specific price

Exhibit 10.4
Ahla Wa Sahla Company, General Price-Level Income Statements for the Year
Ended December 31, 19X3

	Historical Cost	Replacement Cost	Net Realizable Value
Revenues	$18,000[a]	$18,000	$25,000[g]
Cost of Goods Sold	14,000[b]	13,200[d]	18,400[h]
Gross Margin	$3,600	$4,800	$6,600
Interest (10%)	800	800	800
Operating Income	$2,800	$4,000	$5,800
Real realized holding Gains and Losses	(included above)	(1,200)[e]	(1,200)
Real unrealized holding Gains and Losses	(not applicable)	(560)[f]	(560)
General price level Gains and Losses	(360)[c]	(360)	(360)
Net Income	$2,440	$1,880	$3,680

[a]$15,000 × 144/120 = $18,000
[b]$10,000 × 144/100 = 814,400
[c]See Exhibit 10.6.
[d]$11,000 × 144/120 = $13,200
[e]500 × ($22 × 144/120) − ($20 × 144/100) = F(1,200) 200 ($26− ($20 × 144/100) = $(560)
[f]818,000 + ($35 × 200 units) = $25,000
[g]$13,200 + ($26 × 200 units) = $18,400

level, because it relies on historical cost, rather than replacement cost or net realizable value, as the attribute of the elements of financial statements.

Mexico's accounting pronouncement B-10 requires the use of a historical cost-constant purchasing power model. The income statement under Mexican B-10 requirements is as follows:

Sales
− GPL cost of goods sold
− Revalued depreciation
Gross profit
− Selling, general, and administrative expenses
Operating profit
− Net interest expense
− Net foreign exchange loss
+ Monetary gain or loss

Exhibit 10.5
Ahla Wa Sahla Company, General Price-Level Balance Sheets For the Year
Ended December 31, 19X3

	Historical Cost	Replacement Cost	Net Realizable Value
Assets			
Cash	$16,200	$16,200	$16,200
Inventory	5,760[a]	5,200	7,000
Total assets	$21,960	$21,400	$23,200
Equities			
Bonds (10%)	$8,000	$8,000	$8,000
Capital	11,520[b]	11,520	11,520
Retained earnings			
Realized	2,800	2,800	2,800
Unrealized	(not applicable)	(560)	1,240[c]
General price-level			
Gains or losses	$(360)	(360)	(360)
Total equities	$21,960	$21,400	$23,200

[a]$4,000 × 144/100 = $5,760
[b]$8,000 × 144/100 = $11,520
[c]Unrealized operating gains $1,800 ($7,000 − $5,200) + unrealized holding gains ($560)

Pretax income

− Taxes

Net income

How should we evaluate the general price-level-adjusted, historical cost financial statements presented in Exhibits 10.4. and 10.5? First, they are interpretable. General price-level-adjusted, historical cost financial statements are based on the concept of purchasing-power money maintenance. The attribute being measured is NOD in some cases and COG in other cases. Hence, general

Exhibit 10.6
Ahla Wa Sahla Company, General Price-Level Gain or Loss for the Year Ended December 31, 19X3

	Unadjusted Amount	Conversion Factor	Adjusted Amount
Net monetary assets on January 1, 19X3	$8,000	144/100	$11,520
Add: Monetary receipts during 19X3 sales	$15,000	144/120	$18,000
Net $ monetary items	23,000		$29,520
Less: Monetary payments			
Purchases	$14,000	144/100	$20,160
Interest (10%)	800	144/144	800
Total	$14,800		$20,960
Computed net monetary assets December 31, 19X3			$8,560
Actual net monetary assets December 31, 19X3	$8,200		$8,200
General price level gain or loss			$(360)

price-level adjusted, historical cost income and all balance sheet figures, with the exception of cash (and monetary assets and liabilities) may be interpreted as NOD measures. Only the cash figures (and monetary assets and liabilities) may be interpreted as COG measures. Second, only the cash figures (and monetary assets and liabilities) are relevant, because they are expressed as COG measures.

In summary, general price-level-adjusted, replacement-cost financial statements contain timing errors, contain no measuring-unit errors, are interpretable, and provide relevant measures of COG only for cash figures (and monetary assets and liabilities).

General Price-Level-Adjusted, Replacement-Cost Accounting

General price-level-adjusted, replacement-cost accounting is characterized primarily by the use of replacement cost as the attribute of the elements of financial statements, the use of general purchasing power as the unit measure, the realization principle, the dichotomization of operating income and real realized holding gains and losses, and the dichotomization of real realized and real unrealized holding gains and losses.

Accordingly, general price-level adjusted, replacement-cost income is equal to the difference between realized revenues and their corresponding replacement costs, both expressed in units of general purchasing power. Similarly, general price-level-adjusted, replacement-cost financial statements eliminate "fictitious holding gains and losses" to arrive at "real holding gains and losses." Fictitious holding gains and losses represent the general price-level restatement that is required to maintain the general purchasing power of nonmonetary items. We can see from Exhibit 10.4 that general price-level, replacement-cost income is equal to $1,880. Included in the $1,880 income figure is a $(360) general price-level loss, computed as shown in Exhibit 10.5. The $1,880 figure represents Ahla Wa Sahla's replacement-cost net income, expressed in units of general purchasing power at the end of 19X3. Such a measure of income has all the advantages of replacement-cost accounting income and the added advantage of being expressed in units of general purchasing power.

For these reasons, general price-level-adjusted, replacement-cost accounting constitutes a net improvement over replacement-cost accounting, because this accounting model not only adopts replacement cost as the attribute of the elements of financial statements, but also employs general purchasing power as the unit of measure. Despite these improvements, however, general price-level-adjusted, replacement-cost income contains the same timing errors that replacement-cost income contains. Second, general price-level-adjusted, replacement-cost income contains no measuring-unit errors, because it takes into account changes in the general price level. In addition, this measure of income takes into account changes in the specific price level, because it adopts replacement cost as the attribute of the element of financial statements.

How should we evaluate the general price-level-adjusted, replacement-cost financial statements presented in Exhibits 10.4 and 10.5? First, they are interpretable. General price-level-adjusted, replacement-cost financial statements are based on the concept of purchasing-power, productive-capacity maintenance. The figures on both the income statement and the balance sheet are expressed as COG measures. Second, general price-level-adjusted, replacement-cost financial statements are relevant, because they are expressed as COG measures. Note, however, that COG is in the input market rather than the output market.

In summary, general price-level-adjusted, replacement-cost financial statements contain timing errors, contain no measuring-unit errors, are interpretable, and provide relevant measures of COG in the input market.

General Price-Level-Adjusted, Net Realizable Value Accounting

General price-level-adjusted, net realizable value accounting is characterized by the use of net realizable value as the attribute of the elements of financial statements, the use of general purchasing power as the unit of measure, the abandonment of the realization principle, the dichotomization of operating income and real holding gains and losses, and the dichotomization of real realized and real unrealized gains and losses.

Accordingly, general price-level-adjusted, net realizable value net income is equal to the sum of net realizable value operating income and holding gains and losses, both expressed in units of general purchasing power. The general price-level-adjusted, net realizable value operating income is equal to the sum of operating income arising from sale and operating income on inventory, both expressed in units of general purchasing power. From Exhibit 10.4, there is (1) general price-level-adjusted, net realizable operating income of $5,800 (2) real realized holding losses of $1,200 (3) real unrealized holding losses of $560, and (4) a general price-level loss of $360.

Again, the general price-leveled-adjusted, net realizable value net income of $5,800 is composed of general price-level-adjusted, net realizable value operating income on sales of $4,000 and general price-level-adjusted, net realizable value operating income on inventory of $1,800.

In addition to the advantages of net realizable value net income, general price-level-adjusted, net realizable value income is expressed in units of general purchasing power. For these reasons, general, price-level-adjusted, net realizable value represents an overall improvement on net realizable value accounting, because it not only adopts net realizable value as an attribute of the elements of financial statements but also employs general purchasing power as the unit of measure.

Thus, general price-level-adjusted, net realizable value income involves no measuring-unit errors, because it is expressed in units of general purchasing power.

How should we evaluate the general price-level adjusted, net realizable value financial statements presented in Exhibits 10.4 and 10.5? First, they are interpretable. General price-level-adjusted, net realizable value financial statements are based on the concept of purchasing power, productive capacity maintenance. The figures on both the income statement and balance sheet are expressed as COG measures. Second, these financial statements are relevant, because they are expressed as COG measures. Note, however that COG is in the output market rather than the input market.

In summary, general price-level-adjusted, net realizable value financial statement contain no timing errors, do contain measuring-unit errors, are interpretable, and provide relevant measures of COG in the output market.

Such statements, therefore, meet all the criteria established for the comparison and evaluation of the evaluation of the alternative accounting models, as shown in Exhibit 10.7.

A TAXONOMY OF PRICE CHANGE MODELS

Description of Price Change Models

The differences between price change models rests on the differences in their implicit and explicit specification of (1) a valuation model, or a measured attribute for assets and liabilities, and (2) a capital maintenance concept. Various studies have provided a taxonomy of price change models based on a useful algebraic approach.[6] Chasteen's approach will be used here to illustrate the different price change models.[7] He based his analysis on the following assumptions and price change data. The twelve price change models, based on an attribute measured/capital maintenance concept, were:

1. historical cost/nominal dollars (HC/N$) model
2. historical cost/constant dollars (HC/C$) model
3. historical cost/constant dollars model according to Ijiri
4. historical cost/constant dollars model using the one-line adjustment
5. current cost/nominal dollars (CC/N$) model
6. current cost/constant dollars (CC/C$) model
7. current cost/physical capital (CC/PC) model
8. current cost/physical capital model that incorporates purchasing power gains and losses on monetary items based on specific price changes
9. current cost/physical capital model that incorporates both specific price changes adjustment as in the previous model and a "gearing" adjustment
10. current exit value/nominal dollars (EV/N$)
11. current exit value/constant dollars (EV/C$) according to Sterling
12. current exit value/constant dollars according to Chambers

The algebraic formulation of each model is as follows:

A. A firm begins operations at a time $t = 0$ with monetary assets of M, nonmonetary assets acquired at a price of N, and monetary liabilities of L. Thus, at $t = 0$, the firm's financial position is given by $M + N = L + R$, where R equals equity and $R > 0$.

B. No transactions occur from $t = 0$ to $t = 1$.

C. During the time interval from $t = 0$ to $t = 1$, the following price changes occur:

Exhibit 10.7
Error-type Analysis

ACCOUNTING MODEL	TIMING ERROR		MEASURING-UNIT ERROR	INTERPRETATION		RELEVANCE
	OPERATING PROFIT	HOLDING GAINS		NOD	COG	
1 Historical Cost Accounting	Yes	Yes	Yes	Yes (Income statement)	No	No
2 Replacement Cost Accounting	Yes	Eliminated	Yes	Yes (Income statement)	Yes (Asset Figure)	Yes (Asset Figure)
3 Net Realizable Value Accounting	Eliminated	Eliminated	Yes	Yes (Income statement)	Yes (Monetary Assets and Liabilities)	Yes (Monetary Assets and Liabilities)
4 General Price-Level Adjusted Historical Cost Accounting	Yes	Yes	Eliminated	Yes (Income statement)	Yes	Yes
5 General Price-Level-Adjusted Replacement Cost Accounting	Yes	Eliminated	Eliminated	Eliminated	Yes	Yes
6 General Price-Level-Adjusted Net Realizable Value Accounting	Eliminated	Eliminated	Eliminated	Eliminated	Yes	Yes

NOD = number of dollars
**COG = command of goods

	At $t = 0$	At $t = 1$
General price index	1	$(1 + p)$
Current cost of nonmonetary assets	N	$(1 + s_1)$
Current exit value of nonmonetary assets	N	$(1 + s_1)$

where

p = proportional change in the general level of prices (divide by 100)

s_1 = proportional change in the asset's current cost (divide by 100)

s_2 = proportional change in the asset's-current exit value (divide by 100)

4. For simplicity, assume that p, s_1 and $s_2 > 0$ and that p, s_1, and s_2 are not necessarily equal.

1. The historical cost/nominal dollars model is represented as follows:

$$M + N = \underbrace{L + R}_{(t = 1 \text{ capital})} \tag{1}$$

Both inventory and equity security may be reported at $n(1 + s_1)$ or if s_1 and s_2 are negative, at $N(1 + s_2)$.

2. The historical cost/constant dollar model is represented as follows:

$$M + N(1 + p) = L + \underbrace{R(1 + p)}_{(t = 1 \text{ capital})} \qquad \underbrace{-p(M - L)}_{(\text{income [loss]})} \tag{2}$$

3. The historical cost/constant dollars model based on Ijiri's interpretation[8] is represented as follows:

$$M + N(1 + p) = L + \underbrace{R(1 + p)}_{(t = 1 \text{ capital})} \qquad \underbrace{+ Np - Rp}_{(\text{income [loss]})} \tag{3}$$

4. The historical cost/constant dollars model based on the one-line adjustment[9] is represented as follows:

$$M + N = L + \underbrace{R(1 + p)}_{(t = 1 \text{ capital})} \qquad \underbrace{-Rp}_{(\text{loss})} \tag{4}$$

5. The current cost/nominal dollars model[10] is represented as follows:

$$M + N(1 + s_1) = \underbrace{L + R}_{(t = 1 \text{ capital})} \quad \underbrace{+ Ns_1}_{(\text{income})} \tag{5}$$

allowing the disaggregation of the firm's replacement or current cost income into two elements: (a) the current operating profit (revenues less the current costs of earning the revenues) and (b) holding gains (Ns_1).

6. The current cost/constant dollars model is represented as follows:

$$M + N(1 + s_1) = \underbrace{L + R(1 + p)}_{(t = \text{ capital})} \quad \underbrace{+ N(s_1 - p) - p(M - L)}_{(\text{income (loss)})} \tag{6}$$

where $N(S_1 - p)$ is the holding gain or loss resulting from the specific price level changes, and $p(m - L)$ is the purchasing power gain or loss resulting from the general price level changes.

7. The current cost/physical capital model is represented as follows:

$$M + N(1 + s_1) = L + \underbrace{(R + Ns_1)}_{(t = 1 \text{ capital})} \tag{7}$$

where, unlike in the current cost/nominal dollars model, the holding gains are considered a capital maintenance adjustment rather than an element of income.

8. The current cost-physical capital model that incorporates purchasing power gains and losses on monetary items based on specific price changes[11] is represented as follows:

$$M + N(1 + s_1) = L + \underbrace{(R + Rs_1)}_{(t = \text{ capital})} \quad \underbrace{- s_1(M - L)}_{(\text{income [loss]})} \tag{8}$$

9. The current cost/physical capital model that incorporates both a specific price change adjustment and a "gearing" adjustment[12] is represented as follows:

$$M + N(1 + s_1) = L + (R + Ns_1 \frac{P}{(L + R)} \tag{9}$$

$$\underbrace{+ Ms_1 \frac{R}{(L + R)})}_{(t = 1 \text{ capital})} + \underbrace{(Ns_1 \frac{L}{(L + R)} - Ms_1 \frac{R}{(L + R)})}_{(\text{income})}$$

where the gearing adjustment is calculated by allocating the holding gain (specific price increase) on nonmonetary assets between income and capital as follows:

$$\text{Income} = \text{portion } \frac{L}{L + R}(Ns_1)$$

$$\text{Capital maintenance portion} = \frac{R}{L + R}(Ns_1)$$

10. The current exit value/nominal dollars is represented as follows:

$$M + N(1 + s_2) = \underbrace{L + (R}_{(t = 1 \text{ capital})} \underbrace{+ Ns_2}_{(\text{income})} \tag{10}$$

11. The current exit value/constant dollars model according to Sterling[13] is represented as follows:

$$M + N(1 + s_2) = \underbrace{L + R(1 + p)}_{(t = 1 \text{ capital})} \underbrace{+ N(s_2 - p) - p (M - L)}_{(\text{income})} \tag{11}$$

where the nonmonetary assets are valued at exit prices instead of replacement costs.

12. The current exit value/constant dollars according to Chambers[14] is represented as follows:

$$M + N (1 + s_2) = \underbrace{L + R(1 + p)}_{(t = 1 \text{ capital})} \underbrace{+ Ns_2 - R_p}_{(\text{income})} \tag{12}$$

The 12 models described in this section represent some of the models that can be used and/or adapted by any country to account for inflation.

Illustration of Price Change Models

Chasteen used the following numerical example to illustrate the 12 model equations:

Let

$$
\begin{array}{ll}
M = \$200 & p = .10 \\
N = \$1,000 & s_1 = .24 \\
L = \$400 & s_2 = .30 \\
R = \$800 & C = \text{capital at } t = 1 \\
& I = \text{income (loss)}
\end{array}
$$

The beginning ($t=0$) financial position is:

$$\$200 + \$1000 = \$400 + \$800$$
$$M \qquad N \qquad\quad L \qquad R$$

Ending ($t=0$) financial position statements for each price change model are:

$$\$200 + \$1000 = \$400 + \underbrace{\$800}_{C} \qquad\qquad (1)$$

$$\$200 + \$1000(1.10) = \$400 + \$800(1.10) - 0.10(\$200 - \$400) \qquad (2)$$
$$\$200 + \$1100 = \$400 + \underbrace{\$880}_{C} + \underbrace{\$20}_{I}$$

$$\$200 + \$1000(1.10) = \$400 + \$800(1.10) - \$1000(0.10) - \$800(0.10) \qquad (3)$$
$$\$200 + \$1100 = \$400 + \underbrace{\$880}_{C} + \underbrace{\$20}_{I}$$

$$\$200 + \$1000 = \$400 + \$800(1.10) - \$800(0.10) \qquad\qquad (4)$$
$$\$200 + \$1000 = \$400 + \underbrace{\$880}_{C} - \underbrace{\$80}_{I}$$

$$\$200 + \$1000(1.24) = \$400 + \$800 + \$1000(0.24) \qquad\qquad (5)$$
$$\$200 + \$1240 = \$400 + \underbrace{\$800}_{C} + \underbrace{\$240}_{I}$$

$$\$200 + \$1000(1.24) = \$400 + \$800(1.10) + \$1000(0.24$$
$$- 0.10) - 0.10(\$200 - \$400) \qquad (6)$$
$$\$200 + \$1240 = \$400 + \underbrace{\$880}_{C} + \underbrace{\$140}_{I} + \$20$$

$$\$200 + \$1000(1.24) = \$400 + \$800 + \$1000(0.24) \qquad\qquad (7)$$
$$\$200 + \$1240 = \$400 + \underbrace{\$1040}_{C}$$

$$\$200+\$1000(1.24)=\$400+\$800+\$800(0.24)-0.24(\$200-\$400) \qquad (8)$$

$$\$200 + \$1240 = \$400 + \underbrace{\$992}_{C} + \underbrace{\$48}_{I}$$

$$\$200 + \$1000(1.24) = \$400 + \$800 + 2/3(\$1000)(0.24) \qquad (9)$$
$$+ \ 2/3(\$200)(0.24) + 1/3(\$1000)(0.24) - 2/3 \ (\$200)(0.24)$$

$$\$200 + \$1240 = \$400 + \underbrace{\$992}_{C} + \underbrace{\$48}_{I}$$

$$\$200 + \$1000(1.30) = \$400 + \$800 + \$1000(0.30) \qquad (10)$$

$$\$200 + \$1300 = \$400 + \underbrace{\$800}_{C} + \underbrace{\$300}_{I}$$

$$\$200 + \$1000(1.30) = \$400 + \$800(1.10) + \$1000(0.3 - 0.10) \qquad (11)$$
$$- \ 0.10(\$200 - \$400)$$

$$\$200 + \$1300 = \$400 + \underbrace{\$880}_{C} + \underbrace{\$220}_{I}$$

$$\$200+\$1000(1.30) = \$400+\$800(1.10)+\$1000(0.30)-\$800(0.10) \qquad (12)$$

$$\$200 + \$1300 = \$400 + \$220$$

$$\underbrace{\quad C \quad}_{} \quad \underbrace{I \quad}_{}$$

CURRENCY TRANSLATION IN INFLATIONARY ENVIRONMENTS

A problem arises when a firm consolidates the financial statement of foreign affiliates from inflationary environments. The problem is how to treat the effects of changes in the exchange rate and the effects of changes in the specific and general price levels on the financial statements of foreign affiliates simultaneously. The first option is simply to restate the foreign account balances to reflect the changes in the general price level of the foreign country, then translate the adjusted amounts to their domestic currency equivalent. This option is known as the restate-translate option.

The limitations of this method include the fact that the end result reflects units measured in terms of different purchasing power, as well as counting the effects of inflation twice, given that exchange rates reflect the effects of inflation.

The second option is first to translate the foreign-account balances to the domestic currency of the parent company, and then to adjust for the general price-level change equivalents. Advantages of this method include the ease of computation and the use of a single standard of measurement, which is dollars of domestic purchasing power.

The use of one method versus the other results in significant differences in the consolidated results. In any case, the currency translation problem related to inflation is not solved by either SFAS 33 or SFAS 52. Appropriate modifications were introduced by SFAS 89.

The requirements of SFAS 89 are illustrated in Exhibit 10.8. There are basically two requirements of SFAS 89. In the first, if the U.S. dollar is the functional currency, the requirements of SFAS 33 apply and no others. In the second, the U.S. dollar is not the functional currency and the following two situations arise.

Situation 1. If the firms measuring their operations in functional currencies other than the dollar have historical-cost/constant-dollar disclosure, they are exempted from disclosures.

Situation 2. If current-cost disclosures are feasible, then the financial statements are first restated to current cost before either a translate-restate or a restate-translate option is chosen. Under the translate-restate option, the current costs are translated to dollars, then restated to the U.S. general price level. Under the restate-translate option, the current costs are restated to foreign general inflation, then translated to dollars.

CONCLUSIONS

This chapter has elaborated on the measurement of well-being at the macro level, and well-offness at the micro level. In both cases, the methods adopted lead to different measures and different interpretations. This calls for caution in the understanding and use of accounting and economic data from international sources. For example, in the case of accounting for inflation, countries will be adopting techniques that are either (1) completely identical to one of the alternative asset valuation and income determination models presented in the chapter, (2) a component of one of more of these models, or (3) a combination of these models. The sophisticated user of accounting data should evaluate the method adopted in a given county by (1) determining the attribute used, (2) determining whether the model is expressed in units of general purchasing power, (3) evaluating the method as either including or not including timing and measuring unit errors, (4) determining if it can be interpreted as NOD or COG, and, finally, (5) determining if the data thus obtained are relevant for decision making.

NOTES

1. Nasar, Sylvia, "Why International Statistical Comparisons Don't Work," *New York Times* (March 8, 1992), p. 4.

2. "Interpretation," *Review of Social Economy* (October 1983), pp. 172–177; Horvat, Branko, "Welfare of The Common Man in Various Countries," *World Development* (July 1974), pp. 29–39; Belkaoui, Ahmed, and Mustafa Maksy, "Welfare of the Common Man and Type of Economic Systems: A Sensitivity Analysis," *Review of Social Economy*

Exhibit 10.8
Restatement Methodology for Foreign Operations as Given by SFAS 89

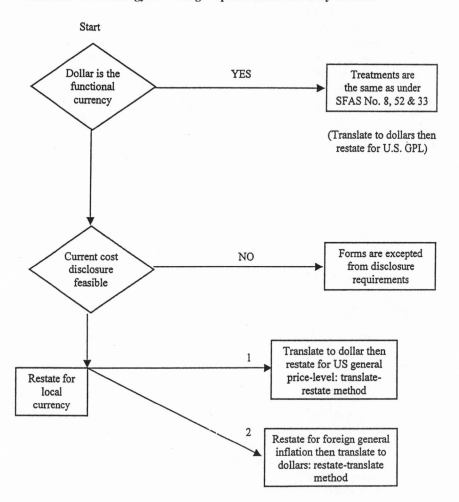

(October 1986), pp. 178–182; Belkaoui, Ahmed, and Mustafa Maksy, "Welfare of the Common Man and Accounting Disclosure Adequacy: An Empirical Investigation," *International Journal of Accounting* (Spring 1985), pp. 82–94.

3. Hicks, T. R, *Value and Capital*, 2nd Ed. (Oxford, U.K.: Clarendon Press, 1946), p. 177.

4. Choi, F. D. S., C. A. Frost, and G. K. Neek, *International Accounting*, 3rd Ed. (Upper Saddle River, NJ: Prentice-Hall, 1999), p. 207.

5. A fourth attribute, the present or capitalized value, is not included here because of its limited application. It refers to the present value of net cash flows expected to be received from the use of the asset or the net outflows expected to be discussed to redeem the liability.

6. Chambers, R. J., *Accounting and Economic Behavior* (Hemel Hempstead, U.K.: Prentice-Hall, 1966); Chambers, R. J., "The Use and Misuse of a Notation: The History of an Idea," *Abacus* (December 1978), pp. 122–144; Barton, A., *An Analysis of Business Income Concepts*, ICRA Occasional Paper No. 7, (University of Lancaster, International Center for Research in Accounting, 1975); Chasteen, Lanny, "A Taxonomy of Price Change Models," *The Accounting Review* (July 1984), pp. 515–523.

7. Chasteen, "Taxonomy."

8. Ijiri, Y., "The Price Level Restatement and Its Dual Interpretation," *The Accounting Review* (April 1976), pp. 227–243.

9. Chambers, "The Use and Misuse of a Notation: A History of an Idea;" Grady, P., "Purchasing Power Accounting," *Price Waterhouse Review* 5 (1975), pp. 3–5; Agrawal, S., and K. Rosenweig, "One-Line Adjustment Methods of Accounting for the Effects of Inflation," in *Collected Abstracts of the AAA Annual Meeting* (Sarasota, FL: American Accounting Association, 1982), p. 29.

10. Edwards, E., and P. Bell, *The Theory and Measurement of Business Income* (Berkeley: University of California Press, 1961); Samuelson, R. A., "Should Replacement-Cost Changes Be Included in Income?" *The Accounting Review*, (April 1980), pp. 254–268.

11. Gynter, R., *Accounting for Price Level Changes* (Oxford, U.K.: Pergamon Press, 1966).

12. "Statement of Standard Accounting Practice No.16: Current Cost Accounting," *Accountancy* (April 1980), pp. 99–100.

13. Sterling, R. R., *Theory of the Measurement of Enterprise Income* (Lawrence: University Press of Kansas, 1970); Sterling, R. R., "Relevant Financial Reporting in an Age of Price Changes," *Journal of Accountancy* 10 (February 1975), pp. 42–51.

14. Chambers, R. J., "NOD, COG and PuPu: See How Inflation Teases!" *Journal of Accountancy* 10 (September 1975), pp. 56–62.

SELECTED READINGS

Basu, S., and J. R., Hanna. *Inflation Accounting: Alternatives, Implementation Issues, and Some Empirical Evidence*. Hamilton, Ontario: The Society of Management Accountants of Canada, 1977.

Chambers, R. J. *Accounting, Evaluation, and Economic Behavior*. Englewood Cliffs, NJ: Prentice-Hall, 1966.

———. "NOD, COG, and PuPu: See How Inflation Teases!" *Journal of Accountancy* 10 (September 1975), pp. 56–62.

Edwards, E. O., and P. W. Bell. *The Theory and Measurement of Business Income*. Berkeley: University of California Press, 1961.

Gynther, R. S. "Capital Maintenance, Price Changes, and Profit Determination," *The Accounting Review* (October 1970), pp. 712–730.

Hanna, J. R. *Accounting-Income Models: An Application and Evaluation*. Special Study No. 8. Toronto: The Society of Management Accountants of Canada, July 1974.

Kerr, Jean St. G., "Three Concepts of Business Income." In S. Davidson et al. (Eds.), *An Income Approach to Accounting Theory*. Englewood Cliffs, NJ: Prentice-Hall, 1961, pp. 40–48.

Louderback, J. G "Projectability as a Criterion for Income Determination Methods." *The Accounting Review* (April 1971), pp. 298–305.

Parker, P. W., and P. M. D. Gibbs. "Accounting for Inflation: Recent Proposals and Their Effects." *Journal of the Institute of Actuaries* (December 1974), pp. 1–10.

Revsine, L., and J. J. Weygandt. "Accounting for Inflation: The Controversy," *Journal of Accountancy* (October 1974), pp. 72–78.

Rosen, L. S. *Current-Value Accounting and Price-Level Restatements.* Toronto: Canadian Institute of Chartered Accountants, 1972.

Rosenfield, Paul. "Accounting for Inflation: A Field Test." *Journal of Accountancy* (June 1969), pp. 45–50.

———. "The Confusion Between General Price-Level Restatement and Current-Value Accounting." *Journal of Accountancy* (October 1972), pp. 63–68.

———. "CPP Accounting: Relevance and Interpretability." *Journal of Accountancy* (August 1975), pp. 42–51.

Sterling Robert R. *Theory of Measurement of Enterprise Income.* Lawrence: University Press of Kansas, 1970.

———. "Relevant Financial Reporting in an Age of Price Changes." *Journal of Accountancy* 10 (February 1975), pp. 42–51.

Wolk, H. I. "An Illustration of Four Price-Level Approaches to Income Measurement." In J. Don Edwards (Ed.), *Accounting Education: Problems and Prospects* (Sarasota, Fla.: American Accounting Association, 1974.

APPENDIX: ILLUSTRATIVE CALCULATIONS FROM SFAS 70 TO COMPUTE CURRENT-COST/CONSTANT-PURCHASING-POWER INFORMATION

Introduction

22. This appendix presents an example of the methodology that might be used to calculate supplementary current cost information for a foreign subsidiary that uses the local currency as its functional currency. To simplify the calculations, the company is assumed to have a fixed asset but no inventory. The mechanics of restating inventory and cost of goods sold on a current cost basis are similar to those illustrated for property, plant, and equipment and depreciation.

23. The methodology used in this example is essentially the same as that illustrated in Appendix E of Statement 33. The major adaptation needed to accommodate the functional currency concept is first to measure not only current cost amounts but also increases or decreases therein for the foreign subsidiary in its local currency and then to translate those amounts into U.S. dollar equivalents in accordance with Statement 52. The effect of general inflation may be measured either (a) after translation and based on the US CPI(U) or (b) before translation and based on the local price index. To prepare consolidated supplementary information, dollar equivalent amounts determined in accordance with either (a) or (b) would be aggregated with dollar equivalent amounts computed in a similar fashion for other subsidiaries with foreign functional currencies and dollar amounts for operations for which the U.S. dollar is the functional currency. Statement 33 (paragraph 27) encourages presentation of information by segments of business enterprises, and it may be helpful to present foreign operations separately.

24. Throughout this illustration, CFC indicates constant functional currency amounts, and CFC$ indicates the translated dollar equivalents of CFC amounts. Nominal functional currency is indicated by FC, and C$E indicates dollar equivalents of FC amounts restated by the U.S. index.

Assumptions

25. The functional currency financial statements of Sub Company appear below:

Sub Company: Historical Cost FC Balance Sheets

	December 31	
	1982	1981
Cash	FC2,500	FC1,250
Equipment	2,500	2,500
Accumulated depreciation	750	500
Net equipment	1,750	2,000
Total assets	FC4,300	FC3,250

Source: Financial Accounting Standards Board (FASB) *Financial Reporting and Changing Prices: Foreign Currency Translation, An Amendment of FASB Statement No. 33*, Statement of Financial Accounting Standard No. 70 (Norwalk, CT: FASB, 1982), par. 9.

Current liabilities	FC600	FC500
Long-term debt	2,000	1,500
Total liabilities	2,600	2,000
Capital stock	500	500
Retained earnings	1,200	750
Total equity	1,700	1,250
Total liabilities and equity	FC4,300	FC3,250

Sub Company:
Historical Cost FC Statement of Income and Retained Earnings
Year Ending December 31, 1982

Revenue	FC5,000
Salaries	2,500
General and administrative expenses	1,000
Depreciation	250
Interest	350
	4,100
Income before taxes	900
Income taxes	450
Net income	450
Retained Earnings—beginning of year	750
Retained Earnings—end of year	FC1,200

26. The fixed asset was acquired on December 31, 1979. It is depreciated on a straight-line basis over ten years and is expected to have no salvage value. There were no acquisitions or disposals of assets during the year.

27. Exchange rates between the functional currency and the dollar are:

December 31, 1981:   FC1=$1.20

Average 1982:   FC1=$1.10

December 31, 1982:   FC1=$1.00

28. Management has measured the current cost of equipment at December 31, 1981 and December 31, 1982 as follows:

	1982	1981
Current cost	FC5,500	FC4,000
Accumulated depreciation	(1,650)	(800)
Net current cost	FC3,850	FC3,200

The "net recoverable amount has been determined to be in excess of net current cost at both dates.

29. Current cost equity is nominal FC at the beginning and end of the year may be computed by adding net monetary items and net property, plant, and equipment at current cost. To determine current cost equity in nominal dollars, those FC amounts are translated at the appropriate exchange rate:

	December 31					
		1982 Exchange			1981 Exchange	
	FC	Rate	$	FC	Rate	$
Monetary items (par. 5): Cash	FC2,550	$1	$2,550	FC1,250	$1,20	$1,500
Current liabilities	(600)	$1	(600)	(500)	$1,20	(600)
Long-term debt	(2000)	$1	(2000)	(1,500)	$1,20	(1,800)
Net monetary liabilities	FC(50)		$(50)	FC(750)		$(900)
Equipment -net (par. 28)	FC3,850	$1	$3,850	FC3,200	$1,20	$3,840
Equity at current cost	FC3,800		$3,800	FC2,450		$2,940

30. The U.S. and local general price level indexes are:

	Local	US
December 1981	144	281.5
Average 1982	158	292.5ᵃ
December 1982	173	303.5ᵃ

ᵃAssumed for illustrative purposes.

The Translate-Restate Method

31. To apply the translate-restate method, amounts measured in nominal FC are first translated into their dollar equivalents. Changes in those dollar equivalent amounts are then restated to reflect the effects of U.S. inflation.

Current Cost Depreciation and Income from Continuing Operations

32. The first step is to determine current cost depreciation for the year as follows:

Current cost—beginning of year	FC4,000
Current cost—end of year	5,550
	9,500
	2
Average current, gross	FC4,750

Current cost depreciation expense for the year measured in average 1982 CFC is CFC475 (FC4,750 × 10%). Computation of current cost depreciation and income from continuing operations does not involve use of a general price level index if measurements are made in average-for-the-year currency units. Accordingly, reported current cost depreciation under the translate-restate method is $523 (FC475 × $1.10).

33. Income from continuing operations on a current cost basis measured in average 1982 CFC is computed by simply replacing historical cost depreciation in income from continuing operations in the primary financial statements with the current cost amount. Accordingly, current cost income from continuing operations measured in average 1982 CFC is:

Net income   + historical cost depreciation − current cost depreciation
                 = income from continuing operations
FC450 (par. 25) + FC250 (par. 25) − FC475 (par. 32) = CFC225

Reported current cost income from continuing operations under the translate-restate method is C$E248 (CFC225 × $1.10).

Excess of Increase in Specific Prices over Increase in General Price Level

34. The second step is to compute the change in the current cost of equipment and the effect of the increase in the general price level. To measure the increase in current cost of equipment in nominal FC dollar equivalents, the effect of the exchange rate change must be excluded (paragraphs 60–62). One way to accomplish that is to translate the 12/31/81 and 12/31/82 FC current cost amounts to dollar equivalents at the average exchange rate and then restate those dollar amounts to average 1982 constant dollar equivalents:

	Current Cost/FC	Exchange Rate	Current Cost/S	Conversion Factor	Current Cost/CSE
Current cost, net- 12/31/81 (par.28)	FC3,200	$1.10	$3520	292.5(Avg. 1982) 281.5(Dec. 1981)	C$E3,658
Depreciation	(475)	$1.10	(523)	a	(523)
Current cost, net- 12/31/82 (par. 28)	3,850	$1.10	4,235	292.5(Avg. 1982) 303.5(Dec. 1982)	4,081
Increase in current cost	FC1,125		$1,238		C$E946

a Assumed to be in average 1982 C$E.

The inflation component of the increase in current cost amount is the difference between the nominal dollar and the constant dollar equivalent amounts:

Increase in current cost	($)$1,238
Increase in current cost (C$E)	C$E946
Inflation component	292

Purchasing Power Gain or Loss on Net Monetary Items

35. The third step is to compute the purchasing power gain or loss on net monetary items. Under the translate-restate method, the translated beginning and ending net monetary liabilities are restated to average 1982 dollars. The U.S. purchasing power gain is then the balancing amount:

	FC	Exchange Rate	$
Net monetary liabilities-12/31/81 (para. 29)	FC750	$1.20	$900
Net monetary liabilities-12/31/82 (para. 29)	50	$1.00	50
Decrease during the year	FC700		$850

	$	Conversion Factor	C$E
Net monetary liabilities-12/31/81	$900	292.5(Avg. 1982) / 281.5(Dec. 1981)	
Decrease during the year	(850)	a	(850)
Net monetary liabilities-12/31/82	$50	292.5(Avg.1982) / 303.5(Dec.1982)	48
Purchasing power gain			C$E37

a Assumed to be in average 1982 C$E.

The preceding computation is the same as that used to compute the purchasing power gain or loss on net monetary items under the original translate-restate provisions of Statement 33. In some circumstances, that procedure will include a part of the effects of exchange rate changes on net monetary items in the purchasing power gain or loss. A more theoretically correct computation that would completely exclude the effect of exchange rate changes would be to compute a separate purchasing power gain or loss for each functional currency operation in a manner similar to that illustrated in paragraph 34 for the increase in specific prices. For example, that alternative method produces a purchasing power gain of $34.

	FC	Average Exchange Rate	$	Conversion Factor	C$E
Net monetary liabilities- 12/31/81 (par. 29)	FC750	$1.10	$825	292.5(Avg. 1982) 281.5(Dec. 1981)	C$E857
Decrease during the year	(700)	$1.10	770	a	(770)
Net monetary liabilities - 12/31/82 (par. 29)	FC50	$1.10	$55	292.5(Avg. 1982) 303.5(Dec. 1982)	53
Purchasing power gain					C$E34

a Assumed to be in average 1982 C$E

However, the first procedure illustrated is less costly because it can be applied on a consolidated basis, and it generally provides a reasonable approximation Accordingly, that method is acceptable.

Reconciliation of Equity

36. Although neither Statement 33 nor this statement requires disclosure of a reconciliation of equity, such a reconciliation serves as a check of the calculations and is a convenient way to compute the translation adjustment:

Equity at 12/31/81 in average 1982 C$ $2,940 (par. 29) × 292.5/281.5		C$3,055
Income from continuing operations (par. 33)	C$E248	
Purchasing power gain (par. 35)	37	
Excess of increase in specific prices over increase in general price level (par. 34)	946	
Translation adjustment (par. 37)	(624)	
Increase in equity in terms of US purchasing power		607
		C$3,662
Equity at 12/31/82 in average 1982 C$ $3,800 (par. 29) × 292.5/303.5		C$3,662

Translation Adjustment

37. The translation adjustment is the amount needed to balance the reconciliation of equity. The translation adjustment determined under the translate-restate method may be checked by translating the beginning- and end-of-year equity on a C$ basis into FC amounts and using the FC amounts.

	C$	Exchange Rate	FC
Equity at 12/31/81 in average 1982 C$ (par. 36)	C$3,055	$0.833[a]	FC2,545
Equity at 1/31/82 in average 1982 C$ (par. 36)	3,662	$1.00	3,662
Increase in equity	C$607		FC1,117
Restated opening equity		FC2,545	
Exchange rate change during 1982 ($1,20-$1.00)		x (.10) $509	
Plus increase in equity		FC1,117	
Difference between ending exchange rate and average rate for 1982 ($1.10-$1.00)		x (.10) $(112)	
Translation adjustment		$(621)	

[a] IFC $1.20 = $0.833.

The difference of $3 ($624 − $621) between the translation adjustment computed above and the translation adjustment that appears in paragraph 36 reflects the $3 difference ($37 − $34) between the short-cut and theoretically correct procedures illustrated in paragraph 35.

The Restate-Translate Method

38. To apply the restate-translate method, the steps illustrated in paragraphs 31–35 are followed except that all restatements to reflect the effects of general inflation are made before translation to dollar equivalents and using the local general price level index.

Current Cost Depreciation and Income from Continuing Operations

39. Current cost depreciation and income from continuing operations are CFC475 and CFC225, respectively, as determined in paragraphs 32 and 33.

Purchasing Power Gain or Loss on Net Monetary Items

40. To apply the restate-translate method, the FC amount of net monetary items at the beginning of the year, changes in the net monetary items, and the amount at the end of the year are restated into average 1982 CFC. The purchasing power gain or loss on net monetary items is then the balancing item:

	FC	Conversion Factor	CFC
Net monetary liabilities 12/31/81 (par. 29)	FC750	158(Avg. 1982) 173(Dec. 1982)	CFC823
Decrease during the year	(700)	a	(700)
Net monetary liabilities 12/31/82 (par. 29)	FC50	158(Avg. 1982) 173(Dec. 1982)	46
Purchasing power gain			CFC77

ª Assumed to be in average 1982 CFC.

Excess of Increase in Specific Prices over Increase in General Price Level

41. Under the restate-translate method, the local index is used to restate the beginning and ending current cost/FC amounts into average 1982 CFC:

	FC	Conversion Factor	CFC Cost/CFC
Current cost, net – 12/31/81	FC3,200	158(Avg. 1982) 144(Dec. 1981)	CFC3,511
Depreciation	(475)	a	(475)
Current cost, net – 12/31/82	(3,850)	158(Avg. 1982) 173(Dec. 1982)	(3,516)
Increase in current cost	FC1,125		CFC480

ª Assumed to be in average 1982 CFC.

The inflation component of the increase in current cost amount is the difference between the nominal functional currency and constant functional currency amounts:

Increase in current cost (FC)	FC1,125	
Increase in current cost (CFC)	CFC 480	
Inflation component	645	

Reconciliation of Equity

42. As with the translate-restate method, a reconciliation of equity acts as a check of the calculations. A reconciliation of equity also is a convenient point at which to translate the functional currency amounts determined in the preceding paragraphs into dollar equivalents and is a convenient way to compute the translation and parity adjustments.

43. If opening and closing equity are restated to average 1982 CFC using the local index, the reconciliation of equity under the restate-translate method would be:

	CFC	Exchange Rate	CFCS
Equity at 12/31/81 in average 1982 CFC FC2,450 (par. 29) x 158/144	CFC2,688	1.20	CFC$3,225
Income from continuing operations (par. 39)	225	1.10	248
Purchasing power gain (par. 40)	77	1.10	248
Excess of increase in specific prices over increase in general price level (par. 41)	480	1.10	528
Translation adjustment (par. 44)			(616)
	CFC3,470		CFC$3,470
Equity at 12/31/82 in average 1982 CFC FC3,800 (par. 29) x 158/173	CFC3,470	1.00	CFC$3,470

Translation Adjustment

44. The translation adjustment is the amount needed to balance the CFC$ reconciliation of equity. The adjustment may be computed as (a) the change in exchange rates during the period multiplied by the restated amount of net assets at the beginning of the period plus (b) the difference between the average exchange rate for the period and the end-of-period exchange rate multiplied by the increase or decrease in restated net assets for the period. Accordingly, the translation adjustment under the restate-translate method is:

Restated opening equity (par. 43)	CFC2,688
Exchange rate change during 1982 ($1.20 − $1.00)	× (.20)
	$(538)

Plus (equity at 12/31/82) minus equity at 12/31/81 = $3,470 − 2,688)	CFC 782
Difference between ending exchange rate and average rate for 1982 ($1.10 − $1.00)	× (.10)
	(78)
Translation adjustment	$(616)

Parity Adjustment

45. The reconciliation of equity in paragraph 43, in which beginning-of-year and end-of-year equity are stated in average 1982 CFC, is needed to calculate the translation adjustment in CFC$. However, beginning-of-year and end-of-year equity and increase in equity must be stated in average 1982 constant dollars in the supplementary current cost information. Beginning-of-year and end-of-year equity in average 1982 constant dollars are C$3,055 and C$3,662, respectively, as computed in paragraph 36. The overall increase in U.S. purchasing power for the year thus is C$3,662 − C$3,055 = C$607. The difference between that amount and the increase of CFC$245 (CFC$3,470 − CFC$3,225) that appears in the reconciliation of equity of paragraph 43 is the parity adjustment needed to adjust the ending net investment and the increase in the net investment to measures in average 1982 constant dollars (paragraph 74). Accordingly, the parity adjustment is C$607 − CFC$245 = $362. That amount represents (a) the effect of the difference between local and U.S. inflation from December 31, 1981, to average for 1982 on the restatement of opening equity to average units plus (b) the effect of the difference between local and U.S. inflation from average for 1982 to December 31, 1982, on the restatement of ending nominal dollar equity to average units:

Equity at 12/31/82 (par. 29)	$2,940
Difference between local and US inflation from 12/31/81 to average 1982 (158/144 − 292.5/281.5)	× 0.0581
	$ 171
Plus equity at 12/31/82 (par. 29)	$3,800
Difference between US and local inflation from average 1982 to 12/31/82 (292.5/303.5 − 158/173)	× 0.0504
	$ 191
Parity adjustment	$ 362

For display purposes, the parity adjustment is combined with the $(616) translation adjustment (paragraph 43). Accordingly, the net translation adjustment disclosed in the supplementary current cost information prepared using the restate-translate method would be $(616) + $362 = $(254). The components of current cost information based on the restate-translate method thus would be:

Beginning-of-year equity	C$3,055
Income from continuing operations	CFC$248

Purchasing power gain	85	
Excess of increase in specific prices over increase in general price level	528	
Translation and parity adjustments	(254)	
Increasing in equity in terms of US purchasing power		607
End-of-year equity		C$3,662

Index

About the Author

AHMED RIAHI-BELKAOUI is CBA Distinguished Professor of Accounting in the College of Business Administration, University of Illinois at Chicago. Author of numerous Quorum books, published or forthcoming, and coauthor of several more, he is also a prolific contributor to the scholarly and professional journals of his field, and has served on various editorial boards that oversee them.